This is a volume in the Arno Press Series

NATIONAL BUREAU
OF
ECONOMIC RESEARCH
PUBLICATIONS
IN REPRINT

See last pages of this volume
for a complete list of titles.

American Agriculture, 1899-1939

A Study of Output, Employment and Productivity

by Harold Barger
and Hans H. Landsberg

ARNO PRESS
A New York Times Company
New York - 1975

Editorial Supervision: Eve Nelson
Reprint Edition 1975 by Arno Press Inc.

NATIONAL BUREAU OF ECONOMIC RESEARCH
PUBLICATIONS IN REPRINT
ISBN for complete set: 0-405-07572-3
See last pages of this volume for titles.

Manufactured in the United States of America

Library of Congress Cataloging in Publication Data

Barger, Harold.
American agriculture, 1899-1939.

(National Bureau of Economic Research publications in reprint)
Reprint of the ed. published by National Bureau of Economic Research, New York, which was issued as no. 42 of its Publications.
1. Agriculture--United States. 2. Agriculture--Economic aspects--United States. I. Landsberg, Hans H., joint author. II. Title. III. Series. IV. Series: National Bureau of Economic Research. General series ; no. 42.
HD1761.B3 1975 338.1'0973 75-19693
ISBN 0-405-07574-X

Publications of the

National Bureau of Economic Research, Inc.

Number 42

American Agriculture, 1899–1939: A Study of

Output, Employment and Productivity

American Agriculture, 1899-1939

A Study of Output, Employment and Productivity

by Harold Barger
and Hans H. Landsberg

National Bureau of
Economic Research, Inc.

NEW YORK 1942

National Bureau of Economic Research, Inc.

1819 Broadway, New York

Manufactured in the U. S. A. by

American Book–Stratford Press, Inc., New York

Director's Note

THIS report is one of several dealing with the trends of production and productivity in American industry since the opening of the twentieth century. Other volumes already published are *The Output of Manufacturing Industries, 1899–1937* by Solomon Fabricant (1940); and *Employment in Manufacturing, 1899–1939: An Analysis of Its Relation to the Volume of Production,* by the same author (1942).

The study upon which this volume is based was made possible by funds granted by The Maurice and Laura Falk Foundation of Pittsburgh. The Falk Foundation is not, however, the author, publisher, or proprietor of this publication, and is not to be understood as approving or disapproving by virtue of its grant any of the statements made or views expressed herein.

William J. Carson
Executive Director

National Bureau of Economic Research, Inc.
December 1942

Preface

As ITS subtitle indicates, this book deals with certain aspects only, albeit important aspects, of agricultural development since the end of the last century. The limitations upon its scope are deliberate and require brief explanation.

Farming is much more than just another industrial segment; it has indeed been called a way of life. It is one of the oldest, and still one of the most important, ways of getting a living. Throughout the ages it has been the subject of an extensive literature: writers have treated it from every point of view. It has a sociological interest which is barely touched on in this volume. Changes in the farmer's standard of living, or in his cultural attainments, his reactions to governmental incentives, the changing fortunes of different farming areas, problems of migration and the farm-city interchange—all these lie outside the scope of a volume such as the present and will be mentioned only incidentally. Questions of a more strictly commercial nature, such as the marketing methods pursued by the farmer, and the processes of price formation in the case of farm products, also remain undiscussed. These restrictions are necessary limitations, for without them it would be impossible, within the compass of a single volume, to accord adequate treatment to our chosen topics—output, employment and productivity.

The structure of the book is briefly as follows. Part One, consisting of Chapter 1, describes some peculiarities of agricultural enterprise and furnishes a definition of agricultural output. Chapters 2 to 4, in Part Two, provide an extended discussion of the size and composition of farm output. The factors which have influenced this size and composition from one period to another are treated in considerable detail. Thus, in Chapter 2 the general reader will find the new index of output and a summary of changes in its composition. Chapter 3, which is concerned with the output behavior of each individual product in turn, will be of interest chiefly to specialists. Chapter 4 regards agriculture as the source of the nation's food supply, and examines the bearing of nutritional standards upon farm output in general. In particular, new estimates are offered for the per capita consumption of calories, vitamins and other food elements.

Part Three, which deals with employment and productivity, comprises three chapters. Of these, Chapter 5 reviews the history of technological changes in agriculture, and considers the extent to which well-known innovations have actually been adopted in different farming areas. Chapter 6 offers estimates of agricultural employment. In the first section of Chapter 7 the trend in output per worker is examined; in succeeding sections direct labor requirements and yield per acre for different crops are analyzed and reconciled with estimates already given for employment and output per worker.

In Part Four, Chapter 8 sets forth our conclusions and discusses their bearing upon the outlook for agriculture as a segment of the nation's economy.

Harold Barger
Hans H. Landsberg

Authors' Acknowledgments

THROUGHOUT the study helpful advice and criticism were given by a National Bureau staff committee consisting of Moses Abramovitz, F. C. Mills (chairman) and Leo Wolman; in addition we are indebted to Solomon Fabricant for almost continuous counsel and advice. The manuscript was read, in whole or in part, and useful comments were made, by other members of the National Bureau staff, A. F. Burns, W. C. Mitchell and G. H. Moore; by several Directors of the National Bureau; by G. L. Johnson, R. S. Kifer and O. C. Stine of the Bureau of Agricultural Economics; by I. H. Siegel of the Bureau of Labor Statistics, Wilfred Malenbaum of the Office of Strategic Services and Horst Mendershausen of Bennington College; by O. S. Morgan and H. C. Sherman of Columbia University; by E. J. Working of the University of Illinois and D. R. Kaldor of Iowa State College; by M. K. Bennett, J. S. Davis and A. E. Taylor of Stanford University; by Asher Hobson of the University of Wisconsin, G. R. Cowgill of Yale University, J. S. Gow of the Falk Foundation, Dr. R. M. Wilder of the Mayo Clinic and H. L. Boyle of the International Harvester Company.

We are indebted to the following for the use of unpublished material and for numerous suggestions during the course of the study: C. L. Harlan, S. A. Jones and J. B. Shepard of the Agricultural Marketing Service; O. E. Baker, C. A. Burmeister and E. E. Vial of the Bureau of Agricultural Economics; W. H. Shaw of the Bureau of Foreign and Domestic Commerce, Frederick Strauss of the War Production Board, S. W. Shear of the University of California, Holbrook Working of Stanford University, and F. J. Hosking of the Corn Industries Research Foundation.

We are grateful to several coworkers who assisted us in different phases of the study. Many of the computations were performed by Corolynn L. Lee and Céleste N. Medlicott. Edna Deutsch rendered bibliographical assistance. The charts were drawn by H. Irving Forman. Finally, the volume owes much to its editor, Bettina Sinclair, whose suggestions led to numerous improvements.

H. B.
H. H. L.

Contents

Part Four
SUMMARY AND CONCLUSIONS

APPENDICES

Text Tables

Appendix Tables

Charts

Part One

Introduction

Chapter 1

Agriculture as a Segment of the Nation's Industry

SLIGHTLY more than thirty million persons, nearly 25 percent of the population of the United States, live on farms. Some of them work at nonagricultural occupations, but nearly ten million, or about one third of the farm population, are apt to be actively engaged, at one season or another, in agricultural production. In 1940 one out of every six gainfully occupied persons in the United States tilled the soil or tended farm animals, although many of these were working only intermittently, for example at harvest time. The average number of persons actually employed in agriculture throughout the year is difficult to determine exactly, but it is probably of the same order as the average number employed in manufacturing (9.8 million in 1937), and must be very much larger than the average for any other single industrial division. Judged by its contribution to national income, however, agriculture is much less important than manufacturing: in 1937 it contributed only 9 percent to the income of the nation as a whole, whereas manufacturing accounted for 23 percent.[1]

Still more striking is the contrast in the size of the productive unit. Manufactured commodities are derived from fewer than 200,000 establishments, some of them very large indeed, whereas there are in the United States over 6 million farms, the average size being about 160 acres. To be sure, the scale of agricultural operation is far from uniform. Farms vary from the acre or so cultivated by the part-time agricul-

[1] Simon Kuznets, *National Income and Its Composition, 1919–1938* (National Bureau of Economic Research, 1941), Table 12.

turalist to the ranch embracing several hundred sections in a single pasture; from the farm that changes hands every year and boasts no permanent equipment to the domain with an investment of over $100,000; from the patch worked by the tenant with one mule to the 10,000-acre plantation.[2]

In the cultivation of the soil there is discernible scarcely any tendency toward that growth in the size of the entrepreneurial unit which has characterized other types of industry. True, in 1900 only 0.8 percent of all farms exceeded 1,000 acres, and only 24 percent of all farm land was concentrated in such holdings, whereas by 1935 the percentages had risen to 1.3 and 29 respectively.[3] But the increase appears to have been concentrated in the Pacific, and especially the Mountain states where many new large farms were established.[4] There is little evidence of the consolidation of existing farms in other parts of the country: indeed the increase during the same period in the proportion of very small farms (under 20 acres) might appear to indicate an actual disintegration of existing holdings. The smallest size groups, however, are covered rather spasmodically by the Census, and in any case include many farms cultivated by tenants who exercise no real entrepreneurial control independently of their landlords. All things considered, the scale of agricultural operations in general appears to have undergone little change since the turn of the century. The number of producing units remains very large compared with most branches of manufacturing or mining. This generalization applies even to the more specialized types of fruit and vegetable production where concentration of control has alone made any real progress.[5]

[2] E. W. Zimmermann, *World Resources and Industries* (Harpers, 1933), pp. 159-60.

[3] *Statistical Abstract of the United States, 1940,* p. 642. Most of the change appears to have occurred between 1925 and 1930.

[4] A. L. Meyers, *Agriculture and the National Economy,* Monograph 23 (Temporary National Economic Committee, Washington, 1940), Table 6.

[5] *Ibid.,* Table 7.

The fact that agriculture is still, relatively speaking, a field for small-scale undertakings has precluded any significant incursion of corporate enterprise. Although farms are sometimes owned by corporations (often unwillingly, as the result of mortgage foreclosure), the number subject to corporate operation as well as ownership is extremely small. Corporate control is, however, exercised indirectly in some specialized lines of production and in a few regions by processors contracting in advance—as much as a year or more—for the individual farmer's output or part of it. Such arrangements reduce both the number and the extent of the entrepreneurial functions normally attributable to the farmer. Though he may still own the farm, the farmer is subject to company control in the execution of his plans and in some cases is an employee in all but name.[6] Situations of this sort are common among sugar-beet growers, many of the fruit and vegetable farmers on the Pacific Coast, and some other groups dealing largely in truck crops. Nevertheless, for the agricultural picture in the large, such phenomena represent deviations from the norm. Farming is still conducted, in overwhelming degree, by individual entrepreneurs, roughly half of whom own the land they cultivate.[7] And of farm output as a whole, perhaps one fifth is sold through cooperative marketing associations; [8] the remainder, except that consumed on the farm, is placed on the open market or (in the case of fruit and vegetables) sold to canners under contract. In recent years less than 10 percent of this output has been exported.

[6] *Violations of Free Speech and Rights of Labor,* Hearings before a Subcommittee of the Committee on Education and Labor, U. S. Senate, 76th Congress, 3rd Session, Pt. 62 (Washington, 1940), pp. 22773-815.

[7] Of all farm operators in 1940, 50.6 percent were full owners, 10.1 percent were part owners, 0.6 percent were managers and 38.7 percent were tenants. However, four out of every ten farmers owning their farms reported mortgages. The average equity held by the farmer in such cases was 57 percent of the value of the farm.

[8] Such associations marketed $1,684 million of products in 1938–39 (U. S. Department of Agriculture, *Agricultural Statistics, 1940,* Table 809).

Perhaps what distinguishes agriculture most sharply from other segments of industrial activity is the fact that it furnishes not only a living, but a complete way of life. The factory employee, even the professional man or civil servant, keeps more or less fixed hours and lives away from his job: he "goes to work" each morning. Even a storekeeper runs his shop during a more or less definite period of the day. On the other hand a farmer and his family live with—and on—the job; for them the farm is both home and workshop. The hours they work vary with the season and with the crop or type of livestock, but are largely outside their control. Often, also, isolation throws the members of a farming community together in a manner unknown to those who follow urban pursuits. On this account agriculture possesses a sociological interest quite unlike that of other vocations. And there is still another peculiarity of agricultural activity. For a large number of farmers the production of agricultural commodities is not carried on as a means of making money, but rather as a mode of existence. Where production is undertaken primarily for consumption by the farm family itself, the farmer may live almost entirely by this means—on a subsistence basis —or he may use his agricultural activity to supplement other forms of income, such as a pension or wages from a nearby factory. The noncommercial farmer has no counterpart in any other sphere of economic activity. Partly because of the prevalence of farming of this character, in which the produce is consumed on the farm itself, but also because of the very large number of small farms, only half the nation's farms were responsible, in 1929, for the production of almost 90 percent of all farm products *marketed;* the other half—especially farms in the South—contributed the remaining 10 percent.[9]

[9] O. E. Baker, *A Graphic Summary of the Number, Size, and Type of Farm, and Value of Products,* Misc. Pub. 266 (U. S. Department of Agriculture, 1937), p. 68. The same study reveals that almost 30 percent of products sold were in that year contributed by no more than 250,000 farms.

From a more technical viewpoint also agricultural production has certain characteristics all its own. In the first place it is highly seasonal as to its absorption of labor and materials and its output as well. This is notably true of crops, and especially of crops whose geographic distribution is narrow and whose tolerance of climatic variations is small (e.g., cotton and various fruits); but it applies also, though in less degree, to livestock and dairy production. In the second place, the output of a single season depends in large measure upon the accident of weather. In this respect, too, livestock and dairy production are somewhat less sensitive than crops: as may be seen from Chart 5, the fluctuation from year to year in the series for livestock, milk, poultry and wool is less violent than in the case of other branches of agriculture.

Finally, the demand for agricultural products is, in the aggregate, highly inelastic, for the *total* amount of agricultural products purchased by the public will not be reduced (or increased) to any important extent by a rise (or fall) in price, though for individual products the reverse may be true. Considered from another angle, since the public buys fairly fixed amounts of agricultural products, unusually large supplies can be disposed of only if the price is reduced severely, while short supplies will sell at high prices because buyers will seek eagerly to secure their customary quota. For the individual farmer, the price of his crop is determined in the competitive mechanism of the market, which he as an individual cannot hope to influence: his withdrawal from the market will not raise the price, but will proportionately reduce his receipts. In the short run, therefore, a fall in price will discourage output appreciably only in the extreme case in which prices are so low that harvesting costs exceed prospective receipts; in such circumstances the crop may be left to rot unharvested. For the operator who hires little labor this point is rarely reached since he will continue to work, however low the reward for his own efforts, so long as he is at least reimbursed for materials used. Incidentally, the farmer's status of self-employer goes far to explain why he has always been reluctant to give up his vocation. Even from one season to another the farmer may fail to react easily or quickly to price changes. Inertia, in part the result of technical conditions, may impede or prevent adjustments which would be achieved readily enough in other industries. In the case of many crops both prices and production fluctuate notoriously from year to year, frequently showing marked inverse correlation.

These are some of the considerations which must be borne in mind by anyone attempting to interpret the behavior of agricultural output. Almost in a textbook sense, agriculture has been "the last surviving stronghold of pure competition." [10] But it is also a sector of the economy in which the adjustments we have been taught to associate with a competitive market are peculiarly difficult to achieve in any smooth and orderly fashion.

THE BOUNDARIES OF AGRICULTURE

In contrast to manufacturing, which constantly discards old and adopts new activities, the boundaries of agriculture have changed little throughout history. If any trend is discernible, it is the gradual transference of agricultural functions to industry—breadmaking from the farm oven to the commercial bakery, buttermaking from the home churn to the dairy plant, slaughtering from the farm to the packinghouse, spinning from the wooden wheel to the textile factory.[11] In this way the functions of agriculture have been whittled down to the growing of raw materials exclusively. Farm processing of

[10] Meyers, *op. cit.*, p. 9.

[11] Breadmaking and clothmaking are on a slightly different footing from the other activities mentioned, since they were functions of the farm household (as well as of the urban household) as consumer rather than as producer or seller.

food or fiber, in many instances even for home use, has become the exception rather than the rule.

This change in the character of agricultural operations to some extent vitiates long-range comparisons, for agricultural production has a narrower and more specialized meaning than it had a hundred years ago. Even at the turn of the present century agriculture had been stripped of most of its processing functions, with the exception of the production of butter, three fourths of which was still made on farms in 1899.[12]

Apart from the transfer of processing from the farm to the factory the content of agriculture has scarcely changed. The principal functions are still the growing of some sixty to seventy crops to provide food and industrial raw materials and the raising of livestock for dairy products and for slaughter.

Although it is simple enough to define agriculture, it is a more difficult matter to measure the volume of output which must be termed agricultural. Perhaps the most important reason for the introduction of further qualifications is the fact that basic data on output are derived in the main from Census canvasses. These, in turn, are confined to holdings classified as farms by the Census authorities:

> A "farm," for census purposes, is all the land which is directly farmed by one person conducting agricultural opera-

[12] E. E. Vial, *Production and Consumption of Manufactured Dairy Products*, Technical Bulletin 722 (U. S. Department of Agriculture, 1940), pp. 6-7. Little more than 5 percent of all cheese was made on farms in 1899. Slaughter too was at that time carried on mainly in commercial establishments, and the transfer from farms has continued since then:

Number of Animals Slaughtered on Farms as Percentage of Total Number Slaughtered[a]

	1899	*1939*
Cattle	8.3	4.3
Calves	17.5	8.5
Hogs	26.7	20.7
Sheep and lambs	4.2	3.1

[a] *Agricultural Statistics, 1940,* Tables 475, 498, 533.

> tions either by his own labor or with the assistance of members of his household or hired employees. The term "agricultural operations" is used as a general term referring to the work of growing crops, producing other agricultural products, and raising domestic animals, poultry, and bees. . . . Do not report as a "farm" any tract of land of less than 3 acres, unless agricultural products to the value of $250 or more were produced on such tract in 1929. . . .[13]

From the outset, therefore, we must disregard all crops or livestock raised in places not considered farms, since they are not accounted for in available production statistics. This limitation is more serious in some fields of activity than in others, and probably most disturbing in the attempt to estimate the output of vegetables,[14] since a large amount of vegetables entering the market originates in gardens in urban, and more especially in rural, nonfarm areas. Poultry and milk cows also are kept to some extent in establishments not classified as farms.[15] Furthermore, as the above excerpt from the Census instructions indicates, lower limits are placed upon the acreage and value of farms whose output is recorded. These limits—three acres and $250, respectively—have applied since the Census of 1910; in 1900 no lower limit was set in terms of either acreage or value of products. The effect of the restriction has been found to be small,[16] and it is mentioned here only to define unequivocally the *area* treated in this book as "agriculture."

We have followed the Bureau of the Census with respect to its definition of a farm by size and value of products, but have further delimited the scope of "agriculture" by disre-

[13] *Fifteenth Census of the United States, 1930, Agriculture,* Vol. IV, p. 952.

[14] See pp. 129-32 below.

[15] The last Census year in which animals not on farms were the subject of a special canvass was 1920.

[16] J. D. Black and R. H. Allen, "The Counting of Farms in the United States," *Journal of the American Statistical Association,* Vol. 32 (Sept. 1937), pp. 439-63.

garding certain activities included by the Census. The Census considers as farms nurseries, greenhouses, hatcheries and apiaries, even though it is doubtful to what extent enterprises of this sort were actually covered prior to 1930. Difficulties of statistical treatment rather than conceptual considerations have led us to omit not only such establishments, but also fish hatcheries, stockyards, fur farms, etc., which the Census likewise excludes.[17] For the same reason we have excluded forest products, although the Census reports their value when forestry is conducted in conjunction with other farming operations. Although almost 20 percent of all farmland is woodland, gross farm income from forest products contributes only 1 to 2 percent of the total. Regionally, of course, there are wide differences; many farms in the Piedmont section, in New England, and in the Northwest derive a considerable part of their income from forestry. Moreover, changes in the pattern of Southern agriculture have evoked increased attention to farm forest problems. But data on production and prices are almost nonexistent, partly because so much of the lumber cut is farm-consumed. It should be noted that maple sugar and sirup are not ordinarily regarded as forest products, but rather as a form of crop production: unlike lumber, therefore, they are included in the present study.

Finally, agriculture has to be distinguished from mining, manufacturing and other nonagricultural pursuits.[18] This is not always as easy as it sounds. Where the operations of an entire enterprise fall on one side of the line or the other, there is no special difficulty. But where two or more types of

[17] *Census of Agriculture, 1935,* Vol. III, p. 12. The Census counts such places as farms, if farming operations are carried on, but does not collect data on nonfarm activities.

[18] Manufacturing production is treated in Solomon Fabricant's *The Output of Manufacturing Industries, 1899–1937* (National Bureau of Economic Research, 1940). Mr. Fabricant's study of manufacturing is continued in *Employment in Manufacturing, 1899–1939* (National Bureau of Economic Research, 1942); and output, employment and productivity in mining, and in transportation and public utilities will be the subject of further volumes which the National Bureau hopes to publish shortly.

activity contribute to the production of a single enterprise, even of a single product, a rather intricate accounting problem arises. In such endeavors as fruit drying or the production of cane sugar, the line of demarcation between the agricultural operation and the manufacturing process remains more or less arbitrary.

THE MEANING OF AGRICULTURAL OUTPUT

There remains the question as to what portions of agricultural production as here circumscribed we seek to cover in our measure of output. Agricultural products fall naturally into two broad classes: (1) crops and (2) livestock and livestock products. Crops may be grown for a variety of purposes: to be consumed in the farm household; to be fed to livestock; to serve as seed; to be sold to other farmers for the same variety of purposes; to be sold to nonagricultural consumers either for direct consumption or for processing into goods consumed both on and off farms, at home and abroad. Livestock is raised either for the products derived from it (milk, eggs, wool, leather) or for direct consumption as meat; the distribution may be similar to that of crops, except that quantitatively much less is fed to livestock (milk fed to calves is practically the only instance). Since output consumed on the farm itself during the production process reappears as other output at a later stage, it is appropriate to exclude the amount consumed in this manner. Consequently the definition of farm output turns mainly upon the deductions from gross output which are necessary to measure the production of a single enterprise or of the industry as a whole.

Output may embrace—in its broadest connotation—the entire harvest of a given crop; it may be confined to the portion sold; or it may be regarded even more narrowly as the amount sold to people other than farmers. For a study that centered on changes in the fortunes of a particular crop, the entire amount harvested (which we call gross output) would no doubt be the appropriate measure.[19] But if we are interested in farm output as a whole, the duplication implicit in such a treatment becomes an insurmountable obstacle to accuracy. Milk, for example, would represent merely feed that has been processed by a "feed-milk converter," i.e., a dairy cow. It is obvious that crops (and milk) fed to livestock would be counted twice over if we were to include them both in the "raw" stage and again in the "converted" stage. Consequently we have defined output as consisting of those products which are not consumed in further processing within agriculture but are available for consumption elsewhere.[20] This is the "net output" which alone figures as a constituent of our output indexes.[21] In it we include products sold to nonfarm purchasers, products used by farm families as consumers rather than as producers,[22] and those not yet disposed of for sale or home consumption. Additions to inventory, in other words, are treated as output. The latter point assumes im-

[19] Since net output is obtained from gross output by deducting feed and seed requirements, the difference between the two measures is most marked in the case of the grains, and particularly corn and oats: four fifths of the gross output of these two crops is excluded from net output. With hay the same situation applies. The quantitative relationship between gross and net output in the case of the grains and hay is further considered below, pp. 47, 50n and 139-40.

[20] As will be seen from the notes in Appendix A, duplication was not always eliminated as completely as the authors would have wished.

[21] Thus the index for crops excludes feed and seed; the index for livestock products excludes milk fed to calves. The problem could have been solved also by measuring the gross output of crops (excluding only seed), and deducting feed (as well as milk fed to calves) in computing the index for livestock products. An identical index for agricultural output as a whole would have resulted, although the calculations would naturally have required a different weighting system in combining crops and livestock from that used in this volume. The work would have been more intricate, and the method does not appear to possess advantages over that actually adopted.

[22] This distinction is one of the fundamental concepts used in measuring income and will be preserved here. The value given to this portion for purposes of index-number weighting has been taken as the price of the portion marketed.

portance mainly in the case of livestock,[23] where output thus consists of the number of animals slaughtered or sold for slaughter, plus or minus the increase or decrease in the number on hand on farms over the year. Let us illustrate by an extreme example: if in one year no sales of hogs are made, but all newborn hogs are added to the existing stock, production, so far from being zero, must be treated as equal to the net addition to existing herds.[24] Crops not harvested, or those given away for charity are, of course, excluded from output.

SCOPE AND ORGANIZATION OF THE STUDY

The foregoing definitions of farming and of farm output may serve, in some degree at least, to delimit our subject matter. The aims of the book—to assemble indexes of total agricultural output and of its constituent parts, to explain their movements as well as the shifting pattern of output, and finally to compare the behavior of output with changes in the volume of agricultural employment—fall naturally under two heads. Part Two (Chapters 2 to 4) deals with output; Part Three (Chapters 5 to 7), with employment and its relation to output. The former opens with a discussion of the new index of agricultural output, presented annually since 1899, and of indexes for the output of some fifteen major groups of farm products. These will be found in Chapter 2, which also contains a discussion of trends in farm output, and comparisons of experience before and after the first World War. However, in undertaking a rather thorough analysis of the behavior of farm output, and of the factors which influenced it from one period to another, we found that in some ways our index numbers concealed more than they revealed and that special discussion of the peculiar circumstances surrounding

[23] Crops may also be stored on farms, but here additions to inventory are automatically included, since we rely on harvest data.

[24] For further discussion, see notes to Table A-1, Appendix A.

individual commodities was needed to complete the picture. Accordingly, in Chapter 3 individual products are considered separately and an attempt is made to offer explanations, in terms of demand and supply, for their differing fortunes. Among the various sets of factors influencing agriculture from the side of demand three are of primary importance: the utilization of farm products by industry, the export situation and the domestic demand for foodstuffs. Because the last of these is of greatest quantitative significance and at the same time most interesting from a sociological aspect, it is accorded separate treatment in Chapter 4, which is given over to an analysis of trends in domestic food consumption.

In Part Three we consider employment and productivity. Chapter 5 contains a review of the history of technological advance in farm machinery, and of developments in plant improvement and animal breeding. Our main interest here is naturally with economies in labor, increases in yield, and the growing substitution of controls and indicators for the otherwise uncontrollable or unpredictable forces of nature. Chapter 6 is devoted to a discussion of the validity of the available estimates of farm employment. In Chapter 7 output and employment, linked by technology, are brought together in an analysis of changes in productivity during the forty-year period; here an attempt is made to distribute changes in productivity among products and types of farming enterprise.

The broad conclusions that have been reached in the preceding chapters are assembled in Part Four (Chapter 8). Here, following an evaluation of existing trends, the discussion is projected into the future with an appraisal of the outlook for American agriculture.

Part Two

Output

Chapter 2

The Behavior of Agricultural Output

To COMPUTE measures of the physical volume of agricultural production as a whole it is necessary to weave together into a single series output data for a wide variety of commodities. These data, and the formulae used to combine them, are given in detail in Appendix A. Here it must suffice to say that as many farm products as possible have been included, and that farm prices have been used as weights throughout. In this chapter results are presented in the form of an over-all index, intended to show the movement of the entire physical output of agriculture, supplemented by fifteen partial indexes for individual groups of commodities.[1]

THE OVER-ALL INDEX

The index for the aggregate product of agriculture is shown in Table 1 and Chart 1. It will be seen that over the forty-year period net farm output increased by about one half, and that during 1937–39, it stood at a level higher than any attained previously.[2] The rise since 1899 reflects a much less

[1] The over-all index is based upon data for 88 commodities; some of the data are available for only part of the long period since 1899, some (like dairy products) are themselves composites of more than one series, others (like oranges or prunes) are regional or functional subdivisions of a single crop. The fifteen partial indexes are neither exhaustive when taken together, nor free from duplication. For the precise commodity coverage of each index, see p. 331 below. A comparison between the new index for farm output as a whole and various other published indexes of agricultural output will be found in Appendix C.

[2] The five-year average value for 1935–39 is 47.7 percent above the corresponding figure for 1897–1901. As is pointed out in Appendix A, this result depends essentially upon four Edgeworth comparisons, linked in 1909, 1919

rapid rate of growth than that of manufacturing output, which quadrupled in the same period.[3] Indeed, as may be seen from Chart 2, agricultural output grew even more slowly during these years than the population of the United States, which rose about 75 percent. The reasons for this comparatively slow development, and the question as to whether further increases in agricultural output are to be expected in the future, will be discussed in subsequent chapters.

Meanwhile we may comment briefly upon the behavior of the over-all index. The original figures are compared, in Chart 1, both with a five-year moving average derived from them and with an exponential trend fitted to the data. Over the forty-year period farm output grew on the average at a rate of about one percent a year (Table 4). In the original series, there is observable an almost uninterrupted rise between 1897 and 1914, disturbed only slightly by a minor drop in 1901, a peak and recession in 1906–07, and a minor decline in 1913. In the following period, extending roughly from 1915 to 1922, rises and falls alternate, resulting in a horizontal trend. It is not until 1923 that the 1915 high—itself largely attributable to the record cereal yields of that year—is finally surpassed in any substantial measure. Thereafter the rate at which agricultural production increases is far slower than the pace prevailing before 1915. In 1926 the upward movement levels off, to be succeeded after 1931 by the most precipitous drop recorded at any time during the period of observation. By 1934 the index has fallen almost to the level of 1916 and

---

and 1929. By contrast, a direct Edgeworth comparison between the two periods indicated suggests a slightly smaller rise, 42.1 percent. (This comparison excludes some products for which data are not available in 1897–1901; the output of these products expanded rapidly, and their exclusion is partly responsible for the difference in result.) The use of other formulae would doubtless also yield slightly differing results.

[3] Solomon Fabricant, *The Output of Manufacturing Industries, 1899–1937* (National Bureau of Economic Research, 1940), p. 6; *The Relation between Factory Employment and Output since 1899,* Occasional Paper 4 (National Bureau of Economic Research, 1941), p. 37.

1921, but that year is a turning point followed by an exceptionally rapid rise, so that in 1939 production exceeds the 1934 low by almost a third.

TABLE 1

INDEX OF AGRICULTURAL OUTPUT, 1897–1939

1899:100

Year	*Basic Index*	*Five-year Moving Average*	*Year*	*Basic Index*	*Five-year Moving Average*
1897	95	..	1919	125	127
1898	100	..	1920	130	128
1899	100	100	1921	118	128
1900	101	102	1922	130	131
1901	99	103	1923	132	132
1902	103	104	1924	137	138
1903	104	106	1925	138	140
1904	109	110	1926	146	143
1905	108	111	1927	141	145
1906	118	113	1928	147	146
1907	110	113	1929	144	147
1908	112	114	1930	145	147
1909	111	114	1931	150	146
1910	114	117	1932	144	141
1911	117	118	1933	140	139
1912	123	122	1934	120	136
1913	119	125	1935	133	137
1914	129	125	1936	134	140
1915	129	125	1937	153	148
1916	119	127	1938	152	..
1917	124	127	1939	159	..
1918	130	127			

The year-to-year fluctuations are relatively mild. Save for the turbulent 1930's, changes of 2 or 3 points in the index seem to be the rule, and rises or declines of 7 or 8 points the exception. Manufacturing activity, in contrast, ordinarily changes at a rate of 5 to 10 points from one year to another, and in the period preceding the first World War sometimes shifted as much as 30 points.[4]

[4] Fabricant, *The Output of Manufacturing Industries,* pp. 44-45.

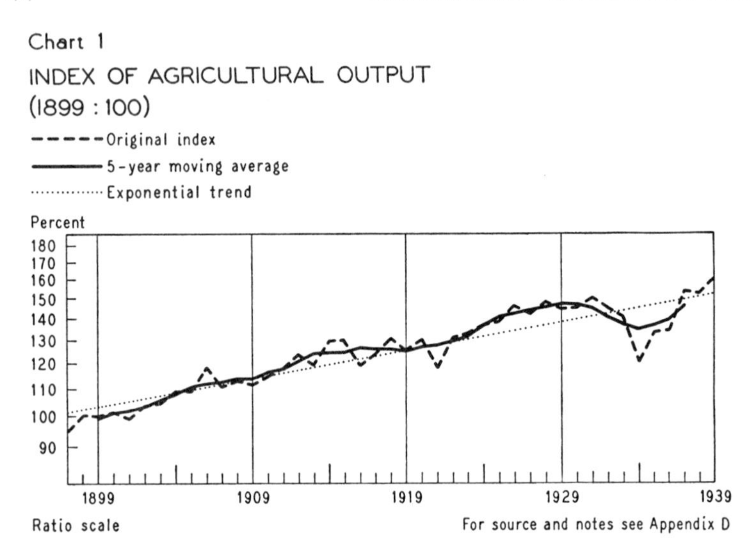

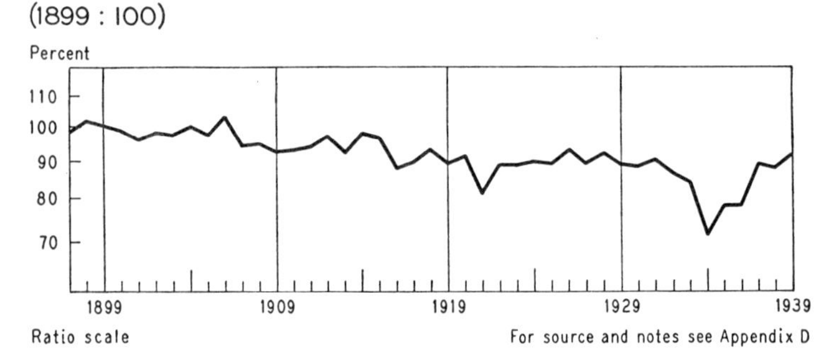

The comparative stability of agricultural output in the short run is not difficult to explain. Yields are largely a function of the weather, and as the weather is rarely either uniformly good or bad throughout the country, low and high yields in different localities tend to offset one another, except

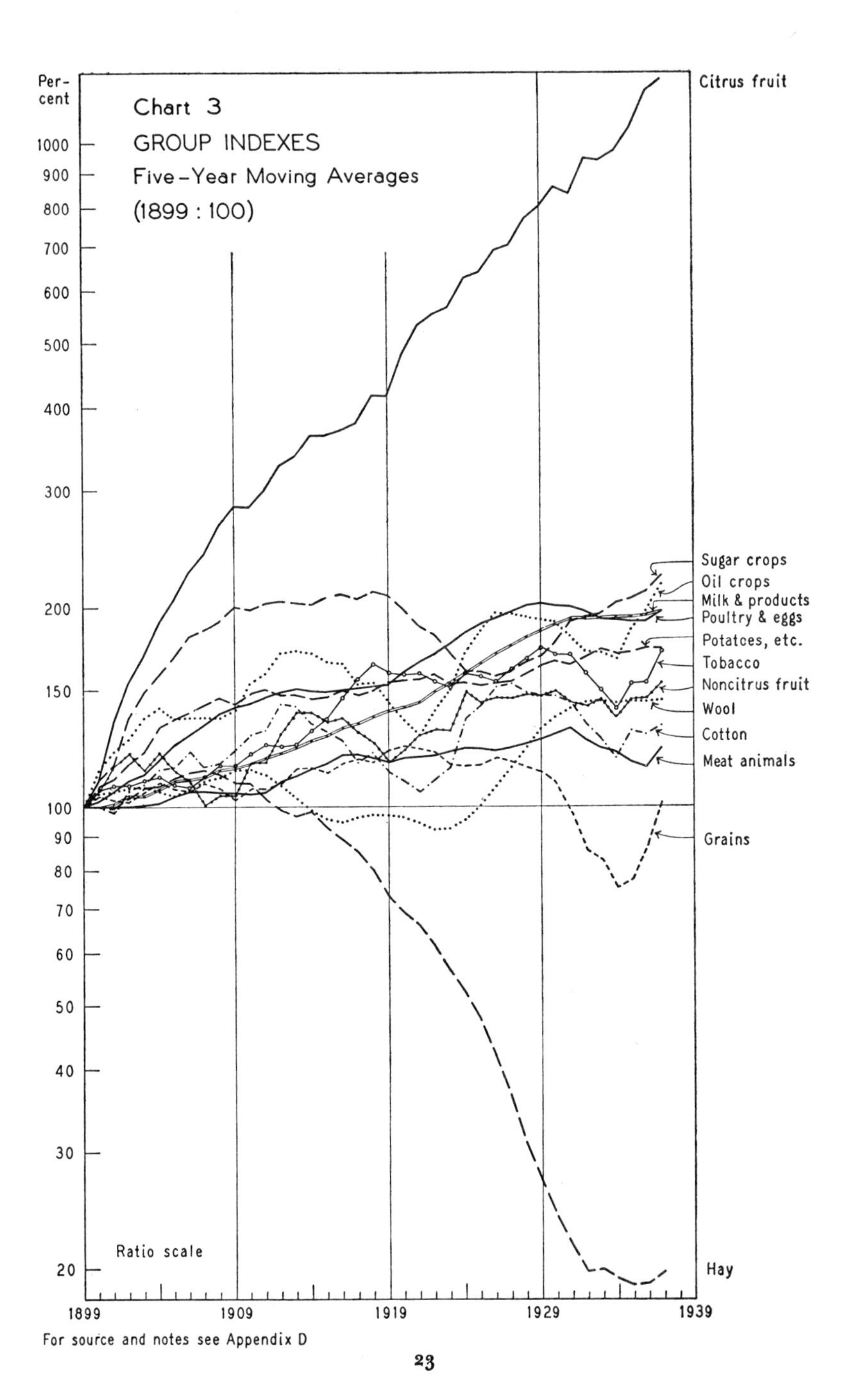

For source and notes see Appendix D

of course in years of general drought like 1934.[5] Moreover, the farmer is subject to considerable inertia; for example, he must develop breeding and crop rotation programs, which cannot be quickly changed. Unless induced by government to do otherwise, he usually plants a fairly constant acreage year by year; once an area is planted he will tend to harvest and sell or use the entire product, unless it appears that prospective returns will not even repay the cost of harvesting. As for the demand for agricultural output, it is probably as inelastic, in the short run, as the supply. Consequently, the burden of adjustment falls upon prices rather than upon production; the course of farm prices has always been marked by much more violent fluctuations than has that of farm output.

Breakdowns of the kind shown in Chart 4 and Table 2 suggest that about 81 percent of net farm output in 1897–1901, and about 84 percent in 1935–39, was destined for consumption as human food. But the size of the human stomach is limited. Clearly, unless a nation's foreign customers absorb the surplus, the boundaries of agricultural expansion, as compared with the growth of manufacturing, are reached rather quickly. This must not be taken to imply that the nation's consuming capacity, estimated upon a physiological rather than a pecuniary basis, has ever been reached. On the contrary, experts are agreed upon the presence of large "nutritional deficits." It is estimated that if all the nation's families were to enjoy what may be defined as "good" diets, consumption would have to increase by the following amounts: milk, 20 percent; butter, 15 percent; eggs, 35 percent; tomatoes and citrus fruit, 70 percent; leafy, green and yellow vegetables, 100 percent.[6] However, not even the practical realization of

[5] Even in 1934 as much as one quarter of the entire country remained unaffected. (U. S. Department of Agriculture, *Yearbook of Agriculture, 1935,* p. 15.)

[6] J. P. Cavin, H. K. Stiebeling and Marius Farioletti, "Agricultural Surpluses and Nutritional Deficits," *Yearbook of Agriculture, 1940,* p. 333. Inasmuch as allowance may be necessary for offsetting reductions in other foods, these figures give an exaggerated picture of the potential increase in farm output.

such a program would result in an expansion in agricultural production of the proportions observed in manufacturing, when comparisons are made today with the situation at the beginning of the century.

The physiological barrier to increased food consumption is reflected in a tendency on the part of the population at large to apply increased purchasing power to items other than food, or at least to diversify rather than to amplify the diet. Because of the nature of our index, diversification shows up only in the form of a shift toward higher-priced products. In the long run, however, these more expensive products gradually become cheaper (citrus fruit is a good example) as sales volume, output and marketing facilities expand, and thus the qualitative improvement in the aggregate food intake affects the index in steadily diminishing degree. If we had available a ready measure that would indicate the changing nutritive value of agricultural output, it might well show a more pronounced rise between 1899 and 1937 than that recorded by the present index, which takes account of qualitative changes only indirectly so far as they influence constant dollar values. In this respect, indexes of agricultural production suffer from the same deficiency as do those for manufacturing. However, in manufacturing there is much wider scope for expansion in the progressive diversification of output, a factor whose comparative absence in agriculture accounts in part for its slower growth, both actual and observed.

When we compare agricultural production with population increase, the lagging growth of the former becomes still more apparent. An index of agricultural output per capita, shown in Chart 2, has fluctuated in recent years around a level from 10 to 20 percent below that prevailing at the beginning of the present century. The combined index, as might be expected, conceals wide variations in the movement of individual products. This dispersion, which is depicted in Chart 3, is discussed in the next section.

CHANGES IN THE COMPOSITION OF FARM OUTPUT

Changes in the composition of agricultural output are at least as noteworthy as changes in its total, whose behavior we have just reviewed. The contribution of different products to total output can be computed, of course, only in value terms, but changes in the physical composition of the aggregate between different dates may be measured with the help of a comparison in constant prices. For this purpose we have chosen the initial and final five-year periods, 1897–1901 and 1935–39, multiplying the average output of each commodity in each period by its average farm price for all ten of the years specified. To insure comparability only those items were included for which data were available for both periods.[7] The resulting weighted quantities for each product and group were then transformed into percentages of the aggregate for either period. These percentages are what we have in mind when in the discussion to follow we speak of "contributions" or "shares" of individual products or groups. The results are shown in Table 2 and Chart 4.

Grains, meat animals, and dairy products underwent the most striking changes. Grains as a group declined in relative importance from 17.7 percent of the total in the initial period to only 12.6 percent in the second.

Meat animals showed less of a decline, decreasing as a share of the total from 32.5 to 27.2 percent. The loss is fully accounted for by the diminishing importance of cattle and hogs. The declining output of meat animals contrasts with the increased contribution of the poultry group, which advanced in relative importance by about one third between the two periods. By far the greatest absolute expansion took place in dairying, which accounted for 22.1 percent of the total in

[7] This qualification eliminates nuts and truck crops and tends to overstate the relative importance of all items in the second period, since data for the crops that have shown the greatest rise—certain fruit and vegetables—are omitted. See note d to Table 2.

TABLE 2

PERCENTAGE COMPOSITION OF OUTPUT, 1897–1901 and 1935–39[a]

	1897–1901	1935–39
Grains	*17.7*	*12.6*
Wheat	10.1	6.6
Corn	5.0	3.9
Rye	.2	.2
Oats	1.7	.8
Barley	.5	.6
Buckwheat	.1	e
Rice	.1	.6
Cotton (lint only)	*9.8*	*8.8*
Tobacco	*2.5*	*3.0*
Sugar crops	*.4*	*1.1*
Sugarcane	.3	.3
Sugar beets	.1	.7
Potatoes, etc.	*3.3*	*4.1*
Potatoes	2.6	2.8
Sweetpotatoes	.6	.7
Dry edible beans	.2	.6
Hay	*2.1*	*.3*
Fruit, citrus	*.2*	*1.9*
California	.2	1.0
Florida	e	1.0
Fruit, noncitrus	*3.2*	*3.1*
Apples	2.8	1.9
Apricots	.1	.1
Grapes	.3	.8
Dried prunes	.1	.2
Oil crops	*1.8*	*2.2*
Cottonseed[b]	1.1	1.4
Flaxseed[c]	.5	.2
Peanuts	.2	.6
Hops	*.1*	*.1*
Milk and milk products	*15.9*	*22.1*
Poultry and eggs	*9.2*	*12.4*
Chickens	3.5	4.6
Eggs	5.7	7.8
Meat animals	*32.5*	*27.2*
Cattle	14.2	10.7
Calves	1.0	1.8
Hogs	15.8	13.1
Sheep and lambs	1.5	1.7
Wool	*1.2*	*1.1*
TOTAL[d]	100.0	100.0

[a] Based on average quantities produced (excluding seed and feed) in either period, weighted by average farm prices for the ten years 1897–1901 and 1935–39.

[b] In computing the group output indexes of this chapter and Chapter 3, cottonseed has been included both in the index for cotton and cottonseed and in the index for oil crops.

[c] In computing the group output indexes of this chapter and Chapter 3, flaxseed has been included both in the index for the grains and in the index for oil crops.

[d] The total includes only the products shown, for which data are available in both 1897–1901 and 1935–39. Products excluded from the comparison, for which no data are available in 1897–1901, comprise the following: sugarcane sirup, sorgo sirup, maple sugar and sirup, soybeans, broomcorn, pears, peaches, plums, other prunes, strawberries, cranberries, olives, figs, citrus fruit outside California and Florida, walnuts, almonds, pecans, truck crops (artichokes, asparagus, snap beans, beets, cabbage, cantaloups, carrots, cauliflower, celery, sweet corn, cucumbers, eggplant, lettuce, onions, green peas, green peppers, spinach, tomatoes, watermelons), mohair, turkeys and peppermint. These items had a value in 1937 of $570 million, and the value of all items shown in the table in the same year was $8,540 million, making a total value of agricultural products of $9,110 million. The value of products omitted from the comparison was therefore about 6 percent of the value of the net output of all agricultural products in 1937.

[e] Less than 0.05.

1935–39 as compared with 15.9 percent in 1897–1901. This sharp gain in importance made dairy products the second largest group in 1935–39, with almost twice the weight of grains, whereas in the early period the contribution of grains had exceeded that of dairy products by about one eighth.

Among other outstanding changes are the almost tenfold increase in the contribution of citrus fruit (from 0.2 to 1.9 percent), the virtual elimination of the net output of hay (from 2.1 to 0.3 percent), the sevenfold increase in sugar beets (from 0.1 to 0.7 percent), and the decline in the importance of apples (from 2.8 to 1.9 percent). The increase in oil crops is slightly understated, since soybeans are excluded from the computation. If we included them by assuming their production in 1897–1901 to have been nil, and by inserting their average value for 1935–39, the percentage contribution of oil crops in the latter period would be 2.4 percent instead of 2.2.

INDEXES FOR GROUPS AND COMMODITIES

The changes in the composition of farm output over the period as a whole reflect the markedly dissimilar behavior of different products. In examining the relative growth of these products we could of course make use directly of the data for individual commodities assembled in Appendix A. However, because of the obvious affinities among various products, already suggested in Table 2, it was found preferable to compute separate partial indexes for the entire period on the same plan, with the aid of the formula used in the construction of the over-all index presented above.

We may first compare the fortunes of crop raising and livestock production, for agricultural output can be divided between vegetable products of every kind (all of which can be termed "crops" for the present purpose) on the one hand, and meat, poultry products, wool and dairy products on the other. Indexes in the form of five-year moving averages are

Chart 4
COMPOSITION OF AGRICULTURAL OUTPUT

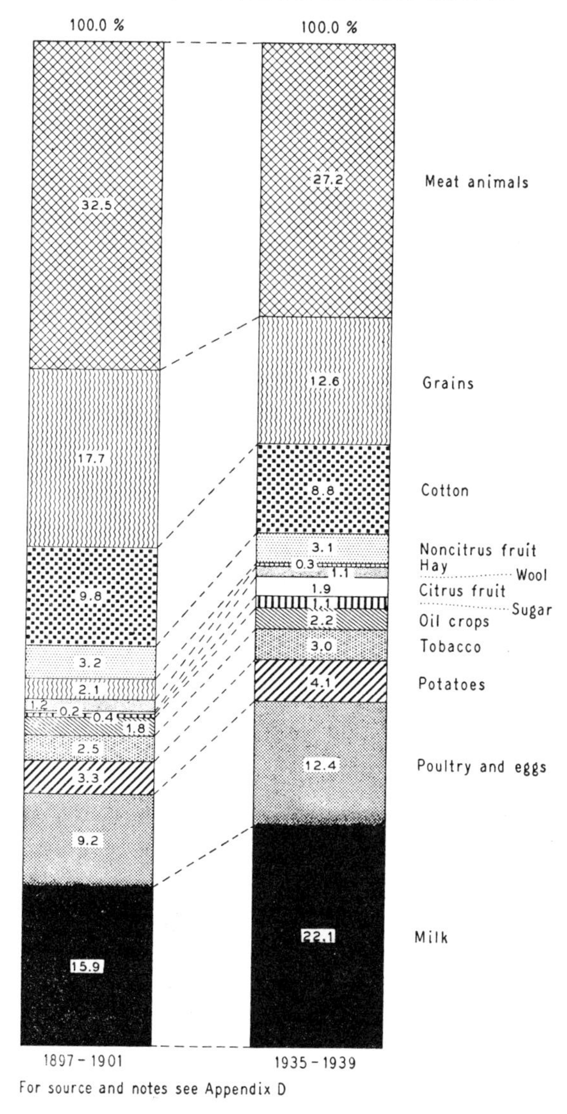

For source and notes see Appendix D

shown in Table 3 for these two categories. The remarkable growth, during most of the period, of dairying at the expense of the raising of cash crops is clearly apparent. On an 1899 base, to be sure, livestock products did not outstrip crops until about the year 1915, but thereafter the disparity increased rather steadily. If the growth of dairying has not been confined to any particular area, it has of course resulted in an increased demand for feed. We may say, if we like, that corn which forty years ago would have been sold as such is now marketed as milk or eggs. The increase in crops produced for feed is not of course reflected in the index of crop production shown in Table 3; but the augmented feed requirements have been no more than a partial offset to the decline in the per capita demand for cereals for human food (see pp. 163-66 below). The enlarged fraction of agricultural resources devoted to dairying has probably reduced the need for regional specialization and lessened dependence upon the weather. It has tended also to regularize the farmer's work year, for cattle require a much less fluctuating amount of labor from one season to another than do crops. The shift of labor from cropping to caring for animals has been all the more substantial because of the fact that labor requirements per unit of output have diminished in cropping, but in dairying have remained almost unchanged.[8]

As the next step in the analysis, in order to explore the behavior of different types of output, fifteen partial indexes were computed for groups of products. The indexes for thirteen of these groups are shown, in the form of five-year moving averages, in Chart 3.[9] Divergence in behavior is extremely marked. The most extreme movements are revealed, not by any of the staples, but by hay and citrus fruit respectively.

[8] See Chapter 7 below.

[9] The fifteen indexes are given in numerical form in Tables 5 and 6 in the next chapter. Only thirteen of them are reproduced in Chart 3 because two of the fifteen (truck crops and tree nuts) are not available for the early years of the period.

The virtual disappearance of the city horse reduced sales of hay off the farm by four fifths. Growing popularity and ease of distribution raised the output of citrus fruit tenfold. For

TABLE 3
CROPS AND LIVESTOCK
Net Output, Five-Year Moving Averages[a]
1899 (1897–1901): 100

Year	*Combined Index*	*All Crops*[b]	*All Livestock Products*	*Year*	*Combined Index*	*All Crops*[b]	*All Livestock Products*
1899	100	100	100	1919	127	124	129
1900	102	103	100	1920	128	124	131
1901	103	103	102	1921	128	123	133
1902	104	107	103	1922	131	125	136
1903	106	109	104	1923	132	125	139
1904	110	114	106	1924	138	133	142
1905	111	113	109	1925	140	135	145
1906	113	115	111	1926	143	139	147
1907	113	115	112	1927	145	140	150
1908	114	116	113	1928	146	139	153
1909	114	114	114	1929	147	138	155
1910	117	119	115	1930	147	137	157
1911	118	120	116	1931	146	132	159
1912	122	125	119	1932	141	124	156
1913	125	129	121	1933	139	122	154
1914	125	127	124	1934	136	115	153
1915	125	125	126	1935	137	123	151
1916	127	127	128	1936	140	128	150
1917	127	124	129	1937	148	139	156
1918	127	125	129				

[a] Based on Table A-3, Appendix A.
[b] Some readers may prefer to compare the output of livestock products with the gross rather than with the net output of crops. A rough check shows that an index for crops which measured gross output (including seed and feed requirements) would report practically the same change over the period as does the index given here for net output (which of course excludes these items). This result is due to the combined effects of two opposing tendencies which neutralize each other. Thus, on the one hand, increased use of the grains and hay for feeding livestock has raised the gross output of these products relatively to their net output (see pp. 47, 139, below). On the other hand, (1) even their gross output has risen less rapidly than the output of crops in general; moreover, (2) the substitution of their gross for their net output gives them a heavier weight in the index for crops as a whole. The second consideration appears to be slightly more important than the first, so that an index for the gross output of all crops would stand at the end of the period about one percentage point below the net output index shown in the table.

other products the rises or declines were much more moderate. Sugar, oil crops, poultry and dairy products each roughly doubled in output, while grains hardly rose at all. The remaining groups gained somewhat, although several of these, if the series were converted to a per capita basis, would show declines.

These contrasts in the behavior of different types of product have been responsible for considerable variation in the fortunes of different farming areas. By 1900 wheat growing in California was already declining, but since then the phenomenal development of the citrus industry has led to an expansion of agricultural activity in that state; the same influence has been at work in Florida. Wheat growing has continued to decline in the East, and the raising of this crop is being confined more and more closely to the North Central states. Between 1917 and 1930 wheat farming spread into the western counties of the Dakotas, Nebraska and Kansas, and into the Oklahoma panhandle, but a succession of years with low rainfall discouraged this enterprise during the following decade. Drought also pushed the margin of corn cultivation eastward, and led to the substitution of wheat, which requires less moisture than corn, in the eastern parts of Kansas and Nebraska.[10] Other crops also have undergone regional changes. The center of the nation's cotton acreage, for example, has shifted westward toward Texas,[11] but the decline in cotton farming in the deep South has been counterbalanced to some extent by an increase in livestock production.[12] Among other noteworthy developments are the introduction

[10] U. S. Department of Agriculture release, "Regional Adjustments to Meet War Impacts" (Washington, 1940).

[11] See pp. 76-77 below.

[12] The number of cattle on farms in the Delta Cotton area (Arkansas, Louisiana and Mississippi) increased by 35 percent between 1907–11 and 1937–41 (averages for January 1); the corresponding increase for the United States was roughly 12 percent. See U. S. Department of Agriculture, *Livestock on Farms, January 1, 1867–1935* (Washington, 1938); U. S. Department of Agriculture, *Agricultural Statistics, 1941,* Tables 458 and 460.

of the sugar beet into California, the advent of the soybean and the growth in the importance of truck farming, especially in the neighborhood of the larger cities.

THE MEASUREMENT OF TRENDS

The volume of agricultural production is subject only in part to control by the producer. To a great extent it is determined by weather conditions, or by the activity of insect pests and plant diseases, which are unpredictable and in large measure uncontrollable. Consequently year-to-year changes in the output of individual products will tend to be erratic, and to conceal, perhaps for several years at a time, any underlying tendency for production to expand or contract as a result of economic conditions. Such a tendency, operating as it must through changes in acreage and in agricultural technique, can be expected to emerge only over a period of years of indeterminate length. It may readily be seen from Charts 1 and 5 that while the fluctuations in agricultural output as a whole are comparatively mild, the output of several of our groups of products fluctuates from year to year with considerable violence. Because of this situation, only a vague impression concerning trend movements can be derived from a casual inspection of the series. In order to summarize the movements of these series, we have therefore fitted trend lines to the total and to the fifteen partial indexes. For this purpose the simplest appropriate computed trend appears to be one which allows for a constant percentage change from one year to the next: in other words, an exponential growth curve fitted to the original output data. The computation, when carried out by Glover's method, is not laborious.[13] In the accompanying chart the various trend lines obtained in this

[13] Commonly called an exponential growth curve, it may conveniently be fitted by the method of moments. The constants are readily obtained from tables.

Chart 5

GROUP INDEXES AND TRENDS

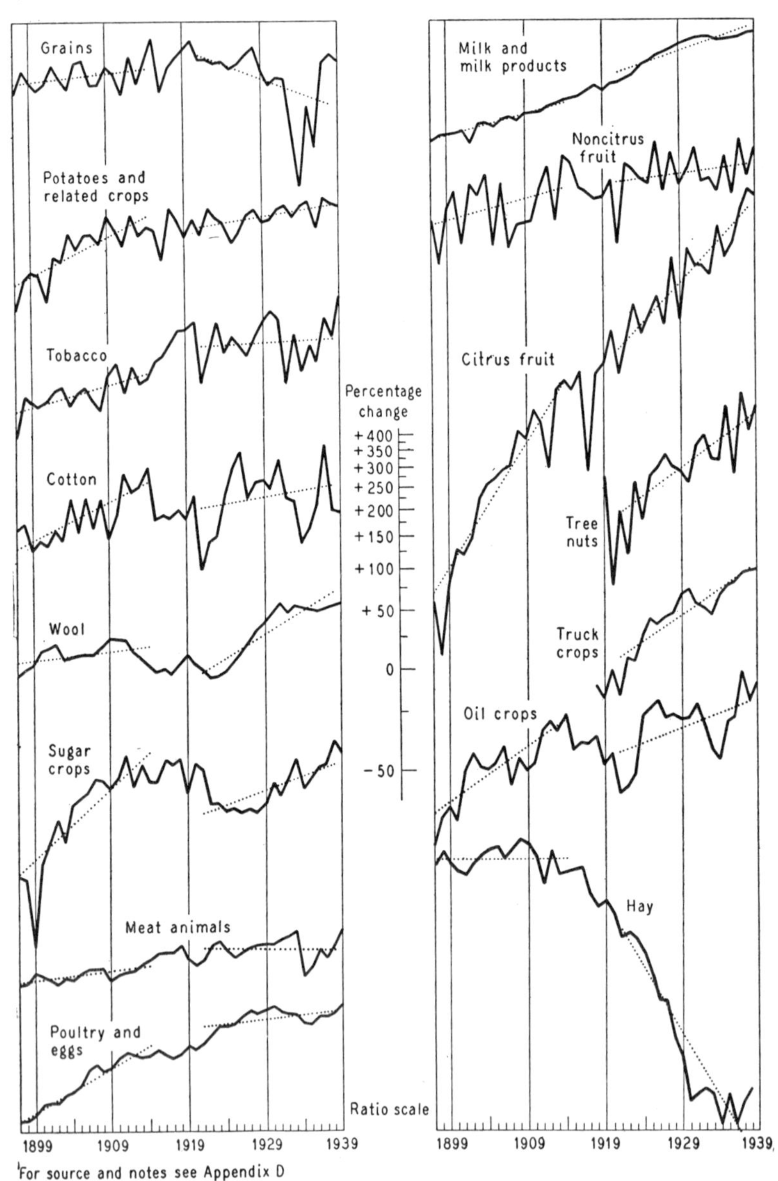

For source and notes see Appendix D

fashion have been superimposed upon the crude movements of the indexes. Since the chart is drawn on a logarithmic scale the growth curves appear as straight lines.

Besides describing the trend during the period as a whole, the same technique may be used to determine whether there has been retardation of growth. Thus the period studied—1897 to date—falls naturally into two parts, more or less equal in length, divided by the first World War. That conflict left the output of some crops comparatively unaffected, but markedly increased the output of others. Retardation of growth, as a secular phenomenon, can therefore best be studied if we omit the war years, and institute a comparison between annual growth rates in the pre- and post-war periods respectively. For this purpose we have arbitrarily chosen the eighteen-year subperiods 1897–1914 and 1921–38. The influence of the war did not affect any of our groups until 1915 [14] at the earliest, and by the year 1921 wartime demand had disappeared.[15] The legacy of war of course remained: changes in migration, foreign trade, indebtedness and price levels persisted, and there was a further impetus to technical change. It is this legacy, in large part, that distinguishes the post-war from the pre-war period.

The average annual percentage rates of growth are assembled for comparison in Table 4. They merely afford a convenient summary of the dominant tendency of the series under observation. It is unwise, however, to regard the trend lines to which they correspond, shown as dotted lines in Chart 5, simply as substitutes for the original series. Not only does the average rate of growth hide deviations from the central tendency as computed; but the choice of terminal dates in comput-

[14] It is well to remember in this connection that the crop harvested in the fall of 1914 had been sown prior to the outbreak of the war and was thus largely unaffected by it.

[15] See also A. B. Genung, "Agriculture in the World War Period," *Yearbook of Agriculture, 1940*, p. 278.

TABLE 4

GROUP INDEXES OF OUTPUT

Average Annual Percentage Change, by Groups[a]

Group	*1897–1914*	*1921–38*	*1899–1937*
Grains	+ .6	−2.0	− .2
Potatoes and related crops	+2.8	+ .9	+1.0
Tobacco	+1.5	+ .3	+1.3
Cotton	+2.6	+ .9	+ .6
Wool	+ .6	+3.3	+ .9
Sugar crops	+5.0	+2.0	+ .7
Meat animals	+ .7	− .1	+ .6
Poultry and eggs	+3.1	+ .6	+1.7
Milk and milk products	+1.5	+1.8	+2.1
Noncitrus fruit	+1.5	+ .7	+ .9
Citrus fruit	+8.9	+5.9	+5.8
Oil crops	+3.8	+2.1	+1.2
Tree nuts	b	+3.9	b
Truck crops	b	+3.6	b
Hay	nil	−8.6	−4.2
TOTAL AGRICULTURAL OUTPUT	1.5	.5	1.0

[a] The groups for which percentage changes are shown in the table are neither exhaustive nor entirely free from duplication. For a list of products contained in each group, see Appendix A. The order in which the groups are presented is of no significance. The results are derived from the material in Table 5.

[b] Data not available.

ing the trend affects to some extent the results obtained.[16] If agricultural production moved in more or less regular cycles, we might choose our terminal points, in computing the annual rate of growth, in such a way as to represent approximately similar phases of these cycles.[17] Unfortunately the

[16] The behavior of noncitrus fruit may be cited as an extreme example of this waywardness. Because 1921 was a year of abnormally low yield, the average annual percentage increase for 1921–38 is as high as .7; whereas for 1922–38 (17 years instead of 18) the increase amounts to only .1 percent per annum. Similarly in the case of cotton and cottonseed the growth rate for 1921–38 is .9 percent, but for 1921–37 (omitting the final year) 1.3 percent per annum.

[17] This was the procedure adopted by Arthur F. Burns to measure trends in industrial production; *Production Trends in the United States Since 1870* (National Bureau of Economic Research, 1934).

behavior of agricultural output is too irregular to lend much value to such a procedure. The same standard pairs of terminal dates have therefore been used in computing trends for all the agricultural output series.

For the reason indicated particular significance should not be attached to small variations among the growth rates computed in Table 4. However, even when due allowance has been made for the type of bias mentioned, changes in growth rates between the two periods stand out clearly enough. For every group except wool and dairy products the rate of increase in the post-war period is the smaller of the two, and in three cases an average annual increase in the earlier period turned into a decline in the later period. To be sure, we have no data for truck crops or tree nuts in the earlier period—groups which (with the exception of citrus fruit) grew most rapidly during 1921–38. Nevertheless the available evidence points toward retardation in the growth of agricultural output as a whole.

FACTORS INFLUENCING AGRICULTURAL OUTPUT

Before proceeding to an interpretation of changes in the output of individual groups and products, we may briefly recapitulate the outstanding findings of the preceding pages.

First, we have seen that the movement of agricultural output as a whole is marked by an absence of either regular or violent fluctuations.

Second, the increase in agricultural output for the period under observation has failed to keep pace with population growth. Even for a year of record output like 1939, per capita production fell short of the level prevailing at the turn of the century by as much as 10 percent.

Third, significant changes in the composition of total output have taken place during the four decades. Grains, hay and meats have lost ground, while poultry, eggs and milk have accounted for a growing share of total output. Citrus fruit and sugar production too have increased their shares of the total, but still account only for a small proportion of aggregate output.

Fourth, changes in the composition of total output are confirmed by the establishment of trends for the major groups. Grains, hay and meat animals, again, show the least rapid rates of growth, while citrus fruit, dairy products, and poultry and eggs rank highest. Furthermore, rates of growth for the post-war period, in all instances but two, are lower than for the pre-war period. The two exceptions are dairy products and wool.

These changes in the amount and character of agricultural production are to be interpreted mainly in terms of two types of influence: foreign trade on the one hand, domestic demand on the other. The fraction of the wheat crop exported has fallen perhaps from a third to an eighth, of cotton from two thirds to less than half, of beef and pork products from nearly one fifth to practically nothing. Tobacco alone among agricultural products has come near to holding its own in the export market. Every agricultural export has to compete with products from countries other than the United States. To the extent that the United States has lost out in foreign markets, the products of other countries have been available to foreigners more cheaply, or have been preferred by them for political or sentimental reasons. Moreover agricultural protection has closed the markets of many European countries to imports of cereals and livestock products from any outside source. Of no product is the United States sole producer, but it comes close to monopoly, perhaps, in the case of certain types of tobacco. This fact may explain why exports of tobacco have been somewhat less severely hit than have exports of most other products.

From the viewpoint of the domestic market the output of agriculture consists primarily of food materials. Ordinarily, as we have seen, more than four fifths of all farm produce is destined for consumption as human food. The remainder consists of raw materials supplied to a great variety of industries other than those manufacturing food products. The chief industries in this second group are those processing tobacco, cotton, wool and leather; industries making or using starches and oils; and industries making wine, beer and distilled spirits. The industrial demand for materials of this kind produced by domestic agriculture depends partly upon the availability of similar materials from abroad, and partly upon the competition of substances not of agricultural origin. The principal domestic products subject to competition from imports are sugar, vegetable oils, wool and hides, and in the case of at least two of these—sugar and wool—domestic output has been powerfully influenced by the availability of imported supplies.[18] The competition of nonagricultural products is felt mainly in respect of fibers: there can be little doubt that rayon has cut into the demand for cotton and possibly for wool also.

As we have seen, food accounts for the largest part of the domestic consumption of agricultural output, either directly or through the intermediary of the processing industries. For physiological reasons per capita demand for food as a whole, whether measured by weight or by calorific value, is rather stable. Yet there is some evidence of a shift from low- to high-priced foods; and the behavior of individual foodstuffs is even more variable. For instance, we have seen that the output of citrus fruit increased much more rapidly than did population; cereal production, on the other hand, hardly rose at all, and, if measured on a per capita basis, actually declined. Clearly changes of this kind have been influenced by the export of foodstuffs; but they are also a function of changing dietary habits among our own citizens. Thus in the case of wheat, had per capita domestic consumption not declined,

[18] See Chapter 3 below.

population increase would have more than compensated for the loss of exports.[19] On the other hand, the sensational advance in the production of citrus fruit was due in the main to a rise in per capita consumption within the United States.

These summary reflections represent as much as it is possible to say within the compass of the present chapter. The output history of individual products, and the detailed evidence surrounding each, are reviewed in Chapter 3. The material is organized by groups of products and by individual commodities. Not all products are treated in equal detail: some commodities are more important than others, or present points of special interest, and the reader will find that these are discussed at greater length.

[19] Per capita wheat consumption per annum fell between 1909 and 1939 about 1.3 bushels; on the basis of the population in the latter year this amounts to about 170 million bushels. Exports of wheat averaged 150 million bushels during 1900–09 and 70 million bushels during 1930–39.

Chapter 3

The Output of Individual Products

As WAS indicated by the trend measures given in the preceding chapter, there has been wide diversity in the development of the different groups and individual products of American agriculture since 1899. Most products have expanded in volume, though at varying rates, but some have actually declined. Limited by two extremes—citrus fruit, with the greatest increase, and hay, with the largest decline—the products have each followed a distinctive pattern of output, changes in which can be detected even from year to year.

In Chapter 2 we tried to summarize the behavior of each group by means of a few simple trend values, comparing the ranks with reference only to two periods, an initial and a final one. Here we shall consider the year-by-year course of each group and of a number of individual products, and at the same time suggest explanations for the diversity of movement so clearly evidenced by Tables 5 and 6.

GRAINS

As a concentrated source of carbohydrates the grains are unsurpassed among foodstuffs. According to our estimates, presented in Chapter 4 below, the grains used for human food alone have supplied, on the average, around 50 percent of the total carbohydrates consumed by the population of the United States during the last two decades, or, in terms of calorific value, somewhat less than one third of the total food supply. They resemble one another not only in regional distribution and methods of cultivation, but also in ultimate destination.

TABLE 5

INDEXES OF OUTPUT FOR SELECTED GROUPS AND PRODUCTS, 1897–1939[a]

1929:100

Year	*Combined Index*	*Grains*	*Potatoes and Related Products*	*Hay*	*Cotton*	*Tobacco*	*Sugar Crops*	*Wool*	*Meat Animals*	*Poultry and Eggs*	*Milk and Milk Products*	*Fruit, Non-citrus*	*Fruit, Citrus*	*Oil Crops*	*Truck Crops*	*Tree Nuts*
1897	66.0	85.7	55.1	380	70.6	45.9	60.3	69.7	75.9	46.8	51.9	77.7	14.5	42.5	..	..
1898	69.5	99.9	66.9	413	74.4	59.3	59.3	72.9	77.0	47.3	53.9	58.1	9.9	51.3	..	..
1899	69.5	91.8	71.0	370	61.5	56.8	37.2	75.5	82.6	48.8	54.3	82.9	16.6	54.8	..	..
1900	70.1	87.2	69.5	353	66.1	55.6	67.4	82.6	81.0	52.5	54.8	96.4	20.9	50.2	..	..
1901	68.8	90.8	58.2	350	64.1	57.8	78.5	84.4	79.3	52.9	55.7	66.9	20.1	70.0	..	..
1902	71.8	102.9	79.0	380	70.9	62.6	89.2	87.0	76.2	52.6	51.1	100.6	22.6	79.3	..	..
1903	72.5	93.6	75.8	407	66.2	63.7	77.3	77.9	79.9	56.2	58.6	92.7	29.8	71.6	..	..
1904	75.7	87.7	93.0	420	88.5	55.9	99.0	79.4	79.7	57.2	58.8	106.8	32.7	71.0	..	..
1905	75.3	104.5	83.3	427	70.4	61.3	103.7	80.5	82.6	60.0	57.8	66.4	33.7	74.3	..	..
1906	81.7	107.4	92.4	390	88.2	63.5	108.3	81.4	84.8	66.9	60.1	101.1	36.0	83.0	..	..
1907	76.3	89.7	90.6	420	72.4	57.8	119.4	81.4	85.2	69.5	60.9	65.4	36.7	63.9	..	..
1908	78.1	91.5	85.8	447	87.6	54.5	116.9	85.8	85.5	65.9	59.6	76.4	47.2	76.2	..	..
1909	77.4	102.3	104.2	433	67.2	68.8	111.3	91.1	79.0	67.5	62.8	77.0	44.1	70.5	..	..
1910	79.4	96.9	94.9	400	78.7	74.5	119.9	89.9	82.1	72.6	62.9	78.4	54.4	73.7	..	..
1911	81.5	85.4	85.2	327	105.0	61.4	138.9	88.7	83.5	75.8	63.1	98.5	49.5	91.7	..	..
1912	85.6	109.3	105.5	410	92.2	72.9	112.7	81.9	84.2	73.7	65.7	114.3	36.6	98.9	..	..
1913	82.8	91.0	91.1	353	95.5	64.7	130.0	78.9	88.3	73.4	66.8	79.0	62.5	92.4	..	..
1914	89.6	109.5	96.8	357	109.3	67.6	116.0	74.6	91.0	73.8	68.2	122.3	66.4	102.9	..	..
1915	89.9	125.4	94.9	360	76.3	75.5	116.1	71.7	94.4	76.6	69.4	117.4	62.3	80.8	..	..
1916	82.3	86.0	76.9	367	78.8	78.7	134.9	72.5	95.2	74.0	70.4	97.5	70.3	85.5	..	..

[a] Data relate to crop years in the case of crops, calendar years in the case of livestock and livestock products. See Appendix A.

TABLE 5 (concluded)

Year	Combined Index	Grains	Potatoes and Related Products	Hay	Cotton	Tobacco	Sugar Crops	Wool	Meat Animals	Poultry and Eggs	Milk and Milk Products	Fruit, Non-citrus	Fruit, Citrus	Oil Crops	Truck Crops	Tree Nuts
1917	85.9	100.9	110.4	303	77.2	86.5	129.8	70.5	94.5	72.4	73.1	94.9	35.5	84.3	..	..
1918	90.2	109.9	101.4	280	82.0	94.2	136.2	75.6	100.0	74.5	75.7	90.9	68.8	88.9	53.7	..
1919	87.1	114.5	90.2	290	77.3	94.2	107.6	80.2	90.5	78.3	73.4	91.6	74.0	73.1	49.4	96.3
1920	90.0	122.6	101.6	267	89.6	98.5	130.9	74.9	86.8	76.4	76.7	102.8	92.6	79.3	59.9	45.8
1921	81.9	108.1	92.0	227	54.0	65.6	126.4	72.3	89.6	80.4	77.2	66.7	69.3	59.8	50.3	73.8
1922	90.3	107.9	110.2	233	65.7	81.8	98.5	68.3	100.4	85.6	79.6	115.2	90.0	62.8	64.8	56.6
1923	91.9	105.0	103.5	223	68.1	99.0	99.9	68.9	102.7	90.4	81.5	111.4	111.0	68.8	63.3	92.4
1924	94.9	106.1	99.2	203	91.9	81.2	94.7	71.5	95.9	89.6	86.8	104.3	90.9	103.0	74.8	71.6
1925	95.8	100.6	86.8	173	108.8	89.8	96.5	76.2	91.8	91.5	88.8	100.2	103.7	107.9	85.3	97.8
1926	101.3	104.4	93.5	147	121.9	84.1	93.7	81.6	95.9	97.4	92.6	134.1	117.7	113.6	81.5	103.4
1927	98.2	110.8	105.1	147	87.8	79.0	96.5	87.6	98.6	101.2	95.0	95.8	96.9	100.6	85.4	113.1
1928	102.4	116.6	109.1	117	98.1	89.6	94.0	95.9	99.6	98.3	97.0	124.7	154.6	102.8	87.8	103.0
1929	100.0	100.0	100.0	100	100.0	100.0	100.0	100.0	100.0	100.0	100.0	100.0	100.0	100.0	100.0	100.0
1930	100.4	90.3	100.6	73	93.9	107.5	115.2	107.2	100.0	103.0	101.8	111.7	162.9	100.8	103.6	92.9
1931	104.0	94.9	109.9	77	114.9	102.1	104.6	114.4	104.2	98.7	104.5	129.0	144.9	110.9	93.9	119.8
1932	100.0	94.3	111.8	80	87.8	66.4	119.1	106.5	105.9	98.0	105.0	102.4	145.1	94.6	91.0	129.3
1933	97.4	66.8	104.1	77	87.4	89.5	136.0	113.0	109.7	97.7	105.1	104.3	136.3	80.6	87.3	108.7
1934	83.5	44.8	112.3	63	65.4	70.6	110.6	111.5	80.2	91.6	102.5	95.9	191.4	76.3	100.4	108.4
1935	92.2	77.7	115.8	77	72.1	84.6	120.2	110.0	86.1	90.8	102.9	122.4	154.9	97.5	106.4	156.8
1936	93.0	59.0	97.3	63	84.4	75.4	128.0	108.6	97.1	97.2	104.8	93.9	171.0	102.2	109.1	98.5
1937	106.3	104.7	119.1	73	128.3	102.0	129.9	110.5	91.7	95.9	105.3	136.3	216.0	138.5	115.9	170.8
1938	105.4	111.5	113.7	80	81.1	89.8	154.0	112.4	100.0	98.7	108.5	107.0	247.4	115.3	118.2	132.1
1939	110.7	107.0	110.6	77	80.1	120.6	143.3	114.9	111.3	104.9	109.1	127.5	237.5	128.8	118.9	156.6

TABLE 6

INDEXES OF OUTPUT FOR SELECTED GROUPS AND PRODUCTS, FIVE-YEAR MOVING AVERAGES, 1899–1937

1897–1901: 100

Year	*Combined Index*	*Grains*	*Potatoes and Related Products*	*Hay*	*Cotton*	*Tobacco*	*Sugar Crops*	*Wool*	*Meat Animals*	*Poultry and Eggs*	*Milk and Milk Products*	*Fruit, Non-Citrus*	*Fruit, Citrus*	*Oil Crops*
1899	100.0	100.0	100.0	100.0	100.0	100.0	100.0	100.0	100.0	100.0	100.0	100.0	100.0	100.0
1900	101.7	103.7	107.5	100.0	100.1	106.0	109.6	104.5	100.0	102.2	99.8	106.0	109.7	113.6
1901	102.6	102.4	110.3	99.6	97.8	107.6	115.5	105.8	100.8	105.8	101.5	115.1	134.1	121.2
1902	104.4	101.4	117.2	102.3	105.8	107.3	136.0	106.9	100.0	109.3	103.1	121.3	153.6	127.1
1903	105.9	105.3	121.5	106.2	107.0	109.3	148.1	106.2	100.4	112.3	104.3	113.5	169.4	136.1
1904	109.6	108.9	132.1	108.4	114.1	111.4	157.9	105.5	101.8	117.9	105.9	122.4	188.9	140.9
1905	110.9	106.0	135.7	110.5	114.6	109.6	167.8	104.0	104.2	124.7	109.6	113.2	206.0	135.3
1906	112.6	105.6	138.8	112.7	121.0	106.4	180.8	106.1	105.6	128.6	110.0	108.9	227.3	137.0
1907	113.1	108.8	142.4	113.4	114.7	111.1	185.0	109.1	105.4	132.8	111.3	101.2	240.7	136.8
1908	114.3	107.1	146.0	112.0	117.1	115.8	190.2	111.6	105.2	137.8	113.3	104.3	266.3	136.6
1909	114.2	102.3	143.7	108.6	122.1	115.1	200.5	113.5	104.9	141.4	114.4	103.5	282.8	139.8
1910	116.9	106.6	148.4	108.0	127.9	120.5	198.3	113.6	104.7	143.1	116.1	116.4	282.1	152.8
1911	118.3	106.5	150.1	103.0	130.3	124.3	202.6	111.8	105.3	146.1	118.7	117.0	301.0	158.7
1912	121.8	108.0	147.7	98.9	142.8	123.8	204.1	107.5	108.3	148.5	120.7	128.9	328.5	170.8
1913	124.9	114.3	147.7	96.8	142.2	124.1	203.0	102.9	111.5	150.1	123.1	139.1	338.2	173.4
1914	125.1	114.5	145.1	98.9	134.3	130.5	201.7	98.7	114.4	149.5	125.9	138.9	363.2	171.2
1915	125.2	112.6	146.6	93.2	129.9	135.4	207.3	95.7	117.0	148.9	128.7	133.8	362.0	165.8
1916	127.4	116.8	150.0	89.3	125.9	146.1	209.3	94.8	119.9	149.5	132.0	136.9	369.9	164.5

TABLE 6 (concluded)

Year	Combined Index	Grains	Potatoes and Related Products	Hay	Cotton	Tobacco	Sugar Crops	Wool	Meat Animals	Poultry and Eggs	Milk and Milk Products	Fruit, Non-Citrus	Fruit, Citrus	Oil Crops
1917	126.6	117.9	147.7	85.7	116.3	155.7	206.4	96.2	119.8	151.3	133.8	128.8	379.0	153.3
1918	126.7	117.2	149.9	80.7	120.4	164.1	211.4	97.1	117.9	151.1	136.6	125.0	415.6	152.8
1919	126.5	122.1	154.6	73.2	112.9	159.3	208.6	97.0	116.5	153.7	139.0	117.0	414.4	143.3
1920	127.8	123.6	154.6	69.5	109.5	157.7	198.2	96.5	118.1	159.2	141.4	122.3	480.8	135.3
1921	128.3	122.5	155.2	66.4	105.3	159.3	186.3	94.7	118.7	165.4	143.6	127.6	532.6	127.9
1922	130.6	120.6	158.0	61.8	109.8	154.6	182.0	92.5	120.1	170.0	148.6	131.0	553.3	138.8
1923	132.3	115.8	153.4	56.8	115.5	151.5	170.6	92.7	121.3	176.1	153.0	130.4	566.7	149.6
1924	137.9	115.0	153.8	52.5	135.7	158.3	159.8	95.2	122.9	182.9	158.8	147.9	625.2	169.5
1925	140.2	115.7	152.3	47.9	142.2	157.2	159.2	100.1	122.5	189.1	164.5	142.9	633.8	183.6
1926	143.3	118.2	154.0	42.1	151.1	153.9	157.2	107.3	121.6	192.4	170.2	146.3	686.8	196.3
1927	144.7	116.9	154.3	36.6	153.5	160.6	159.0	114.5	122.7	196.6	175.0	145.3	698.4	195.2
1928	146.1	114.6	158.7	31.2	149.0	167.2	165.1	122.6	124.7	201.2	179.9	148.3	770.3	192.6
1929	146.9	112.5	163.8	27.5	147.0	173.7	168.6	131.2	126.9	201.8	184.3	146.9	803.2	191.4
1930	147.4	108.9	165.8	23.9	147.0	169.0	176.2	136.1	128.8	200.4	188.0	148.7	862.3	189.2
1931	145.9	98.0	164.3	21.8	143.8	169.0	190.1	140.5	131.3	200.2	190.9	143.3	839.7	181.0
1932	141.1	85.8	168.2	19.8	133.6	158.3	193.6	143.5	126.3	196.8	191.9	142.3	951.2	172.1
1933	138.7	83.1	172.9	20.0	127.0	149.9	195.2	144.3	122.7	192.0	192.2	145.0	941.5	171.0
1934	135.6	75.2	169.0	19.3	118.0	140.3	203.0	142.7	121.0	191.3	192.2	135.9	973.2	167.7
1935	137.4	77.5	171.1	18.9	130.0	153.2	206.4	143.8	117.3	190.3	192.4	144.6	1,060	184.0
1936	139.8	87.3	174.1	19.1	128.1	153.4	212.4	143.6	114.9	190.7	193.7	145.4	1,195	197.0
1937	147.7	101.0	173.6	19.8	132.5	171.5	223.3	144.5	122.7	196.2	196.1	153.7	1,251	216.5

Their share in farm output fell over four decades from nearly one fifth to about one eighth (Table 2). Together they account for over 60 percent of the country's total crop acreage, but furnish only one out of every ten dollars of gross farm income.

The grains group includes the following crops: wheat, rye, corn, oats, barley, flaxseed, rice and buckwheat.[1] These, in turn, may be divided into food grains and feed grains, although the lines separating the two classes are rather flexible and to some degree arbitrary. By far the largest portion of the feed grains is consumed on the farms where it is grown and thus never enters the "organized" market.[2] At the same time the retention of the various grains for use as feed is influenced by the prevailing market situation. None of the grains is used exclusively for human food or exclusively to feed animals; nevertheless some are used predominantly for the one purpose, some mainly for the other. Wheat, rice and rye are primarily the food grains; corn, oats, barley and, to an

[1] There seems to exist some doubt as to whether it is proper to include flaxseed and buckwheat in the group. In strict scientific usage the term cereal is restricted to members of the grass family whose fruits or seeds are farinaceous (i.e., can be ground into a mealy substance) and suitable for food. The term grains, in turn, properly refers only to the fruits of grasses so defined, but is often used as a synonym for cereal. In commercial usage, moreover, the term grains is broadened to include even such crops as beans, peas, lentils, etc.

Buckwheat, being an herb and not a grass, is therefore not a cereal proper, but its inclusion in the grains group may be justified by its utilization as a substitute for other grains. On the other hand, flaxseed, a cereal neither by plant classification nor by utilization, has often been included with grains because of regional affinity and similarities in its handling and marketing. N. Jasny, *Competition Among Grains* (Food Research Institute, Stanford University, 1940), p. 5, objects to the inclusion of flaxseed with grains, holding that the latter term should properly be confined to cereals. On the other hand, the inclusion of buckwheat, also not a cereal, is accepted by Jasny. It would seem that for our purposes these distinctions should not be given too much consideration. Flaxseed, for instance, we have included both in the grains and in the oil materials group (as already noted, the classification exemplified in Table 5 is intended to be neither exhaustive nor free from duplication), while buckwheat seems to fit into the grains group better than into any other.

[2] This portion, as explained in Chapter 1, is excluded from our indexes of output.

increasing degree, buckwheat, make up the feed group. Flaxseed stands alone as an industrial raw material. The approximate distribution of the gross output of each of the eight crops among seed, feed and net output is shown in Table 7. These figures suggest sharp increases, for the majority of grains, in the relative importance of feed utilization—a trend which reflects the expansion that has occurred in the output of dairy products.

TABLE 7

GRAINS

Percentage Distribution of Gross Output, 1897–1901 and 1935–39[a]

	1897–1901			*1935–39*		
Crop	Seed	Feed	Net Output	Seed	Feed	Net Output
Wheat	11.0	4.5	84.6	11.3	13.2	75.6
Corn	b	b	20.0	b	b	22.2
Oats	b	b	30.0	b	b	17.1
Rye	15.6	15.0	69.4	21.4	35.1	43.5
Barley	b	b	50.0	b	b	37.4
Rice	8.9	3.7	87.4	5.0	1.3	93.7
Buckwheat	6.2	30.0	63.8	5.8	54.3	39.9
Flaxseed	8.0	0	92.0	10.8	0	89.2

[a] Data for 1935–39 are estimates by the Department of Agriculture. Data for 1897–1901 were assembled by the authors from various sources (see Appendix A); in most cases they are only rough approximations.

[b] Not separately available.

Corn is raised in every state of the Union—Iowa, at the top of the scale, has more than 10 million acres in corn crops; Nevada and Rhode Island, at the bottom, have less than 10 thousand each. Nor is there a state in which oats are not raised. Wheat is grown in forty states, barley in thirty-six and rye in thirty-four. Although the grains are widely dispersed, some areas are far more important producers than others. To-

Chart 6
GRAINS: NET OUTPUT

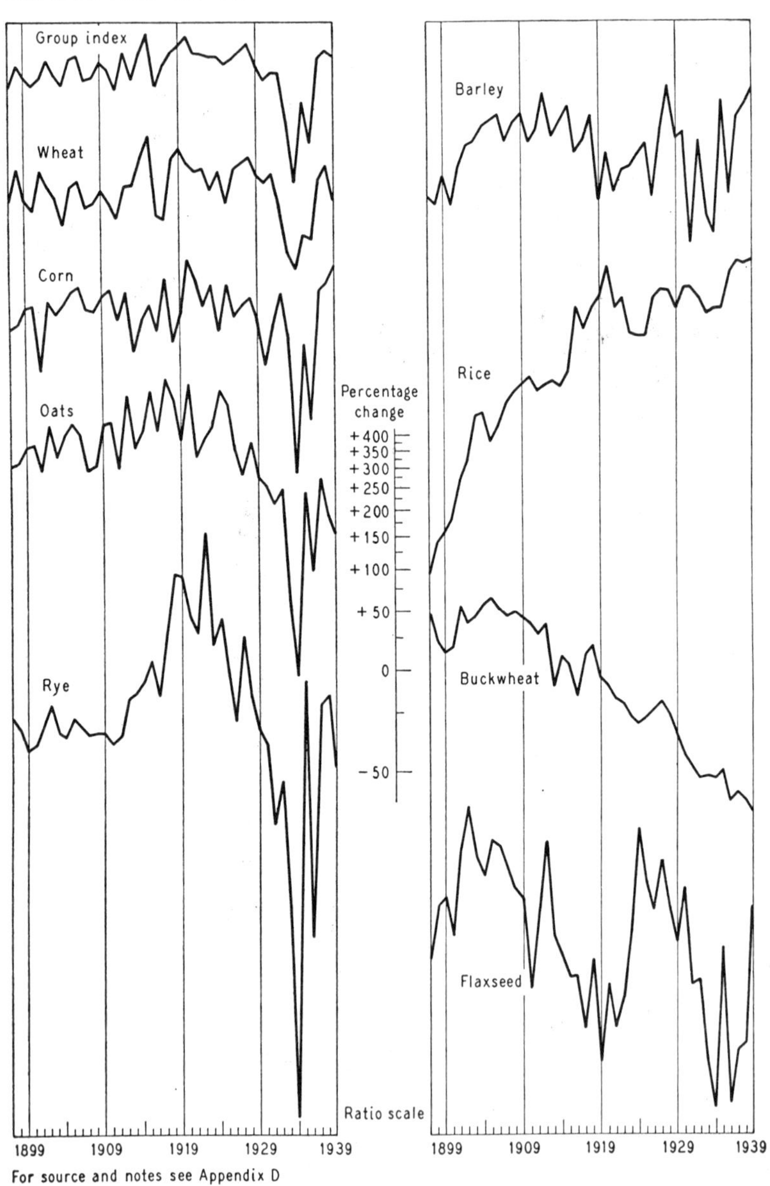

For source and notes see Appendix D

day grain growing is centered in the North Central region:[3] on the average during the past decade this territory has been responsible for 85 percent of all rye production, 80 percent of oats, 70 percent of corn, and 60 percent of wheat. Today Iowa (oats and corn), Kansas (wheat), North Dakota (rye), and Minnesota (barley), are the principal producing states.

Table 8 shows, for grains as a group and for each separate crop, annual average rates of change for the periods before and after the war of 1914–18.[4] These data of course refer not to the whole crop, but to net output only.[5] The combined grain index shows an annual average rate of growth for the period 1897–1914 of 0.6 percent, whereas the post-war period is characterized by an average decline of 2.0 percent per annum. The grains group and hay, to which we shall turn later in this chapter, are the only groups whose rate of growth has not merely slackened but has actually turned into a decline.[6] Yet

[3] Ohio, Indiana, Illinois, Michigan, Wisconsin, Minnesota, Iowa, Missouri, North Dakota, South Dakota, Nebraska, Kansas.

[4] For the method used in these comparisons see above, pp. 33-37.

[5] As explained in Chapter 1, our production data should be adjusted to exclude the portion used for seed or fed to livestock without leaving the farm economy, i.e., to include only the part consumed by the farm family or sold to a nonfarm consumer. Provided that this could be done, it would leave us with production series which, in the case of the feed grains, would exclude most of the farm demand for feed. Unfortunately, it is rarely possible to determine even roughly the distribution of total sales from farms according to utilization. Thus, some transactions are undoubtedly farmer-to-farmer sales for feed or seed, and to that degree are included only because we lack the data required to eliminate them. Another portion represents sales to commercial feed and seed dealers and feed processing plants, a third part is sold for eventual human consumption and a fourth for nonfood industrial uses. Our aim is to include in the case of each crop only that portion which is sold "off farms," i.e., leaves agriculture—regardless of the purpose for which it is used thereafter. The technical difficulties involved in arriving at such "net output" series are discussed in the Notes to Table A-1, pp. 353-71. It is clear from the foregoing that our "net values" are identical with what is commonly designated as "gross income." In order to avoid the impression that the entire crop is referred to we have preferred not to use the term "gross."

[6] See Table 4 above: the production of meat animals also showed a negative trend for 1921–38, but of such negligible proportions that it hardly can be considered significant.

during the same period (1921–38) population grew roughly 20 percent, or a little more than 1 percent per annum.[7]

TABLE 8

GRAINS

Average Annual Rates of Change in Net Output, 1897–1914 and 1921–38[a]

Crop	*1897–1914*	*1921–38*
	(Percent)	
Wheat	+0.3	− 1.7
Corn	+0.4	− 2.0
Oats	+1.1	− 5.3
Rye	+1.2	−12.8
Barley	+3.1	+ 1.1
Rice	+6.6	+ 1.9
Buckwheat	−0.6	− 4.2
Flaxseed	−0.9	− 5.3
ALL GRAINS	+0.6	− 2.0

[a] The data in this table are computed in the same manner as, and afford a partial breakdown of material to be found in, Table 4.

For each crop the annual average rates of change for the two periods reveal considerable dispersion, but in each period those for wheat and corn are closest to the central tendency. This is to be expected, in view of the relative importance, in terms of value, of the several crops (Table 9). In all Census years but one (1909) wheat accounted for more than 50 percent of the total net value of the grains crop, and even in 1909 it contributed 50 percent. Corn, second in importance throughout the long period 1899–1937, contributed between 25 and 30 percent. Oats declined from 11 percent in 1899 to 6 percent in 1937, with barley, rice, flaxseed, and

[7] Over our entire period of study the net output of the grains as a whole showed on balance practically no change (Table 6 above). If a direct comparison is made between the average for 1897–1901 and the average for 1935–39, the net output of the group is found to have fallen by 0.3 percent. By contrast, the combined *gross* output of the eight grains expanded 7.2 percent. The difference between the two results reflects the increased use of grain for feed disclosed by Table 7 above.

buckwheat following in the order given. The main influence on the behavior of the group is to be found, therefore, in the production of wheat and corn.

TABLE 9
GRAINS
Percentage Contributions of Individual Crops to Total Net Value of Group[a]

Crop	*1899*	*1909*	*1919*	*1929*	*1937*
Wheat	54.1	50.0	58.2	53.0	56.9
Corn	25.3	29.0	25.2	29.4	27.3
Oats	11.0	11.6	7.3	7.2	6.0
Rye	1.4	1.2	2.8	1.3	1.5
Barley	3.7	4.1	2.0	3.1	4.2
Rice	1.0	1.4	3.4	2.8	2.9
Buckwheat	.6	.5	.3	.3	.2
Flaxseed	2.9	2.1	.8	2.9	1.1
ALL GRAINS	100.0	100.0	100.0	100.0	100.0

[a] Each figure represents the product of net output and average season farm price, expressed as a percentage of the sum of these products for all eight grains. See Table A-2, p. 372.

Wheat is predominantly and typically the food grain. The explanation for its declining trend (see Chart 6) must be sought in shrinking per capita consumption at home, aggravated by a receding demand for American wheat in markets formerly supplied by this country. There is abundant evidence of the influence of both factors.

The decline in per capita consumption of wheat flour is not a phenomenon confined to the years after 1918, even though the slackening in population growth, coupled with the loss of former markets, tends to create that impression. As early as 1926 it was pointed out [8] that per capita flour consumption had dropped over 21 percent between 1904 and 1923; yet these years witnessed no decrease in aggregate production, since population increased at a rate more than suffi-

[8] Holbrook Working, "The Decline in Per Capita Consumption of Flour in the United States," *Wheat Studies*, Vol. II (Food Research Institute, Stanford University, 1926), p. 265.

cient to offset the decline in per capita consumption. Recent data released by the Department of Agriculture indicate that between 1909–14 and 1935–39 per capita wheat flour consumption fell off by 26 percent.[9] This downward trend has been fairly persistent; it has been reversed occasionally, but never for more than one year at a time.

The decline in wheat consumption can be appreciated only as part of the general shift in the pattern of the nation's food supply during the past three or four decades. For this reason it becomes necessary at this point to refer to the general discussion of trends in food consumption contained in Chapter 4, below. The factors listed there go far toward interpreting the statistical picture encountered in this section of our analysis. They suggest, further, that the rate of decline shown for the post-war period is not due primarily to the severe damage wrought by the drought years, though no doubt those years of extreme depression—1930, 1934 and 1936—are a contributory cause. From the consumption trends alone, one might well guess that any recovery to former output levels is unlikely; even the maintenance of wheat production on its present scale seems by no means certain.

The consequences of declining per capita consumption at home have been aggravated by the disappearance of foreign markets and the emergence of powerful competitors abroad. To summarize a development whose roots reach down to the beginning of the century, and which has left in its wake one of the basic problems in agricultural adjustment that this country has had to face, we present Table 10 which shows the annual percentages of net wheat output represented by wheat exports (both grain and flour). If we divide the period at 1925, regarding the years following as the post-war period—and for the history of wheat exports this would be quite justified—we find that exports averaged 15.8 percent of net output for 1926–38, whereas for 1897–1925 exports av-

[9] See Appendix Table B-1.

TABLE 10

WHEAT[a]

Ratio of Exports to Net Output, 1897–1938

Year	*Percent*	*Year*	*Percent*
1897	38.4	1918	37.3
1898	31.8	1919	26.9
1899	33.2	1920	50.3
1900	41.5	1921	40.5
1901	34.0	1922	31.6
1902	33.0	1923	26.0
1903	21.3	1924	36.9
1904	9.6	1925	19.2
1905	16.1	1926	30.7
1906	22.7	1927	27.8
1907	30.7	1928	21.1
1908	20.7	1929	22.5
1909	14.5	1930	20.3
1910	12.7	1931	19.7
1911	16.1	1932	7.5
1912	22.9	1933	9.2
1913	23.2	1934	6.0
1914	42.6	1935	3.5
1915	27.3	1936	4.9
1916	39.8	1937	16.0
1917	26.4	1938	15.9

Source: Exports from U. S. Department of Agriculture, *Agricultural Statistics, 1940,* Table 1; net output from Appendix A. Data are for crop years.

[a] Grain and flour (converted to wheat equivalent).

eraged 28.5 percent. Moreover the pre-war years for which amounts exported are low are years of weak yields (1904, 1911), or years immediately following such poor years (1917), or years of bumper crops (1915 and 1919) when the large quantities exported still amounted only to a small fraction of the total. In contrast, the proportion exported since 1925 has been low regardless of the size of the crop.

Increasing self-sufficiency in Europe and expanding production on the part of competing non-European countries have contributed to the shrinkage of wheat exports from the United States. Between 1909–13 and 1934–38 wheat output in Europe rose almost 20 percent.[10] And Canada, which at the beginning of the century produced only about 56 million bushels a year—or one tenth of United States production—harvested during the 1920's close to 400 million bushels on the average—more than half of United States production—

Chart 7

WHEAT: GROSS OUTPUT IN VARIOUS COUNTRIES

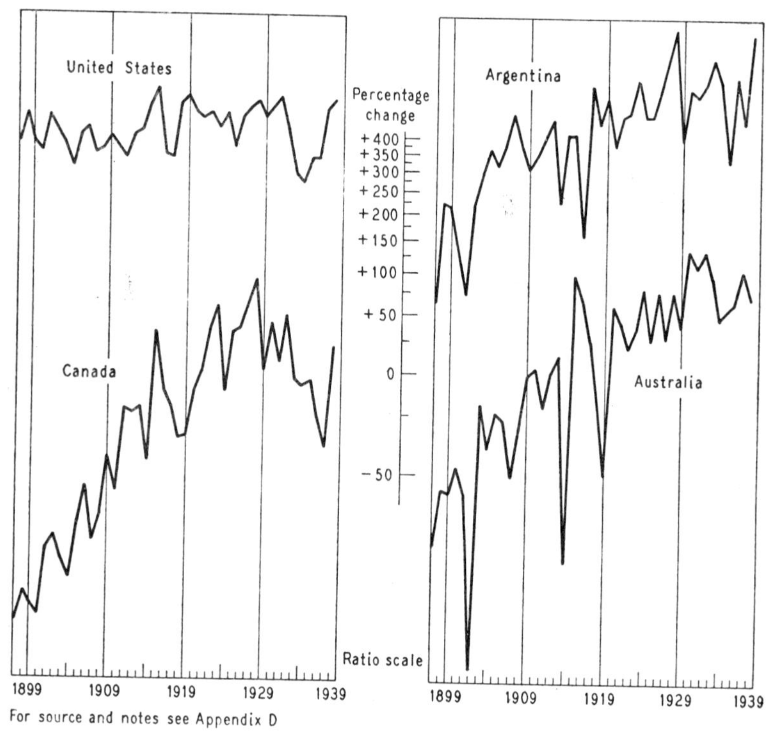

For source and notes see Appendix D

and in each of the years 1928, 1939 and 1940 raised more than 500 million bushels. The story of Australia and Argentina resembles that of Canada on a smaller scale (see Chart 7). As a net result, the contribution of the United States to the

[10] Excluding the U.S.S.R.; M. K. Bennett, "Wheat and War, 1914–18 and Now," *Wheat Studies*, Vol. XVI (Nov. 1939), p. 84.

world's total wheat production [11] dropped from 29 percent at the turn of the century to 23 percent in the mid-1920's, and again to 20 percent by the late 1930's.

The decline in American wheat exports may be attributed primarily to agricultural protection on the continent of Europe, and, so far as the United Kingdom is concerned, to the preferential treatment it has accorded Canada and Australia for political, and Argentina for commercial, reasons. As long as the European farmer continues to be protected from outside competition, and the policy of Great Britain remains inspired by the chimera of Imperial self-sufficiency, it seems idle to expect any substantial or permanent recovery in the export of wheat by this country. And since the scale of wheat exports in the United States from one period to another is powerfully influenced by such matters, it seems probable that the days when one third of the wheat crop was regularly exported are gone forever.

Corn is put to a multitude of uses (see Chart 8) and for this reason the explanation of its declining volume is much more complicated than in the case of wheat. Although it has never been subject to the hazards of the export market and is affected only indirectly by the human consumption factor, it slumped at least as fast as wheat during the years following the first World War (Chart 6). During 1937–39, however, net corn output [12] was the highest ever attained in three successive crop years. In order to understand this development, we must first disentangle and appraise the large number of influences that operate upon the demand for corn. This is not an easy task; indeed the effort to follow corn products down the numerous channels through which they reach the consumer has caused much difficulty to seasoned statisticians. Of the roughly 2.5 billion bushels normally grown in this country,

[11] Excluding the U.S.S.R. and China.

[12] We may remind the reader that net output excludes consumption for feed and seed: in the case of corn this is a particularly important reservation.

Chart 8

THE CORN REFINING INDUSTRY

For source and notes see Appendix D

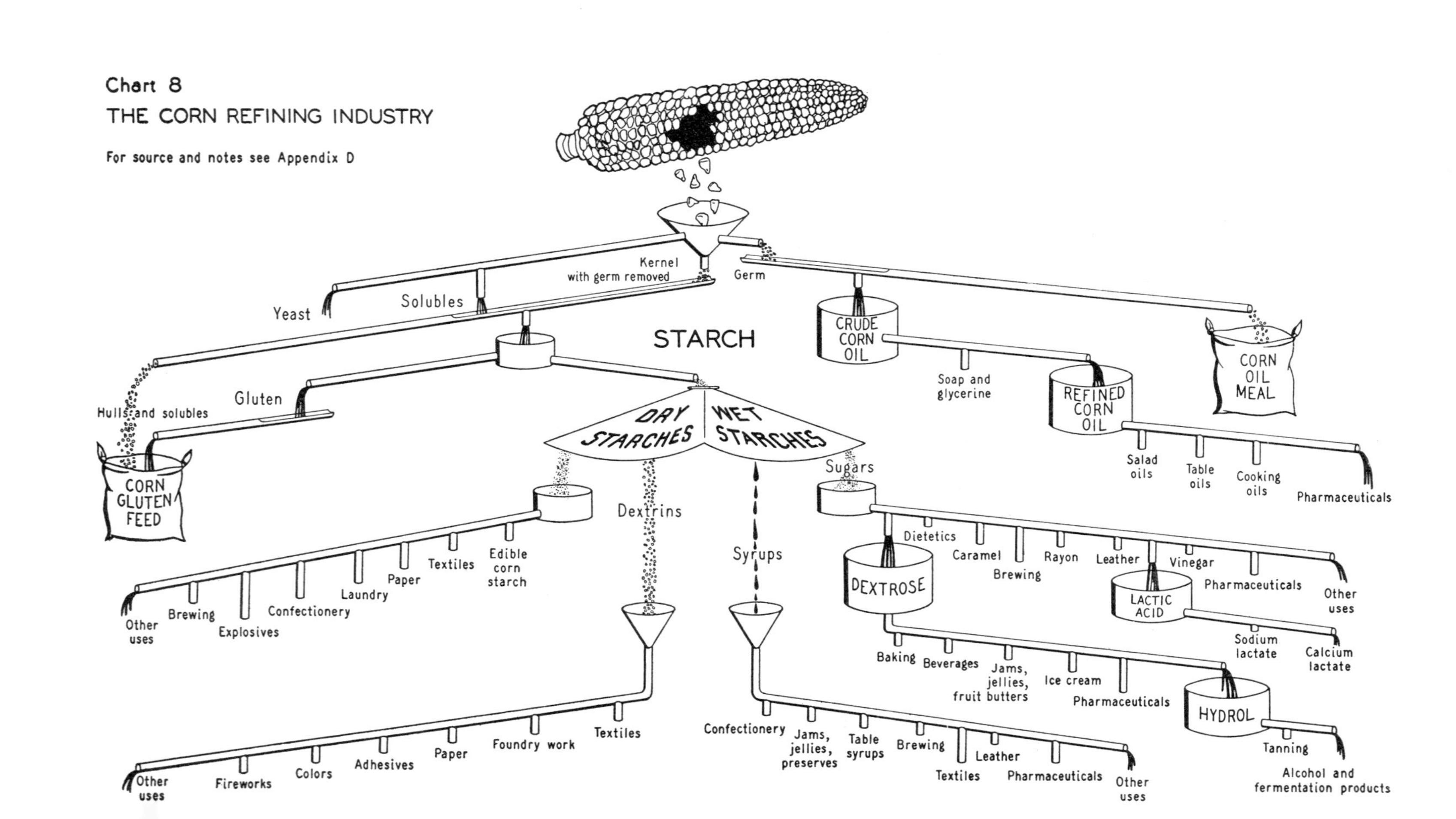

some 10 to 20 percent is harvested for silage or "hogged off." Of the remainder about 1.5 billion bushels are harvested for grain and consumed as feed on the farm where grown. This leaves a balance of around 500 million bushels sold by growers, and it is this amount for which data on disposition are not readily available. From one source it is indicated that "about 9 percent of the domestic crop of 2½ to 3 billion bushels is used for all 'city' purposes, including the production of starch." [13] These 250 to 300 million bushels, then, may be taken to represent at least one half of the amount of corn reported as sold, and to include the basic material for the large variety of products emerging from both the dry- and the wet-milling processes.[14]

In all its commercial uses corn has to compete fiercely with a host of other products, agricultural and otherwise. Starch, for example, is easily obtained from a variety of other sources; so also are sirups, vegetable oils and other corn derivatives. Hence the extent to which corn enters the processing industries depends largely on its relative price. So far the absorption of corn in the wet-milling process has ranged from a low

[13] U. S. Department of Agriculture, *Yearbook of Agriculture, 1940,* p. 620.

[14] The following is based on a survey entitled *Regional Research Laboratories, Department of Agriculture,* Sen. Doc. No. 65, 76th Congress, 1st Session (Washington, 1939), pp. 22-25.

The dry-milling process yields mainly food products derived both from the starchy kernel (endosperm) and from the germ. The former is the source of hominy, grits, corn meals and flours, processed flour, flaked products and prepared cereal foods, while the germ yields corn oil and stock feed. Nonfood uses of dry-milled corn are cold-water paints and pastes, foundry flours, and fillers or sizing products.

The wet-milling process, the more extensive and promising one for nonfood industrial purposes, also yields commercial feed and oil from the germ factor, but the main product is starch, which is the basis of a multitude of derived products, dextrins, gums, sirups, dextrose or corn sugar—not quite so numerous as the derivatives of coal tar, but economically almost as diverse. A variety of manufactured food products is based in turn on these modified starches. Among nonfood uses we find corn entering into laundry starch, textile sizes, explosives, adhesives, colors; the leather and rayon industries also make extensive use of it in their processing phases; distillation and fermentation, finally, provide another outlet in which malt liquor and the conversion of corn into industrial alcohol are easily the most prominent.

of 55 million bushels in 1934–35 to a high of 88 million bushels during the season of 1927–28. The distribution of that portion of the corn crop which is used for manufacturing of one sort or another may be summarized as follows: roughly one half of the processed products goes to food uses, one fourth reaches the farmer in the form of feeds and the remaining fourth is used industrially for purposes other than the manufacture of food.[15]

When to this amount we add the portion sold to other farmers directly or by way of feed dealers without intervention of processors—an amount that must run to at least another 200 million bushels—it becomes abundantly clear that our net output series is a composite, subject to many influences. It is determined on the one hand by the size of the entire crop,[16] and on the other by a variety of industrial demands largely dependent upon the changing position of corn in the price pattern of a large number of agricultural products.

[15] The approximate nature of these estimates is demonstrated by a comparison with other sources. Thus, a recent release (U. S. Bureau of Agricultural Economics, "Consumption of Agricultural Products," Washington, 1941) puts corn consumption as food at roughly 9 billion pounds of shelled corn, i.e., some 160 million bushels of corn. Since this estimate includes nonfood industrial products of the wet-grinding process (according to a written communication from the director of the study, Miss Elna Anderson) and thus would appear to exclude only industrial alcohol, it falls a good deal short of the estimate cited in the text. Another estimate, made by N. L. Gold (*Agricultural Land Requirements and Available Resources,* Pt. III of the Supplementary Report of the Land Planning Committee of the National Resources Board, Washington, 1935, p. 5) indicates that food consumption of corn was about 160-180 million bushels during the 1920's. This estimate presumably excludes all nonfood uses and thus would come closer to the figure of 250 million bushels mentioned at the outset. Finally, we have a third estimate for recent years, according to which 115 million bushels enter the dry-milling industry, 80 million bushels are absorbed in wet-milling, and close to 40 million go into the manufacture of distilled and fermented liquors. See D. W. Malott and B. F. Martin, *The Agricultural Industries* (McGraw-Hill, 1939), pp. 252-53.

[16] Statistics of sales vary directly with the size of the crop, a phenomenon which may not be altogether unconnected with the way in which such estimates are obtained.

Oats appear to have reached peak output during the first World War (Chart 6), possibly as a result of the army's demand for horse feed.[17] From then on, with occasional reversals in trend usually resulting from high yields (as in 1920 and 1924), the net output of oats declined at an accelerating rate until by 1934, after a precipitous decline beginning in 1928, it had fallen to not quite 60 million bushels, or less than one seventh of the wartime high (1917). The computed post-war rate of decline (Table 8) was 5.3 percent, more than twice that of grains as a whole. Though output has expanded since then, the level prevailing prior to 1929 has not again been touched, nor is it likely to be reattained in the future, since the eclipse of oats is no doubt associated with the gradual disappearance of the horse. From the scanty statistics available it is reasonably certain that most farmers' sales of this crop eventually find their way into animal feed, if for no other reason than that oats are the preferred diet for horses. The quantity utilized for human food—largely in the form of breakfast cereals (oatmeal, rolled oats)—and for industrial non-food purposes—oat hulls for furfural, a plastics material—is much less important. Using Gold's estimates [18] one would arrive at total annual oatmeal consumption of between 30 and 40 million bushels, as compared with sales of oats by farmers totaling on the average more than 200 million bushels per annum.[19] Unless the horse should stage a comeback, it is improbable that oats will regain the position it held prior to the first World War, when it contributed some 11 percent to the total net value of grains.

Rye, as its percentage contribution to the net value of grains indicates (between 1 and 2 percent; see Table 9), is of very minor importance. This low percentage was exceeded

[17] Exports of oatmeal also were exceptionally high during the final months of the war, amounting to the equivalent of 20 million bushels of oats.

[18] See footnote 15.

[19] These estimates are confirmed in a U. S. Department of Agriculture release, "The National Food Situation" (Washington, 1941).

only during and immediately after the first World War period (1919 percentage contribution: 2.8), when there occurred a sudden bulge in the curve of output (Chart 6), occasioned both by the relatively high price of rye—exceeding the price of wheat during the spring of 1918—and by the drought conditions which had prevailed in the Dakotas in 1916 and 1917.[20] A peak was reached in 1922, when net output stood at four times its pre-war level. Nor was that level accidental in the sense of the 1927 bulge which was due entirely to a record yield; for in 1922, although that year saw the largest rye yield ever recorded, acreage had expanded to about three times the pre-war level, with exports reaching an all-time high of more than 50 million bushels.[21] From that level rye output declined most precipitously until 1934, exceeding even oats in its rate of fall. In the last four years, however, there has been a return to the level obtaining between 1897 and 1909, so that the average annual rate of decline of nearly 13 percent per annum computed for the period 1921–38 is attributable primarily to the abnormally low output of the middle 1930's.

Barley cultivation is concentrated in the North Central area, and especially in its western part. Minnesota, Wisconsin and the Dakotas alone were responsible, during the period 1929–38, for over half the average crop. California for many years has contributed one tenth of the annual total.

Barley holds a peculiar position among the grains in that

[20] As has been pointed out by B. B. Hibbard, *Effects of the Great War upon Agriculture in the United States and Great Britain* (Oxford University Press, 1919), p. 33, in explaining this phenomenal increase in rye cultivation, "over seven-eighths of the increase in the rye acreage of the country took place in those two states, and as a matter of fact pretty much all of this in North Dakota. The North Dakota farmers were getting desperate. They must raise something. Wheat had been a comparative failure for two years. A winter crop stands the summer drought better than a spring crop. They cannot sow winter wheat, so they are trying rye."

[21] Rye exports were practically zero prior to the World War, but far into the 1920's the temporary elimination of Russia as an exporter enabled the United States to unload upon the European market a great part of its war-swollen rye crop. See "Rye in its Relations to Wheat," *Wheat Studies*, Vol. IV (March 1928), pp. 198-202.

it appears in the human diet almost exclusively in the form of malt, and more particularly as fermented malt liquor. In terms of bushels consumed in the manufacture of alcohol, distilled spirits and fermented malt liquor, it has now outstripped its closest grain competitor, corn; since the repeal of the 18th Amendment, barley has become twice as important as corn in this connection. However, even the large amount utilized for beverages is secondary to the portion fed to livestock, above all to hogs. Only in times of extreme emergency has barley-meal been used as a flour substitute. In 1917–18, approximately 20 million bushels of barley were ground into flour.[22] In normal times not more than a few million bushels are likely to find their way into the human diet as pearl barley, yeast and vinegar, breakfast foods, and malt preparations other than beverages.[23]

Gold's figures [24] indicate that aggregate consumption of barley as malt stood at about 45 million bushels prior to the first World War, and at between 15 and 20 million bushels during the prohibition era. For 1937, barley consumed in the form of malt has been estimated at 61 million bushels,[25] with minor quantities going into barley flour and breakfast foods. During the past 30 years the use of barley as feed on the farms where it is produced has more than doubled, so that by now feed can be said to be the main destination of barley. Though it is true that only certain types of barley can be used for malting purposes, there can be little doubt that prohibition acted as a stimulus in the shift of barley from a malt material to a feed, especially since, as Jasny points out,[26] the dividing line between malting and non-malting barley is determined to a considerable extent by crop conditions.

[22] Raymond Pearl, *The Nation's Food* (W. B. Saunders, Philadelphia, 1920), p. 53.

[23] U. S. Tariff Commission, *Agricultural Staples and the Tariff*, Tariff Information Series No. 20 (Washington, 1920), p. 108.

[24] See footnote 15.

[25] *Regional Research Laboratories*, p. 43.

[26] Jasny, *Competition Among Grains*, p. 106.

Peculiar demand conditions must be held responsible for the fact that barley is one of the two grains (the other is rice) that showed a positive rate of change both before and after the first World War, even though the post-war rate is less than half the pre-war rate, 1.1 percent as against 3.1 percent (Table 8). In this drop is reflected the influence of prohibition, for the net output curve shows the decline to lower levels setting in with the 1919 crop (Chart 6). A temporary upsurge lasted from 1927 to 1930; and in two of these years, 1927 and 1928, exports took up 50 percent and more of the commercial crop. Since 1930 net output has fluctuated widely, but in general has tended upward to regain its average prewar level which it exceeded for the first time in 1937. It has not declined since then, and in 1939 it came within 2 million bushels of the record net output of 1927.

Rice differs from the other grains in almost every respect. It is the one crop that registered consistent gains throughout the period and did not suffer a relapse after its wartime expansion (Chart 6). Rice growing is confined to Louisiana, Texas, Arkansas, and California. The climate of these states is radically different from that of the North Central region, the principal source of the other grains, so that rice was unaffected by the drought years. Rice is one of the few crops to have experienced a secular rise in yield per acre: where 35 bushels per acre constituted a record yield at the beginning of this century, present yields average close to 50.[27] Between 1897 and 1938 acreage tripled, and average yield per acre doubled. Since the end of the World War usually half the crop has been shipped to United States territories and foreign countries, and although exports to foreign countries fell off heavily during the depression, shipments to Hawaii, Alaska, and Puerto Rico have continued at the same pace. The favored position of the United States in these territories, in which per capita consumption of American rice is 20 to 40

[27] See Table 50, below.

times the per capita consumption in the continental United States, and in which rice imports from other countries are practically barred, has been and continues to be an important factor in the steady development of rice growing in this country.

Buckwheat, grown mainly in the hilly sections of New York, Pennsylvania, and parts of New England, has little economic importance. Its principal advantage is that it will thrive even when it is planted late in the spring, in climate and soil unsuitable for other grains. Scarcely entering commercial channels, except as flour for griddle cakes, its net output—and more recently even its gross output—has declined steadily throughout the past three decades, with its impending eclipse as a commercial crop only temporarily delayed by the first World War. The chief current use of buckwheat is as feed in regions where more desirable crops are not easily grown.

Flaxseed, which is not a cereal or a food, is included among the grains because of its place in crop systems and the similarity in methods of farming.[28] Classification by use would put it clearly into the oil crops group, since in this country practically all flax is planted for its seed and not for its fiber. It is only on a small acreage in Oregon that fiber flax is cultivated, amounting, in terms of value, to less than 0.5 percent of the $40 million worth of linen and fiber annually imported into the United States. It has been estimated that imports could be replaced by the yield from 500,000 acres, allowing for rotation of crops.[29]

Like buckwheat, flax has been a pioneer crop, doing well on newly broken soil and preparing virgin land for cultivation of wheat or other grain during subsequent years. Con-

[28] See above, p. 46n.

[29] *Regional Research Laboratories,* p. 105. The use of flax fiber in the manufacture of cigarette paper, long a potential market for flax, has, with the cessation of imports after the fall of France, become a reality, though so far the approximate volume of utilization can be gauged only by the $5 to $6 million annually paid for imported cigarette paper.

sequently, it is not surprising that output reached its peak around the turn of the century and suffered an almost continuous decline for the following two decades; in 1919 net output amounted to barely more than one sixth of its 1902 level. At that time, there began a resumption of flax growing which, by 1924, in the short span of five years, had carried output up to a level second only to that of 1902. Another steep decline ensued, however, and in 1934 and again in 1936 net output was below even the trough of 1919. Recovery from those levels was well under way in 1939 and 1940.

The explanation of these rather violent changes is to be found partly in the relationship of flax to other grains, and partly in its sensitiveness to the price of other vegetable oils. Flaxseed production is concentrated in a narrow area in Minnesota and North Dakota.[30] To follow in any detail the trend of flaxseed production would therefore involve tracing the interrelationship of the principal grains grown in the spring wheat belt. In this connection it is significant that the doubling of flaxseed production in 1924 followed upon a year of extremely poor yields in both wheat and rye, a year, furthermore, in which the spread between the price of flaxseed and that of wheat had widened in favor of flaxseed. This spread is believed to have an important bearing upon the acreage planted to flax in the succeeding year.[31] While flax competes for land with wheat, corn and oats, the derived product, linseed oil, competes with other oils, both domestic and imported. This country since about 1910 has usually been on an import basis with regard to flaxseed, so that the price is scarcely affected by the size of the domestic flaxseed crop. And as the size of the domestic crop is largely conditioned by the world market price of linseed oil and its relationship to the price of domestic wheat, major fluctuations from year to year are not surprising. Since the first World War, these fac-

[30] More recently Kansas and California have begun to acquire status as flaxseed growing states.

[31] *Flaxseed Prices and the Tariff*, Sen. Doc. No. 62, 76th Congress, 1st Session (Washington, 1939), p. 8.

tors, with rare exceptions, have combined to make the cultivation of flaxseed appear less profitable than that of alternative crops; increasing tariffs on both seed and oil have relieved, but not eliminated, the comparative unprofitability of the crop.

POTATOES AND RELATED CROPS

This group comprises three staple foods which, although vegetables, are not counted as truck crops: potatoes, sweetpotatoes, and dry edible beans. By virtue of their high starch content, they are closer to the grains than to other vegetables. In its year-to-year fluctuations the group is dominated by the behavior of potatoes, but the rapid rise in dry edible beans has increased its relative importance over the whole period. The combined contribution of the three crops to total output rose from 3.3 percent in 1897–1901 to 4.1 percent in 1935–39 (Table 2).

Potatoes, like corn and oats, are raised in every state. Production, however, is not highly concentrated, although it is more so in some areas than in others. Maine, the largest potato state, produced only 10 percent of the total during the past decade. Yet this small percentage supplies almost half the cash income of the Maine farmer. Altogether only 3 million acres —or one in every hundred crop acres on farms—are devoted to potato growing, but the yield per acre is exceedingly high: by weight, between 8 and 9 times that of wheat. Output in bushels is almost half that of wheat. Usually one fifth of the potato crop is retained as food for the farm household, a much larger portion than in the case of either wheat or corn.[32]

[32] Production for use in the farm household is of course included in net output as we compute it. Since in some states potatoes are mainly a cash crop, the percentage retained for food naturally shows a great deal of variation from state to state. Thus, in 1938 only 1 to 3 percent of total production was home-consumed in Maine, Idaho, Colorado, California, while 50 percent or more was retained for food in Indiana, Illinois, Iowa and other states.

Sweetpotatoes, grown on an acreage usually less than one third that devoted to potatoes, are mainly a southern crop, even though they may be found on a few thousand acres in Iowa, Indiana and Illinois. The bulk of the crop originates east of the Mississippi and south of the Mason-Dixon line, with the lower Atlantic states contributing more than one third of the total. To a much larger extent than potatoes,

Chart 9

POTATOES AND RELATED CROPS: NET OUTPUT

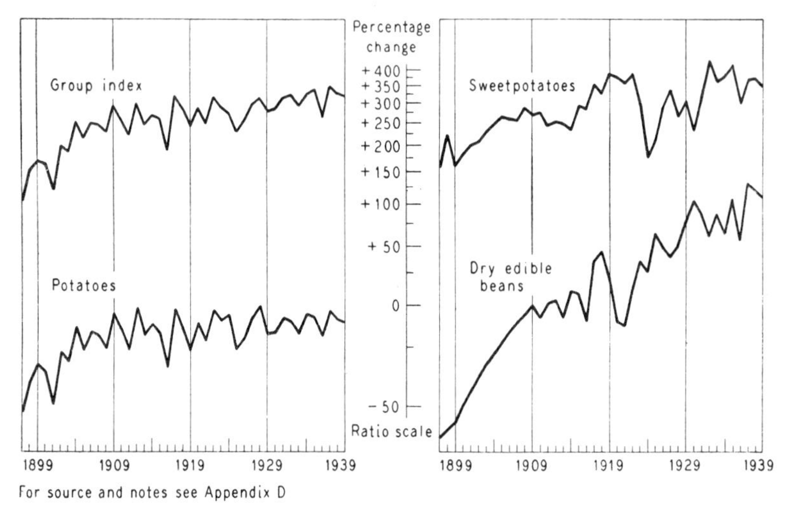

For source and notes see Appendix D

sweetpotatoes are grown for home consumption: usually less than one third of the crop is sold.

Dry edible beans, predominantly a cash crop, come from three widely separated areas: lower Michigan and western New York; California; and more recently, certain areas in the Mountain states, particularly Colorado and Idaho, along the western border of the Great Plains. Michigan and California together account for over one half of the country's crop.

The combined output of the potato group showed a fairly rapid rise up to about 1909 (Chart 9), after which expansion slowed down noticeably. The computed annual average rate of growth for the group amounts to 2.8 percent for the pre-war period, but to only 0.9 percent for the post-war period (Table 4 above). This retardation of growth is explained in part by a decided contraction in per capita potato consumption, amounting to some 25 percent since 1909. In fact population growth has just sufficed to keep total consumption

Chart 10
POTATO CONSUMPTION PER CAPITA, 1909 - 39

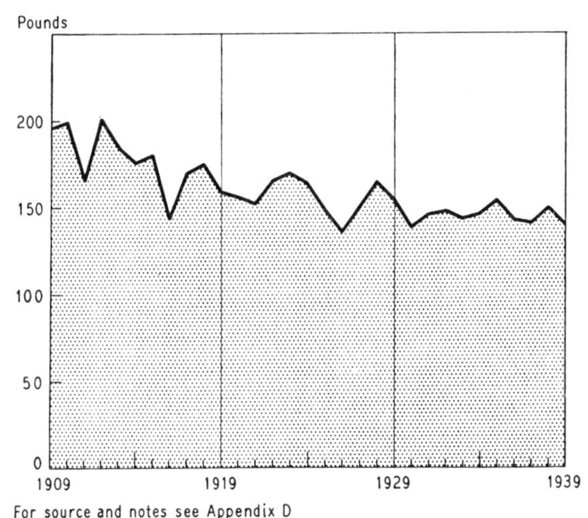

For source and notes see Appendix D

steady. The rapid rise in the production of beans and the moderate advance in the output of sweetpotatoes suggest that there has been a substitution in their favor.

It is pertinent to remark on the substantial increase in potato yields over the past two decades, a gain which appears to have helped maintain post-war levels of potato output: whereas in every year since 1922 more than 100 bushels per acre have been harvested, in only 9 years during the long period 1866–1921 were there any yields of similar magnitude.[33] Expansion in sweetpotatoes and beans, on the other hand, has been due to additional acreage; in fact sweetpotato yields seem to have passed their peak (Table 50 below).

TOBACCO

Tobacco is purely a cash crop, and perhaps its most important characteristic is its unusually high monetary value per acre. Grown in an area amounting to no more than one half of 1 percent of the nation's entire crop acreage, tobacco has in recent years contributed between 2 and 3 percent to gross farm income, and between 3 and 4 percent to cash income. The crop is distinguished also by the marked qualitative variations—there are 28 officially recognized types—that originate in differences of climate, soil, seed and curing processes. Tobacco growing is highly localized and occupies an especially prominent place in the economy of North Carolina, Kentucky and Tennessee. In 1935, for example, its sales supplied the farmers of North Carolina with 40 percent of their gross income, 54 percent of their cash income.[34] The three states together have produced more than 70 percent of all domestic tobacco during the past 10 years. The remainder of the crop is derived from 17 states, most of which raise only small amounts of special varieties. And finally, when we turn to foreign trade, we find tobacco not only the oldest article of export,[35] but also high up in the list of farm products sent to foreign markets at the present time. Although, for reasons set out below, a decreasing fraction of total tobacco production

[33] See Table 50 and Chart 47 below. Fertilizer and certified seed appear to have been the two agents responsible.

[34] U. S. Bureau of Agricultural Economics, *Farm Value, Gross Income and Cash Income from Farm Production, by States and Commodities, 1934–1935* (Washington, 1936).

[35] As early as 1618 the colonies shipped tobacco, in that year only 20,000 pounds, to England. See W. W. Garner, E. G. Moss, H. S. Yohe, F. B. Wilkinson and O. C. Stine, "History and Status of Tobacco Culture," *Yearbook of Agriculture, 1922,* p. 448.

has been entering export channels, this crop has accounted for a growing percentage of aggregate agricultural exports since the War of 1914–18. This development too is treated in greater detail below.

Before attempting to analyze such changes in tobacco output as have occurred over the past few decades, we shall briefly sketch the actual course of output and the measures of change that are yielded by our standard procedures (Chart 11). The opening year of our period finds tobacco output at the end of a series of years during which it had shown practically no change. The next year, 1898, marks the permanent transition to the million-acre level as well as the first 800-pound-per-acre yield since 1875. With the exception of three years—1899, 1900 and 1913—yields above 800 pounds per acre remained the rule until after the War of 1914–18.[36] To some extent this sudden jump from 1897 to 1898 accounts for the high annual average growth rate for the period 1897–1914 of 1.5 percent; for practically no change in output occurs until 1909, when another substantial increment in acreage carries tobacco production to a new level [37] around which it oscillates until 1914. Though the increase in acreage was larger between 1908 and 1909 than between 1897 and 1898 (20 percent as against 15), output expanded relatively less in the more recent period, since it was not accompanied, as it had been in 1898, by a corresponding spurt in yield per acre.

Since the first World War fluctuations in output have been erratic, as may be seen from Chart 11, and the computed annual rate of growth of 0.3 percent has little meaning. Because there was a spectacular rise in the short span of four years (1915–18), our computed rates of growth for the pre- and post-war periods give little hint of the substantial difference between the pre-war and post-war volumes of production. The

[36] See Table 50 and Chart 47 below.

[37] A glance at the price statistics of the period suggests that the upward movement was not unconnected with the substantial rise in tobacco prices which had preceded it.

high level of output attained in 1918, 1919 and 1920 gave way, in a number of years to follow, to a crop more reminiscent of the average size prevailing between 1909 and 1916, but in other years, notably 1923, 1929–31 and, most recently, 1937 and 1939, the 1920 peak was surpassed. It appears that the wartime expansion in acreage has left a permanent mark on tobacco growing, much as it has on wheat growing and on

Chart 11

TOBACCO: NET OUTPUT

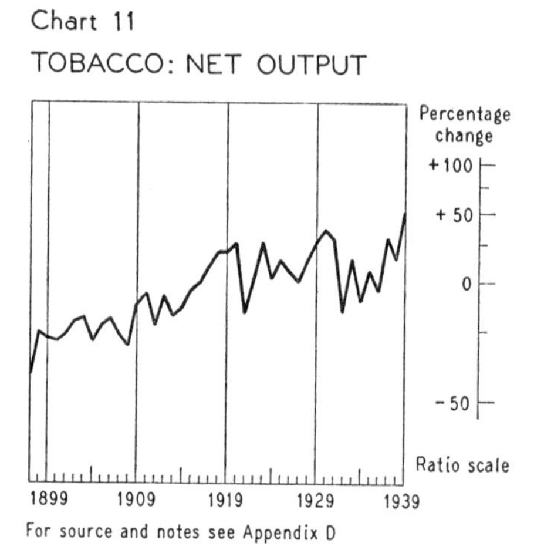

For source and notes see Appendix D

other types of farm enterprise which, in a period of falling prices, have refused to embrace output contraction as a means of economic salvation. Two years of abrupt decline in acreage, 1921 and 1932, were both preceded by a season of plunging prices. Acreage contraction during the 1930's serves to explain why post-war output has not risen to a greater extent than the annual 0.3 percent mentioned above.

Shifts in both domestic demand and foreign trade have had their effect on tobacco raising. Indeed the emergence of the cigarette and the attendant changes in the composition of American tobacco output fall within the period under study. More recent years have witnessed also the slow process by which United States tobacco has been shut off increasingly from its export markets.

Domestic demand, as revealed in per capita consumption data, rose almost without interruption from 1900 to 1913, amounting to an average of 1.8 percent per year as compared to the annual growth rate of 1.5 percent from 1897 to 1914. Per capita consumption began another brief but rapid rise in 1915, and by 1917 it reached the unprecedented (and so far not repeated) level of 7.74 pounds per person. Of this total, one sixth represented consumption of cigarettes, whereas only three years earlier, at the outbreak of the war, cigarettes had accounted for scarcely 10 percent of all tobacco consumed. It is common knowledge that the first World War accelerated the spread of cigarette smoking, which to this day has apparently not reached its culmination (Table 11).

The effect of increased cigarette smoking upon the output of tobacco during the World War becomes clear when we trace the development of tobacco by types. It is then seen that the real upswing occurred in flue-cured tobacco,[38] the type that is grown in the Atlantic states and used predominantly in the manufacture of cigarettes; tobacco for cigars and pipes showed little tendency to expand. Naturally, the growth in output was paralleled (and presumably stimulated) by rising prices for flue-cured tobacco which far outran prices of other types.[39] This tendency was furthered by the development of blends that used less Turkish and more domestic tobacco, particularly when imports of Turkish tobacco were temporarily interrupted during the war.[40] Thus the shift toward cigarette smoking also meant a decline in import requirements and became a boon to the domestic producers of flue-cured tobacco.

Both per capita consumption and exports have been unable

[38] Garner et al., *op. cit.*, p. 412.

[39] *Ibid.*, p. 442.

[40] Malott and Martin, *The Agricultural Industries*, p. 380. Import statistics indicate that imports from San Domingo temporarily took the place of imports from Turkey, but the lapse was considerable and the total volume remained low.

TABLE 11

TOBACCO PRODUCTS

Per Capita Consumption, 1900–39

Pounds

Calendar Years	*Cigars*	*Cigarettes*	*Chewing Tobacco*	*Smoking Tobacco*	*Snuff*	*Total*
1900[a]	1.33	0.14	2.39	1.31	0.20	5.37
1905[a]	1.59	0.15	2.09	1.92	0.25	6.00
1910	1.59	0.34	2.17	2.30	0.34	6.74
1911	1.65	0.40	1.98	2.23	0.31	6.57
1912	1.65	0.49	1.96	2.28	0.33	6.71
1913	1.72	0.60	1.96	2.27	0.34	6.89
1914	1.67	0.62	1.84	2.28	0.31	6.72
1915	1.58	0.67	1.77	2.36	0.33	6.71
1916	1.71	0.93	1.90	2.37	0.34	7.25
1917	1.79	1.29	1.98	2.34	0.34	7.74
1918	1.65	1.39	1.76	2.25	0.36	7.41
1919	1.61	1.59	1.53	2.17	0.34	7.24
1920	1.87	1.56	1.43	1.98	0.34	7.18
1925	1.39	2.07	1.10	2.14	0.33	7.03
1930	1.17	2.73	0.80	1.87	0.33	6.90
1931	1.08	2.58	0.69	1.95	0.32	6.62
1932	0.89	2.32	0.57	1.93	0.29	6.00
1933	0.89	2.53	0.55	1.87	0.29	6.13
1934	0.94	2.87	0.56	1.87	0.29	6.53
1935	0.96	3.01	0.89	1.49	0.28	6.63
1936	1.03	3.40	0.90	1.51	0.29	7.13
1937	1.04	3.55	0.89	1.44	0.28	7.20
1938	0.97	3.54	0.82	1.53	0.29	7.15
1939	0.99	3.71	0.81	1.50	0.29	7.30

Source: U. S. Department of Agriculture, *First Annual Report on Tobacco Statistics,* Statistical Bulletin 58 (Washington, 1937), Table 16; *Annual Report on Tobacco Statistics, 1940,* Table 25. Data for 1939 are preliminary.

[a] Year beginning July.

to maintain the heights they reached during the World War. Consumption quickly receded from its record-breaking performance of 1917 to a low in 1922, yet this low equaled the highest level attained in pre-war years. With the exception of a steep decline during the depression of the 1930's, beginning

TABLE 12

LEAF TOBACCO USED IN MANUFACTURE OF VARIOUS PRODUCTS

Five-year Average	*Cigars*		*Cigarettes*		*Tobacco and Snuff*		*Total*	
	1000 lbs.	Percent	1000 lbs.	Percent	1000 lbs.	Percent	1000 lbs.	Percent
1897–1901	95,941	25.7	14,628	3.9	262,069	70.3	372,638	100.0
1907–1911	141,134	26.4	26,576	5.0	366,896	68.6	534,606	100.0
1917–1921	154,180	23.7	146,272	22.5	349,991	53.8	650,442	100.0
1927–1931	144,292	18.8	325,009	42.5	296,249	38.7	765,550	100.0
1934–1938	119,770	14.5	438,394	53.0	269,247	32.5	827,411	100.0

Source: U. S. Department of Agriculture, *First Annual Report on Tobacco Statistics,* Statistical Bulletin 58 (Washington, 1937), Table 13; U. S. Agricultural Marketing Service, *Annual Report on Tobacco Statistics, 1940* (Washington, 1940), Table 20. Data relate to calendar years, except for cigars and cigarettes in 1897–1901 and 1907–11 where figures are for years beginning July.

in 1930 and not overcome until 1936, per capita consumption has remained stable at just about seven pounds per head of population. Whether the high level of 1939 marks the beginning of another upswing, paralleling the experience of the first World War, it is too early to predict. It seems unlikely, however, that any such striking development as the popularization of the cigarette, or the spread of smoking among women, is to be anticipated in the future. Throughout the period, cigarettes have continued to grow in importance, so that by now more than 50 percent of all leaf tobacco processed is used in the production of cigarettes (Table 12). At the same time per capita use of tobacco in other forms has tended to decline (Table 11).

Exports, which up to 1930 had remained substantially above the pre-war level, have suffered a severe decline since that year; nonetheless, the share of tobacco in total agricultural exports (in terms of value) was much higher in the 1930's than in the preceding decade.[41] In 1935, the percentage of the tobacco crop exported was lower (except for 1931) than at any time since 1917, yet in that same year tobacco's share of aggregate agricultural exports registered a high of over 18 percent—as against 5 to 7 percent in the peak export period 1918–19—so severe had been the decline in exports of other agricultural commodities (Chart 12). In comparison with other farm products, tobacco's hold on the export market has been tenacious, even in the face of import restrictions by European countries, preferential tariffs granted to Empire nations by the United Kingdom, increased domestic growth of flue-cured tobacco in China (formerly one of our most important customers), and the continuous shrinkage in exports of fire-cured tobacco.[42] At the same time exports have

[41] Frederick Strauss, *The Composition of Gross Farm Income since the Civil War,* Bulletin 78 (National Bureau of Economic Research, 1940), Table 7.

[42] B. S. White, Jr., "Our Changing Tobacco Exports," *The Agricultural Situation,* March 1939.

Chart 12

TOBACCO EXPORTS

Ratio to Total Farm Exports

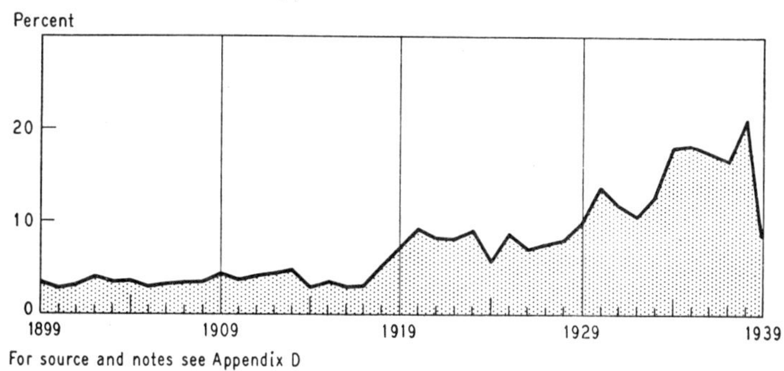

For source and notes see Appendix D

Chart 13

TOBACCO EXPORTS

Ratio to Gross Farm Income from Tobacco

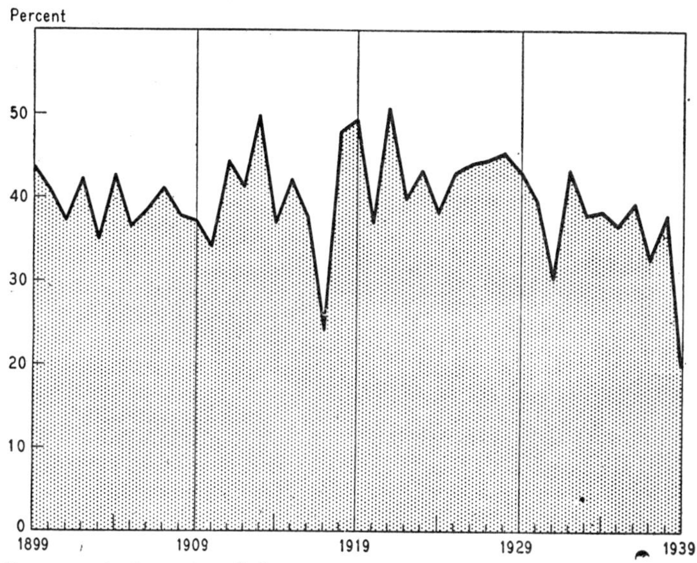

For source and notes see Appendix D

amounted to less than 40 percent of tobacco output in every year since 1932, and are likely to sag still further, temporarily at least, since tobacco has been one of the first victims of the shipping shortage of the current war. The threat of surplus production, ever present since war-born expansion first swept acreage to the 2-million mark, overhangs the industry. Indeed it is believed that the 600,000 tobacco-raising families in the South could "produce readily at least 50 percent more than the world now consumes." [43] It is difficult to imagine changes in smoking habits here or abroad which would result in absorption of such tremendous quantities. To expect a continuation of the rising output trend which began in 1932 therefore seems visionary; even maintenance of the level prevailing during the 1920's may prove an impossible task.

COTTON

Among nonfood products of agricultural origin cotton is easily the most important, measured by any standard. But even when compared with food products, cotton ranks high. One out of every ten farm acres tilled is usually planted to cotton, and the contribution of this crop to farm income, cash or gross, is greater than that of any other single crop.

Its limited tolerance in respect of climatic conditions makes cotton a highly localized product, and one of enormous significance in some states. It has been estimated that "sixty percent of the southern farm families are dependent on cotton for their primary source of income." [44] In Mississippi in 1935, farmers received as much as 70 percent of their cash income, and about half their gross income, from cotton (including cottonseed); in a few other states the ratios are almost as high. Cotton had its greatest expansion in the mid-1920's when over 45 million acres were planted. Texas alone, between

[43] U. S. Department of Agriculture release, "Regional Adjustments to Meet War Impacts" (Washington, 1940), p. 18.

[44] *Ibid.*, p. 16.

1919–20 and 1925–26, put some 5 to 6 million additional acres into cotton and became responsible for about one third of the total acreage. At the same time the importance of the older cotton regions of Georgia and the Carolinas, the Coastal Plains and the Piedmont, steadily declined. More recently the largest reductions in cotton acreage have occurred in precisely those areas to which production had shifted in the 1920's: acreage in the South Central states,[45] for instance, was halved—from 34 to 19 million—between 1930 and 1940.[46]

Chart 14

COTTON: NET OUTPUT

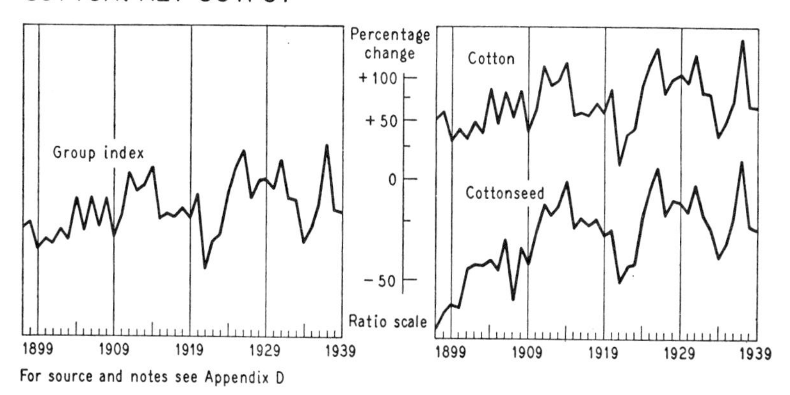

For source and notes see Appendix D

The computed rates of growth for cotton and cottonseed combined are 2.6 percent per annum for the period 1897–1914, 0.9 percent for the period after 1921, but only 0.6 percent for the four decades as a whole (Table 4 above). This anomaly is explained by the severe slump in cotton output between 1914 and 1921 (Chart 14). During this interval cotton production fell from 16 to 8 million bales, cottonseed produc-

[45] Kentucky, Tennessee, Alabama, Mississippi, Arkansas, Louisiana, Oklahoma and Texas.

[46] In Texas the decline was from 16.1 to 8.5 million acres. See *Agricultural Statistics;* also Bureau of Agricultural Economics release, "Cotton Revisions: Acreage, Yield and Production, Crop Years 1866–1935, by States" (1936). Because of rising yields per acre production has been reduced proportionately less.

tion from 6 to 3 million tons. This period saw the heaviest boll weevil infestation,[47] combined with a decline of cotton exports and a consequent accumulation of large carryovers which further discouraged the cultivation of the crop. The year 1921, characterized by a reduction in yield of over 30 percent due to weevil damage,[48] appears to have marked the turning point in weevil control and the resumption of exports on a pre-war scale: by 1926 output had exceeded that of 1914, the record year of the pre-war era. Since then output has fluctuated about the 10 million-bale level, with a corresponding production of cottonseed, and in 1937, largely because of the highest yield ever registered, the record of 1926 was outstripped.

Cotton's place in agriculture, as gauged by its contribution to total production, declined only slightly between 1899 and 1937. In the former year it contributed 10.8, in the latter, 10.2, percent to agricultural output as a whole (Table 2). Of this contribution, one tenth was derived from cottonseed in 1899, one seventh in 1937. The increased importance of cottonseed as compared with cotton reflects a growth in the fraction of cottonseed absorbed into commercial channels: it will be recalled that we do not count as output cottonseed used as seed, feed or fertilizer.

Just as cotton has until recently retained its relative position in domestic agriculture, it has also maintained its place in the scheme of agricultural exports, but only because other exports have shrunk more than cotton. This is illustrated by Charts 15 and 16 which give the percentage contribution of cotton to total agricultural exports, and the percentage contribution of cotton exports to gross income from cotton. While the first series shows little trend, the second is marked by an abrupt decline early in the World War. With occasional reversals, the proportion of income from cotton repre-

[47] W. C. Holley and L. E. Arnold, *Cotton* (National Research Project, Philadelphia, 1938), p. 92. The boll weevil first appeared in the Southwest in 1892 and by 1920 had affected substantially the whole of the cotton area.

[48] *Ibid.*, p. 93.

sented by exports has continued to fall ever since. The era when two thirds of gross farm income from cotton was regularly derived from exports ended before the first World War.

There are many reasons for this shift in the export situation: [49]

(a) Exports of cotton textiles from the United Kingdom reached a peak in 1911 and have been declining ever since.

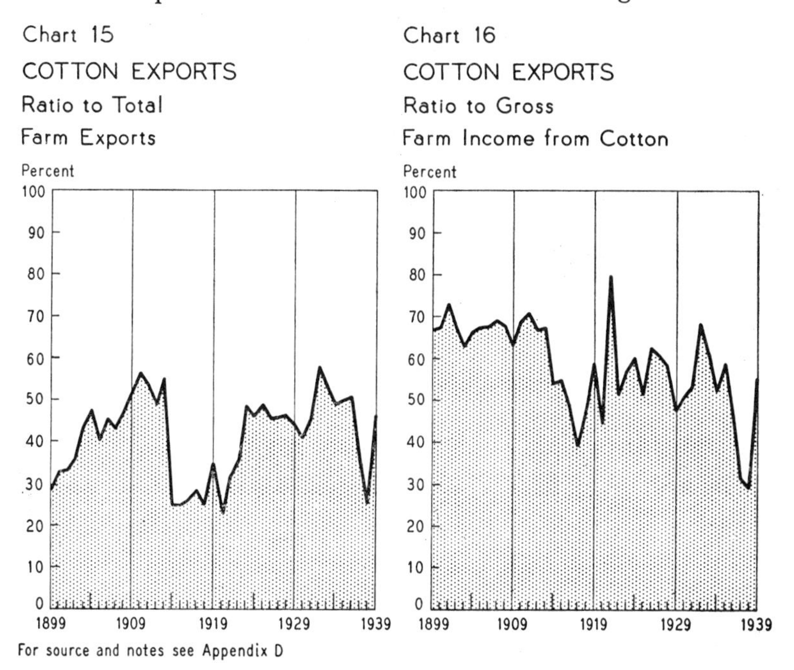

For source and notes see Appendix D

This decline, in turn, affected the United States more than other cotton exporters since about 80 percent of Great Britain's raw cotton imports before the World War were of American origin. In addition, an increasing portion of Great Britain's cotton imports has been derived from competing areas (e.g. British India, Egypt and the Sudan) so that only

[49] This discussion is based on a Bureau of Agricultural Economics release by M. R. Cooper entitled "Some Effects of the World War on Cotton" (1937); and Malott and Martin, *The Agricultural Industries,* pp. 162-67.

about one half of its imports now comes from the United States.

(b) The countries to which cotton manufacturing has shifted —Japan, China, India and Brazil—use larger proportions of non-American cotton than Great Britain did,[50] mainly be-

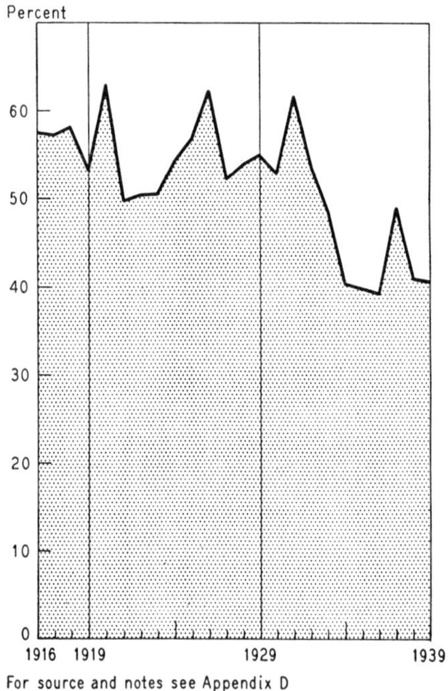

cause of the more favorable location of non-American growers, and also because of the high prices of American cotton which prevailed during the early 1920's. Those high prices

[50] Nonetheless, Japan and China have been using relatively more American cotton than before the World War, and this has been the only offsetting factor among the changes in the foreign trade situation.

furthermore seem to have been instrumental in stimulating foreign production which has grown much faster than United States output (Chart 17).

(c) This country's relative contribution to the raw cotton imports of continental Europe has declined severely, though not so much as in the case of British imports.

Chart 18

COTTON CONSUMPTION PER CAPITA

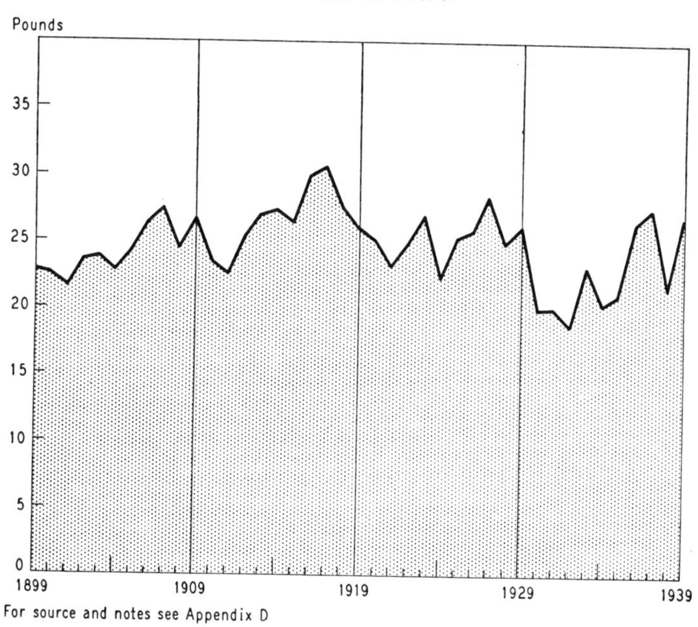

For source and notes see Appendix D

(d) In recent years competition from other fibers has cut severely into the foreign demand for cotton.

Since cotton has ceased to be predominantly an export commodity, trends in domestic per capita consumption have acquired increased significance, but have failed to compensate for the shrinkage in exports. Indeed, per capita consumption on the domestic market declined, on the average, more than 20 percent between the period of peak consumption during the first World War and the trough of the depression of the 1930's. This drop assumes even larger proportions when we compare the years of highest and lowest consumption, 1917 and 1932 respectively, between which consumption fell almost 40 percent. Despite recovery in recent years, consumption still remains below World War levels (Chart 18).

Competition from rayon, which in 1939 furnished 10 percent by weight of all apparel fibers consumed in the United States—as against less than 4 percent in 1929 and 0.3 percent in 1919—has been a potent factor in curtailing the consumption of cotton. That increased rayon consumption has made greater inroads on cotton than on wool is suggested by the data presented in Chart 19. These show that the share contributed to total fiber consumption by wool shrank very abruptly between the two fiscal years 1897–98 and 1898–99,[51] i.e., almost two full decades before rayon appeared, while the shrinkage in relative cotton consumption proceeded *pari passu* with the growth of rayon. It is possible also that rayon assumed the role that would otherwise have fallen to silk, and so may have been responsible for the failure of silk consumption to increase.

Despite the decline in its importance, cotton continues to occupy the predominant position among textile fibers.[52] However, there is general agreement that in the long run cotton acreage will have to be curtailed still further: cotton growing will have to be replaced by other farm enterprises or by nonfarm employment if a full adjustment is to be effected in the economy of the southern states.

51 For a further explanation of this break, see p. 88 below.

52 The consumption of imported cotton in pounds, itself a negligible fraction of all cotton consumed in the United States, still normally exceeds total imports of silk, a fiber we are accustomed to regard as taking pride of place among textile materials of foreign origin.

Chart 19
APPAREL FIBERS
Percentage Distribution of U. S. Consumption, 1892 – 1939

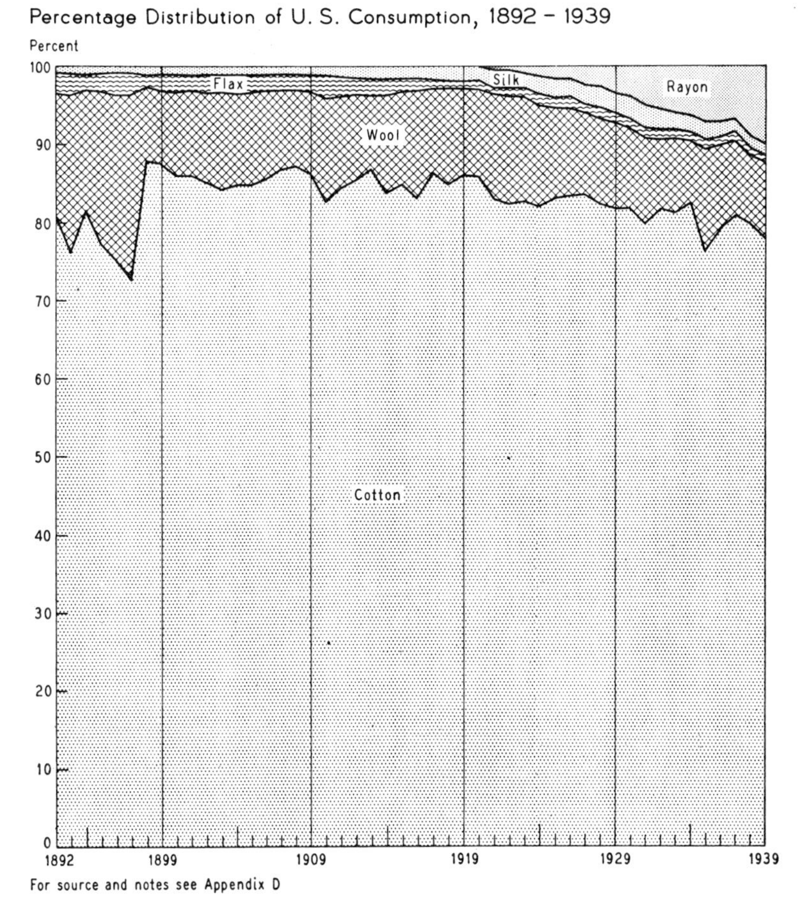

For source and notes see Appendix D

WOOL

Although some wool is shorn [53] in every state, its production is concentrated in the western states, which usually are responsible for half the output. Another 20 percent originates in Texas, the largest single producing state, and the balance is scattered over the rest of the country, with the 17 Atlantic states contributing a negligible amount. The prominence of Texas dates only from the middle 1920's: between 1920 and

TABLE 13

APPAREL FIBERS

Percentage Distribution of Domestic Consumption[a]

Fiber	*1892–99*	*1900–09*	*1910–19*	*1920–29*	*1930–39*
Cotton	80.2	85.8	84.9	83.1	80.0
Wool[b]	16.5	11.0	11.7	11.8	10.0
Silk	.8	1.0	1.4	2.1	2.0
Rayon	..	..	.2	1.7	6.9
Flax	2.5	2.2	1.8	1.3	1.1
TOTAL	100.0	100.0	100.0	100.0	100.0

Source: R. B. Evans and R. F. Monachino, *Trends in the Consumption of Fibers in the United States, 1892–1939* (U. S. Bureau of Agricultural Chemistry and Engineering, New Orleans, 1941), Table 9.

[a] The distributions are in terms of weight. Periods shown relate to fiscal years ended June 30, 1892–1917; calendar years, 1918–39.

[b] Including mohair and camel's hair.

1928 wool production almost doubled, and by 1940 it had doubled once more. Even so, income derived from wool in the last few years has contributed only around 5 percent to the total gross income of Texas farmers.

The behavior of wool output is distinguished by the fact that its growth rate for the post-war period amounts to more

[53] Only shorn wool is considered here, since pulled wool is really a product of the meatpacking industry and its production and value are reflected in the series dealing with sheep and lambs. Mohair is included from 1909 on, but is not accorded separate treatment because it amounts only to a small percentage of wool production.

than five times that of the pre-war years: 0.6 percent for 1897–1914, and 3.3 percent for 1921–38 (Table 4). The war years themselves show no discernible trend, but the prolonged period of shrinkage, beginning in 1909 and not reversed till 1922, results in an average growth rate for the entire period of only 0.9 percent. Increase during the postwar period is confined entirely to an 8-year span, 1923–31,

Chart 20

WOOL: NET OUTPUT

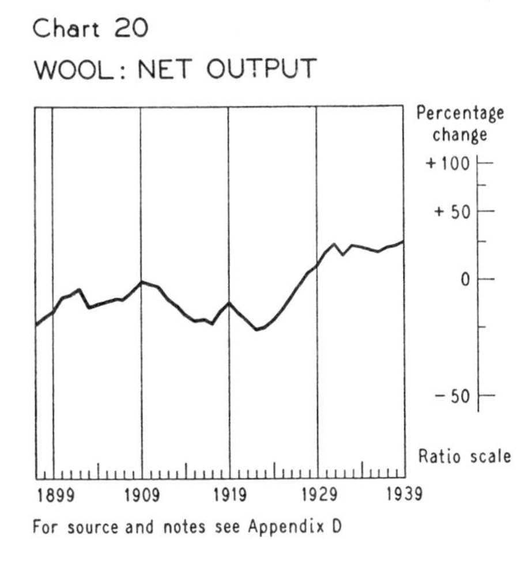

For source and notes see Appendix D

during which output increased by more than 60 percent; since 1931 an almost constant level has prevailed, with deviations from the 1931–39 average measuring not more than 5 percent in either direction for any year.

Comparing the terminal years with a view to assessing the place of wool in total agricultural production, we find that in 1935–39 it contributed only slightly less than in 1897–1901: 1.1 percent and 1.2 percent respectively (Table 2). This observation checks with the computed average growth rate of 0.9 percent which is close to that for agricultural output as a whole. It is interesting also to compare the contribution of wool with that of sheep and lambs as meat animals; here we find that between the two 5-year periods the contribution

Chart 21

APPAREL WOOL

Ratio of Imports to Domestic Consumption, 1892 – 1939

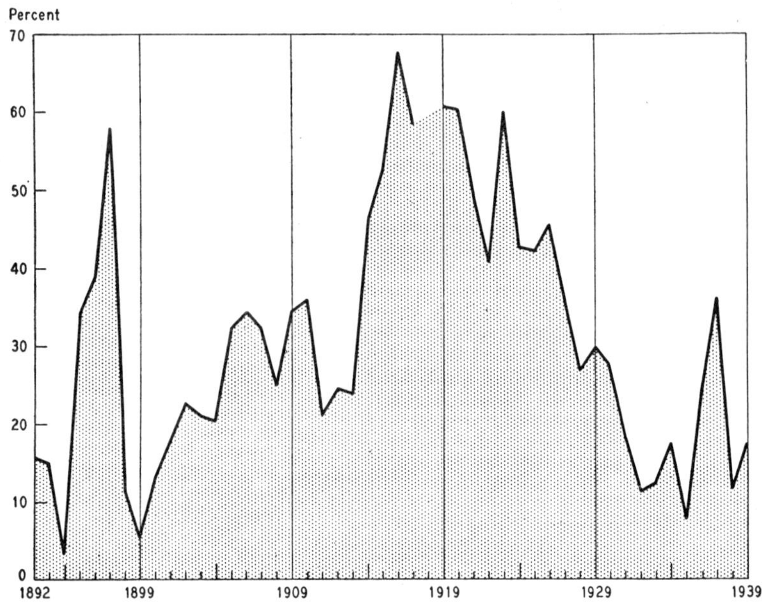

For source and notes see Appendix D

Chart 22

APPAREL WOOL

Per Capita Consumption, 1892 – 1939

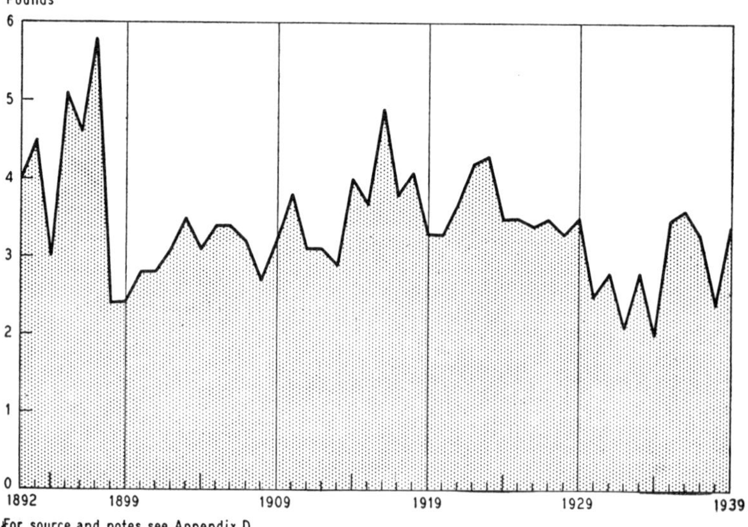

For source and notes see Appendix D

represented by the utilization of sheep and lambs for purposes of food advanced in relation to that made by wool shearing, so that by 1935–39 sheep and lambs contributed as meat more than 1½ times as much as they did as wool; in 1897–1901 this lead amounted to only 25 percent.[54]

Confronted with the task of explaining the changes in output, we cannot simply refer to demand for wool as reflected in per capita consumption estimates. For domestic output has been conditioned more by changes in the tariff situation and by ease of import from competing countries—above all Australia and South America—than by domestic demand. Indeed, as Charts 20-22 show, there is a close resemblance in movement of per capita consumption and imports, while domestic output usually runs counter to both these series. Thus the highest demand for apparel wool arose during the war years 1914–18, with a peak of 4.9 pounds per capita in 1916. Yet during these years domestic output stood at lower levels than obtained either before or after, and imports rose sharply from 31.5 percent of all apparel wool made available for consumption in 1910–14 to 61.6 percent in 1915–19.[55] By 1935–39 the import ratio had dropped back to 19.4 percent of total consumption—one third or one fourth of the war-time volume—and domestic output soared to record levels. Indeed, the sustained expansion in domestic output during 1923–31 was paralleled by an equally sustained shrinkage in imports, which by 1932 had virtually ceased. In the same way, the earlier shrinkage in domestic output which began in 1909 had almost coincided with a sharp upturn in imports (after 1911) which culminated in the war years. The influence of the tariff may be traced in two instances, although it is difficult to say just how strong a force the change in duty alone

[54] This comparison is in terms not of weight but of values at constant prices. See pp. 26-27 above.

[55] R. B. Evans and R. F. Monachino, *Trends in the Consumption of Fibers in the United States, 1892–1939* (U. S. Bureau of Agricultural Chemistry and Engineering, New Orleans, 1941), Tables 6 and 18.

exerted in either case. These two instances are the arrival of free wool in 1894 and again in 1913,[56] and the return to the tariff in 1897 and 1921 respectively.

The situation that developed in 1897 perhaps deserves special consideration since that very year marks a transition from a high level of wool consumption, both absolute and relative to other fibers, to a much lower one (Charts 19 and 22, and Table 13). Although during the past decade curtailed wool consumption may have resulted in part from the competition of rayon, this was not true at the turn of the century. What happened was that greatly increased imports during the period of free wool (1894–97), and particularly during the months preceding the reimposition of the tariff in July 1897, led to a high apparent level of consumption; similarly, smaller imports than had prevailed throughout the preceding ten years rendered wool consumption extremely low during the remaining two years of the century. While these happenings account for the sudden break in 1897, they do not explain why wool consumption did not again, save for isolated years, reach the level of the 1890's. Probably the chief causes were increasing competition from cotton, and the emergence of rayon. Indeed, it seems to have been during the era of free wool that farmers in the West, from sheer desperation, began to market sheep and lambs for meat rather than for wool.

As is easily seen from the foregoing summary, the complete story of the wool growing enterprise would require a much more thorough analysis of tariff policies and their effects than the scope of our study allows. But this much is obvious: domestic demand has affected domestic supply only indirectly through the import situation, and periods of high per capita consumption have usually coincided with years of low output.

[56] The 1913 tariff law never received a fair trial, since military exigencies soon counteracted any effects it might have had.

SUGAR CROPS

This group combines the yield of two totally different plants, sugarcane and sugar beet. Since the resulting foodstuffs are identical, the two crops are treated together in this discussion.

Sugar is the most important food item derived principally from areas outside the North American continent.[57] The

Chart 23

SUGAR CROPS: NET OUTPUT

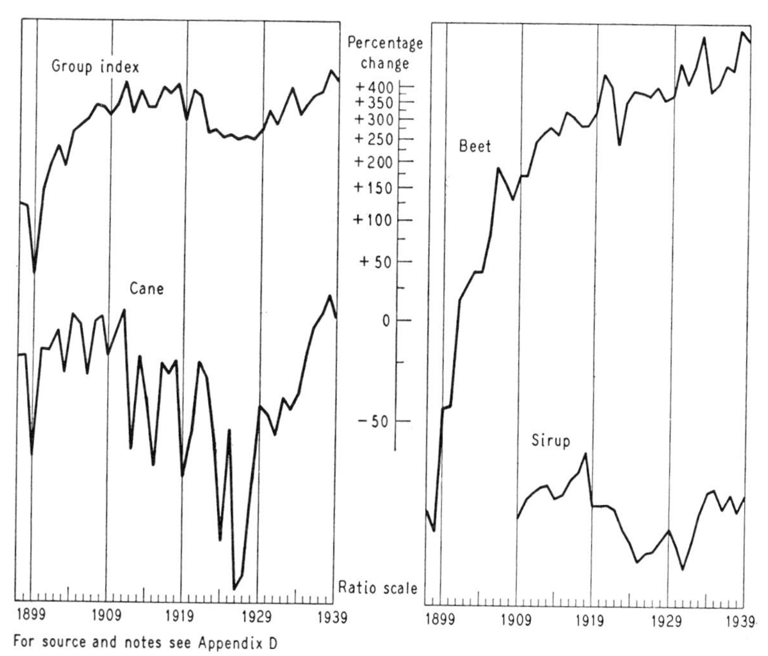

For source and notes see Appendix D

period of our study has witnessed drastic changes in the sources of sugar supply. The trend, observable in Table 14, has been toward independence of foreign sources of cane sugar, and more recently even of areas outside the continental United States. All imports from insular possessions and from

[57] Of food products in the wider sense only coffee looms as large in our import balance.

foreign countries consist of cane sugar, while beet sugar is restricted to the amount obtained from beets grown in the United States.[58]

Sugar was first extracted from home-grown cane in this country in 1791,[59] but the raising of sugar beets lagged almost one hundred years behind, notwithstanding sporadic attempts to introduce beet-sugar manufacture earlier in the nineteenth century.[60] The real rise of sugar-beet growing started with the Tariff Act of 1890 which replaced the tariff by a cash bounty payable directly to growers; various states added bounties of their own. Succeeding tariffs have been high enough to promote the growth of beet sugar as depicted in Chart 23. By 1906 more sugar of domestic origin was derived from beets than from cane, and the positions have not since been reversed.

Louisiana contributes 90 percent of all domestic sugarcane grown for sugar production. The cultivation of beets, though widespread, is concentrated in three areas: between 50 and 60 percent is grown in the Rocky Mountain states and in western Nebraska; a secondary area embraces Ohio and Michigan; and a third is California. Neither the cane nor the beet crop contributes more than 10 percent to gross farm income in any state, but in particular counties the picture may well be different.[61]

Our usual trend measures, which in this case fail to separate the different periods altogether satisfactorily, indicate an annual growth of 5 percent for 1897–1914 and of 2 percent for 1921–38 (Table 4 above). Actually, the period falls rather naturally into two phases of growth (1897 to 1911 and

[58] The amount of beet sugar occasionally imported from European countries is entirely negligible.

[59] P. G. Wright, *Sugar in Relation to the Tariff* (McGraw-Hill, 1924), p. 36.

[60] Only 0.19 percent of sugar consumed was domestic beet sugar in 1890. *Ibid.*, p. 68.

[61] See, for example, L. K. Macy, L. E. Arnold, E. G. McKibben and E. J. Stone, *Sugar Beets* (National Research Project, Philadelphia, 1937), p. 2.

TABLE 14

SUGAR

Percentage Distribution of Domestic Consumption by Sources, 1897–1939

Crop Years	*Continental United States*		*United States Insular Possessions*[a]	*Foreign*[b]
	Cane	Beet		
PERIOD				
1897–1901	11.1	3.2	14.8	70.9[c]
1902–1906	11.3	8.1	18.2	62.3[c]
1907–1911	10.5	14.1	23.9	51.6[c]
1912–1916	5.7	17.5	25.5	51.3[c]
1917–1921	5.1	18.4	23.9	52.6[c]
1922–1926	2.9	16.5	23.0	57.5
1927–1931	2.3	17.1	33.1	47.4
YEAR				
1931	2.8	19.1	43.5	34.5
1932	4.1	22.6	47.8	25.6
1933	3.8	27.0	49.7	19.5
1934	4.2	19.3	36.0	40.5
1935	5.8	19.2	40.8	34.2
1936	6.6	21.2	43.0	29.1
1937	7.5	22.2	43.5	26.8
1938	8.7	27.1	40.7	23.5
1939	7.1	24.8	36.2	31.9

Sources: 1897–1931: U. S. Tariff Commission, *Report to the President on Sugar,* Report No. 73, Second Series (Washington, 1934), p. 159; percentages refer to total market deliveries for consumption.

1931–39: *Statistical Abstract of the United States, 1940,* Tables 701, 703; percentages refer to sugar available for consumption, regardless of stocks at beginning and end of year.

[a] Hawaii, Philippines, Puerto Rico, Virgin Islands (since 1917).

[b] For the past three decades, almost exclusively Cuba; prior to 1903, when Cuba was granted preferential tariff, also Java, Germany, San Domingo and some South American countries (notably Peru) although even then Cuba was usually the largest *single* source abroad. For some years following 1903 imports from countries other than Cuba continued until expanded Cuban production forced the sugar price to a level at which other countries were squeezed out.

[c] Includes a small amount (less than 1 percent) of undetermined origin.

1928 to 1939), one of stagnation (1911 to 1921) and one of depression (1922 to 1928). Total domestic sugar crop production, according to our index, reached a peak in 1911, thanks to the rapid rise of beet cultivation, and for the succeeding decade kept fairly close to that level. At the start, decline in cane output was balanced by the continued growth of sugar-beet production. But once the rate of growth of beet output had begun to slacken in 1921, a succession of low-output years ensued until 1929, when both sugarcane and beets moved upward; thereafter production expanded year after year (except for 1934 when drought affected the crop) to reach an all-time high, more than 50 percent above the 1929 level, in 1938.

The fluctuations of the past 20 years are attributable largely to the changing fortunes of sugarcane cultivation. Although cane production fluctuated but little up to the first World War, it had shrunk to about half its former dimensions by the onset of the immediate post-war depression; and in the mid-1920's it stood at about one sixth its pre-war level. Recovery in the 1930's was equally rapid. These violent fluctuations must be charged primarily to the damage wrought in the Louisiana [62] cane fields by the so-called mosaic disease,[63] which had obtained a firm footing by 1919. Beginning with 1921 this plague caused both per-acre yield and acreage harvested to shrink year after year, while government experts were busy trying to develop disease-resistant strains. In this they succeeded: yields rose after 1926, acreage after 1927. Wider distribution of resistant strains has subsequently helped to bring about yields per acre not recorded since 1909, the year for which the first yield data are available. The extent of both the depression and the ensuing recovery may be gauged by Chart 24.

[62] Florida entered sugarcane production only recently and contributes but a small fraction to total sugar output.

[63] U. S. Department of Agriculture, *Technology on the Farm* (Washington, 1940), pp. 141-42.

Chart 24
SUGARCANE FOR SUGAR IN LOUISIANA
Production, Acreage and Yield, 1909 – 39

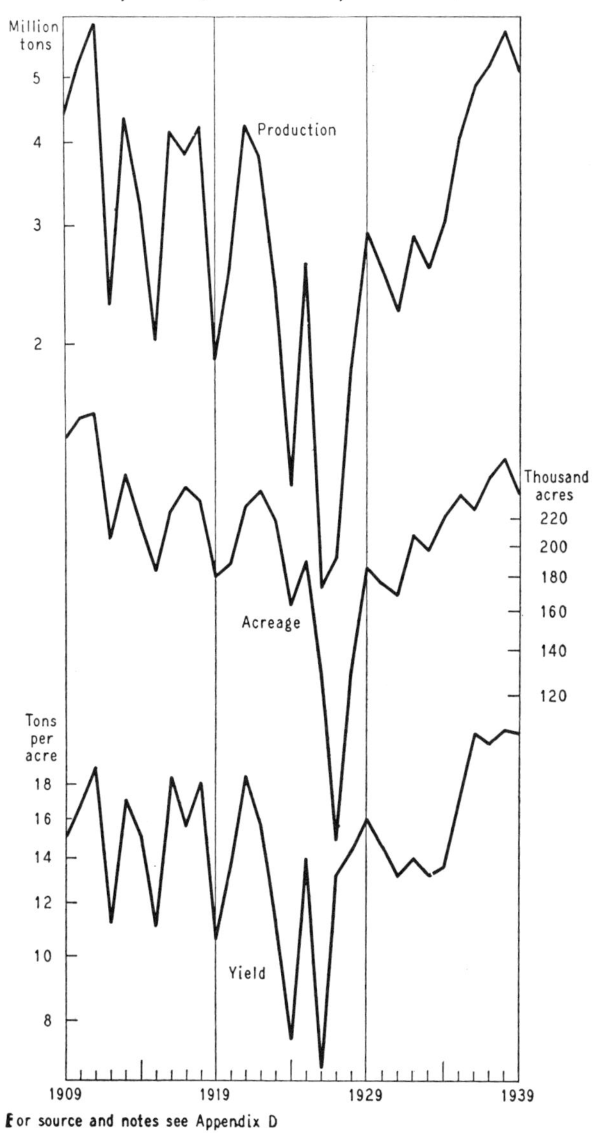

For source and notes see Appendix D

Although the assumption is a tempting one, it is quite unlikely that the slackening of domestic production in the 1920's was related to the approaching stability of per capita sugar consumption in the United States. The argument against a correlation is supported by the fact that in 1928 output resumed its upward trend in the face of a decline, though a minor one, in per capita consumption. The latter development deserves special mention, since rising per capita sugar consumption has been one of the most striking developments in human nutrition, much to the regret, it must be noted, of the nutritionists.[64] Whether the present stability signifies a genuine saturation of the demand for sugar or reflects the teachings of the experts it is hard to say.

Compared with beet and cane sugar, the other sugars and sweetening agents—maple sugar and sirup, sugarcane sirup, sorgo sirup, etc.—are of slight importance in the scheme of consumption, although in terms of gross income the four products just named have together accounted for a little more than 20 percent of the gross income derived from sugar crops as a whole.

Of the minor sugar products, sugarcane sirup is the most important; it roughly maintains the level it held in 1909, the first year for which we possess reliable data. It is of interest that the ups and downs of cane grown for sugar apply only to a negligible degree to cane grown for sirup. This is probably because the latter is more widely distributed geographically than the former, and thus escaped the plight of sugarcane in Louisiana. More than half the output of cane sirup comes from states which no longer contribute to sugar production (South Carolina, Georgia, Alabama, Mississippi, Arkansas, Texas), and in these states the bulk of the output is consumed in the grower's household, being consequently much less exposed to the vicissitudes of the market.[65]

[64] See pp. 163-64 below.

[65] Sugarcane sirup consumed by farm households is included in our index so far as statistics allow.

The three remaining crops, maple sugar, maple sirup, and sorgo sirup are too unimportant to treat in detail, the two former contributing even in Vermont not more than 2 to 3 percent of gross farm income. Other sugars such as glucose or grape sugar are manufactured products and thus do not come within the scope of this study.

MEAT ANIMALS

This group comprises only cattle, calves, hogs, sheep, and lambs, i.e., the animals which provide the raw material of the meat-packing industry. Horses and mules are excluded, and other livestock products (milk, shorn wool) are treated elsewhere, as is also the poultry enterprise.

Since we are interested in the relationship of production to employment, we have chosen to account not only for the number of animals slaughtered, but also for additions to, or deductions from, herds. Clearly, if we assume that in a given year no animals are sold for slaughter or are slaughtered on farms, but that all young stock are added to existing herds, we still cannot consider the output of such a year as zero. Net output is therefore defined as the number of animals slaughtered—this being the closest approximation to the total number of heads disposed of on farms and ranches either by slaughter or by sale for slaughter [66]—plus or minus the increase or decrease in the number on hand between the beginning and the end of the year.

This procedure raises the awkward problem of assigning a price to the computed change in inventory. To use for this purpose the price received by farmers for animals sold for slaughter is to introduce an artificial element. What we are in fact assuming is that if the addition to herds had been marketed it would have sold at the average annual farm price, or in the opposite case, that the number of animals sold from

[66] Animals reshipped (so-called stockers or feeders) are omitted, since such transfers take place within the enterprise itself.

herds beyond the point of replacement went at the average price realized for all animals. Neither calculation is altogether correct, yet neither can be dispensed with except through a lengthy investigation of the changing age and sex composition of the herds.[67] However, since we are not dealing with income estimates, but require prices merely as statistical weights in estimating production, these prices are thought sufficiently accurate as indicators of the relative importance of the various animals in question.

The omission from our indexes, both for livestock and for output as a whole, of horses and mules also calls for some explanation. This apparent deficiency stems in the main from the impossibility of securing reliable data concerning the movement of horses and mules to nonagricultural areas and occupations. In principle there is a strong case for treating the sale of horses to urban areas, adjusted for changes in inventory, as a form of agricultural production.[68] However, apart from the fact that the methods available for estimating sales of horses off farms are rather unsatisfactory, we face the added difficulty that for many years the number thus disposed of (corrected for the change in number on hand) yields a negative result. The net output of horses may indeed have been negative, but the statistical evidence is very insecure.

[67] It might be argued that certain types of changes in livestock inventories should be regarded as fluctuations in the volume of capital equipment, and that such changes should not be treated as additions to or deductions from current output. The only type of animal for which this argument has real justification is, of course, the dairy cow. However, since the final destination even of most dairy cows is the slaughterhouse, we may consider changes in the number of dairy cows as a measure of changes in their production, without being guilty of a major inconsistency. As always, our decision was shaped by the availability of data, the amount of work required to follow a more refined method, and the probable difference in the final result.

[68] As in the case of the milk cow, it might seem preferable to regard the farm horse as a form of equipment. If changes in the number of horses were counted as part of production, additions to buildings and permanent improvements might be thought to possess an equal claim to inclusion in the volume of production; in fact so might everything on which farm labor is expended. Such a treatment, even if desirable, is obviously not feasible.

For all these reasons, it was finally decided to omit both horses and mules altogether.

The production of meat animals is by far the most important branch of the farm economy. Around 1899, according to our measurements (Table 2), it accounted for 32.5 percent of all physical output, and in spite of its diminished significance

Chart 25
LIVESTOCK: NET OUTPUT

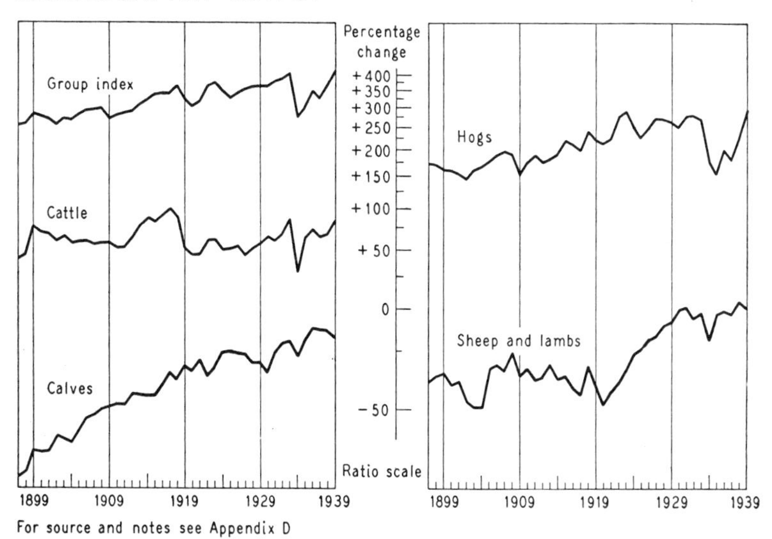

For source and notes see Appendix D

it still contributed 27.2 percent in 1937. As between the different kinds of animals, hog raising had a slight lead over cattle raising at the beginning of the period under discussion and has since retained it;[69] in fact hog raising itself represents the second largest farm enterprise, being surpassed only by dairy farming. Cattle, hogs and sheep are found throughout the country, but their significance in the farm economy differs widely from state to state, both in absolute number

[69] In terms of gross income, cattle and calves combined have overtaken hogs by a narrow margin since 1937.

raised and in their relation to other enterprises. Thus, in the late 1930's, the 50,000 cattle on the farms of Delaware contributed about 3 percent to the gross farm income of that state, while during the same period Iowa farms derived more than 20 percent of their gross income from their 4.5 million cattle.

Notwithstanding these differences, livestock raising [70] is perhaps the least concentrated type of agricultural activity. In recent years only one state, Iowa, has been responsible for as much as 10 percent of all gross income derived from cattle and calves; two states, Iowa and Illinois, occupy a similar place in hog raising; no state has a lead of equal proportions in sheep and lamb production. The Corn Belt states naturally figure most prominently: about half the cattle and calves slaughtered originate in the twelve North Central states,[71] and the western seven of these have recently accounted for about 70 percent of hog production. Sheep production, on the other hand, is most heavily concentrated in the West.

Livestock production as a whole has increased rather steadily throughout the past four decades with only one serious interruption—the drought year 1934 (Chart 25). The computed rate of growth is 0.6 percent per annum, slightly higher for the pre-war period and practically zero for the post-war period (Table 4 above). Yet we should hesitate to conclude from these data that retardation of growth in the production of meat animals has already set in, for the absence of a positive growth rate for the period 1921–38 is evidently due to the exceptional conditions which affected all four species during 1934–37. It is clear, nevertheless, that meat animal production has not grown as fast as farm output as a whole, which increased at around 1 percent per annum on the aver-

[70] Within this section the term "livestock" is used as a synonym for "meat animals." Throughout the remainder of the book "livestock" includes both meat animals and livestock products.

[71] Ohio, Indiana, Illinois, Michigan, Wisconsin, Minnesota, Iowa, Missouri, North Dakota, South Dakota, Nebraska, Kansas.

age. Thus the contribution of meat animals to net physical output fell from 32 percent in 1899 to 27 percent in 1937 (Table 2 above).[72]

Calves, of the four categories, have shown the greatest increase over the period: whereas in 1899 one calf was killed for every 2.8 mature animals, the ratio, by 1939, had increased to 1:1.6. In 1916 the output of calves (in terms of liveweight pounds) for the first time exceeded the output of sheep and lambs. Even at the peak, however, calves contributed less than 10 percent to total meat animal production.

Sheep and lambs come next in order of increase, showing a rise of more than 60 percent over the period 1899–1937. But again the contribution to total livestock output is below 10 percent, so that the course of this output as a whole is influenced only slightly by the expansion of the output of either calves or sheep and lambs.

Cattle and *hogs,* in contrast to the two expanding, but minor series, have changed but little over the 40 years. Hog output in the 5-year period centered on 1937 was just 17 percent above the output of the half decade centered on 1899; and cattle output had risen by barely 8 percent over the same period. These gains are, of course, smaller than the increase in population.

For an explanation of the virtual stagnation of cattle and hog production, we have to consider—as in the case of wheat, sugar and many other items—both the changing diet of the American people and the loss of export markets. The first topic is dealt with in Chapter 4, and will not be treated further here; but the development of foreign trade requires some discussion at this point (see Table 15). Before we can proceed, however, we must distinguish between the export of cattle and beef products, and that of hogs and pork prod-

[72] The decline in the contribution of meat animals is probably understated, inasmuch as truck crops, which appear to have increased greatly in relative importance, are unrepresented in the comparison undertaken in Table 2.

ucts. Though both items are alike in that they began to be major factors in the export situation at the same time, and though the export of both has now declined to negligible proportions, they differ with respect to the time this decline set in and to the events which caused it.

As is well known, the rise in meat exports was closely connected with the spread of refrigeration, which dates from the 1870's. By 1880, this country was exporting (in terms of gross

TABLE 15
BEEF AND PORK
Exports as Percentage of Gross Farm Income from Each, 1894–1937

Period	*Live Cattle and Beef Products*	*Pork and Pork Products*
1894–98	16.4	18.8
1899–1903	15.5	20.9
1904–08	13.7	17.2
1909–13	4.9	13.3
1914–18	7.4	18.8
1919–23	5.0	21.1
1924–28	2.4	12.4
1929–33	1.2	6.9
1934–37	0.5	2.7

Source: Frederick Strauss, *The Composition of Gross Farm Income since the Civil War,* Bulletin 78 (National Bureau of Economic Research, 1940), Table 6. Data are averages for calendar years shown.

farm income) 15 percent of its beef production, including live cattle; thereafter there was a decline resulting from import restrictions imposed by European countries, but once the restrictions were relaxed, in 1887, the proportion exported rose again, and remained close to 15 percent until about 1907. At that time Argentina was rapidly overtaking the United States in the competitive market.[73] Although that country exported

[73] Figures on Argentine exports from L. R. Edminster, *The Cattle Industry and The Tariff* (Macmillan, 1926), p. 150; on United States exports, U. S. Agricultural Marketing Service, *Livestock, Meats and Wool Market Statistics and Related Data, 1940* (Washington, 1941), p. 56.

only 6.6 million pounds of beef [74] in 1896, it shipped abroad an average of 245 million pounds during each year of the period 1901–05, and this average almost doubled during the succeeding five years; in contrast, United States exports of beef were 360 million pounds in 1896, 400 million pounds a year during 1901–05, but only 270 million pounds in

Chart 26

THE CATTLE CYCLE

Number of Beef Cattle on Farms, January 1st, per Head of U. S. Population, 1867 – 1942

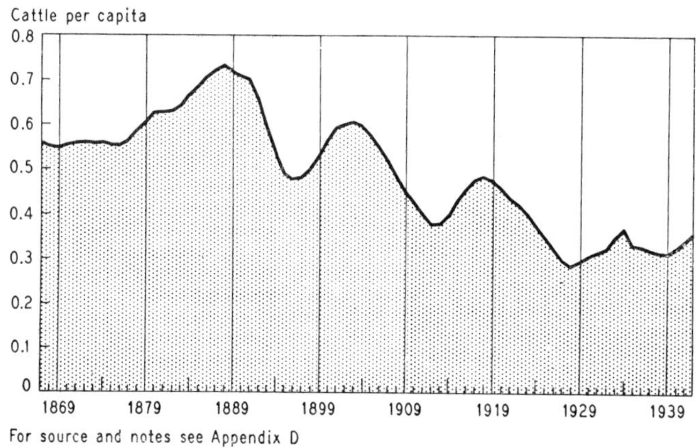

For source and notes see Appendix D

1906–10. By 1913 beef exports from the United States had dropped to a mere 40 million pounds, and even this modest level was never regained after the temporary wartime boom had spent itself in 1920–21.

The question as to what factors were responsible for the replacement of American by Argentine exports is a rather complex one, deserving of more than the summary treatment to which we are limited here. The factors involved in the rather sudden change appear to have been the following:

(a) The slowing down in the expansion of this country's total beef cattle inventory. The peak of the cattle cycle 1896–

[74] Excluding live cattle.

1912 occurred in 1903 and, on a per capita basis, fell below the peak reached in 1888 during the preceding cycle (Chart 26). This development, in turn, may be related to the disappearance of the frontier and the inability of beef raising to compete successfully with other farm enterprises, once the advantages inherent in the open range had been lost.[75]

(b) Both aggregate beef production and per capita consumption continued to rise until 1909. If per capita consumption had remained at the 1899–1901 level, exports could easily have been continued at pre-1907 levels; in other words, it was not so much the inadequacy of current production—though sooner or later the encroachment upon inventories was bound to lead to a decline in output—as the increase in domestic per capita consumption that curtailed the amount available for exports.

(c) It is hardly a mere accident that the decline of United States meat exports coincides exactly with the entry of this country's meat packers into the South American market, though it is difficult to assign cause and effect. Certainly the North American packers took a hand in the South American trade, perhaps because it had already been expanding greatly,[76] and it is also true that their movement into Argentina and Uruguay resulted in further and accelerated expan-

[75] This point is made very forcefully by Edminster, *op. cit.*; unfortunately writing in the 1920's, this author drew his conclusions from Department of Agriculture figures which have since been revised in such a way as to weaken his argument. As is evident in Chart 26, per capita inventory of beef cattle reached a peak in 1888 and a low in 1896. During those years nothing happened to beef exports, although population pressure must have been just as strong as during the succeeding cycle. The relative decline in the beef cattle industry would thus seem to have been a necessary condition, but in no way a sufficient one. Other factors, such as rising domestic costs (Chart 27), the profitability of South American exports during and after the Boer War, and the corresponding reaction of the United States meat packers, must be taken into consideration if a satisfactory explanation is to be found.

[76] About 30 times more frozen meat was exported from South America in 1907 than in 1897, and exports of chilled meat, which were nonexistent in 1897, amounted to half as much again as those of frozen meat in 1907; A. D. Melvin, "The South American Meat Industry," *Yearbook of Agriculture, 1913*, p. 353.

sion of frozen, and particularly chilled, meat exports. Though the opening fanfare in the packers' South American drive was not sounded until 1907, when the largest Argentine firm was acquired by the Swift interests,[77] within three years United States packers controlled over 40 percent of total Argentine and Uruguayan beef exports,[78] and in succeeding years increased exports were attributable largely to the widening activities of the American-controlled establishments.[79]

To summarize, there can be little doubt that although beef exports from this country declined severely after 1907, total exports by United States packers, regardless of the origin of shipments, increased, as export operations were shifted from this country to Argentina and Uruguay. It is unlikely that the packers were forced into this situation by dwindling supplies at home, since on a per capita basis herds began to decline as early as 1888, and it was not until 1909 that the previous low of 1896 was reached (Chart 26). Total production, on the other hand, increased up to 1909, by which time the United States packers were firmly entrenched in Latin America (Chart 27). A low in exports was touched in 1913,[80] the year when the tariff on imports into this country was abolished, and for the next two years large amounts of beef, originating chiefly in South America, were imported to relieve a brief shortage resulting from a decline in production.[81] Temporarily reversed during the war, the downward trend has by

[77] Federal Trade Commission, *Report on the Meat-Packing Industry*, Summary and Part I (Washington, 1919), p. 164.

[78] *Ibid.*, p. 167.

[79] *Ibid.*, p. 166.

[80] Strauss, *The Composition of Gross Farm Income since the Civil War*, Table 6.

[81] From evidence in the Federal Trade Commission reports mentioned above it seems that these imports too were largely under the control of United States packers. It is interesting to note in this connection that the average cost of domestic cattle to United States packers (per pound of live weight) had risen almost uninterruptedly since 1896, and especially sharply between 1911 and 1913 (Chart 27). Comparable costs of imports are not available.

Chart 27

MEAT PRODUCTS: VOLUME AND COST, 1890-1916

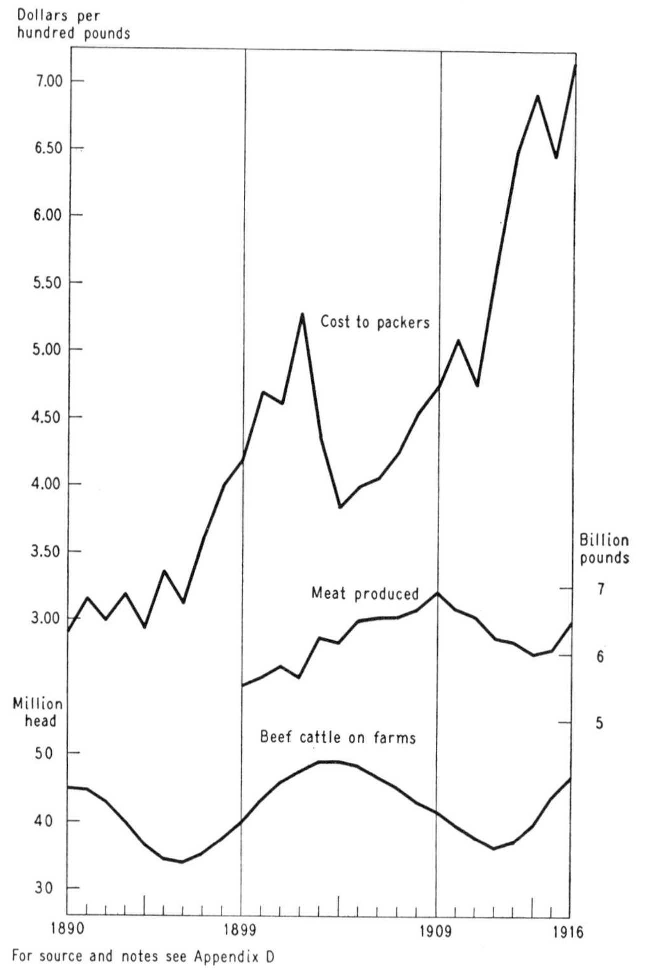

For source and notes see Appendix D

now reached a point where beef exports have practically disappeared.

The turning point in beef exports occurred as early as 1907, but pork exports, despite a slight shrinkage during the years immediately preceding the World War, were rising as late as 1923, in which year they accounted for as much as 19.4 percent of the gross farm income derived from hogs.[82] Then the downward tendency which had been interrupted for about ten years revived with redoubled intensity, so that in the decade 1927–37 there was only one year, 1929, when as much as 10 percent of farm income from hogs was supplied by exports.[83] European competition, rather than the development of South American production, has been in the main responsible for this trend.[84]

Changes in the output of both veal and lamb (including mutton) are little affected by foreign trade. The rise in veal consumption reflects on the one hand a trend toward a lighter and finer type of meat, and on the other a preference on the part of foreign-born elements of the population.[85] Consumption of veal may also have been stimulated by the increased supply of calves for slaughter associated with the expansion of dairying: to some degree milk and calves may be regarded as joint products. The expansion in the output of sheep and lambs is more difficult to trace, since it is intimately connected with wool production and thus must have been influenced by the emergence of Australian and Argentine competition and by changes in the tariff on wool and its price. It appears true in general that the real beginning of expansion was the severe crisis of the 1890's which threatened virtually to wipe out wool growing in this country.[86] As a means of raising cash, the sale of lambs for meat was pushed and, as so often, an emergency measure proved to be the beginning of a trend. Though specific data are lacking, there can be little

[82] Strauss, *op. cit.,* Table 6.

[83] *Ibid.*

[84] Of particular importance appears to have been a preference developed in the English market for Danish-type bacon which cannot easily be shipped from this country.

[85] R. A. Clemen, *The American Livestock and Meat Packing Industry* (Ronald, 1933), p. 268.

[86] M. A. Smith, *The Tariff on Wool* (Macmillan, 1926), pp. 116-17, 120.

doubt that most slaughtered animals classified as "sheep and lambs" around the turn of the century were in fact sheep, and it was only gradually that lamb began to replace mutton.

In conclusion it must be mentioned that the drop shown by the composite index for meat animals as a group for 1934 would be somewhat less severe if we had included the more than 4.5 million cattle and calves which in that year were slaughtered for government account and turned over for the most part to state relief associations. Inclusion of this item would have raised cattle output by about 30 percent and the output of calves by about half as much, so that the livestock index for 1934 would have stood at 91 instead of 80.2.[87] The case of sheep and lambs is analogous to that of cattle, but of little quantitative importance; the same observation applies to hogs, to which we must add that the government purchase of more than 6 million pigs under the emergency control of hog production in 1933 yielded but 100 million pounds of meat which was distributed to needy families.[88] The balance of the slaughter was utilized in the manufacture of tankage, fertilizer, etc.

POULTRY AND EGGS

In absolute numbers chickens far exceed all other farm animals taken together: since 1910 there have never been fewer than 350 million chickens on the country's farms at the beginning of each year; an even larger number are consumed

[87] Whether the item should be included is arguable. On the one hand, we have made it a practice to exclude crops not harvested or donated to charity (e.g., citrus fruit in California); on the other, since our prices of grain, cotton, etc., include loan values, it might have been logical to include the results of government intervention also in this case. It is noteworthy that although slaughter and meat production statistics, as given in *Agricultural Statistics, 1940*, Tables 475 and 498, exclude this item, it is obviously included in a recent recapitulation of total net meat production as released in U. S. Agricultural Marketing Service, *Farm Production and Income from Meat Animals, by States, 1939–1940* (Washington, 1941).

[88] Total pork consumption in 1934 exceeded 9 billion pounds; see Appendix Table B-1.

annually, one third on the farms where produced, and the balance in urban and rural homes. Since they require little in the way of land resources, chickens more than any other farm animal are most often raised by nonfarm families. According to an estimate released in 1930,[89] one chicken is raised off farms for every 20 chickens on farms.

Chicken production is widely scattered. Iowa, the leading state in 1939, contributed a little over 6 percent to total chicken output, Illinois, a bare 5 percent; all other states were responsible for less than 5 percent each. The North Central states together account for about half of total output. Egg production is even more widely dispersed. Some of the New England states have derived as much as 20 percent of their gross farm income from chickens and eggs; Delaware, more than 30 percent. For most states, however, the percentage is less than 10.

Our combined index for eggs and chickens, which after 1929 includes the net output of turkeys as well, gives evidence of remarkably steady growth (Chart 28). The average rate for the four decades is 1.7 percent per annum—a tempo exceeded by two groups only, dairy products and citrus fruit (Table 4).[90] The output of eggs and poultry contracted significantly only during the 5-year span 1931–35, and by 1939 production was above the record levels of 1930. There is some evidence of retardation in the rate of expansion, the annual growth rate being 3.1 percent for the pre-war period, but only 0.6

[89] S. A. Jones, "Method and Procedure in Estimating Production, Disposition and Income from Poultry and Eggs," *Farm Value, Gross Income, and Cash Income from Farm Production,* Part II (U. S. Bureau of Agricultural Economics, 1930), p. 26. Chickens raised off farms are not included in our output index.

[90] We may note that in 1937 the indexes for sugar and for oil crops on a 5-year average basis stood at a higher level in relation to 1899 than the corresponding index for eggs and poultry (223 and 216 respectively against 196; see Table 6). However, relapses suffered at various times by oils and by sugars are not paralleled in the case of eggs and poultry, and the computed growth rate for the latter group consequently exceeds the rates for the two former groups.

percent for the post-war years; yet even the latter exceeds the corresponding rate for agricultural output as a whole (0.5 percent—see Table 4 above). For the four decades together, eggs and poultry have in fact grown almost twice as fast as farm output as a whole; their share in net physical output has expanded from 9 to 12 percent (Table 2). Within the group, the share of eggs rose from not quite two thirds to nearly

Chart 28
POULTRY AND EGGS: NET OUTPUT

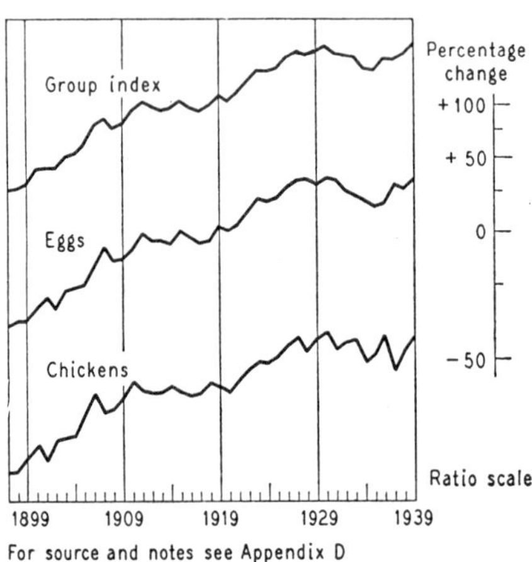

For source and notes see Appendix D

three quarters. Just about twice as many chickens were produced in 1939 as in 1899; but the output of eggs rose to 2.2 times its former level. This shift has resulted mainly from an increase in the number of eggs per laying chicken.[91]

There remains the question whether the inclusion in our index of other types of poultry would materially affect the results just outlined; this is difficult to settle with confidence, but if we were to base a guess on the scanty data available, we would answer in the negative. The dominant position of chicken eggs and the negligible number of birds other than

[91] See Table 50 below. The increases during the months of November and December of each year have been particularly striking.

chickens, as evidenced by early Census data,[92] leads us to believe that the coverage provided by chickens and eggs alone is sufficiently high to yield results applicable to poultry as a whole. Even in 1929 and 1937, years for which we possess data on the output of turkeys, the contribution of the latter to the total value of the group did not amount to more than 3.4 and 6.2 percent, respectively.

MILK AND MILK PRODUCTS

As indicated in an earlier section, dairy farming is the largest single farm enterprise: at the turn of the century it contrib-

Chart 29
MILK AND MILK PRODUCTS: NET OUTPUT

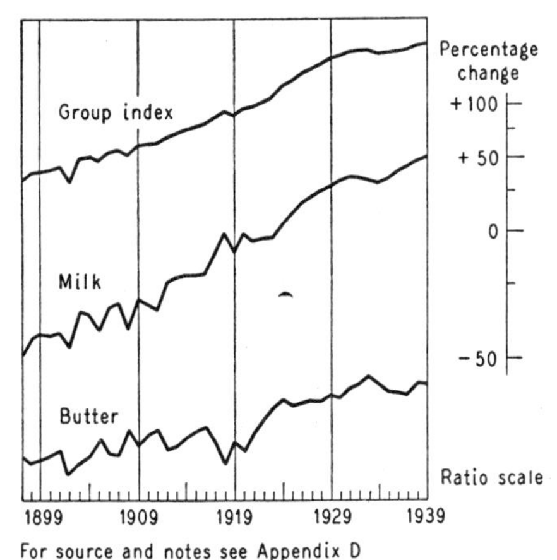

For source and notes see Appendix D

uted 15.9 percent to total output, followed closely by hogs (15.8) and by cattle and calves (15.2); in 1935–39 the percentage contribution of milk and milk products had risen to 22.1, while the share of the nearest competitor—hogs—had dropped to 13.1 (Table 2 above). Dairying ranks high even when com-

[92] Jones, *op. cit.*, p. 7. This report served as the basis for the estimates of chickens and eggs in 1899 (see Appendix A), but lack of supplementary material made it impossible to combine into an annual series the data given for other fowl.

pared to the leading branches of manufacturing. The gross income derived from dairying in 1937 ($1,937 million), when compared with the value of products of leading branches of manufacture, ranks just below the fifth largest manufacturing group (motor-vehicle bodies and parts) and above such important industries as electrical machinery, printing and publishing (newspapers and periodicals), or cigarette manufacture.

As in the case of poultry, no state contributes, in terms of gross income, as much as 10 percent of aggregate production; but in terms of weight in pounds, Wisconsin has for many years turned out more than a tenth of the total.[93] Minnesota, New York and Iowa, in 1939, each accounted for more than 5 percent of the total, but the remainder of the milk output was divided between twelve states producing between 2 and 5 percent each, fourteen states with 1 to 2 percent each, and the remaining states with less than 1 percent each. Geographically, dairying is rather widely dispersed. When production data are broken down in accordance with the use to which milk is put, this statement must be qualified. More than 30 percent of all milk skimmed for sale as cream in 1939 originated in Minnesota and Iowa, more than 50 percent in the seven West North Central states.[94] On the other hand, over half the dairy products consumed on the farms where they were produced were accounted for by the sixteen states in the South Atlantic and South Central regions, which figure only negligibly in the production of milk for sale. For the country as a whole about 25 percent of all milk produced is consumed on the farm on which it originates.

The steady expansion during the past four decades of the output of milk and products derived from it distinguishes this group rather sharply from others considered here. While

[93] This discrepancy is due to the fact that most Wisconsin milk goes into manufactured dairy products and thus earns a lower price per unit.

[94] Minnesota, Iowa, Missouri, North Dakota, South Dakota, Nebraska, Kansas.

the respective shares of liquid milk and of butter in the group total are subject to rather sharp movements from year to year, the growth in the output of the group as a whole has been remarkably smooth (Chart 29). Over the entire period the average annual rate of growth amounts to as much as 2.1 percent, being exceeded only by that of citrus fruit (Table 4 above). The output of dairy products increased more than twice as rapidly as population, and its contribution to net farm output as a whole rose from 16 percent in 1897–1901 to 22 percent in 1935–39 (Table 2). With the exception of wool, milk is the only product that grew more rapidly in the post-war than in the pre-war period.[95] Its average growth rate during 1897–1914 (1.5 percent) equaled that for farm output as a whole; during 1921–38 the group rose (at 1.8 percent yearly) more than three times as rapidly as total farm output (Table 4 above).

From the available data it appears that expansion from 1909 to 1919 was due mainly to an increase in the number of milk cows.[96] For the succeeding decade, numbers did not increase much; but milk production per cow rose 10 percent from 1924 to 1929 [97] and appears to have expanded even more between 1919 and 1924. Since 1929 growth has been attributable again to increase in the number of cows, with production per cow falling from 1929 to 1934 and returning to the 1929 level in 1940.

In constructing our index for this group, we weighted butter and the various forms of fluid milk by their respective farm prices. Consequently the index reflects not only changes in total milk production (measured in gallons), but also shifts between alternative uses. It shows that dairy products in-

[95] However, we have no data for truck crops in the earlier period; possibly they also may be an exception in this respect.

[96] R. G. Bressler, Jr., and J. A. Hopkins, *Trends in Size and Production of the Aggregate Farm Enterprise, 1909–36* (National Research Project, Philadelphia, 1938), Tables A-95 and A-96.

[97] U. S. Agricultural Marketing Service, *Farm Production, Disposition and Income from Milk, 1924–1940, by States* (Washington, 1941), p. 2.

creased 96 percent between 1899 and 1937 (5-year averages) whereas the net output of milk in gallons (i.e., unweighted) rose only 86 percent. The divergence between our index (weighted) and milk output in gallons has been particularly pronounced since the first World War, and it is an indication of the fact that the milk supply has shifted to outlets which have yielded consistently better monetary returns. The de-

Chart 30

MILK AND BUTTER: PRODUCTION

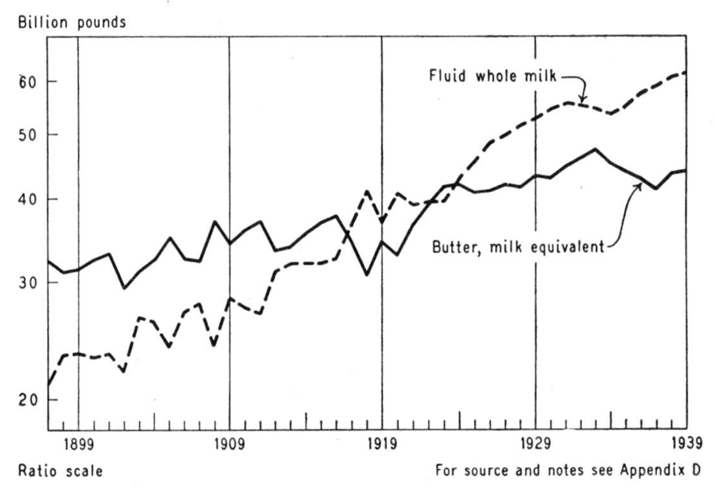

tailed data [98] on milk disposition tell the story: while total butter production increased by less than 40 percent between 1897 and 1939, farmers, over the same period, expanded their sales of fluid whole milk (mainly for consumption in liquid form [99]) roughly threefold. Again, whereas in 1897 more milk

[98] See Appendix A.

[99] Whole milk disposed of in fluid form must not be considered altogether identical with consumption of milk. A sizable proportion of whole fluid milk sales goes into cheese manufacture and a somewhat smaller fraction is turned into evaporated milk, etc. The exact relationship between forms in which milk is sold off farms and in which it is consumed is rather complex and not easily subject to statistical verification; but it appears approximately true that most milk sold as butterfat actually is turned into butter and that little butter is produced from milk sold as whole fluid milk.

left the farms as butter or butterfat than as whole fluid milk, the situation began to be reversed around the end of the World War, and had so changed by 1939 that fluid whole milk sales off farms exceeded farm sales of butter and butterfat by over 40 percent. This shift may be seen in Chart 30.

Another change that has proceeded apace throughout the period and is similarly reflected by the index is the transfer of buttermaking from farm to factory.[100] According to a recent estimate,[101] 1917 was the first year in which more than half the butter produced originated in creameries, and since then factory butter has never relinquished its leadership. Farm butter output reached its peak in the first few years of this century; by now its share of total butter output has shrunk to but little more than 20 percent, and by no means all of this is marketed.[102] It is easily seen that such a shift would tend to depress the index, if we were using unit labor requirements as weights. Though less obviously, weighting by prices of butter and butterfat respectively has the same effect, since the price of farm butter has consistently been above that of an equivalent amount of butterfat.[103]

NONCITRUS FRUIT

Although the climate of most of the states of the Union will support fruit trees, only apples, peaches and cherries are at all widely dispersed. Other kinds of fruit are concentrated on the Pacific Coast, and especially in California. Today California produces 90 percent of all our grapes and apricots, and, with Oregon, over 90 percent of all plums and prunes. California

[100] In contrast to butter, cheesemaking appears to have become predominantly a factory operation by the late 1860's.

[101] E. E. Vial, *Production and Consumption of Manufactured Dairy Products,* Technical Bulletin 722 (U. S. Department of Agriculture, 1940), Appendix Table 5.

[102] Percent of farm butter marketed was about 40 in 1924, 20 in 1939.

[103] To facilitate these comparisons milk, butter and butterfat had to be reduced to comparable milk equivalent units. The technical procedure is described in some detail in Appendix A.

also contributes heavily to peach, pear and cherry production, providing two fifths of the nation's supply of peaches, one third of the pears and more than a tenth of the recorded production of cherries. The main fruit crop for which California does not top the list is apples; the four states—Washington, New York, Virginia and Pennsylvania—yield half the total output of apples, with Washington alone producing a fifth of the entire crop.

The emergence of California and the Pacific Northwest as the leading fruit growing area has probably been the outstanding feature in the recent history of this branch of agriculture. Up to 1900 Washington had produced only one apple crop exceeding 2 million bushels; in 1937 it produced over 30 million bushels. Similarly, pear production in the Pacific Coast states rose threefold between 1919 and 1938, but only about a third in the rest of the country. Production of clingstone peaches in California has increased more than tenfold since 1909, and it now represents 20 to 30 percent of the country's total peach crop.

Our index for noncitrus fruit rests upon data whose adequacy diminishes progressively as they recede beyond 1919. Sometimes output records, sometimes price records, and frequently both, have had to be pieced together in an effort to gauge the development of this important category of agricultural production. While it is believed that long-run tendencies are mirrored in our index with reasonable fidelity, the year-to-year fluctuations are probably much less reliable.[104]

[104] Wherever possible, we have relied on official data; unfortunately, however, revised estimates of fruit production for years prior to 1919 have not yet been released by the Department of Agriculture, so that we had to resort to earlier, unrevised, estimates; those, in turn, were supplemented by estimates made some ten years ago by Dr. O. E. Baker, of the Department of Agriculture, in collaboration with Professor S. W. Shear, of the University of California. Since Professor Shear is an outstanding authority on fruit statistics we did not attempt to improve upon his estimates, but merely tried to reconcile them with such official data for the more recent period as have become available since his estimates were made. The make-up of our series is described in some detail in Appendix A.

Apart from doubts about the validity of our data, short-run fluctuations are of less significance in this group for yet another reason: changes in acreage, i.e., in the number of bearing trees, take place comparatively slowly. Short-run changes in output result from the vagaries of the weather and the incidence of pests and diseases—to which few crops are more susceptible.

Our index includes for a varying number of years, in order of importance, apples, peaches, grapes, strawberries,[105] pears, prunes, apricots, cranberries, plums, figs and olives. It will be remarked that a great many fruits are missing from this list, notably cherries and various types of berries. These omissions are caused entirely by the absence of data [106] and fortunately are of minor consequence; in recent years the total value of the items omitted cannot have amounted to more than 7 or 8 percent of the value of noncitrus fruit as a whole. From the point of view of coverage our index may therefore be accepted as representative, at least from 1909 on; and there is ground for assuming that the representativeness of the index is of a high order even for the first decade.[107]

The noncitrus fruits together (including those omitted from our index) account at present for close to 4 percent of total gross farm income. Forty years ago the four principal fruits—apples, grapes, apricots and prunes—contributed 3.2 percent to agricultural output as defined here (Table 2). If

[105] Strawberries are frequently included among the truck crops, owing to the method of cultivation; in conformity with popular opinion and their place in the pattern of demand we have listed them with the fruits.

[106] Of the twelve states for which cherry production has been recorded, no data are available for seven prior to 1924, and for two prior to 1929. Production of berries, other than cranberries and strawberries, has been unrecorded until very recently.

[107] Among the items missing in the earlier period are peaches and strawberries. For the former we have an output series whose movements conform quite well to those of the index for the group, showing the same direction of change in eight out of twelve years; the lack of a price series for peaches prevented its inclusion. As for strawberries, we know from a comparison of the 1899 and 1909 Censuses that the number of crates of strawberries harvested remained practically unchanged between the two years; so did our index.

we make due allowance for the fruits not included in the earlier year we may conclude that the place of noncitrus fruit in agriculture has changed very little. The total area devoted to this group (excluding acreage of trees not of bearing age) is just over 4 million acres. Yet in 1939 more than $300 million of gross income was derived from these fruits, compared with slightly more than $400 million from wheat grown on an acreage over thirteen times as large.

As may be seen from Chart 31, year-to-year fluctuations in fruit production are exceedingly violent. This fact deprives our computed growth rates for the two subperiods of much of their significance, but we may notice that over the four decades as a whole the output of the group grew at an annual average rate of 0.9 percent, or slightly less than the corresponding rate for farm output as a whole (Table 4 above).

Apples are the dominant noncitrus fruit crop, accounting for close to 40 percent of the total value of all such crops included in our index in 1937; for this reason most of the changes in the group index can be explained with reference to the apple crop. The big 1921 slump is directly traceable to the very large loss inflicted on the apple crop of that year by frost and freeze. All states except those of the Pacific Northwest (which in that very year reaped a record crop) salvaged only a fraction of their customary harvest, and the southernmost fringe of the apple-producing states—Virginia, West Virginia and North Carolina—lost more than nine tenths of their crop. Regardless of the causes of change in the size of the apple crop, there is no doubt that its fluctuations govern the behavior of the index. And because of the relative decline of the apple crop—as against 2.8 percent in 1897–1901 it contributed only 1.9 percent to total output in 1935–39 (Table 2) —the group index fails to register a more decided increase over the whole period. The expansion in the output of grapes has tended, however, to offset the decline in apple production.

Grapes and *peaches* rank next to apples when the crops are

Chart 31

NONCITRUS FRUIT: NET OUTPUT

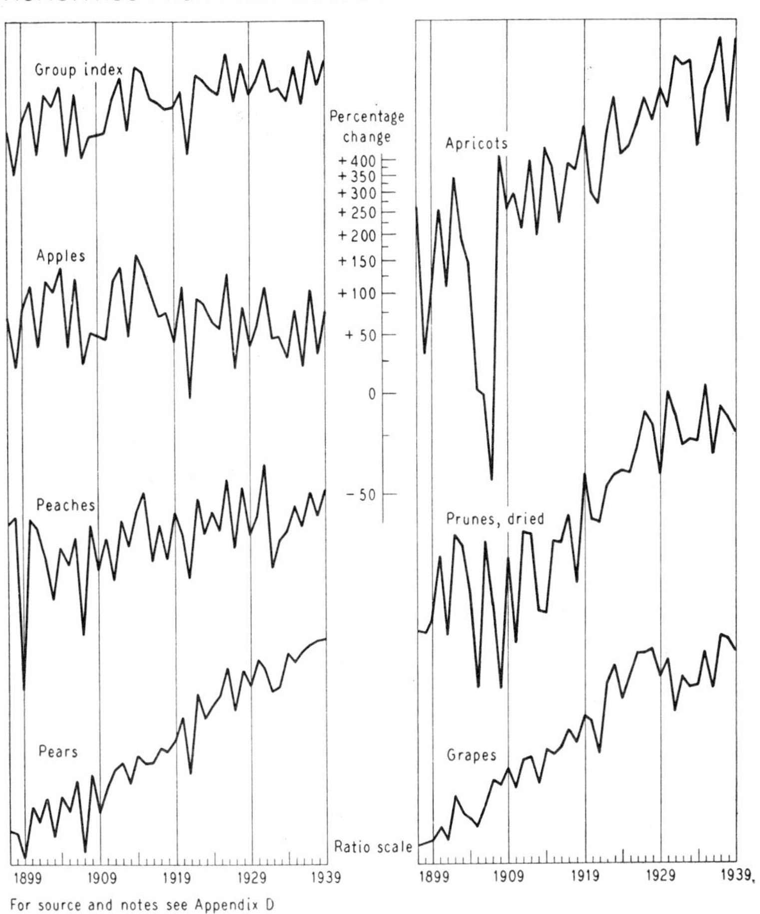

For source and notes see Appendix D

arranged by value of output, and of the two, the grape crop has recently outranked peaches. *Grapes,* produced almost exclusively in California—the source of nearly nine tenths of the nation's supply [108]—have maintained a steady rate of increase. By the mid-1920's production had reached a level some

[108] New York, Michigan and Ohio account for the balance.

three to four times higher than that prevailing during the first decade covered by our index. Since most California grapes are of the raisin type, Prohibition had comparatively little effect upon output. Moreover during the "dry" era there was a shift from wine making to use as unfermented juice stock.[109]

Peaches show none of the expansion evidenced by apples during the pre-war period, but otherwise move in a fairly similar fashion, with neither a rising nor a falling trend since the first World War. In both amplitude and frequency of fluctuations peaches are a close rival to apples. Throughout the 42 years there were only seven instances in which a year of growth was not followed by a year of decline or vice versa, and the change was commonly at least 20 percent.

Pears, which usually amount in physical quantity to not more than 10 percent of the apple crop, tripled in output between the opening years of our series and the second half of the 1920's; since then output has risen only very slightly.

Fresh and canned plums and prunes have also risen substantially, though the data become increasingly unreliable as we trace output back to years before 1919. Since that year, however, output has about doubled.

Dried prunes, by far the most important of the plum and prune group, fluctuate widely; yet over the 42-year period output has increased roughly fourfold.

A sizable portion of total fruit output, both citrus and noncitrus, enters foreign trade and has contributed an increasing percentage to total agricultural exports, as is evident from Table 16. Declines in other fields have helped to boost fruit to third place in the list of agricultural exports (in value terms) in recent years, but the basic export data indicate that this position has not been attained exclusively at the expense of other items. There have been large absolute increases since the first World War in exports of apples, prunes and raisins

[109] *Agricultural Statistics, 1940,* Table 302.

Chart 32
FRUIT EXPORTS, 1913 - 38

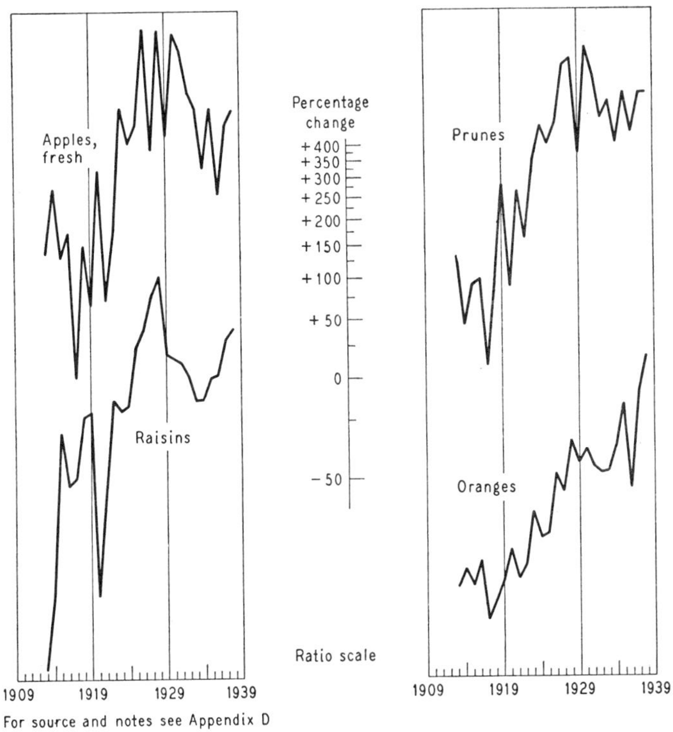

For source and notes see Appendix D

(Chart 32). It is interesting to note that the one important fruit imported, bananas, is usually about equal in weight to the aggregate fruit tonnage exported, including citrus fruit. In terms of value, however, banana imports amount only to about 30 percent of total fruit exports.

CITRUS FRUIT

No other agricultural product even approaches citrus fruit in rapidity and scale of expansion. The average annual rate of growth for the entire period is 5.8 percent, which is nearly

TABLE 16

FRUIT

Relative Contribution to Total Agricultural Exports, 1894–1938[a]

Five-year Average	*Percent*
1894–98	0.9
1899–1903	1.5
1904–08	1.6
1909–13	2.7
1914–18	2.0
1919–23	2.6
1924–28	6.9
1929–33	10.5
1934–38	11.5[b]

Source: Frederick Strauss, *The Composition of Gross Farm Income since the Civil War,* Bulletin 78 (National Bureau of Economic Research, 1940), Table 7. Data relate to years beginning July.

[a] The underlying data are export values.

[b] The 5-year average derived from figures published in *Foreign Crops and Markets,* Annual Supplement (U. S. Department of Agriculture, 1941) was substituted for the 4-year average used by Strauss.

three times as high as that of dairy products, its closest ranking competitor.[110] In sharp contrast to the milk group, however, the average rate at which the citrus enterprise expanded slowed down markedly between the pre- and the post-war periods, from 8.9 to 5.9 percent.

Equally illustrative of the phenomenal development of citrus fruit is its contribution to total production in 1897–1901 and 1935–39, respectively: .2 percent during the former and 1.9 percent during the latter period (Table 2). Indeed, in 1935–39 the share for which citrus fruit was responsible

[110] It must be admitted that our choice of terminal years serves to exaggerate the rise, since Florida's citrus production, which in the early 1890's was still outdistancing that of its younger rival, California, was all but wiped out by the disastrous freeze of 1895. No wonder, then, that our index, particularly in its initial years, records startling percentage increases, for as far as Florida is concerned citrus culture had to be rebuilt from practically nothing.

was double that contributed by sugarcane and sugar beets together, and only slightly smaller than the contribution made by all grains outside of wheat and corn. Since 1933 per capita consumption of citrus fruit has grown progressively larger than that of apples (Chart 34).

California and Florida are the outstanding citrus-producing states. California supplies all the lemons and the two states together produce practically all the oranges grown in this country. Until a decade ago grapefruit cultivation also was confined to the two states named, but in recent years Texas has entered the field and at present contributes close to 40 percent of total grapefruit output. In terms of income Florida is most dependent on citrus fruit, deriving around 40 percent of its gross income from this source, whereas California's income from citrus fruit represents on the average no more than 10 to 20 percent of its total gross farm income.

Though rapid rates of growth have been common features of all citrus crops, there has been considerable inequality among the relative speeds at which their production has expanded. Due weight must of course be given to the fact that the points of time at which these crops began to be exploited on a commercial scale do not always coincide. Inevitably very young industries have very rapid rates of growth, but sooner or later these rates decline even if they remain substantial.

The first shipment of *oranges* left California in 1877,[111] and by 1899 the state had assumed a position of leadership in orange production which it never relinquished thereafter.

[111] Nephtune Fogelberg and A. W. McKay, *The Citrus Industry and the California Fruit Growers Exchange System,* Circular No. C-121 (Farm Credit Administration, 1940), p. 13. The completion of the Southern Pacific railroad in 1876 marks the beginning of the industry on a national scale. Not only did it expedite transcontinental shipments, but it also freed a large army of Chinese railroad laborers for work in fruit orchards; see Carey McWilliams, *Factories in the Field* (Little, Brown, 1939). The navel orange had appeared in Florida as early as 1830, but did not reach California until 1873; Valencia oranges were introduced in both states during the 1870's.

Chart 33

CITRUS FRUIT: NET OUTPUT

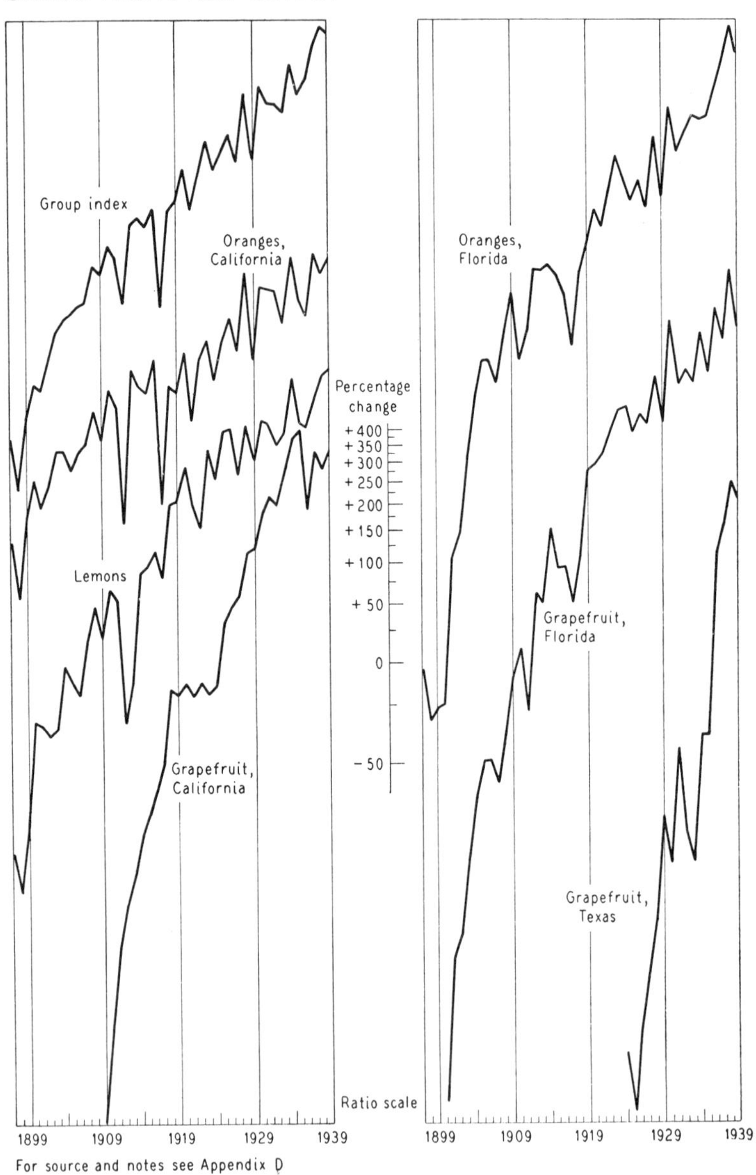

For source and notes see Appendix D

Chart 34

FRUIT CONSUMPTION PER CAPITA, 1909-41

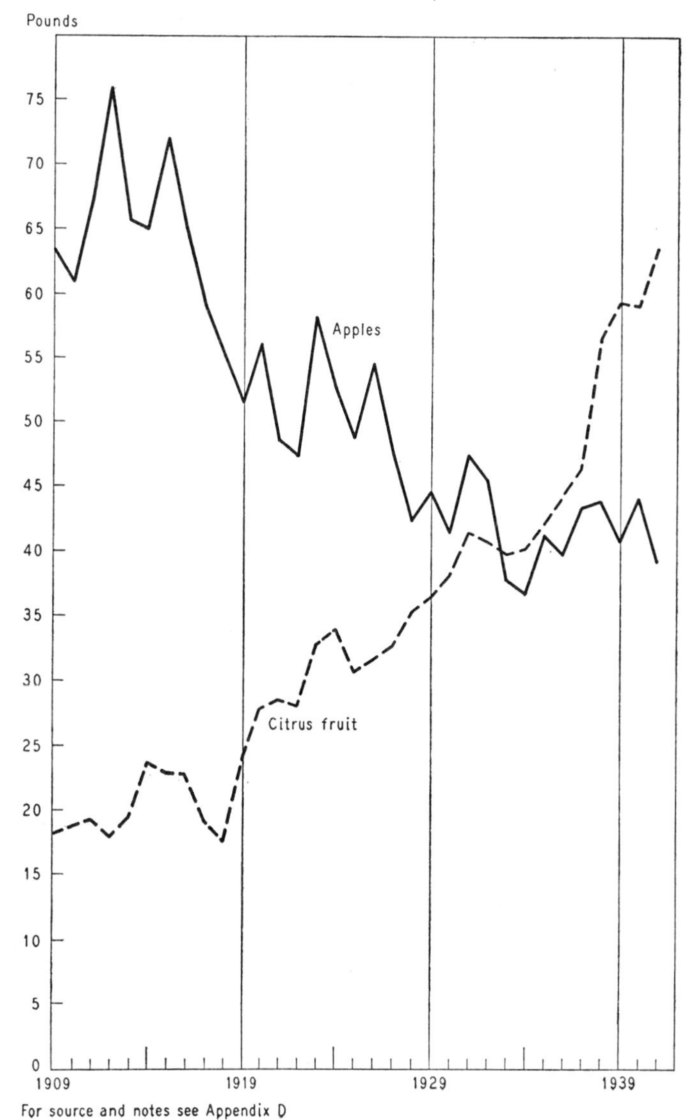

For source and notes see Appendix D

The growth between that year and the present is not as impressive as the rate of increase of other citrus crops, though it amounts to between 500 and 600 percent over the entire period. By 1903 output first reached and surpassed the 10-million-box level; [112] ten years later the figure was 20 million, and by 1934 output had doubled once more. It is difficult to determine how far the early establishment of cooperative marketing is responsible for the position which the California citrus industry has attained.[113] In any case the tight organization under whose tutelage the California industry developed must be considered in any appraisal of its astonishing growth.[114]

In rate of increase, though never in absolute size, Florida orange production, which started from almost zero in 1897, naturally outstrips California output. Once it had regained the volume that preceded the freeze of 1895, its rise slowed down considerably; with the exception of the most recent years, post-1918 output has ranged from two to four times the volume obtaining prior to the war.

Grapefruit has grown more rapidly in output than any other citrus fruit, not only in Florida and California, but very recently in Texas as well. Indeed the speed of its rise has probably not been paralleled by that of any other agricultural product during the period covered by our data (Chart 33). The ease with which the fruit lends itself to canning, both in segments and as juice (Tables 17 and 18), has no doubt been

[112] In California and Arizona a box of oranges contains 70 pounds, in Florida and other states 90 pounds.

[113] First attempts at organizing the California fruit growers were made as early as 1885, and the basis for the Exchange System was laid in 1893. There were a number of organizational changes, but the system grew steadily, and finally adopted its present form in 1905; see Fogelberg and McKay, *op. cit.*, pp. 13-20. The Florida Citrus Exchange, modeled in the image of the California Exchange, was not chartered until 1909; nor was it preceded by earlier attempts at organized selling.

[114] For a brief summary of the role played by advertising and research, see *ibid.*, pp. 65-70.

a factor in its meteoric ascent. The industry is, moreover, a very young one. Florida shipped no grapefruit until the 1880's,[115] produced only 20,000 boxes in 1890,[116] and fell a

TABLE 17

GRAPEFRUIT, FRESH AND CANNED

Pounds Consumed Per Capita, 1923–38[a]

Year[b]	*Fresh*	*Canned*[c]
1923	5.7	.2
1924	5.7	.3
1925	4.7	.4
1926	5.5	.7
1927	4.8	.6
1928	6.7	.8
1929	5.7	1.2
1930	8.6	2.1
1931	7.4	.7
1932	6.3	1.4
1933	6.2	1.3
1934	7.9	3.3
1935	7.3	2.3
1936	10.0	5.3
1937	9.9	5.5
1938	11.7	6.9

Source: Statistical Information on the Grapefruit Industry (California Fruit Growers Exchange, Marketing Research Department, 1940), Table 6.

[a] Excluding government purchases for relief distribution.

[b] Beginning in September.

[c] Equivalent number of pounds of fresh grapefruit.

victim to the freeze of 1895 before its output had attained sizable proportions; it was not until 1909 that the yield rose to one million boxes. In California grapefruit was cultivated

[115] *Ibid.*, p. 4.

[116] F. W. Risher, *Statistics of Florida Agriculture and Related Enterprises* (Florida Department of Agriculture, 1932?), p. 7. In Florida and Texas a box of grapefruit contains 80 pounds, and in California and Arizona, 60 pounds.

TABLE 18

CANNED GRAPEFRUIT

Relation to Total Grapefruit Production and Percent Utilized as Juice, 1920–40[a]

Season	Number of Cases Canned		*Juice Pack as Percent of Total Number of Cases Canned*
	Thousands[b]	Percent of Total Production[c]	
1920–21	2	[d]	0
1921–22	10	0.1	0
1922–23	150	1.6	0
1923–24	200	1.9	0
1924–25	350	3.2	0
1925–26	400	4.2	0
1926–27	700	6.4	0
1927–28	600	5.7	0
1928–29	1,162	7.9	17.6
1929–30	1,509	14.8	12.7
1930–31	3,174	15.1	14.6
1931–32	1,248	7.4	27.3
1932–33	2,960	17.6	26.2
1933–34	2,900	18.2	24.4
1934–35	6,267	26.5	42.6
1935–36	4,772	24.5	50.8
1936–37	10,801	30.1	59.6
1937–38	12,670	32.5	69.7
1938–39	16,252	32.0	71.5
1939–40	n.a.	44.5	n.a.

Source: Statistical Bulletin, Season 1939–40 (Florida Citrus Exchange, Nov. 1940), p. 41.

[a] Data relate to output of California, Florida, Texas and Arizona.
[b] Equivalent cases of 24 cans, No. 2 size.
[c] Derived from field boxes used in canning.
[d] Less than 0.05 percent.

even later; in 1909–10 only 19,000 boxes were produced, whereas the 1939–40 crop was one hundred times as large. Of still more recent origin is the raising of grapefruit in Texas and Arizona. Texas, which has enjoyed a more spectacular boom than the other producing states, started with the production of 3,000 boxes in 1919. Within ten years it had surpassed California and by 1939, with a crop of nearly 15 million boxes, was running a close second to Florida, with which it had attained rough equality in respect of total number of trees, bearing and nonbearing, as early as 1935.[117]

Lemons hold a position intermediate between the phenomenal growth of grapefruit and the more gradual expansion of California oranges. Almost wholly confined to California since the Florida freeze, the growing of lemons in this country has a rather long history, though it appears that most of today's lemon crop stems from varieties that were not planted until the 1870's.[118] Once lemon output had approached the million-box level [119]—in 1900 [120]—it did not rise sharply again for several years; nor did it stay permanently above the 2-million-box level until 1914. That year marked the beginning of an accelerated rate of growth, and by the mid-1920's seven lemons were harvested for every one picked in 1900. Since then, with the exception of the most recent years, output has risen but little. However, data on nonbearing acreage indicate a strong likelihood that a prolonged period of rising output is under way, inasmuch as only 4 percent of total lemon acreage was nonbearing in 1927–28, whereas 30 percent was nonbearing in 1936–37, after which plantings dropped somewhat.[121]

Though exports of both oranges (Chart 32) and grapefruit

117 *Census of Agriculture, 1935,* Vol. III, p. 378.

118 Fogelberg and McKay, *The Citrus Industry,* p. 6.

119 A box of lemons contains 76 pounds.

120 This in itself is a remarkably rapid development: in 1887 only 12 carloads had been shipped out of California; see John Perrin, *The Lemon Industry in the State of California,* Special Report No. 5 (Federal Reserve Bank of San Francisco, 1922), p. 4.

121 "Statistical Information on the Lemon Industry" (release by California Fruit Growers Exchange, Marketing Research Department, 1940), p. 5.

have expanded at a rapid rate,[122] possibly faster than total output, their relative importance is so slight as to prove that the main drive toward higher production has originated in the domestic market.

TREE NUTS

This group consists of walnuts, almonds and pecans. Though closely related to the fruits, tree nuts are most conveniently treated in a separate category. With the exception of pecans, commercial production is confined to California and parts of Oregon. In California nut production contributes at most 2 or 3 percent of the state's gross farm income.

For the period 1921–38, average annual growth for the group has been computed at 3.9 percent, a rate surpassed only by citrus fruit (Table 4 above). All three series fluctuate with great violence, but the upward tendency appears to have been strongest in walnut production (Chart 35). Except in some of the southern states, the growing of nuts is a comparatively young enterprise in this country.[123] This fact must be remembered if the rapid rise of nut production is to be assessed in its true light, for, as in the case of citrus fruit, we are really dealing with a new industry.

[122] First separately reported in 1922–23, grapefruit exports then amounted to 252,000 boxes; they rose to a high of 1.3 million boxes by 1938–39. Orange exports have had a longer development. Since exports were not separately reported by quantity until 1907–08, we can gauge their early history only through value data: in 1901–02 they accounted for 5 percent of the value of all fruits exported, in 1907–08 for 11 percent. In the latter year 650,000 boxes were exported, constituting not quite 5 percent of total orange production of that year. In 1913–14, 1.6 million boxes or 6 percent were exported, and in recent years an export of 4 to 5 million boxes has been the rule, equivalent to about 8 percent of output.

[123] Even in Georgia and other parts of the Deep South, long a source of pecans, production on a commercial scale did not start until the end of last century.

Chart 35
TREE NUTS: NET OUTPUT

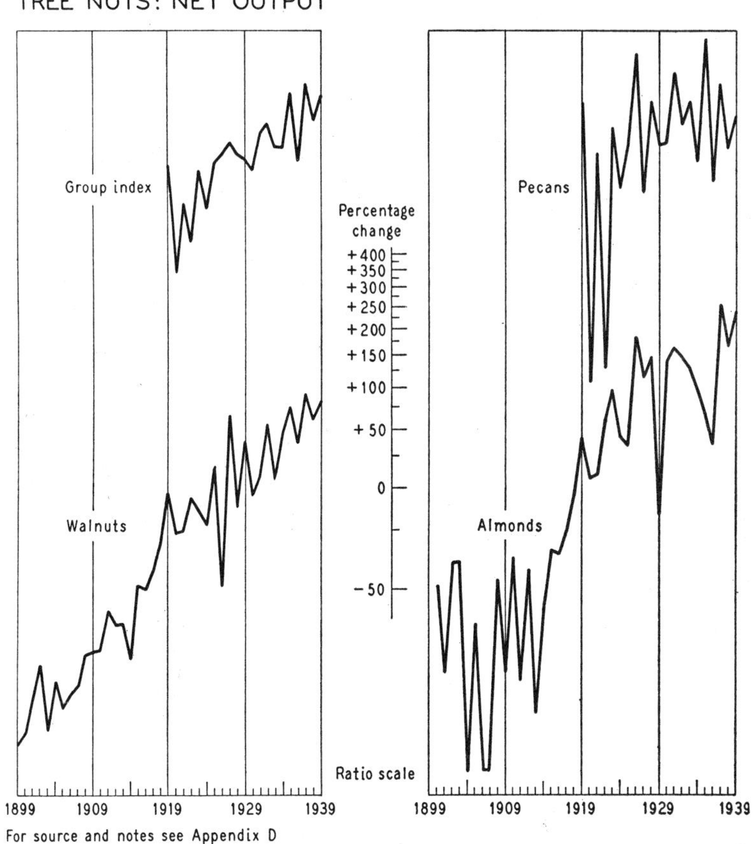

For source and notes see Appendix D

TRUCK CROPS

This group comprises nineteen vegetables, excluding potatoes, sweetpotatoes and dry edible beans,[124] all three of which are grown under conditions substantially different from those attending the cultivation of truck crops proper. We may draw a distinction, for statistical purposes, between four kinds of

[124] These are treated above, pp. 65-68. The nineteen vegetables included in our index (see Chart 5 above) are listed on p. 331.

vegetable production: (1) commercial truck crops for fresh market shipment; (2) commercial truck crops for processing; (3) market garden vegetables; and (4) the produce of farm gardens.[125]

Five states—California, Texas, Florida, New York and New Jersey—usually account for about half the value of the nation's commercial truck crops. The first three ship almost exclusively for fresh consumption, whereas New York and New Jersey divert about a third of their crop to processing channels. The latter two states, plus Maryland and the Corn Belt, account for about 70 percent of the supply of truck crops for processing. Between 10 and 20 percent of the total supply of truck crops is usually processed.

Output data are available only for the first and second categories of production mentioned above; thus market garden vegetables and the product of farm gardens are alike omitted from our index (Chart 5). Nor is this defect unimportant; on the contrary, from figures for gross income it appears that commercial truck crops account for less than half the total output of vegetables (Table 19). Value data suggest, furthermore, that commercial output has risen somewhat faster than

[125] This classification and the following quotations are taken from U. S. Department of Agriculture, *Income Parity for Agriculture* (Washington, 1941), Pt. I, Sec. 14, pp. 2, 11. Distinguishing commercial truck crops is the ". . . extensiveness of cultivation and the concentration of production in fairly well defined areas where soil and climatic conditions are especially adapted to their production." Crops for fresh market shipment are ". . . usually produced in areas some distance from market centers, and shipped by rail or boat in carlots, or trucked to market," while crops for processing (canning or preserving) ". . . are usually produced under processor-grower contracts which provide the processor with considerable control over the output." Market garden vegetables ". . . include primarily those vegetables produced by growers located near large cities. This production is largely trucked to the nearby markets and sold at certain periods of the year in wholesale and retail markets. Cultural practices are intensive. In the estimates of income for this group of vegetables there is also included income from some vegetables grown under conditions similar to commercial truck crops but not of sufficient importance to justify separate estimates." Finally, farm gardens include all vegetables grown on the farm (other than potatoes, sweetpotatoes, and dry edible beans) ". . . for fresh consumption, canned, pickled, or dried for home use."

noncommercial production, so that our index probably has an upward bias. So far as the index for agricultural output as a whole is concerned (Table 1 and Chart 1), this upward bias is tempered by the fact that the truck crop index, which rises more rapidly than total output, is given the weight derived from commercial production only. How far these two types of bias cancel one another cannot be estimated, but it

TABLE 19

GROSS INCOME FROM TRUCK CROPS, INCLUDING FARM GARDENS, AND FARM VALUE OF COMMERCIAL TRUCK CROPS, 1919–39

Million dollars

Year	*Gross Income from Truck Crops including Farm Gardens*	*Farm Value of Commercial Truck Crops*
1919	443	164
1920	486	175
1921	415	161
1922	464	192
1923	509	219
1924	530	234
1925	586	266
1926	547	236
1927	541	236
1928	576	267
1929	601	289
1930	563	276
1931	492	220
1932	405	172
1933	428	173
1934	433	205
1935	506	233
1936	516	252
1937	562	276
1938	511	247
1939	534	259

Source: Col. 1: U. S. Department of Agriculture, *Income Parity for Agriculture* (Washington, 1941), Pt. I, Sec. 14, p. 17. Col. 2: U. S. Department of Agriculture, *Agricultural Statistics, 1941,* Table 368. Data relate to calendar years.

is certain that the error in the total index since 1919 on this account is very small.[126]

Truck crops grew at an average annual rate of 3.6 percent from 1921 to 1938; this far exceeds the rate for agricultural output as a whole and is surpassed for this period only by the growth of citrus fruit and tree nuts (Table 4). A significant difference may be observed between the behavior of crops intended for processing and those sent to market for fresh consumption, the latter being characterized by large increases, whereas only one or two of the processed crops have expanded in volume. The increase in fresh vegetables might have been still larger had not yields declined somewhat from 1920 to 1935; during this period yields were reduced by roughly 25 percent. Recovery in recent years, accompanied by retardation of output expansion, has not been sufficient to meet previous levels; in contrast, vegetables for manufacture, which also suffered from sagging yields during the second half of the 1920's, have registered record crops in the last three years (Chart 36). By far the most rapid rise has occurred in the production of fresh peas, which increased roughly fifteenfold during the two post-war decades and boosted the income of the growers from slightly over $1 million in 1918 to more than ten times that amount in recent years. Snap beans, carrots, spinach and lettuce—the latter being one of the leading truck crops—have increased as much as fivefold during the period under consideration. Fresh beets, though of secondary importance, are distinguished by the tenfold increase which they achieved within a space of five years (1923–28). Other truck crops—cabbage, sweet corn, onions, tomatoes—have expanded only slightly or not at all.

OIL CROPS

This group comprises four crops which in part or in their entirety constitute the raw material from which crushing

[126] See Appendix A, pp. 327-29.

Chart 36
TRUCK CROPS
Indexes of Acreage and Yield
(1924-29 : 100)

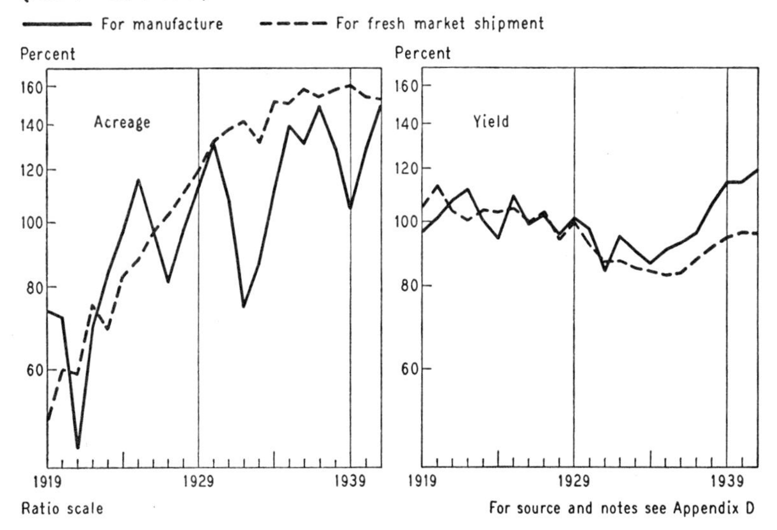

mills manufacture vegetable oils of varying composition for a number of purposes. Two of them—cottonseed and flaxseed—have already been discussed earlier in this chapter.[127]

Of the four, *cottonseed* is by far the most important; indeed with minor exceptions [128] the oil-crops index closely resembles the cotton index (in which, it will be recalled, cot-

[127] Pp. 76-78 and 63-65, respectively.

[128] As has been mentioned earlier in this chapter, we include only the amount of cottonseed which is used neither for feed nor for fertilizer. This amount is equivalent to mill deliveries. At present roughly 80 percent of the total crop is thus utilized, but at the beginning of our period less than 50 percent was crushed, and even that percentage represented a vast increase over the preceding decade when only one quarter of all cottonseed harvested went to the oil mills. (U. S. Department of Agriculture, *Fats, Oils and Oleaginous Raw Materials,* Statistical Bulletin 59, Washington, 1937, Table 40.) The divergences between cotton production and cottonseed production are thus largely due to differences in *net* rather than *gross* output. This is particularly noteworthy for the years 1897–1905, a period during which cotton and cottonseed production show very diverse movements.

tonseed has also been included). Cottonseed output has always accounted for more than 50 percent of the output of oil crops, and after 1909 its share grew substantially larger. However, since sizable amounts of vegetable oils are imported, cottonseed oil constitutes a somewhat smaller proportion of all oils consumed.

Of the remaining three crops, *soybeans* did not attain commercial importance as an oil-producing crop until the late 1920's; and *flaxseed* outranked *peanuts* until just before the War of 1914–18. At that time the "insufficiency of vegetable oils for use in the manufacture of munitions and butter substitutes," [129] coupled with the crisis in cotton planting which was just then beginning, led to an expansion in the planting and commercial utilization of peanuts.

Peanuts ceded second place to flaxseed in the mid-1920's—the period in which there was a sudden revival of flaxseed growing [130]—but, after a few years of approximate equality, regained it in 1931. This crop continued to rank second until 1939, when rising soybean output pushed it into third place.

Over the four decades oil-bearing crops as a group have grown at an annual rate of 1.2 percent. The expansion of the group is brought out more vividly when we compare indexes of 5-year moving averages based on 1897–1901 as 100. Such a comparison shows oil crops to have passed the 200 mark by 1935–39, outdistanced only by citrus fruit and sugar (Table 6).

The reason why annual rates of growth are less impressive than moving averages is to be found in the severe decline suffered by the group from 1914 to 1921. This slump, mainly a reflection of cottonseed contraction (except in 1919 when all three constituents registered sizable losses), almost cut output in two, depressing it from a high of 102.9 (1929:100)

[129] *Prices and Competition among Peanut Mills,* Sen. Doc. No. 132, 72nd Congress, 1st Session (Washington, 1932), p. 15.
[130] See p. 64 above.

in 1914 to 59.8 in 1921. And it is precisely this span of years which would have no effect upon a comparison of terminal years, or upon the trend rates of our customary half-periods.

Summarizing the various measures, we may say that this

Chart 37

OIL CROPS: NET OUTPUT

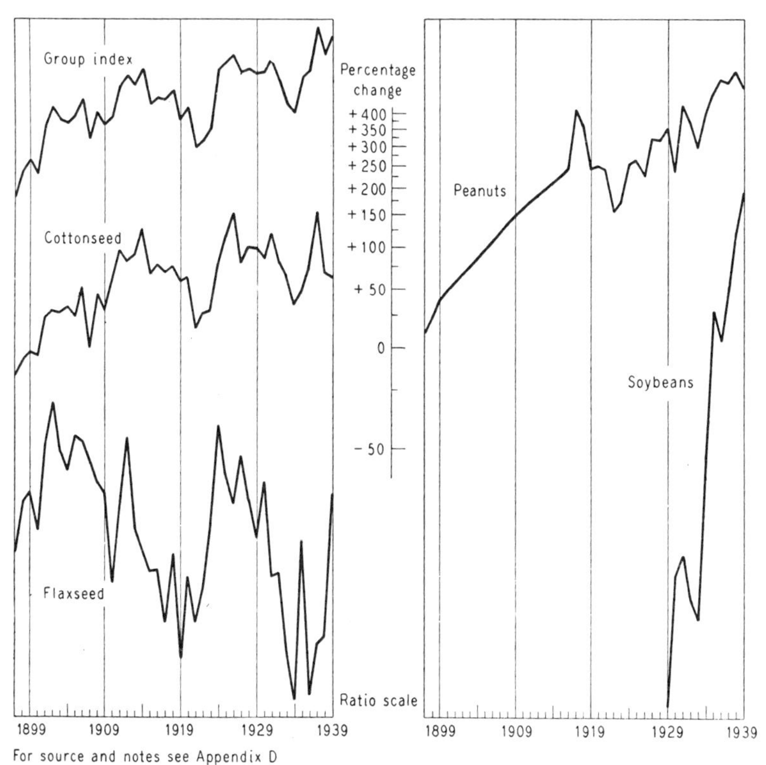

For source and notes see Appendix D

group is one of the most thriving of the fifteen considered here. As additional evidence of its resilience, we can point to the fact that it took only three years after each of the two major declines—1921 and 1934—for output to regain or exceed the previously recorded peak (Chart 37).

Since the domestic oils discussed above are replaceable in varying measure by imported oils, and since relative price positions and tariff policies have much to do with their development, to trace further the reasons for the differences in growth of the various oils would lead us far beyond the framework of this study.[131] Regarding other aspects of the individual series, it should be pointed out that only a minor fraction of total *peanut* output is converted to oil; the principal destinations of peanuts harvested as such are the peanut stand and the confectionery shop. The amount going to the crushing mills is largely determined by the price of peanuts in relation to that of competing oil crops, and year-to-year fluctuations in crushings are therefore violent. Since in addition a large amount of peanuts—in some years equivalent in magnitude to the entire net output—is not picked and threshed but used as feed, it is hard to classify peanuts in any of our groups.

As mentioned earlier, the net output of peanuts advanced only gradually up to the World War, when it enjoyed a sudden upswing which by 1917 had carried it to almost twice the 1910 volume. However, this volume of output was neither maintained nor reached again until 1931. Since then a high level has prevailed and from 1935 on net output has stayed above the billion-pound mark. Governmental efforts toward crop diversification in the South, coupled with intensified research into new uses of peanuts, have no doubt fostered the recent expansion.

One of the most remarkable developments in contemporary agricultural history has been the rise of the *soybean*. Though long known in this country, its domestic cultivation had al-

[131] A great deal has been written on the subject, and particular reference may be made here to two studies: (1) U. S. Tariff Commission, *Report to the Congress on Certain Vegetable Oils, Whale Oil, and Copra,* Report No. 41, Second Series (Washington, 1932); (2) G. M. Weber and C. L. Alsberg, *The American Vegetable-Shortening Industry,* Fats and Oils Studies No. 5 (Food Research Institute, Stanford University, 1934).

ways been secondary to its importation, and it was not until after the war that soybeans became a domestic crop.[132] In 1922, the first year for which we have reliable data, no more than 159,000 bushels were crushed and the value to the growers was just over $300,000. In 1939, however, more than 57 million bushels were delivered to the mills,[133] yielding the growers a return of roughly $43 million.[134]

The increasingly wide variety of uses for soybeans pertains for the most part to the crushed bean and its derivatives, oil and meal, rather than to the whole bean which is used largely for feed and for some food products. The spectacular growth of the industry is indicated by the following comparison of production figures for soybean oilmeal, linseeed oilmeal and cottonseed meal in 1925–26 and 1935–39.[135]

	1925–26	*1938–39*
	(thousand tons)	
Soybean oilmeal	8	1,050
Linseed oilmeal	750	506
Cottonseed meal	2,800	2,023

At first principally used as a drying oil in the manufacture of paints and varnishes, soybean oil was long considered unfit for human consumption because of its unpleasant odor. But suitable processing led, in 1930, to its introduction into

[132] The large imports of soybean oil during the war years stimulated interest in the crop, and tariffs on oil (1921) and beans (1922) further promoted its growth.

[133] An additional 30 million bushels harvested for beans in 1939 were used for purposes other than crushing. These are not included in our index, even though a small amount no doubt enters nonagricultural markets. Most of this portion presumably consists of beans for human consumption, but statistics are scanty. Excluded also, of course, is the portion that is fed to livestock as silage or in other unprocessed forms.

[134] The value of imported soybean oil in the same year amounted only to about $150,000, that of soybeans to $5,000. Gross income for 1939 came to more than $50 million, i.e., exceeded the income derived from any grain except corn and wheat.

[135] K. J. Maltas, "Utilization and Merchandising of Soybeans," *Papers Presented at the Program on Grain Marketing* (University of Illinois, 1940).

oleomargarine; ten years later it represented a third of all oils and fats used in making this product.[136] By 1940, moreover, almost 80 percent of all soybean oil consumed in factories was concentrated in the food industries, despite the fact that its keeping qualities are still inferior to those of other vegetable oils. In terms of total factory consumption of all oils, soybean oil ranked fourth, behind cottonseed oil, in-

TABLE 20

FATS AND OILS

Percentage Distribution of Factory Consumption,[a] 1931–40

Year	*Cotton-seed Oil*	*Coconut Oil*	*Linseed Oil*	*Palm Oil*	*Soy-bean Oil*	*Other Vegetable Oils*	*Animal Fats and Oils*
1931	30.2	15.7	7.9	6.2	0.7	9.1	30.1
1932	32.3	16.4	6.5	6.2	0.8	6.6	31.2
1933	31.7	16.6	6.9	6.6	0.7	7.9	29.7
1934	34.2	14.6	6.4	4.8	0.5	7.9	31.6
1935	29.7	13.0	6.5	5.6	2.0	12.9	30.3
1936	27.3	12.6	6.4	6.3	3.9	14.0	29.6
1937	34.0	8.6	7.6	6.7	3.6	12.9	26.7
1938	33.2	12.0	6.4	5.5	5.1	9.4	28.4
1939	27.5	11.0	7.2	5.6	7.7	9.8	31.1
1940	27.0	11.1	8.2	3.3	9.1	8.1	33.2

Source: U. S. Bureau of the Gensus, *Animal and Vegetable Fats and Oils* (Washington, 1936 and 1941). Data relate to calendar years.

[a] Including butter.

edible tallow and coconut oil, having within the preceding four years overtaken linseed oil, palm oil, grease and fish oils (see Table 20).[137]

The data on soybean output, however regarded, cannot

[136] U. S. Bureau of the Census, *Animal and Vegetable Fats and Oils, 1936–40* (Washington, 1941), p. 27; also U. S. Tariff Commission, *Fats, Oils and Oil-Bearing Materials in the United States* (Washington, 1941).

[137] *Animal and Vegetable Fats and Oils*, pp. 21-24.

fail to impress the reader as a record of rapid and continuing growth. Present indications, furthermore, point to broader industrial utilization of soybean derivatives, which are already so numerous as to rival the catalog of corn products. When used in paint, soybean oil dries more slowly than linseed oil, but has the advantage that it does not yellow with age. It is also used in soap manufacture and as a constituent of printers' ink. Soybean meal, which contains a residue of oil, is converted primarily into commercial feeds, but it has also been used as a base for the manufacture of glues and adhesives, plastics, synthetic fibers and linoleum.[138]

MISCELLANEOUS CROPS

Of the crops that are not readily allocated to any homogeneous group, *hay* is much the most important. Closely related to the feed grains, it differs from them in that it is used exclusively for feeding animals—on farms or elsewhere. Of the gross output of hay, much the largest part—79.5 percent in 1897–1901, 97.0 percent in 1935–39, as closely as we can estimate—is used for feeding livestock on the farm itself and forms no part of net output. The remainder—about one fifth of total production at the turn of the century, but only 3 percent today—is used for feeding horses not on farms, mainly in cities. A sharp fall in net output (Chart 5), occasioned by the disappearance of the city horse, reduced the contribution of hay to the aggregate net output of agriculture from 2.1 percent to 0.3 percent (Table 2). It should not be thought, however, that hay is any less important in the farm economy

[138] For a description of present and suggested uses see the previously cited survey, *Regional Research Laboratories.* See also H. E. Barnard, "Prospects for Industrial Uses for Farm Products," *Journal of Farm Economics,* Vol. XX (Feb. 1938), pp. 119-33; and E. W. Grove, *Soybeans in the United States; Recent Trends and Present Economic Status,* Technical Bulletin 619 (U. S. Department of Agriculture, 1938).

as a whole: indeed the gross output of tame hay increased by about one third between 1899 and 1937.[139]

Hops is a crop that cannot conveniently be included in any category, except the very broad one of "industrial raw materials." Since the sole purpose for which hops are grown is the manufacture of beer and other fermented malt liquors and cereal beverages, our output series registers a substantial setback during the "dry" years. From a pre-Prohibition level of 40 to 60 million pounds, production of hops receded to less than 30 million pounds beginning in 1918, and did not again touch the 40-million level until 1933, when beer was restored to legality. The contribution of hops to total agricultural output has never been more than 0.1 percent, though concentration of cultivation in a very narrow area—Oregon, California and Washington—invests it with some local importance. In 1935–37 over one half of the domestic hops produced and nearly one sixth of the world's output of hops was centered in Oregon,[140] and in this state between 7 and 8 percent of the farmer's income is derived from hops.

139 Frederick Strauss and L. H. Bean, *Gross Farm Income and Indices of Farm Production and Prices in the United States, 1869–1937,* Technical Bulletin 703 (U. S. Department of Agriculture, 1940), p. 62. In fact there is some difficulty in estimating the fraction of gross output leaving agriculture, a fraction which, as mentioned in the text, has steadily declined. The series we have employed (*ibid.,* Table 24) is based on the number of animals not on farms and their estimated per capita consumption of hay. The diminishing number of city horses alone would be sufficient to impart a downward tendency to such a series. However, recent data published in U. S. Bureau of Agricultural Economics, *Disposition of Hay, Crop Years 1909–1936, by States* (Washington, 1939), based on sales, agree closely with our series for the early years (1909–12) though they remain above our series thereafter. Since this second series represents total sales, including sales within agriculture, it is quite certain that year by year it overstates to an increasing degree the amount "sold off farms"; for this reason the series presented here is probably more satisfactory for our purposes.

140 G. W. Kuhlman and R. E. Fore, *Cost and Efficiency in Producing Hops in Oregon,* Bulletin 364 (Oregon Agricultural Experiment Station, 1939), p. 6.

Chapter 4

Agriculture and the Nation's Food

BETWEEN 80 and 90 percent of our agricultural output eventually finds its way into the food basket of the nation. Because the volume as well as the character of agricultural production are intimately related to changes in dietary habits, we have made the demand for food the subject of a separate chapter whose findings will have some bearing upon every group of foodstuffs dealt with in the preceding pages.

THE MEASUREMENT OF FOOD VALUES

The diet of a country [1] at any given moment is determined by many factors. The natural resources, including climate and soil, the state of the industrial arts, transportation and distribution facilities, the composition of the population, progress in the science of nutrition, the course and distribution of real income in the community—all these jointly influence food consumption. But the choices exercised by the consumer in deciding what to eat are not, for the most part, in terms of the nutrients of which food materials are composed. A housewife buys a quart of milk or a loaf of bread; she does not ask for a thousand calories or a milligram of riboflavin. Yet we cannot appraise the food supply in a physi-

[1] In this chapter we are concerned exclusively with changes in food consumption of the population as a whole. Consequently, we must deal in averages. The reader should be aware that the dispersion about this average may be as important as changes within it. The present emphasis is thought important, however, since there is available a large amount of material on differences in food expenditure by income groups, whereas little research has been undertaken on the development of food consumption as a whole.

ological sense, judge its adequacy, or examine the scope for its improvement in the future, unless we talk in terms of food values rather than of foods themselves. Nutrition is a science of comparatively recent growth: but there are signs that it may already have influenced dietary habits, and it can be expected to do so in increasing measure in the future.

The energy-yielding qualities of a food material are measured in calories,[2] which are derived from three broad classes of chemical substances known respectively as proteins, carbohydrates and fats. Besides these three classes of nutrient, which together with water account for the major part of the bulk and weight of most foodstuffs, minute quantities of numerous other substances are necessary to the maintenance of the health of humans and animals alike. So far as is now known, the latter consist of vitamins—complex organic substances—and individual chemical elements such as calcium, phosphorus and iron.

The present extent of our knowledge may be indicated most conveniently by a brief survey of the more important discoveries in the field of nutrition. As a starting point, in order to illustrate the state of the science of nutrition at the turn of the century, we may mention the researches carried on at that time by W. O. Atwater to whom the first systematic description of the energy content of various foods is to be credited,[3] and whose results have been superseded only to a minor extent. Perhaps inevitably Atwater stressed energy content almost to the exclusion of other aspects of foods. His views, which are characteristic of his era, have been summarized as follows:

[2] Throughout the chapter reference is to so-called "large" calories, the unit commonly employed in nutritional analysis. This represents the amount of heat required to raise the temperature of one kilogram of water one degree centigrade; or 4 pounds of water one degree Fahrenheit, approximately.

[3] See *Chemistry and Economy of Food,* Experiment Station Bulletin 21 (U. S. Department of Agriculture, 1895); W. O. Atwater and A. P. Bryant, *The Chemical Composition of American Food Materials,* Experiment Station Bulletin 28 (1896; reprinted 1906).

He believed that if he knew the chemical composition and the fuel values of all important foods and feeding-stuffs, in terms of their content of protein, carbohydrate, and fats, and the digestibility factors for these, together with the energy requirements of human beings and animals, it would be possible to place nutrition of man and animals on a sound economic basis. He set to work, with the support of the U. S. Department of Agriculture, to analyze all American foods . . . Atwater regarded fruits and water-rich fresh vegetables, eggs, etc., as extravagant food purchases. He saw no reason why one should not remain in health while taking a diet selected from the cheapest dried food products.

Atwater visualized the coming of a time when farmers should be able to consult tables showing the cost of protein and energy in various farm crops, and taking into account digestibility of their food elements, to select the cheapest sources of these nutrients for compounding their rations for feeding animals. Fortunately for his peace of mind he never saw the effects of restricting animals or men to diets which might have been compounded on his advice. It is also very fortunate that housewives did not, so far as we are aware, attempt to follow his advice in the feeding of their families.[4]

At the time Atwater wrote, cornmeal was much the cheapest source of calories: it followed that an economical diet would consist predominantly of this substance.[5]

The need for an adequate supply of calories, and therefore of the basic dietetic constituents (proteins, carbohydrates and fats) is of course still recognized. But the problem of determining the food value of proteins has turned out to be more complicated than was earlier supposed. Besides contributing calorific value, proteins are the principal source of nitrogen compounds needed by the body; in fact they supply, through

[4] E. V. McCollum, Elsa Orent-Keiles, and H. G. Day, *The Newer Knowledge of Nutrition* (5th ed; Macmillan, 1939), pp. 10-11. However, although he neither realized the importance of minerals, nor suspected the existence of vitamins, Atwater continually urged that more research was needed.

[5] Atwater, *Chemistry and Economy of Food,* pp. 139-40.

degradation, products essential to tissue-building in growth and maintenance, to reproduction, lactation and other functions of life. These degradation products belong to a large class of organic compounds known as amino acids, some of which are much more useful than others for tissue-building or other specific purposes. Different proteins yield quite different assortments of amino acids, and therefore vary greatly in food value. Some of the amino acids can be synthesized in the body; but the synthesis of others, and therefore of the proteins containing them, cannot be accomplished within the organism. Obviously the true nutritive value of a protein is related to its content of this latter group, the so-called essential amino acids. The systematic appraisal of protein-contributing foodstuffs along these lines has not yet been possible, though it appears that animal-derived proteins rank above all others.[6] For most purposes this question does not appear to have immediate practical importance, however, for the range of proteins available in most diets, except perhaps under siege conditions, is more than sufficient to secure an adequate distribution of amino acids on digestion.[7] Carbohydrates and fats are important chiefly as a source of energy, and their deficiency is easily recognizable in any given diet; moreover the body tolerates the substitution of one carbohydrate or fat for another, so that neither of these elements in nutrition presents a serious problem under ordinary conditions. Our knowledge of protein, carbohydrate and fat requirements in the diet represents in a sense merely an extension of what was already known half a century ago.

Practical recognition of the importance of vitamins may be said to go back to the use of lemon juice by the British navy in 1804, or even earlier, as a preventive of scurvy.[8] Real

[6] McCollum, Orent-Keiles and Day, *op. cit.*, p. 130.

[7] However, it has been suggested that lack of biologically superior protein may contribute to the beriberi of the Indies and the pellagra of our own southern states.

[8] Henry Borsook, *Vitamins* (Viking, 1941), p. 93. The juice of the Mediterranean lemon, known at that time as "lime" juice, was used; it is an important source of vitamin C.

knowledge concerning their properties and availability dates from much more recent times, however. Although it had been suspected as long ago as 1881 that small quantities of definite but complex substances in the diet were essential to the maintenance of health, the beginning of our systematic knowledge concerning vitamins dates only from about the year 1905. Since then experiments in chemical analysis and in the feeding of animals and human beings have led to the isolation of a number of organic substances, all necessary to health, of which in 1940 no fewer than seven had been synthesized commercially.[9] Vitamins are to be distinguished from other complex organic substances important to health, such as hormones, by the fact that (except for vitamin D) they are not manufactured by, and (except for vitamins A and D) are not stored to any great extent by, the human body itself, but must be regularly supplied from outside; hence their importance in diet.

The vitamins are not closely related to each other in a chemical sense, but they have in common (1) that they are necessary in diet only in relatively minute quantity; and (2) that the lack of any one of them invites sooner or later a more or less pronounced pathological condition which, if it does not become too severe, can be cured by restoration of the vitamin to the diet. It is probable also that some of the vitamins actively assist the assimilation of other foodstuffs, although information on this score is still scanty. In general the absence of a vitamin from the diet is not noticed except as a nutritional deficiency disease appears, and the need for vitamins has therefore been described as "hidden hunger," in contrast to the actual hunger resulting from an insufficiency of calories. For the same reason our data on health tell us little about the occurrence of malnutrition, and deaths due to deficiency diseases do not loom large in our vital statistics. Indeed the condition may easily escape notice, or may be

[9] *Ibid.*, p. 7.

wrongly diagnosed,[10] for ". . . in the present state of our knowledge concerning the diagnosis of malnutrition due to many of the specific nutritional factors a wide borderline zone exists between nutritional inadequacy and diagnosable malnutrition." [11]

Vitamin A, discovered in 1913, is necessary to growth and to effective vision, particularly in a dull light, and it also increases resistance to a wide range of infections. It is peculiar among vitamins in that certain related substances, or "precursors," such as the carotenes, can readily be transformed by the body into the vitamin itself, and are therefore satisfactory substitutes. We may regard foodstuffs containing these precursors as containing vitamin A for all practical purposes, and this treatment is usually adopted in nutrition studies. The chief sources of vitamin A (or its precursors) are liver (especially fish liver oils), butterfat, eggs and leafy green and yellow vegetables. Because of the close association with growth, it has sometimes been suggested that this vitamin is less necessary to adults than to children, but this has not been established.[12]

Vitamin B_1 (thiamin), first isolated in 1926, is usually known as the antineuritic vitamin, because its deficiency leads to beriberi, a disease of the nerves of the feet and legs. Its existence was first discovered by the observation that Asiatic populations fed on polished rice contracted beriberi, but recovered when their diet was changed to unpolished rice. Besides its negative function of preventing beriberi it influences normal metabolism, especially of carbohydrates, and even mild deficiency leads to loss of appetite, debility and inefficiency. Vitamin B_1 is widely distributed among food

[10] Norman Jolliffe, J. S. McLester, and H. C. Sherman, "The Prevalence of Malnutrition," *Journal of the American Medical Association,* Vol. 118 (March 21, 1942), pp. 944-50.

[11] *Ibid.,* p. 948. See also pp. 175-78 below.

[12] H. C. Sherman, *Chemistry of Food and Nutrition* (6th ed; Macmillan, 1941), p. 412.

materials, occurring in lean meat, eggs, wholewheat flour, nuts and to a small extent in milk and some fruits and vegetables. However, it is largely lost when flour is refined or rice is polished, and, being soluble in water and susceptible to heat, may disappear in cooking. Vitamin B_2 (or G, riboflavin) resembles vitamin B_1 in that it is water-soluble, plays an important part in the metabolism of the body, and is found in about the same foodstuffs. It was discovered much later, however, and was not isolated until 1933. Another member of the B group, the pellagra-preventive vitamin (nicotinic acid, or niacin) has been discovered still more recently.

The existence of an antiscorbutic factor had been suspected by the early nutritionists, but it was not definitely identified as vitamin C (ascorbic acid) until 1931. Besides preventing scurvy, this vitamin seems to have a general function in cell building. Its availability in food materials is practically confined to fruits and vegetables, and it is found especially in citrus juice. Since vitamin C is water-soluble and easily destroyed by oxidation, losses in processing, storage and cooking are important and probably more serious than in the case of other nutrients. Consequently we have not been able to make estimates for its consumption by the methods followed generally in this chapter.

The antirachitic vitamin D, which is fat-soluble and appears in numerous forms, involves an extremely complicated chemical problem that has not yet been fully solved. Its physiological importance derives from its influence upon calcium metabolism, since its presence is indispensable to bone building. Like vitamin A, it is to be found in liver; it is present also in small quantities in other food materials of animal origin, but is not supplied by vegetables. Data on the vitamin D content of foodstuffs are not at present adequate to permit estimates of its consumption by the methods adopted here. Moreover the problem is complicated by the fact that exposure to sunlight brings about a synthesis of this vitamin within the human body: the degree to which this occurs effectively is related to several factors, among them latitude, smoke in the atmosphere and other conditions. Unfortunately, therefore, estimates of the amount of vitamin D present in foods eaten by a given population may be of little value. The existence of several other vitamins has been established, but too little is known about them to permit one to make estimates of their consumption.

Among individual chemical elements, calcium and phosphorus are important for bone building, and as such are specially needed by growing children. Since both these elements are stored by the body on a much larger scale than any of the vitamins, temporary deficiencies are not so serious, but continuing deficiencies, in children and adults alike, lead to ill health. Calcium and phosphorus are found in milk and eggs, and in smaller quantities in most vegetables.

Iron is a vital constituent of the blood, and as such must be regularly replaced for the maintenance of health. It is found in lean meat, eggs, wholewheat flour, and in many vegetables. An adequate iodine supply is necessary to the proper functioning of the thyroid gland, but we have not been able to measure its consumption here. Apparently numerous other elements also are necessary in minute quantities, although risk of deficiency is slight in most modern diets.[13]

For a more exhaustive discussion of the present state of our knowledge of nutrition the reader is referred to the numerous treatises upon the subject that have appeared in recent years. A complete catalog of the substances necessary for the maintenance of health and efficiency, or even of life itself, cannot yet be compiled. But we do know at least that three broad types of nutrient are indispensable—energy-producing foods (proteins, carbohydrates and fats), vitamins and minerals. How adequate is our food supply, we are naturally

[13] McCollum, Orent-Keiles and Day, *The Newer Knowledge of Nutrition*, Chs. VII-XI; Sherman, *Chemistry of Food and Nutrition*, Chs. XII-XV.

tempted to ask, in terms of these various nutrients? What changes would be called for, in the sphere of agricultural production, by a rise in nutritional standards? In the present chapter we attempt to answer these questions.

THE STATISTICS OF FOOD CONSUMPTION—CALORIES

In principle, if we know the amount consumed of each kind of food, and also its calorie, vitamin or mineral content, we can calculate the average intake of calories (proteins, carbohydrates and fats), vitamins and minerals for the population as a whole. The constitution of common foodstuffs in terms of proteins, carbohydrates and fats is fairly well established. Moreover these energy-producing nutrients account for a major portion of the total weight of most foodstuffs. For these reasons measurement of the per capita intake of calories back to 1899, undertaken in this section, is not a difficult matter. In the case of vitamins and minerals the situation is much more complicated. These nutrients comprise only a minute fraction—and often a highly variable one—of the food materials from which they are supplied. The estimation of per capita consumption of vitamins and minerals is consequently a more formidable undertaking, and the results of the calculations are surrounded by a much larger margin of error than in the case of proteins, carbohydrates and fats. Consequently our estimates for vitamin and mineral consumption (to be presented in subsequent sections of this chapter) are necessarily tentative and confined to recent years.

We shall begin, then, by considering the consumption of energy-producing foods.[14] At the outset, however, it is necessary to sound a warning lest the reader be tempted to place too much reliance upon individual figures. In the first place, consumption data on food are for the most part derived by adjustment of output estimates for imports, exports, changes

[14] The derivation of the estimates presented in the remainder of this chapter is described in detail in Appendix B.

in stocks, and use for nonfood purposes; they suffer therefore from possible weaknesses not only in the output estimates, but in these adjustments as well. In the second place, we have found it necessary to assume that the composition of each food item remained unchanged over the period reviewed, although this cannot have been exactly the case. There is evidence, for instance, that the tendency toward leaner meats may have altered the relative proportions of protein and fat. In the third place, the reduction of the animal carcass (in the case of meat) to fats and proteins in itself depends upon estimates of unknown reliability. Finally, waste, for which we have not been able to allow, undoubtedly occurs at numerous points. Nonfood by-products and the inedible portion of foodstuffs have indeed been excluded, but no allowance has been made for losses in transportation, storage, processing or retailing, in the kitchen or on the table. Our estimates really relate therefore to potential consumption rather than to actual ingestion. For all these reasons changes over long periods of time are to be regarded as more significant than absolute amounts shown for particular years.

First, as to aggregate consumption by weight, official estimates are available for the per capita [15] daily consumption of all foodstuffs in pounds,[16] and this series is shown in Table 21 and Chart 38. It appears, as might be expected, that per

[15] To facilitate clarity of exposition, we have refrained from correcting the population figures used here for changes in age or sex composition. See discussion below.

[16] U. S. Bureau of Agricultural Economics release, "Consumption of Agricultural Products" (1941). The actual poundage eaten is overstated by this series (Table 21, column 1, below), for such items as manufactured dairy products (except butter), canned and dried fruit, fruit juices, and canned vegetables were reconverted by the compilers into their unprocessed equivalents. In the case of dairy products this procedure inflates the total by more than 80 pounds per capita per annum, and in the case of fruit and vegetables the overstatement is almost equally large. An additional overstatement in the Department of Agriculture series reproduced here results from the failure to exclude corn used in the manufacture of nonfood products. On the other hand these data (like all others in this chapter) omit the consumption of fish. A rough check indicates the total overstatement to be around 10 percent.

TABLE 21
DAILY PER CAPITA[a] FOOD CONSUMPTION, 1897–1939

Year	*Pounds*[b]	*Proteins*	*Fats*	*Carbo-hydrates*	*Calories*
		(grams)			
Average, 1897–1901	..	100	132	502	3,590
1909	5.12	96	131	481	3,490
1910	5.15	94	129	478	3,453
1911	5.04	93	135	471	3,471
1912	5.18	95	132	484	3,506
1913	5.08	93	132	478	3,471
1914	5.06	92	136	467	3,453
1915	5.04	89	130	457	3,353
1916	4.94	89	136	457	3,410
1917	5.00	91	131	468	3,410
1918	4.87	88	136	438	3,324
1919	4.87	87	133	451	3,349
1920	4.87	87	128	451	3,306
1921	4.68	83	128	433	3,213
1922	4.99	87	132	462	3,388
1923	4.95	87	139	440	3,359
1924	4.99	87	141	452	3,425
1925	4.93	87	139	445	3,377
1926	5.00	88	140	461	3,457
1927	4.98	88	141	447	3,411
1928	5.01	88	142	467	3,498
1929	5.02	87	144	451	3,449
1930	4.93	87	142	438	3,378
1931	4.90	86	142	439	3,382
1932	4.80	85	141	423	3,299
1933	4.71	83	141	407	3,227
1934	4.73	83	139	420	3,265
1935	4.85	81	128	415	3,136
1936	4.91	84	136	418	3,230
1937	5.01	85	138	411	3,223
1938	5.10	85	139	415	3,252
1939	5.11	86	145	415	3,306

Source: Appendix B, except as otherwise noted. Calendar year data.
[a] Based on population as of midyear, unadjusted for sex and age differences.
[b] Based on U. S. Bureau of Agricultural Economics, *Consumption of Agricultural Products* (Washington, 1941), p. 13; coffee and tea excluded.

capita consumption by weight is remarkably stable. In only one year during the period 1909–39 did the series deviate by as much as 5 percent from its 31-year average. However, the actual number of pounds of food consumed is a somewhat misleading concept which may hide as much as it reveals. Weight, for example, is often due to water content. Few cuts of meat contain less than 40 to 50 percent of water: as purchased, a medium fat loin of beef contains over 50 percent, and a similar loin of pork over 40 percent of water.[17] Fruits and vegetables, of course, are even richer in water. The constitution of the more solid foods varies greatly also, and here the more important question relates to the amounts of proteins, vitamins and other nutrients they can supply. Indeed the popular notion of "heavy" foods refers to digestibility or to calorie content rather than to weight.

The logical procedure, then, is to convert each variety of food consumed into its equivalent in terms of each of the different nutrients of which it is composed. The pioneer study in this field was published in 1920 by Raymond Pearl.[18] Although aware of the importance of vitamins, Pearl was forced to confine his statistical treatment to the estimation of proteins, carbohydrates and fats in the diet, which he did for the years 1911–12 through 1917–18. For these years he found a per capita consumption of about 3,400 calories per day, but the period he considered was not long enough for his figures to reveal any significant downward trend in the intake of calories. Since the publication of Pearl's findings the efforts of the Department of Agriculture have led to a considerable improvement in the data on food consumption. In the present chapter it is our purpose to develop estimates for the per capita consumption of proteins, carbohydrates and fats an-

[17] Atwater and Bryant, *The Chemical Composition of American Food Materials*, pp. 21, 38.

[18] *The Nation's Food* (W. B. Saunders, Philadelphia, 1920). A comparison between our estimates for per capita calorie consumption and those given by Pearl will be found in Appendix B.

nually, back to 1909; in addition we present the best estimate we can make for the period 1897–1901.

For years since 1909 we were able for the most part to rely upon official estimates of food consumption; but where necessary for this period, and for all foodstuffs in 1897–1901, we developed estimates of our own. The next step was to convert each foodstuff into its equivalent of proteins, carbohydrates and fats. For this purpose we supplemented Atwater's data with other estimates of food value where this procedure seemed desirable. The aggregate amounts of each of the three kinds of nutrient were then converted into calories with the following conversion factors:

1 gram of protein = 4 calories
1 gram of fat = 9 calories
1 gram of carbohydrate = 4 calories

These take into account energy losses incurred in the course of digestion [19] and are therefore slightly lower than the factors used by Pearl. The results of the calculation are shown in Table 21 above; the consumption data and conversion factors are presented in Appendix B. Since in the field of fuel elements we are less interested in absolute than in relative levels, and since the composition of the population in terms of energy-requirement units has not altered sufficiently to affect year-to-year changes in per capita consumption appreciably, we have not recomputed population data on the basis of age and sex composition.[20]

As we can see at a glance from Table 21 and Chart 38, per capita calorie consumption has decreased materially over the past few decades. In terms of selected 5-year averages, as shown in Table 22, the reduction between 1897–1901 and

[19] See Sherman, *Chemistry of Food and Nutrition,* pp. 127-28.

[20] From tests we have made it appears that for the last four decades a correction factor of .81 will express satisfactorily the actual population in terms of requirement units. (Such a unit represents the estimated average requirement for males age 20-59.) See also discussion below, pp. 157-58.

Chart 38
FOOD CONSUMPTION PER CAPITA
(1909 : 100)

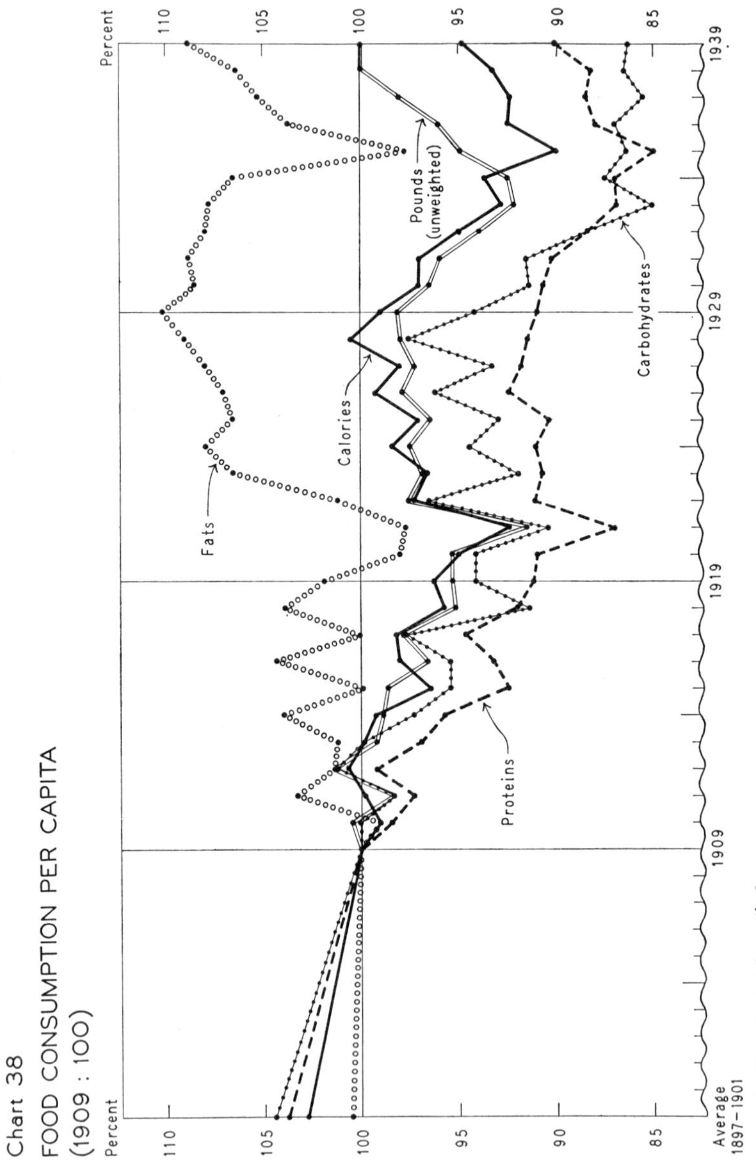

For source and notes see Appendix D

1935–39 has amounted to about 10 percent.[21] However, when we not only compare the initial and final period but observe the year-to-year changes, we discover that the diminution in consumption has not been of a continuous nature; for we can distinguish four stages, two of decline, 1899–1921 and 1928–35, and two of increase, 1921–28 and 1935–39. In fact consumption of calories varies with business activity, and exhibits rather clear cyclical movements. But it is subject also to a declining trend, for per capita calorie consumption is lower in 1935–39 than in earlier quinquennia (Table 22).

TABLE 22

CALORIES

Daily per Capita Consumption

Period	*Calories*
1897–1901	3,590
1909–1913	3,478
1917–1921	3,320
1925–1929	3,438
1930–1934	3,310
1935–1939	3,229

Source: Table 21, above.

Comparing per capita figures for tonnage and for calories in index form (Chart 38), we find the two moving together —with a slight tendency for calories to exceed tonnage both on the downgrade and on the upgrade—until 1934; in 1934 the two indexes part, the calorie index remaining stable and the tonnage index rising very steeply. In fact, from 1933 to 1939 per capita calorie consumption rises only 2.4 percent, while per capita tonnage consumption goes up 8.5 percent over the same period.

Anticipating the findings of subsequent sections we must

[21] About 12 percent in terms of "equivalent adult males." See below, pp. 157-58.

ascribe this divergence almost entirely to the increased consumption of fruit and vegetables, low in calorie content, high in weight.[22] One is naturally tempted to relate this recent change in diet to consumer education, but discussion of this aspect must be deferred to the following section.

Summarizing, we may say that a decided decrease in per capita calorie consumption, amounting to roughly 10 percent, is evident for the period 1899–1939, and that even during the years of highest post-war consumption, 1925–29, per capita calorie intake remained 5 percent below the 1899 level. As the data for the most recent years demonstrate, a measure of consumption by physical weight may be inadequate as a gauge of calorie intake when there are shifts in the selection of foods. In terms of weight of food consumed we eat about as much as did our grandparents; but we get along with 10 percent less calories. It is interesting to inquire briefly as to the factors that may have brought about this change.

There is naturally no way of establishing a definite causal link between changes in our mode of living and shifts in our demand for foodstuffs, nor is it feasible to subject any of the motivating factors to a rigid statistical test. Nonetheless, it is possible to outline major changes in the sociological factors, and to compare the results they would be expected to yield with observed trends in food consumption. Indeed, this has so frequently been done in a general way that the influence upon diet of certain sociological factors may be regarded almost as axiomatic. There may, however, be legitimate doubt as to the relative importance of the factors involved, and in this field there is still ample room for speculation. We have to differentiate between influences upon the *amount* and upon the *kind* of food consumed; generally it is much easier to trace the source of quantitative change than of qualitative

[22] During the period 1933–39 domestic production of truck crops increased 36 percent, of noncitrus fruit 22 percent, of citrus fruit 74 percent; see Table 5 above.

shifts, though in a very strict sense the two are interrelated.

Among the factors that have led to a diminished consumption of calories we must count: (1) increased mechanization of productive operations, both in industry and in agriculture, and a consequent lessening of physical exertion; (2) relative decrease in the agricultural population whose calorie requirements tend to be relatively high (because of hard work, heat-losses through outdoor activity and poor provision for heating in buildings); (3) shifts in the occupational distribution in favor of clerical and other nonmanual employments involving less physical exertion (especially sedentary occupations); (4) reduction in hours of work; (5) improved heating in buildings and transportation facilities, preventing losses of body heat; (6) improved and expanded transportation systems, decreasing the need for walking. Other tendencies, such as decreased body weight per person,[23] may also have had their influence.

The diminished per capita consumption of calories in the United States is sometimes attributed also to the higher average age of the population, in addition to the factors already enumerated: in 1900 the median age was twenty-three, in 1940 twenty-nine. Since the energy requirements of persons sixty years of age and over are substantially below similar requirements for adults in the lower age groups, and since the percentage of old people in the population has been increasing rather rapidly, it might be thought that the decline in per capita calorie intake could be accounted for, partially at least, in this fashion. Surprisingly enough it appears, on the contrary, that when the energy requirements of the various age groups are taken into consideration the calorie needs of the population on a per capita basis have actually gone up

[23] Holbrook Working, "The Decline in Per Capita Consumption of Flour in the United States," *Wheat Studies*, Vol. II (Food Research Institute, Stanford University, 1926), p. 286.

during the last forty years.[24] This is because the decline in the percentage of children, whose energy requirements are also lower than those of young adults, more than outweighs the increased proportion of aged persons in the nation. If the estimated calorie requirements for different age groups are correct, therefore, the increase in the average age of the population cannot have lowered the per capita need for calories, but must actually have raised it between 2 and 3 percent.

The bearing of this result on the interpretation of the observable decline in per capita calorie intake is not completely clear. Only if actual calorie consumption by different age groups conformed to physiological requirements could we say that changing age composition had worked in the opposite direction, and that the observed decline was that much more significant. Though we cannot make a definite statement to this effect, it seems to have been what occurred. The adjustment of calorie consumption to actual needs appears to be more or less automatic. As Working has remarked, "the adjustment of the appetite to the needs of the body for energy-producing foods is so completely unconscious that most people, perhaps, are entirely unaware of its action." [25] In other words, if the physiological need for energy-producing foods declines, so also will their consumption.

While this line of analysis perhaps offers a rational explanation of the decline in the per capita intake of calories, it does little to clarify such shifts in food consumption as that

[24] Using Stiebeling's (H. K. Stiebeling and E. F. Phipard, *Diets of Families of Employed Wage Earners and Clerical Workers in Cities,* Circular No. 507, U. S. Department of Agriculture, 1939) requirement scale and applying it to the age and sex structure as revealed by successive population Censuses, we find that the population, adjusted to an "equivalent adult male" basis, grew 65.3 percent between 1900 and 1930 as against a 61.9 percent increase shown by the uncorrected population figures.

The ratios of corrected to uncorrected population are:

1900	*1910*	*1920*	*1930*
.809	.816	.816	.826

[25] Working, *op. cit.,* p. 281.

toward dairy products, and fresh fruits and vegetables. To such questions we now turn.

COMPOSITION OF THE CALORIE SUPPLY

Calories do not tell the whole story. We must now try to determine how the three groups of nutrient—proteins, carbohydrates and fats—share in supplying energy. The data pertinent to this question are shown in percentage form in Table 23, and the situation is depicted graphically in Chart 39. It will be seen that between proteins, carbohydrates and fats as

TABLE 23
CALORIES
Percentage Contributions of Proteins, Fats and Carbohydrates to Total Consumption

	1897–1901	*1909–13*	*1925–29*	*1935–39*
Proteins	11.1	10.8	10.2	10.4
Fats	33.0	34.1	37.0	38.2
Carbohydrates	55.9	55.0	52.9	51.4
TOTAL	100.0	100.0	100.0	100.0

Source: Appendix B.

alternative sources of calories little or no substitution has occurred. The slight replacement of carbohydrates by fats is unimportant in terms of energy; but, as we shall see below, the changes that have caused this shift are closely connected with the availability of vitamins. They have some bearing also upon the balance of animal and plant proteins in our diet, insofar as the substitution of fat for carbohydrates reflects the replacement of cereals and sugar by milk, meat, and poultry.[26] That such a substitution has occurred, at least to some extent, is evident from a breakdown of total protein consumption, by groups. Here we see that a rising proportion

[26] Substitution of edible oils for cereals and sugar leaves the protein balance unaltered.

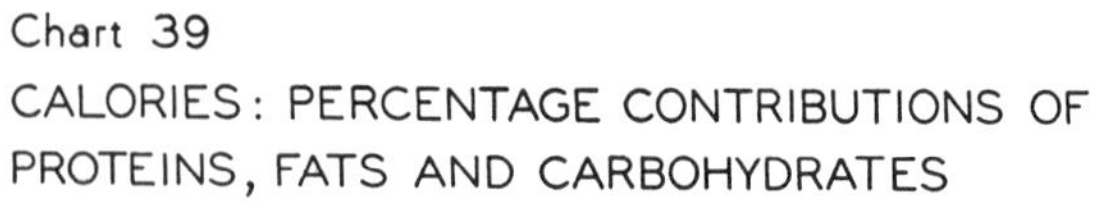

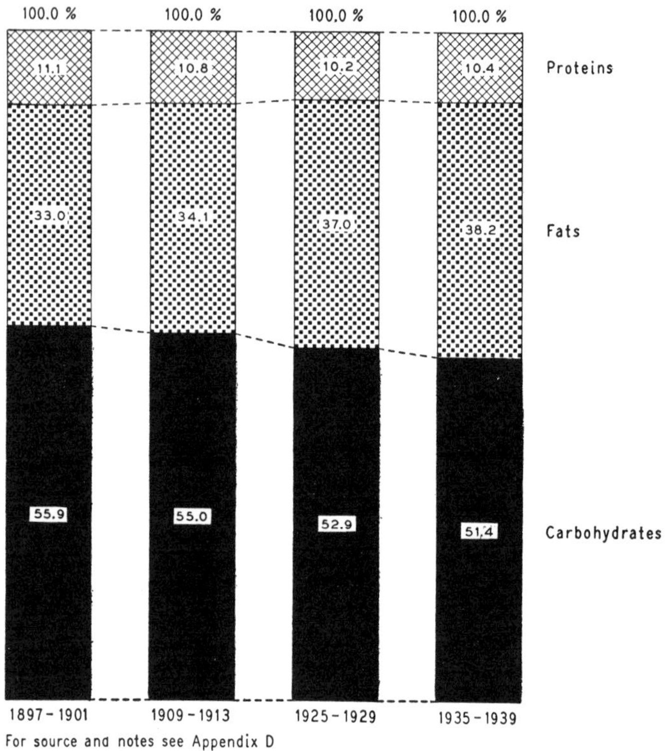

For source and notes see Appendix D

of protein has been accounted for by milk and poultry products, though the share of meat has remained fairly stable (Table 24).[27]

[27] As will be remembered, we have used a constant conversion factor for each meat animal. If the tendency toward leaner meats could be expressed in changing factors, it is likely that the protein derived from meats would also show an increase over the period under observation. As to the contribution of protein to total calories, between 10 and 11 percent, it should be remembered that we have omitted fish, a high-protein food. Its inclusion would probably raise total protein consumption some 3 or 4 percent, or the protein contribution .3 to .4 percentage points.

Chart 40
CALORIES: PERCENTAGE CONTRIBUTIONS OF DIFFERENT FOODS

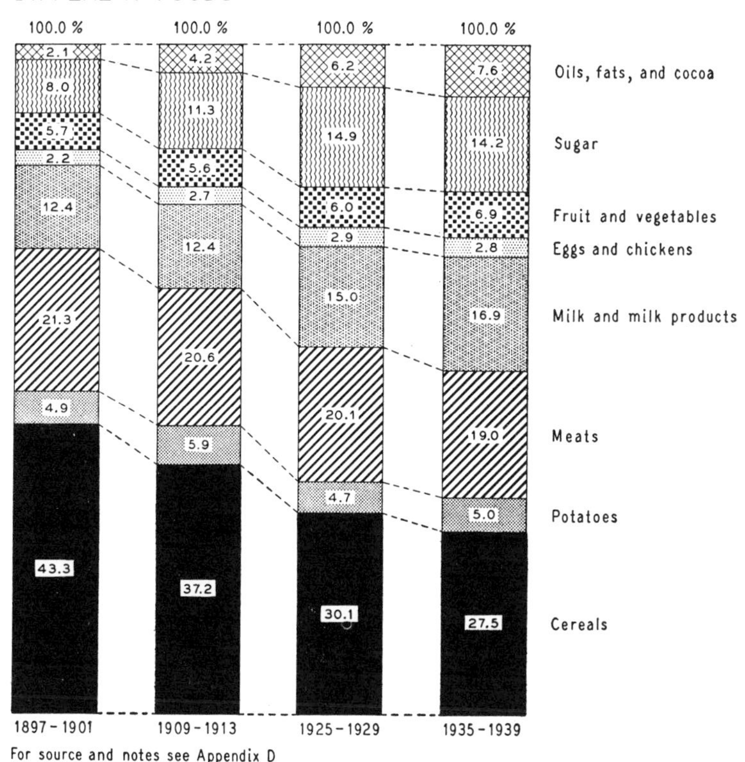

For source and notes see Appendix D

At the turn of the century, animal-derived proteins contributed 44.3 percent to aggregate protein consumption. By 1909–13 the share had risen to 48.3, by 1925–29 to 54.6, and by 1935–39 to 56.8 percent.[28] We can think of no bias in our data so consistent that it would continue year by year to raise those particular items at the expense of the others. It may

[28] The League of Nations' Nutrition Committee of 1937 suggested that 50 percent of protein consumption be of animal origin. See *Final Report of the Mixed Committee of the League of Nations on the Relation of Nutrition to Health, Agriculture and Economic Policy* (Geneva, 1937), p. 60.

TABLE 24

PERCENTAGE CONTRIBUTIONS OF DIFFERENT FOODS TO CONSUMPTION OF CALORIES, PROTEINS, FATS AND CARBOHYDRATES

Period	*Cereals*	*Potatoes and Related Crops*	*Meats*	*Eggs and Poultry*	*Milk and Milk Products*	*Fruit and Vegetables*	*Sugar*	*Oils and Fats*	*Cocoa*
				CALORIES					
1897–1901	43.3	4.9	21.3	2.2	12.4	5.7	8.0	2.0	0.1
1909–13	37.2	5.9	20.6	2.7	12.4	5.6	11.3	4.0	0.2
1925–29	30.1	4.7	20.1	2.9	15.0	6.0	14.9	5.6	0.6
1935–39	27.5	5.0	19.0	2.8	16.9	6.9	14.2	6.8	0.8
				PROTEINS					
1897–1901	46.4	4.0	23.9	7.8	12.6	5.1	..	..	0.1
1909–13	41.2	5.1	24.8	9.6	13.9	5.0	..	..	0.4
1925–29	34.0	4.4	23.7	10.9	20.0	5.8	..	..	1.0
1935–39	30.7	4.6	23.7	10.3	22.8	6.5	..	..	1.4
				FATS					
1897–1901	4.5	0.3	56.2	4.2	27.5	1.2	..	5.9	0.2
1909–13	3.5	0.4	52.2	4.8	25.9	1.1	..	11.7	0.4
1925–29	2.4	0.3	47.7	4.8	27.7	1.1	..	15.2	0.9
1935–39	2.0	0.3	43.3	4.5	29.8	1.2	..	17.7	1.2
				CARBOHYDRATES					
1897–1901	65.7	8.0	..	..	3.3	8.6	14.4	..	0.1
1909–13	57.5	9.8	..	..	3.5	8.4	20.6	..	0.1
1925–29	48.9	8.2	..	..	5.1	9.1	28.3	..	0.3
1935–39	46.2	9.0	..	..	6.0	10.4	27.9	..	0.5

Source: Appendix B.

thus be concluded with some confidence that proteins of animal origin, which have been said to be of higher nutritive value,[29] have grown in importance throughout the four decades.[30]

As has been mentioned, the substitution of fat for carbohydrate has also been traceable, though to a much smaller extent, to the expansion of the use of edible oils and fats. Contributing less than 2 percent of all calories consumed in 1899, their share has risen to between 6 and 7 percent in recent years. In the fat balance sheet they have grown from 5.9 percent in 1899 to about three times that amount, matching almost exactly the reduction in the contribution of meats. If we could conclude that consumption has shifted from lard to vegetable oils, the significance of the change would be slight. If, however, the growth of oils has occurred partly at the expense of butter, the substitution has meant a deterioration of diet, since the vegetable oils—and they constitute the bulk of the group—contain no other nutritive elements.[31]

An interesting shift, best discernible in the composition of the carbohydrate supply, has been the substitution of sugar for cereals. From as much as 66 percent in 1897–1901, cereals have dropped to 46 percent of all carbohydrates in recent

[29] McCollum, Orent-Keiles and Day, *The Newer Knowledge of Nutrition*, p. 564.

[30] This result is consistent with the increased share of total farm output for which edible livestock products were responsible in 1935–39 as against 1897–1901, a share which had risen from 57.6 percent to 61.8 percent (see Table 2). Similar evidence is found in a comparison of the movement of the livestock index with that of crops (Table 3). The livestock index increased 56 percent from 1897–1901 to 1935–39 while the crop index rose only 39 percent over the same period.

[31] The movements of our oil crop index—as we have shown in Chapter 3—are dominated by the production of cottonseed oil. The bulk of cottonseed oil in turn is consumed in edible products, and furthermore the bulk of the oils and fats used in foods consists of cottonseed oil. It is therefore interesting to compare the expansion in oil consumption with our output index. The latter increased not quite two and a quarter times from 1897–1901 to 1935–39 while the share of oils and fats in total fat consumption over the same period has risen threefold.

Chart 41
PROTEINS: PERCENTAGE CONTRIBUTIONS OF DIFFERENT FOODS

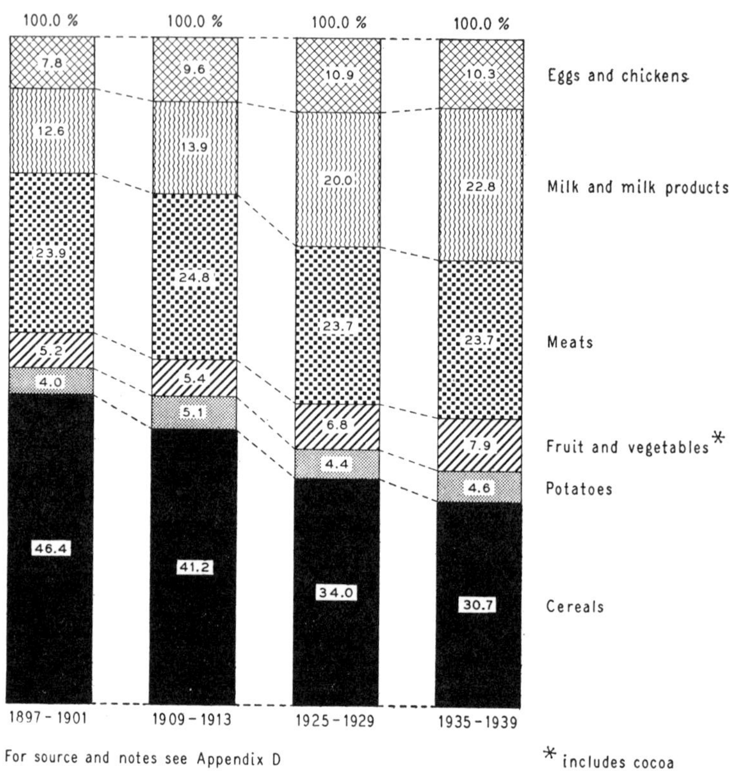

For source and notes see Appendix D

* includes cocoa

years.[32] Over the same period sugar has accounted for a growing share of aggregate carbohydrate consumption, a share that reached its maximum in the middle 1920's, when it amounted to over 28 percent, twice the proportion it had contributed at the turn of the century. For the past 15 years sugar has increased no further, and since 1935 has even shown a declining tendency whose significance cannot yet be assessed.

[32] Rates of change in net output of grains, by kinds, are shown in Table 8 above.

Chart 42
FATS: PERCENTAGE CONTRIBUTIONS OF DIFFERENT FOODS

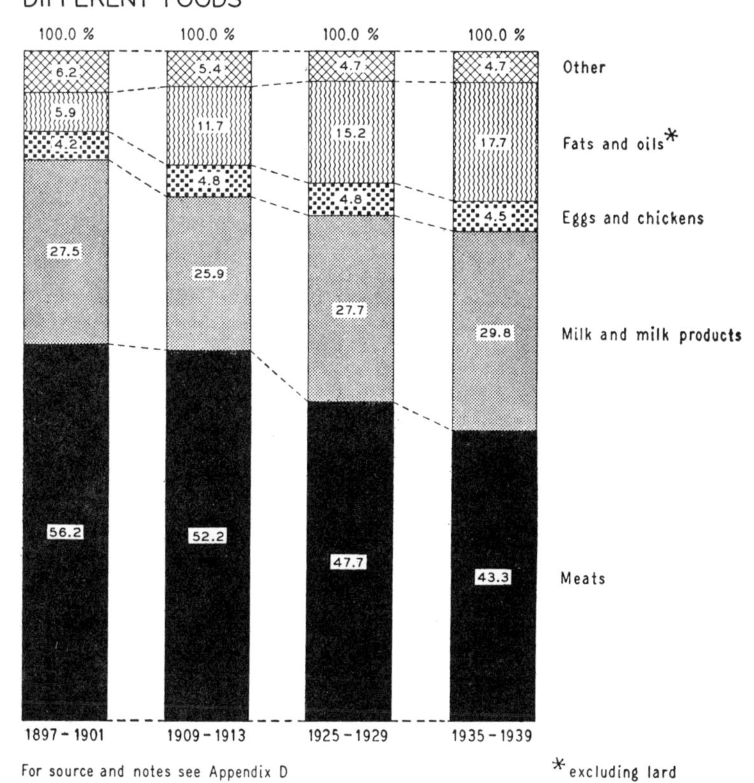

For source and notes see Appendix D

*excluding lard

Since 1900 cereals have declined more rapidly than sugar has risen, so that their joint contribution to the carbohydrate supply has decreased somewhat, from over 80 percent around 1899 to 75 percent in recent years. While the substitution of sugar for cereals must be considered detrimental to the nation's diet—since sugar lacks the protein and the small amounts of vitamins and minerals contained even in highly refined cereal derivatives—the falling share of the two items and their replacement by milk and milk products, and very

Chart 43
CARBOHYDRATES: PERCENTAGE CONTRIBUTIONS OF DIFFERENT FOODS

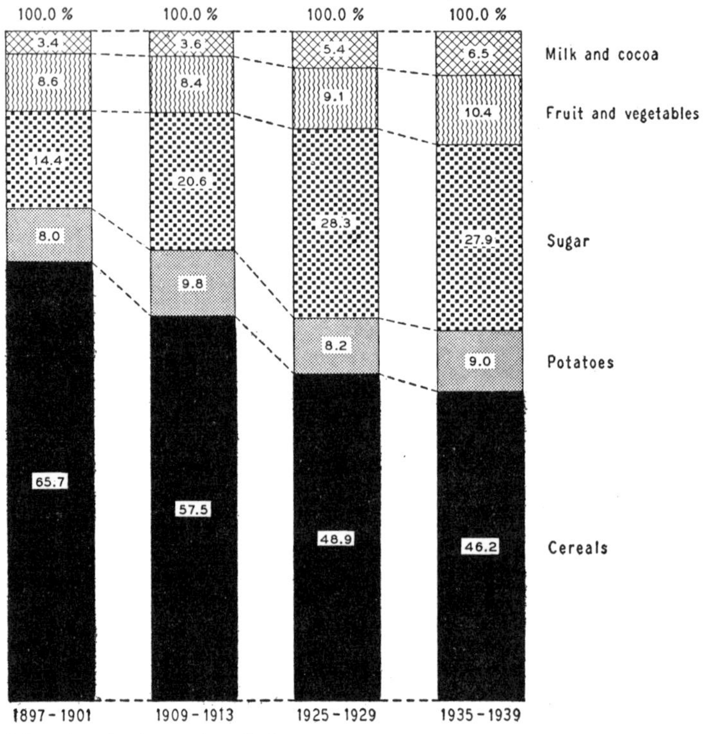

For source and notes see Appendix D

recently by fruit and vegetables, has been a salutary development. The increased representation of fruit and vegetables in the carbohydrate balance—from 8.7 percent in 1933 to 10.8 percent in 1939—must be appraised in the light of the very small carbohydrate content per weight-unit of product. By weight the increase in per capita fruit and vegetable consumption per annum was over 100 pounds between 1933 and 1939,[33] yet the resulting change in the percentage contribu-

[33] "Consumption of Agricultural Products," pp. 11-13.

tion of this group to carbohydrate consumption was very small. However, the nutritional importance of fruit and vegetables derives rather from their vitamins and minerals than from their calorie content.

It is evident that the decline in per capita intake of calories has been accompanied by an increased consumption of dairy products, fruit and vegetables, a development which nutritional experts agree represents a real improvement in diet. The explanation of this trend is more difficult than its recognition, and any attempt to find causes must take account of several diverse factors.

(1) A rising real income has created a demand for greater variety in diet. From many surveys we have learned that at any given time larger income is associated with diversification of food consumption, in which the so-called "protective" foods tend to replace the "heavy," or high-calorie, foods. There can be little doubt that these findings possess historical significance as well. It is noteworthy in this connection that increased vegetable consumption was advocated during the early years of this century because it offered variety of diet.[34] An interesting indication that a higher standard of living (plus ready availability of more expensive foods) will lead to diversified consumption—in the absence of nutritional guidance and even in the face of the consumer's own reasoning against what appear to be "luxuries"—is to be found in the testimony of a housewife as long ago as 1910:

> We are all grown luxurious; little by little it has come about, and we are almost unconscious that a change has been made. When I first began to keep house, ten years ago, we ate cereal, eggs and coffee for breakfast, with fruit occasionally instead of cereal; but now we must have grapefruit every morning, eggs

[34] C. F. Langworthy, "Green Vegetables and Their Uses in the Diet," *Yearbook of the Department of Agriculture, 1911,* pp. 439-52.

> and bacon and hot muffins. We are no better off as far as being nourished goes (sic), but we just somehow want it, and two grapefruit cost as much as did the whole breakfast ten years ago. Then, when I go to market and see fresh beans, cucumbers and spinach, I buy them without really stopping to think; so easily tempted are we.[35]

(2) Improvements in the distribution of perishable products, including transportation, storage, and handling, have made a larger variety of foods available to more people during a greater part of the year, and at lower prices. Yet ability to pay and availability of the newer foods are not of themselves conducive to adequate diet. The palate is not an infallible guide, as we learn from a mass of evidence collected during the past thirty years, obtained from comparative and historical studies of human populations and from experiments upon animals as well.[36] The impossibility of recognizing deficiencies of diet by common sense or intuition has been established only in recent years, and is perhaps not yet popularly admitted. Furthermore, deficiency diseases nowadays rarely advance beyond the subclinical stage, so that the majority escape diagnosis by the medical profession. Unless malnutrition is severe the symptoms are for the most part nonspecific and are apt to be diagnosed as chronic nervous exhaustion, constitutional inferiority and other such vague conditions.

It must be recognized also that in some ways industrial progress has led to a deterioration of our diet. Greater refining and bleaching of flour and the increased availability of sugar have tended directly or indirectly to make our diet

[35] Massachusetts, *Report of the Commission on the Cost of Living* (Boston, 1910), p. 255.

[36] For a summary of this evidence, see McCollum, Orent-Keiles and Day, *The Newer Knowledge of Nutrition*, Ch. XV; also Borsook, *Vitamins*, Ch. II.

less rich in certain minerals and vitamins.[37] This effect has been further enhanced by the increasing commercialization of agriculture. Foods formerly grown and consumed on the farm—cornmeal, molasses, etc.—have been sold for cash, and their place has been taken by commercially refined and nutritionally inferior products like white flour and sugar.[38]

(3) The effect upon popular dietary standards of progress in the science of nutrition is by no means clearly discernible. The state of popular education regarding food values has undoubtedly undergone some change within very recent years, but organized nutritional propaganda can hardly be said to antedate the later 1920's. Indeed, the "newer knowledge of nutrition" itself, though its isolated antecedents can be found before then, emerged as a body only in the third decade of this century. The modern science of nutrition is to be credited with providing us with suitable tools for the analysis of contemporary food consumption, but can hardly be said to have had much influence, at least until very recently, on the diet of the population at large. There is little doubt, however, that in the years to come our newly gained knowledge will be a major factor in determining our diet. Once again, war is acting as a ferment in speeding up and translating into reality a development whose existence had been largely confined to the textbook and the laboratory.

VITAMINS IN THE FOOD SUPPLY

So far as the authors are aware, no estimates of per capita vitamin consumption in the United States, based upon the dis-

[37] "One of the most important factors in lowering the quality of the diet of many millions of Western peoples is the excessive use of refined flour and other cereals, and sugar. There is no valid objection to the use of these foods in certain quantities, provided they are supplemented with sufficient amounts of protective foods, namely milk, eggs, leafy vegetables, and meats. The trouble is that this is not done." McCollum, Orent-Keiles and Day, *op. cit.*, p. 598. On the aspects of "enriched" flour, see A. E. Taylor, "Why Enrichment of Flour?" *Wheat Studies*, Vol. XVIII (Nov. 1941), pp. 77-108; and p. 187 below.

[38] Hazel Kyrk, "Home Economics," *Encyclopaedia of the Social Sciences*, Vol. IV (Macmillan, 1932).

appearance of food materials, have been published.[39] Nor is this omission in any way accidental. The field of vitamin research is newly opened, and the sum of the accurately established results at the disposal of the inquiring statistician is still small. The peculiar difficulty of constructing reliable estimates in this field is caused partly by the fact that the biochemist and the student of nutrition have not yet furnished the economist with all the data he would like to possess, and partly by two characteristics of vitamins themselves. For one thing, vitamins are present in most foodstuffs only in minute quantities, whereas in determinations of the calorific value of nutrients, substantially the whole of the material is accounted for. Proteins, carbohydrates and fats together constitute a large fraction of the total weight of the substance; the remainder consists chiefly of water and mineral elements. The possibility of errors in a food's reported content of these nutrients, or in its calorific value, is somewhat limited by this fact. The protein content of a pound of potatoes cannot of course be ascertained with mathematical exactitude, and there will always be some variation between one sample of potatoes and another. But the true value of the protein content of potatoes in general cannot possibly be as much as twice, or as little as half, its reported value; for to assume

[39] However, Stiebeling and Phipard (*Diets of Families of Employed Wage Earners and Clerical Workers in Cities*) offer estimates based upon family records of food expenditure. This treatment has the advantage that the point of measurement is as close to final ingestion as it can well be outside the laboratory; no account need be taken of losses in processing or distribution, and the task of evaluation in terms of vitamins is simplified. The disadvantage is the difficulty of judging the representativeness of the sample of family budgets. Unfortunately in the study quoted the authors do not give the conversion factors they used; this is all the more regrettable since the results are presented as single values rather than as ranges.

There is also a study of per capita vitamin (A and C) and mineral consumption in the United Kingdom. Though the emphasis of the study is on differences in diets by income levels, yet national food disappearance data were used to correct consumption estimates derived from budget studies. As in the case of the Stiebeling-Phipard study no details of estimation are supplied. J. B. Orr, *Food, Health and Income* (Macmillan, London, 1936).

errors of this magnitude would imply that the various investigators had been so careless as to neglect to weigh their samples of potatoes before they began their analyses. With vitamins, unfortunately, the situation is quite different, for they account usually for only a minute fraction of a percent of the total weight of the food material. It is entirely possible for one sample of a food to have several times the vitamin content of another sample of the same food. Further, small errors in the absolute amounts of vitamin reported in a biological or chemical assay may represent large errors in the percentage vitamin content attributed to the food sample.

The second difficulty in the estimation of vitamin consumption stems from the uneven distribution of vitamins among food materials. There are some foods, for example, whose individual consumption does not have to be worked out with any great accuracy in the computation of the total supply of, say, protein; but it may happen that their share of the total supply of one or another of the vitamins is so great that errors which are unimportant in other connections assume considerable significance. The consumption of liver and kidneys and of fish oils does not have to be estimated accurately when we are computing calories, yet each also contributes a substantial fraction of the total supply of the fat-soluble vitamins A and D. Again, individual fruits and vegetables vary markedly in the amount of vitamins they afford; here too consumption data that are accurate enough for many purposes are scarcely able to support attempts to estimate the vitamin supply. Vitamin content sometimes differs substantially, moreover, as between young and mature crops, or between different varieties of the same vegetable or fruit. These difficulties seriously reduce the precision of any estimates of vitamin consumption, and have in fact prevented us from offering any estimates at all in the case of vitamins C and D. Further, the absence of detailed data on fruit and vegetable consumption for years prior to 1919 precludes the construction of satisfactory estimates of the availability of vitamins during the early part of our period. We have therefore confined the estimates to very recent years.

There can be no doubt that the rather wide ranges reported for the vitamin content of the same foodstuff are to be charged partly to experimental error and partly to the necessity of comparing the results accruing from widely differing types of assay. But there is clearly also rather wide dispersion in the actual contents of samples of a single food, perhaps similar in other respects. Then, too, different portions of the sample specimen will contain varying quantities of vitamins; there is much more vitamin A, for example, in the greener parts of a head of lettuce than in the heart. Differences of this sort would matter less if the ranges in question could be interpreted, even in a very general way, as indicating fiducial limits for averages derived from them. But the number of determinations is too small, and the relative worth of different methods and different investigators too uncertain, to permit such a treatment even by workers much better acquainted with the laboratory aspects of the subject than the present authors. When methods of measurement have become more standardized and the number of determinations in the case of each foodstuff has been substantially increased, the interpretation of the range of the reported estimates as a significant indication of their dispersion would appear to be a more promising line of advance than it is at present.

Something must be said, too, about the question of losses. The estimates for proteins, carbohydrates and fats in the preceding sections almost certainly overstate actual intake by the body because we have not made adequate deductions for waste of the actual foodstuff in processing and distribution, in the kitchen and on the table. With the vitamins, however, and most notably in the case of vitamin C, losses may and do occur even though none of the foodstuff in question is wasted, through chemical disintegration in processing, storage or cooking. To give but one example, fresh snap beans have been observed to lose 42 to 65 percent of their content of vitamin C on storage for six days at a temperature of 1°-3° C., and as much as 58 to 81 percent at 21°-23° C.[40] Processing likewise affects vitamin content, particularly in the case of vitamin C which is easily oxidized when heated in contact with the air. Vitamins of the B group appear to be somewhat more stable,[41] and vitamin A is even less easily destroyed. We have not attempted to make any consumption estimates for vitamin C principally because of the large and uncertain losses of this kind.

Estimates for per capita consumption of vitamins A, B_1 (thiamin) and B_2 (riboflavin) are given in the upper half of Table 25. We compiled the data in the first line of the table under "original range" by taking first the minimum, and second the maximum, published estimate for vitamin value in the case of each food. While the range in the case of any given foodstuff cannot be interpreted as a measure of standard deviation, it is very improbable that the best value should lie at the same end of this range in the case of all foodstuffs, unless indeed the assay methods employed lead to a rather uniform bias. It seemed legitimate therefore to suggest a rather smaller range for our totals than that which results from the procedure just indicated. Accordingly, in the second line of Table 25, under "original range adjusted," are shown the same results, the range being arbitrarily halved, in order to allow for the effects of summation in reducing errors.

With some necessary reservations the estimates of per capita consumption for vitamins A, B_1 and B_2 may be compared with the available data on human requirements. These reservations are of two kinds. In the first place our consump-

[40] Sherman, *Chemistry of Food and Nutrition*, p. 339.

[41] The amounts of B vitamins remaining in cereals after milling may be further reduced in baking; nor have the effects of pasteurization in the case of milk been fully determined as yet. See Taylor, "Why Enrichment of Flour?"

TABLE 25

VITAMINS

Estimated Daily per Capita Consumption and Requirements, 1935–39

	A	*B*$_1$ (*thiamin*)	*B*$_2$ (*riboflavin*)
Consumption	(international units)	(international units[a])	(milligrams)
Original range	3,400 – 11,600	190 – 640[h]	1.64 – 2.20
Original range, adjusted[b]	5,500 – 9,500	300 – 530[h]	1.78 – 2.06
Requirements			
National Research Council, Committee on Food and Nutrition[c]	4,500[i]	480	2.1[i]
Stiebeling and Phipard[d]	5,700[i]	450[i]	1.7[i]
Mayo Clinic[e]		550	
Rose[f]		400 – 500	
Hogan[g]			2 – 3
Sebrell[g]			3

[a] For thiamin, 1,000 international units = 3 milligrams.

[b] The adjustment consists in halving the range reported in the preceding line. See discussion in text.

[c] U. S. Bureau of Home Economics, *Planning Diets by the New Yardstick of Good Nutrition* (Washington, 1941), Table 1.

[d] H. K. Stiebeling and E. F. Phipard, *Diets of Families of Employed Wage Earners and Clerical Workers in Cities*, Circular No. 507 (U. S. Department of Agriculture, 1939), pp. 58-66.

[e] R. D. Williams, H. L. Mason, B. F. Smith and R. M. Wilder, "Induced Thiamine (Vitamin B_1) Deficiency and the Thiamine Requirement of Man," *Archives of Internal Medicine*, Vol. 69 (May 1942), pp. 721-38. These authors report a thiamin requirement of 0.5 mg. per 1,000 calories, which at 3,200 calories equals 550 international units.

[f] Quoted by E. V. McCollum, Elsa Orent-Keiles and H. G. Day, *The Newer Knowledge of Nutrition* (5th ed; Macmillan, 1939), p. 470.

[g] Quoted by H. C. Sherman, *Chemistry of Food and Nutrition* (6th ed; Macmillan, 1941), pp. 381-82.

[h] In reviewing the manuscript of this book, Dr. Russell M. Wilder of the Mayo Clinic reminded the authors that, next to vitamin C, thiamin is subject to greater losses in processing and cooking than are any of the other known vitamins, and suggested that our consumption estimates of this vitamin should be written down by at least a third on this account. Losses of thiamin in the milling of cereals have been allowed for in the calculations, but no account has been taken of losses in other forms of processing or of the destruction of thiamin in cooking. It may well be that our consumption data for thiamin are too high, and that some downward revision, as suggested by Dr. Wilder, would be in order.

[i] Data have been adjusted to the 1930 age and sex distribution of the population.

TABLE 26

VITAMINS

Percentage Contributions of Different Foods to Total Supply, 1935–39[a]

Food	*A*	B_1 (*thiamin*)	B_2 (*riboflavin*)
Milk and dairy products	29.5	20.4	56.4
Eggs	15.0	4.2	7.4
Lean meat, including chickens	.3	22.4	10.1
Meat organs	2.6	1.0	3.8
Cereals	0	14.2	5.3
Fruit	8.0	9.7	3.4
Vegetables	44.5	28.0	13.5
TOTAL	100.0	100.0	100.0

[a] The percentages in this table have been computed on the assumption that the contribution of each food was measured by the midpoint of the range of the vitamin content in each case.

tion figures must be regarded as maximum estimates. They represent measures of the potential supply of vitamins, and take no account of losses of foodstuffs in processing and distribution, or in the home, except that inedible portions of eggs, fruits, and vegetables have been excluded (see Appendix Table B-4). Moreover, losses less serious than in the case of vitamin C may occur through chemical disintegration of vitamins B_1 and B_2, and to a lesser extent of vitamin A, before the food is assimilated. Finally, since the consumption estimates are per capita averages for the entire United States, they take no account of the maldistribution of the vitamin supply which no doubt exists, as between regions, income groups, or other divisions of the population.

The comparison also involves reservations on the side of human requirements. The problem here is primarily a physiological one, and is made no easier by the rather indeterminate character of the information available. Different authorities have focused attention on diverse concepts, such as minimum, normal, standard and optimum requirements.

Sometimes the same, or apparently the same, concept has elicited different estimates. Furthermore, the case of vitamins differs from that of energy-supplying nutrients. For the latter an upper limit exists beyond which the individual may be said to be overeating. In the case of most of the vitamins, however, there appear to be no upper limits beyond which intake becomes definitely harmful.[42] Thus, extensive research, so far restricted to animals, suggests strongly that consumption of various vitamins in quantities two to four times as great as have been generally considered adequate will confer increasing (though not proportionately increasing) benefits on human beings. These benefits appear to be connected with greater resistance to disease, lower death rates throughout the life cycle, and a lengthening of the period generally called "prime of life." [43] For this reason it is premature to assume upper limits to such quantitative intake of vitamins as may be deemed optimal, and our consumption estimates must be appraised in the light not only of minimum requirements but also of ranges many times the minimum. Indeed, vitamin requirements are usually set somewhat above the minimum level that will secure apparent health; for the danger that we may consume too little seems greater than the risk that we may consume too much.

> . . . *optimal diet,* or even optimal intake of an individual factor, is in most cases an *ideal* or an *ultimate* goal which we cannot yet define in precise quantitative terms. . . . It may frequently be desirable to second McCollum's teaching that in nutrition there is or may be an important difference between the merely adequate and the optimal; but it is never desirable to call a diet optimal merely because it is better than barely adequate. . . .[44]

[42] The intake of vitamin D does appear to have such an upper limit, however. See McCollum, Orent-Keiles and Day, *The Newer Knowledge of Nutrition,* pp. 386-87.

[43] Sherman, *Chemistry of Food and Nutrition,* Ch. XXX, *passim.*

[44] *Ibid.,* p. 253n. Italics in original.

The tentative figures we have been able to collect for the daily requirements of each vitamin are shown in the lower half of Table 25. At first sight consumption does not seem to be noticeably below the level of the figures quoted for requirements, at least in respect of the three vitamins shown here. But this conclusion must be qualified by the two important reservations suggested above. As already explained, the consumption estimates relate to the potential supply available in our food rather than to actual intake, and make no allowance for losses in distributive channels or in the home. It is equally obvious that data for per capita consumption must conceal a significant dispersion among individuals.[45] No doubt some dispersion exists in the vitamin requirements of different persons, in addition to that conditioned by age and sex differences. On the other hand we have no reason to expect that the two variables—consumption and requirements—are closely correlated among individuals. In fact variations in consumption are likely to be found mainly on a regional basis, to correspond with the distribution of income, and perhaps to be influenced by a wide range of sociological characteristics which cannot accurately be specified. In the light of these reflections the situation revealed by Table 25 is less satisfactory. Any excess of requirements over per capita consumption as indicated in that table may easily be wiped out by losses in processing. And, finally, an equivalence between per capita consumption and physiological requirements could be considered satisfactory only if the vitamin supply were much more evenly distributed than we have any reason to suppose is the case. We must conclude in fact that our data

[45] In this connection it is interesting to note the results reached in a study of nutrition in Britain. In this study average consumption was estimated for each income group. We combined the results into a per capita average for the entire country by using as weights the estimated population in each income group. In this way it was found that, although average vitamin A consumption was only 6 percent below the assumed requirement, yet one half of the population consumed diets which were deficient in vitamin A (Orr, *Food, Health and Income,* Table VII).

do nothing to disprove the suggestion that a sizable sector of the population subsists on diets which possess no satisfactory margin of safety, and that a fraction, perhaps even larger, fails to obtain adequate amounts of vitamins even to insure a minimum standard of "good" nutrition.[46] Secretary Wickard's recent assertion that "at least three-fourths of us do not have really satisfactory diets" [47] does not appear entirely unreasonable. A more specific evaluation has recently become available in a survey undertaken by the Food and Nutrition Board of the National Research Council:

> Malnutrition is accompanied by manifold signs and symptoms, diverse in nature, and to the casual observer their origin and significance are not always apparent. Some types of malnutrition are strikingly obvious to every one, some are apparent only to the physician who looks for them and some are vague and elusive even to the careful observer using the most accurate specialized techniques. If the first group alone is counted the prevalence of malnutrition will be recorded as low, almost negligible. If the second group is counted it will be recorded as high. If the third group is included then the rate will be sufficiently high to occasion genuine concern.
>
> The evidence at our disposal warrants the conclusion that dietary inadequacies and malnutrition of varying degrees are of frequent occurrence in the United States and that the nutritional status of an appreciable part of the population can be distinctly improved. If optimal nutrition is sought, not mere adequacy, then widespread improvement is possible.[48]

Let us assume, in order to allow for losses and for the dispersion of individual intakes, that an adequate dietary situation, if reflected in levels of apparent per capita consump-

[46] Stiebeling and Phipard, *Diets of Families, passim.*

[47] C. R. Wickard, "Agricultural Policy and National Nutrition," address at the National Nutrition Conference for Defense, Washington, May 27, 1941.

[48] Jolliffe, McLester and Sherman, "The Prevalence of Malnutrition," p. 950.

tion of the kind we have computed, would run somewhat in excess of figures quoted for requirements. In that case the consumption of vitamin A appears to be least inadequate, particularly since losses to be allowed for are probably not serious.[49] For both thiamin and riboflavin the picture is less satisfactory. Some years ago the thiamin consumption reported in Table 25 might have been considered adequate, but recent determinations have suggested a higher requirement level than used to be reported for this vitamin. If, as appears likely, the daily requirement is as high as, or higher than, 500 international units, thiamin consumption is clearly inadequate. This conclusion is strengthened by the fact that thiamin is very susceptible to losses in cooking for which no allowance has been made in the consumption figures.[50] The situation in regard to riboflavin appears even more unfavorable. Recent investigations suggest that a daily intake of between two and three milligrams is necessary, although 1.7 milligrams is accepted as a minimum requirement by Stiebeling and Phipard.[51] Our own consumption estimate is around 2 milligrams, without any allowance for losses prior to ingestion. It seems probable, therefore, that the average American diet fails by a substantial margin to supply riboflavin in adequate amounts. Stiebeling and Phipard concluded, in part at least because of the low requirement with which they reckoned, that "riboflavin appears to be fairly well supplied in average

[49] Our estimates omit fish and nuts as well as some vegetables particularly rich in vitamin A. These omissions, due to the absence of satisfactory data, are revealed, by a rough check, to lead to only a negligible underestimate, since the items involved are consumed in proportions exceedingly small compared to other foodstuffs. On the basis of a trial estimate we feel confident that for none of the vitamins do these omissions lead to a downward bias in our figures of more than 5 percent, if that much. An item like peanut butter, for example, outstandingly rich in both B_1 and B_2, probably contributes no more than three international units of B_1, per day, compared to the total consumption range of 190-640 units per day. The omission of fish affects mainly vitamin A, the intake of which seems least deficient regardless of this omission. See Appendix Table B-3, notes.

[50] See note h to Table 25.

[51] See also Sherman, *Chemistry of Food and Nutrition*, p. 382.

diets." [52] With this exception our results are compatible with the conclusions reached by these authors. The study in question revealed that among white families arrayed according to the vitamin A content of their diet the lowest quarter consumed 2,000 international units or less. For vitamin B_1 the corresponding value was 400 international units.

How may this situation be improved? Table 26 shows the large contributions of dairy products and vegetables to the current supply of all three vitamins for which we have been able to assemble data. In the case of vitamin B_1 (thiamin), meat and cereals are also important sources of supply. In fact the distributions in the table serve to underline the familiar advice that we should do well to substitute dairy products (including milk) for other sources of protein, and to eat more vegetables.[53] The availability of thiamin could be increased further by the substitution of wholewheat flour for white flour, without increasing the total intake of cereals. For example, if all wheat flour were wholewheat, daily per capita thiamin and riboflavin consumption would be raised to 520-770 units and 1.94-2.32 milligrams respectively (adjusted range: see Table 25 above). A successful attack on the problem of losses of vitamins B_1 and B_2 in milling could evidently achieve substantial results without any increase in farm output. As an alternative hypothesis, we may take the increases in consumption which the Department of Agriculture has suggested as essential if the nation as a whole is to enjoy a "good" diet (see pp. 24-25 above). If we assume that there would be no offsetting reductions in the consumption of other foods, the effect of the increases mentioned would be roughly to raise daily thiamin consumption (adjusted range) from 300-530 to 360-620 international units, and riboflavin consumption from 1.78-2.06 to 2.14-2.50 milligrams. Though this would evidently represent a substantial improvement, when checked

[52] *Diets of Families,* p. 99.

[53] Also, of course, more fruit, primarily for the sake of vitamin C.

against requirements (Table 25) even these levels leave but a narrow margin of safety. In the case of vitamin A, the most readily available sources of supply are the fish liver oils. These are not consumed in any quantity in a normal diet, and have been omitted from our estimates; they are of course easily obtainable as special preparations. The other vitamins, too, can be bought in any drug store. Yet it is doubtful whether special preparations are, even apart from questions of cost, an adequate substitute for a balanced diet, however valuable they may be in pathological cases of vitamin deficiency. This is a question to which we shall return in the final section of the chapter.

MINERAL ELEMENTS IN THE FOOD SUPPLY

The task of estimating per capita consumption of minerals is confronted by difficulties not dissimilar to those discussed in connection with the vitamin supply. Both the mineral content of individual food materials and the mineral requirements for human well-being are somewhat more clearly established than in the case of vitamins.[54] Although, as with vitamins, many individual chemical elements comprise a minute fraction of one percent of total food weight, they are much easier to assay and they are not subject to chemical disintegration through storage or cooking. On the other hand a new qualifying factor enters our estimates in the guise of "biological availability." [55] Specifically, although we can compute more confidently the daily consumption of a given mineral eaten as part of a given food, it is frequently impossible for the biologists to tell us with any assurance what fraction of the mineral intake is actually utilized by the body. This difficulty arises in part because minerals are more available in some forms than in others, and in part because some min-

[54] See, however, McCollum, Orent-Keiles and Day, *The Newer Knowledge of Nutrition*, pp. 187-88, on changing mineral content of plant food.

[55] *Ibid.*, pp. 164-68; Sherman, *Chemistry of Food and Nutrition*, pp. 272-73.

erals require the cooperation of other substances for their absorption, notably vitamin D in the case of calcium. It is impossible to take account of these qualifications here,[56] and for this reason our data no doubt offer what are in reality maximum estimates. Furthermore, an ideal treatment of the problem should relate the intake of calcium, for example, to the availability of phosphorus, vitamin D and perhaps also magnesium.[57]

TABLE 27

MINERALS

Estimated Daily per Capita Consumption and Requirements, 1935–39

	Calcium	*Phosphorus*	*Iron*
	(grams)	(grams)	(milligrams)
Consumption	.83	1.31	12.2
Requirements per person[a]	.86	1.24	13.3

[a] These requirements were computed from H. K. Stiebeling and E. F. Phipard, *Diets of Families of Employed Wage Earners and Clerical Workers in Cities,* Circular No. 507 (U. S. Department of Agriculture, 1939), Tables 30, 31 and 33, on the basis of age and sex distributions from the 1930 Census. Allowances computed in accordance with the recommendations of the National Research Council (Table 25, note c) differ slightly—calcium: .92 g., and iron: 11.7 mg. The lower iron requirement is stressed also by H. C. Sherman, *Chemistry of Food and Nutrition* (6th ed; Macmillan, 1941), p. 288, where 12 mg. is considered sufficient.

Estimates for the per capita consumption of calcium, phosphorus and iron are presented in Table 27 and compared with generally accepted requirements. With the above qualifications in mind, we must conclude that the average American diet is almost certainly deficient in all three minerals studied. For, as in the case of riboflavin, estimated average daily consumption is at best equal to the estimated daily requirement. When we allow for losses both in distribution

[56] However, we have treated the calcium content of spinach as nil for dietary purposes, in spite of the fact that it undoubtedly contains this element (see Sherman, *op. cit.*, p. 272).

[57] Sherman, *op. cit.*, Ch. XIV; McCollum, Orent-Keiles and Day, *op. cit.*, Ch. VII.

TABLE 28

MINERALS

Percentage Contributions of Different Foods to Total Supply, 1935–39[a]

Food	*Calcium*	*Phosphorus*	*Iron*
Milk and milk products	77.5	38.2	8.9
Eggs	2.9	7.0	10.3
Lean meat, including chickens and turkeys	1.6	16.7	20.4
Meat organs	[b]	0.9	2.9
Cereals	4.5	19.7	25.5
Vegetables	9.4	11.9	24.0
Fruit	3.3	2.6	6.7
Cocoa	0.7	3.0	1.2
TOTAL	100	100	100

[a] It is interesting to compare this table with a similar one, compiled for the United Kingdom by J. B. Orr, *Food, Health and Income* (Macmillan, London, 1936), Table VIII, even though not all the items are strictly comparable. The left-hand figures refer to the lowest income group, the right-hand figures to the highest income group.

	Calcium	*Phosphorus*	*Iron*
Milk and cheese	61.9–68.4	22.3–34.3	3.1– 5.2
Eggs	2.2– 2.6	2.6– 4.3	3.7– 6.4
Meat	2.1– 1.6	17.3–19.0	24.3–29.6
Fish	.. ..	2.3– 6.1	1.2– 3.2
Cereals	14.7– 5.8	30.6–16.4	30.9–18.4
Vegetables	13.9–15.6	18.5–14.6	26.1–21.7
Fruit	2.8– 3.6	2.5– 2.8	6.7–12.5

[b] Less than 0.05.

and in the home, and for the dispersion in individual consumption, it is plain that a large fraction of the population must consume less than its requirements. Again these results are in line with the conclusions of Stiebeling and Phipard, who found that half of the white families observed subsisted on diets below both the calcium and the iron allowance,[58] with a somewhat more favorable situation in regard to the

[58] If the National Research Council's iron and calcium allowances are nearer the truth (see Table 27, note a), the iron situation is not quite as unfavorable as it would otherwise seem, whereas calcium consumption presents an even less satisfactory picture.

supply of phosphorus. This latter finding is confirmed by our own data. It may be noted that phosphorus intake is apparently more than one and a half times calcium consumption, which is to be regarded as a safe ratio.[59]

Table 28 suggests that improvement of our diet in respect of calcium must depend largely upon an expansion in the production of dairy and poultry products, while for phosphorus and for iron in particular a change in the processing of wheat is needed to retain these minerals. It is worth considering that if all our flour were wholewheat, daily consumption of phosphorus would amount to about 1.93 instead of 1.39 grams, of iron to about 24.6 mg. instead of 13.7 mg.

FOOD AND AGRICULTURAL OUTPUT

It is abundantly clear from the data we have presented in preceding charts and tables that past and present shifts in our national diet have, with two exceptions, led to an improvement. The two exceptions have been the shift from cereals to sugar and from animal fats to vegetable oils. Although the shift toward sugar has come to a halt, and has been replaced by a slight contrary movement, the increasing use of vegetable oils has gathered momentum in recent years. This is an unfortunate change only so far as butter has been replaced. If, as is probable, the shift reflects primarily an increased consumption of vegetable salads, it may be viewed as a concomitant of a thoroughly desirable development.

All other shifts, such as the continuous increase in the consumption of milk, fruit and vegetables, together with the steadiness in egg and poultry consumption, have been toward foods rich in vitamins and minerals; *within* the fruit group the rise of the citrus family—already noted as outstanding in growth among our production series—at the expense of apples has effected a notable increase in our consumption of vitamin C. Similarly, the change in the utilization of milk,

[59] McCollum, Orent-Keiles and Day, *op. cit.*, pp. 172-75.

from butter to fluid milk, has been beneficial in making available vitamins of the B-complex, which are not contained in butter, as well as calcium.

On balance, our findings suggest that actual changes in diet have developed essentially along the lines recommended by the nutritionist; even though the growth in the consumption of fruit and vegetables is of recent origin, it is not too early to assume that the level reached will probably be maintained if not surpassed in the future. It may be that increased consumption in this field has been brought about in part by large-scale advertising,[60] based in its turn on scientific findings, and facilitated by a sagging price structure, owing to increased volume. For example, calculated on the basis of 1925–29:100, retail prices of fruit and vegetables by the end of 1934 were lower than those of any other food group and, with a minor interruption, continued to decline until November 1940, by which time the price index had dropped to 48. At the same time retail price indexes of other foods stood at 82 for meats and eggs, 80 for dairy products, 59 for fats and oils, 84 for cereal and bakery products, and 78 for sugar (Chart 44). Clearly, then, developments in the price pattern of agricultural products have been instrumental in calling forth the shifts in consumption that have been urged by the nutritionists.

Future improvement of the food supply does not depend upon any increase in the calorie intake, or upon greater consumption of proteins, carbohydrates or fats as such. It may be expected to come rather from a substitution of sources of carbohydrates and fats rich in vitamins and minerals for sources poor in these protective nutrients: shifts from sugar and white flour to wholewheat flour as a source of carbohydrates, and from vegetable oils to dairy products as a means of obtaining fats. Additions of fruit and leafy vegetables, low

[60] The producers of citrus fruit publicized the high vitamin content of their crop as early as 1922.

Chart 44

INDEXES OF RETAIL FOOD PRICES, 1929 - 40

(1925 - 29 : 100)

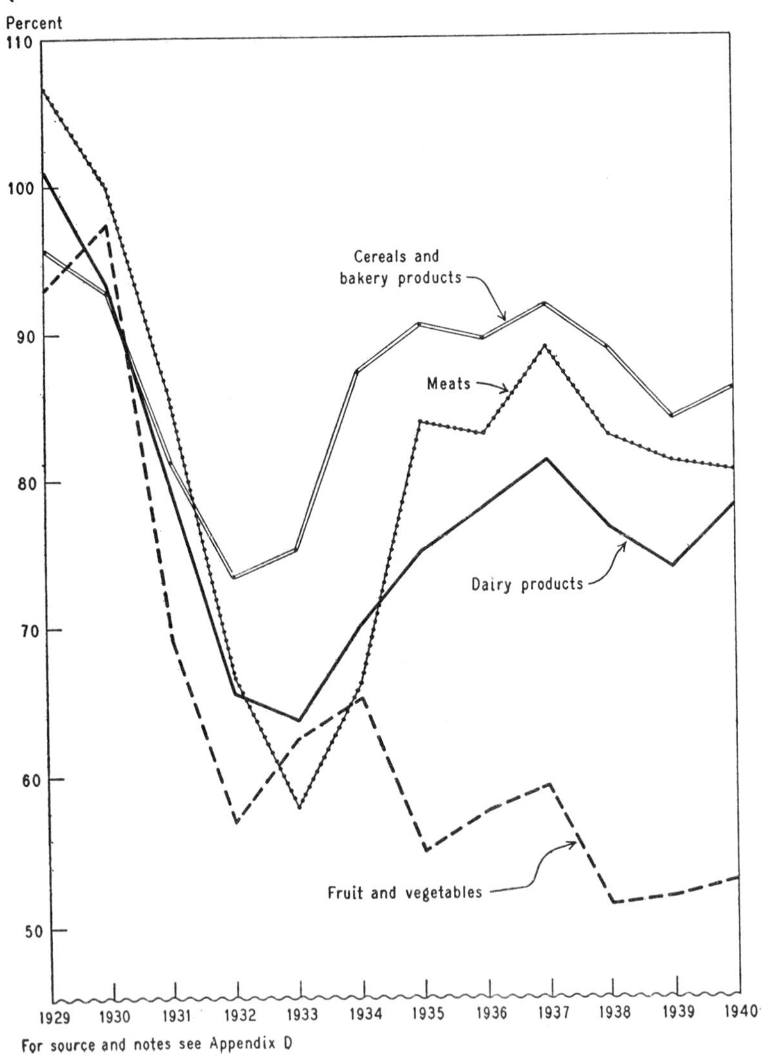

For source and notes see Appendix D

in calories but rich in vitamins and minerals, would also enhance the health-giving properties of the foods we consume. Finally the "enrichment" of existing foodstuffs, such as flour, may play a part.[61]

Our estimates of food consumption have taken no account of commercial preparations of vitamins and minerals which have come to be widely advertised by their manufacturers. The scope of this chapter has been deliberately confined to the study of foodstuffs as such, and we have given slight consideration to individual nutrients appearing under the guise of medicaments. Conceivably, the problem of nutrition might

[61] See Taylor, "Why Enrichment of Flour?" pp. 77-108; J. S. Davis, *Vitamin Enrichment and Fortification of Foods,* Contribution 110 (Food Research Institute, Stanford University, 1941), and "World Wheat Survey and Outlook, May 1942," *Wheat Studies,* Vol. XVIII, pp. 352-54. The following information is taken from the last two of these sources. On October 1, 1941, the Committee on Food and Nutrition of the National Research Council recommended "appropriate enrichment of flour and bread (and perhaps corn meal), the fortification of milk with vitamin D, the suitable addition of vitamin A to table fats and of iodine to salt for dietary use. There is no information available to the Committee at the present time which indicates that it will be desirable to recommend the addition of vitamins and minerals to foods other than those named." The Committee "opposes the addition of synthetic vitamins to carbonated beverages and confectionery." The opposition of the Committee to general and indiscriminate enrichment or fortification of foods is based upon the following grounds: (1) in many cases the necessary technical methods have not been developed; (2) fortification would often be transitory because of losses in cooking; (3) the necessary supplies of specific vitamins are needed for more urgent uses, including enrichment or fortification programs already endorsed; (4) consumers already tend to eat too much of, or to spend too much on, the products in question, to the detriment of their diets; and (5) there is a possibility of creating a vitamin or mineral imbalance (about this little is known at present). On May 27, 1941 the Food and Drug Administration proposed standards for the mandatory enrichment of flour with thiamin, riboflavin, nicotinic acid and iron; and its optional enrichment with, in addition, calcium, vitamin D and wheat germ. Except in the case of riboflavin, supplies of these nutrients have proved readily available, and the flour enrichment program is well under way: bakery sales of enriched bread rose from something like 35 percent of the total late in 1941 to over 50 percent by May 1, 1942. Continued insufficiency of supplies of riboflavin has forced postponement of the date when the Food and Drug Administration program of enrichment is to become mandatory until April 20, 1943. The Administration has also announced standards for the fortification of evaporated milk with vitamin D and of oleomargarine with vitamin A. In 1941 about half the oleomargarine sold was so fortified.

be resolved in the chemical works rather than on the farm. But the increased consumption of such commercial preparations is unlikely to settle the question of a balanced diet for the population in general for two reasons. First, the vitamins and minerals whose physiological requirements are known, and which are commercially available, are believed to represent only a few out of an unknown number of such substances. A diversified diet is likely to supply a much wider range of needed elements than can possibly be obtained at the drug store. Second, since the consumption of manufactured vitamin and mineral preparations tends to be regarded as a form of medication, it is likely, at least in the case of adults, to be sporadic at best and to be resisted by those in apparent good health.[62]

In what directions, then, is progress to be sought? We may assume that the nutritional education of the public at large, through the teaching of home economics or otherwise, will play a larger part in the future than it seems to have played in the past. But whether or not education expands in influence, rising per capita real income seems certain to push food habits somewhat further in directions very similar to those which the nutritional scientist would recommend. The consequences for agriculture would appear to be a continuation of the trend away from cereals and potatoes (and possibly even away from livestock meat products) toward dairy products and fruits and vegetables.

That large changes are still to come may be guessed from the great differences at present observable between the diets of the poor and the diets of the well-to-do. It seems certain that rising standards of living will assimilate the former to

[62] The Committee on Food and Nutrition of the National Research Council "strongly favors the policy of seeing to it that ordinary staple foods will provide a nutritionally adequate diet, reserving administration of synthetic vitamins and vitamin concentrates as such for individual cases under competent medical advice" (Davis, *Vitamin Enrichment and Fortification of Foods,* p. 3). Moreover, the Committee opposes the indiscriminate enrichment or fortification of foods with synthetic vitamins (see footnote 61).

the latter, even if no alteration occurs in the distribution of income. Moreover, the science of nutrition is still young. It may be taken as symptomatic of the continued hold that the old energy concept of nutrition has had upon us until recently that in 1926 Working was still comparing sugar and flour on the economic basis used by Atwater, i.e., cost per unit of energy. True, refined flour is anything but rich in minerals and vitamins, yet there can be little doubt that sugar is a poor substitute, whenever the merits of the two are compared without regard to the balance of other food items consumed with them. It is the energy concept, too, that has served us in the past as a gauge with which to classify foods as "cheap" and "expensive." Thus Working states, "the diversified diet is distinctly more expensive than was the staple diet it has supplanted." [63] This is no doubt sound, if we think in terms of cost per calorie. Whether it is true, too, if we think in terms of cost per unit of vitamin, or per gram of calcium or iron, is at least doubtful. However, it is safe to assume that this heritage from bygone days will stay with us as long as a sizable proportion of our population has to reckon in terms of calories first and almost exclusively—that is, as long as the need to satisfy the "hollow" hunger at the least cost leaves no room for consideration of the "hidden" hunger. In this respect there are definite limits to the effects of nutritional education.

[63] "The Decline in the Per Capita Consumption of Flour in the United States," p. 287.

Part Three

Employment and Productivity

Chapter 5

Changes in Technology

EXCEPT for Part Four, in which we summarize our findings, the remainder of this volume is devoted to a consideration of trends in agricultural productivity. In this discussion we shall be concerned primarily with the comparison of changes in output and changes in employment. But the productivity from one period to another of any industrial segment, in terms of the ratio of output to input of labor, is largely a function of the technological methods in vogue, and trends in this productivity ratio can be understood and interpreted only in the light of the technological state of the industry. In order to provide a background for later discussion, the present chapter will review the development of agricultural technology. It should be regarded, therefore, as an introduction to the statistical treatment of employment and productivity in Chapters 6 and 7.

To agricultural technique as we now know it a great variety of innovations have contributed. Some of these were developed exclusively for the farmer: for example, the combine. Others—gasoline power, for instance—were originally introduced with small thought of their agricultural applications, but were nevertheless adopted eagerly by the farmer once their usefulness in agriculture was established. The discussion of all these various innovations will be grouped under two general topics: changes in farm machinery and equipment and changes in plants and animals.

FARM MACHINERY IN 1899[1]

Much of the machinery commonly regarded as basic to the technique of modern farming had already been invented, and had received considerable development, prior to 1899. The steel plow, many different kinds of cultivating, mowing, harvesting and threshing machinery—all these had decades of experimentation behind them, and had been accepted as standard equipment in one form or another on the larger farms, particularly in the West. By the turn of the century the use of "improved machinery" was widespread; it was commonly considered indispensable to the production even of the much smaller agricultural output of those days,[2] and was looked upon as a vital factor in the development of the West.[3] By "improved machinery" the writers of forty years ago meant apparatus that had already undergone a lengthy process of adaptation since its introduction: gang plows and other four-horse machinery, for example, rather than two- or three-horse machinery;[4] the self-binder rather than the early reapers of the middle nineteenth century; the eight-foot as against the simpler four-foot-cut mowing machinery.[5]

The history of agricultural machinery, as distinguished from hand implements, goes back at least a hundred years,

[1] For an excellent illustrated historical account of agricultural implements prior to 1899, see Leo Rogin, *The Introduction of Farm Machinery in its Relation to the Productivity of Labor in the Agriculture of the United States during the Nineteenth Century* (University of California, 1931); a briefer sketch, with special reference to the harvester and to the priority of its invention, will be found in M. F. Miller, "The Evolution of Reaping Machines," *The Making of America*, ed. R. M. La Follette (Morris, Chicago, 1905), Vol. V. As an original source for the history of agricultural machinery the farmers' journals of the period are of first importance; in the rather summary treatment accorded the subject here we have drawn heavily upon the reprinted material to be found in *The Prairie Farmer*, Jan. 11, 1941.

[2] *Report of the Industrial Commission*, Vol. X (Washington, 1901), pp. 115, 135, 895.

[3] *Ibid.*, p. 96.

[4] W. M. Hays and E. C. Parker, *The Cost of Producing Farm Products*, Bulletin 97 (Minnesota Agricultural Experiment Station, 1906), p. 39.

[5] *Report of the Industrial Commission*, Vol. X, p. 267.

and most of the machines of today appeared in elementary form at a surprisingly early date. In reviewing the technological changes that have occurred during the first four decades of this century—the period selected for the present study—we shall be concerned mainly with the further development and improvement of existing basic types of equipment, and with the introduction of certain new types for special purposes. Above all we shall deal with the application to agriculture of an entirely new source of motive power whose potentialities still went unrecognized in 1899—the gasoline engine. Field implements, which we shall discuss at the outset, fall roughly into three categories according to their use: for tillage, for cultivation, for harvesting. In each category they had made striking progress in the period preceding 1899.

Plowing and Seeding Equipment

The principal instrument of tillage, at once the most ancient and the most universally used agricultural implement, is of course the plow. The typical plow in the eighteenth century was made of wood, faced more or less with metal. Besides being heavy and cumbersome, and needing constant repair, it had the great disadvantage that the shape of a successful instrument could not be freely or accurately reproduced. The standardization of the best model available at any period for any purpose was greatly facilitated by the introduction (by Jethro Wood in 1814–17) of the cast-iron plow, which was also stronger and more manageable than the wooden type. The cast-iron plow found ready acceptance in the East, but would not scour well in the heavier soils of the Mississippi Valley which were then being developed.[6] The next important step came in 1833 or shortly thereafter, when John Lane of Chicago devised the first steel plow from an old saw; he was followed closely by the more famous John Deere, who appar-

[6] Rogin, *op. cit.*, Part I.

ently used the same material.[7] Although considerable variations in shape were to be found, the new models still took the form of the traditionally pointed instrument known as the moldboard plow, which derived its name from the use of a board placed behind the share to mold the furrow. Not until the 1860's, however, was it mounted on wheels, so that the plowman might ride where the terrain was suitable.[8] Riding implements of this type were originally known as *sulky* plows; but this term is now applied to riding plows possessing only one *bottom* or share, which turn a single furrow, in contrast to *gang* plows with two or more bottoms, and which cover correspondingly increased territory.[9] Sulky plows (in this sense) still predominate on the Atlantic coast and in the cotton states; gang plows, which have become steadily more popular, were invented quite early, but made demands upon the source of draft power which could be satisfactorily met only through the development of the tractor.[10] Nevertheless, in 1909 the two-bottom moldboard plow drawn by four or more horses had become standard equipment in the grain areas of the Middle West, and must already have been fairly common in those regions in 1899. At the turn of the century, however, the modern disk plow had not yet evolved from the harrow.

For seeding, drills drawn by horses had long been in use, but the more elaborate implements which open a furrow and plant and fertilize at the same time (especially for corn) had

[7] *Ibid.* See also L. W. Ellis and E. A. Rumely, *Power and the Plow* (Doubleday, 1911), pp. 151-52; J. B. Davidson, *Agricultural Engineering* (Webb, St. Paul, 1918), p. 181. At that period saws imported from Europe provided the easiest available source of high grade steel plate. See also R. L. Ardrey, *American Agricultural Implements* (published by the author, Chicago, 1894), pp. 14-17.

[8] H. P. Smith, *Farm Machinery and Equipment* (McGraw-Hill, 1937), p. 67.

[9] Rogin, *op. cit.*, pp. 36-37.

[10] For some statistics relating to the distribution of moldboard plows by size and region at different dates since 1909, see E. G. McKibben, J. A. Hopkins and R. A. Griffin, *Field Implements* (National Research Project, Philadelphia, 1939), Table 8.

not yet been developed. During the 1850's a corn planter combining the first two of these operations was introduced; drawn by two horses, it had become common by the turn of the century.[11] The two-horse cultivator, dating from about 1861,[12] was still standard equipment in 1914, at least for cultivating corn.[13] Here again real progress had to wait upon the development of mechanical traction, and especially upon the introduction of the all-purpose gasoline tractor of the 1920's which is especially designed to avoid damage to the growing crop.

Harvesting Equipment

By far the most sensational developments of the nineteenth century were in harvesting. The efforts of the early inventors in this sphere, and especially of Hussey and McCormick, were directed toward a lightening of the burden imposed upon the labor supply through the harvesting of small grains by the methods then in vogue. Cyrus McCormick patented his reaper in 1834 [14] and brought it into commercial production during the 1840's, but in its earlier forms the machine was little more than a device for mechanical mowing: [15] the gathering of the grain had still to be performed on the ground

[11] Ardrey, *op. cit.*, pp. 30-31.

[12] Davidson, *op. cit.*, p. 181.

[13] L. K. Macy, L. E. Arnold and E. G. McKibben, *Corn* (National Research Project, Philadelphia, 1938), p. 33.

[14] There were undoubtedly reapers in existence before this date, but none appear to have been practical. The popular interest in the subject may be judged by a quotation from Ardrey (*op. cit.*, p. 42): "In 1814 a theatrical genius by the name of Dobbs invented a reaper, which he advertised by introducing it upon the stage, the latter being planted with wheat and cut by the machine during the course of a play adapted to it." This extraordinary scene apparently occurred somewhere in Britain, where most of the earliest reapers were constructed. The period of incubation of the reaper appears to have been exceptionally long, as inventions go, and in fact lasted almost half a century. The first British patent dates from 1799 and the first American from 1803; the McCormick reaper was first produced in quantity in 1846 when about a hundred were sold (*ibid.*, pp. 41-46).

[15] Rogin, *op. cit.*, pp. 73 *et seq.*

with rakes. The demand for these early machines and the invention of further labor-saving machinery received a sharp impetus from the labor shortage resulting first from the Mexican War and then from the California gold rush; the same stimulus was to operate again even more powerfully during the Civil War.[16] The first harvester, which developed from the reaper and carried men to bind the sheaves, appeared in the early 1850's; and mechanical binding, initially with wire and later with twine, was introduced during the 1870's.[17] Apparently threshing by machinery, of course with the use of animal power, was fairly common as early as the 1830's; but such threshing was carried on as a process entirely independent of harvesting until the combine (harvester-thresher) made its spectacular appearance in California about 1880.[18]

It is always easier to set a date for the invention of a given implement than to say just when its adoption became general. With the exception of the combine, whose introduction was very gradual, most of these machines appear to have made a considerable impression upon actual farming practice within a decade or so of their appearance. In particular, shortage of labor and high grain prices led to rapid mechanization during the Civil War; at its close, according to Rogin, horse-drawn machinery of one kind or another was in almost universal use for harvesting small grains.[19] On the other hand

[16] *The Prairie Farmer,* Jan. 11, 1941, pp. 40-41.

[17] Rogin, *op. cit.,* pp. 107, 110 *et seq.*

[18] *Ibid.,* p. 164; also pp. 119 *et seq.* Experiments with combines had already been made, especially in Michigan, about 1840, but these early attempts seem to have been unsuccessful; see R. B. Elwood, L. E. Arnold, D. C. Schmutz and E. G. McKibben, *Wheat and Oats* (National Research Project, Philadelphia, 1939), pp. 27-28; also *The Prairie Farmer,* Jan. 11, 1941, p. 40.

[19] *Op. cit.,* p. 91. Also, "more harvesting machines were produced in the few years of the Civil War than had been turned out during the entire period which elapsed from the time Hussey sold his first machine in 1833 to the outbreak of the struggle" (p. 93). The effect of the Civil War in furthering the introduction of the reaper seems to have been very similar to the effect of the first World War in stimulating the use of the combine.

it seems probable that public acceptance lagged somewhat as equipment became more complicated; frequently it was necessary to dispatch a mechanic with each machine in order to show the purchaser how to use it—perhaps also to make adjustments which later would become standardized at the factory.[20] This seems to have been true at least of the combine, and perhaps also of the steam tractor for plowing. It has been estimated, for example, that even as late as 1920 less than 5 percent of the nation's wheat crop was harvested by combine; [21] on the other hand we may reasonably suppose that substantially the entire crop was threshed mechanically in that year, whatever the situation may have been in this regard in 1899. It seems fair to conclude that by the turn of the century the use, if not of the combine, at least of the horse-drawn self-binder in conjunction with threshing by steam had become almost standard practice, even in the rice fields of the South where mechanization has always been notoriously slow.[22] Regional variations in practice of course existed. In the Wheat Belt a substantial acreage was probably still cut by header, a machine which clips the stalks below the heads. And it has been estimated that in California two thirds of the wheat acreage was harvested by combine in 1900, although the use of combines elsewhere cannot have been appreciable at that early date.[23] Besides those already discussed, other types of equipment common in 1899, if by no means universally adopted, were the corn harvester, the corn husker and the cotton planter.[24]

All of these machines were at first operated by animal power: for example the combine of the 1880's was commonly drawn by a team of 20 to 24 horses.[25] Such large demands for

[20] *Report of the Industrial Commission,* Vol. X, p. xii.

[21] U. S. Department of Agriculture, *Technology on the Farm* (Washington, 1940), p. 14.

[22] *Report of the Industrial Commission,* Vol. X, p. 772.

[23] Rogin, *op. cit.,* p. 124.

[24] *Report of the Industrial Commission,* Vol. X, pp. 157, 816.

[25] Rogin, *op. cit.,* p. 147.

motive power naturally led to a call upon the steam engine, which had been introduced into agriculture, primarily for threshing, shortly after the Civil War.[26] By 1899 steam was common as a source of stationary power for threshing; it was also in use, particularly in the West, for plowing as well as for the operation of the combines of that day.[27] Indeed steam power was applied to plowing experimentally in Pennsylvania as early as 1858, but the differential was not invented until about 1870, and even by 1890 steam traction (as distinct from stationary power for threshing) was used only under rather exceptional conditions.[28] By 1894, however, steam plowing, according to Ardrey, was "in general use on large farms in the west." [29] The early tractors seem to have been mechanically much less reliable than were the stationary engines of the same period.[30] Even when mechanical difficulties were overcome, however, there could be no doubt that steam engines were expensive, clumsy, and too heavy for use with draft machinery where the ground was soft or very uneven. It must have become clear that a fresh source of power was needed: yet it was not by any means obvious, at the turn of the century, that it was the new-fangled gasoline motor which would furnish this driving force. Even as late as 1901, an author wrote an eloquent description of the future of electricity as a source of power for farmers while making no mention

[26] The steam engine which Horace Greeley noticed on a farm at Watertown, N. Y., in 1850 (Ardrey, *American Agricultural Implements,* p. 114) must indeed have been a curiosity.

[27] Rogin, *op. cit.,* pp. 44, 147-53.

[28] Ellis and Rumely, *Power and the Plow,* pp. 41-43.

[29] *Op. cit.,* p. 20.

[30] *Ibid.,* p. 239. In 1860 the rather hesitant behavior of Mr. Waters' steam plow in Grundy County, Illinois, was described triumphantly as follows: "Ran for 23 minutes; stopped six minutes for wood; ran 13 minutes; stopped 8 minutes for water; ran for 1 minute. Plowed 2.63 acres in 72 minutes, using only six of a gang of 13 plows. Burned 1½ cords of wood. Was managed by a hand and team to supply fuel and water, a fireman, two men to manage the plows, and Mr. Waters." See *The Prairie Farmer,* Jan. 11, 1941, pp. 30-31.

whatever of the internal combustion engine.[31] Although electricity has been widely applied during the last forty years as a source of stationary power on farms, particularly for pumping, it remained for the gasoline tractor to revolutionize the business of hauling draft machinery for plowing, cultivating and harvesting alike.[32]

FARM MACHINERY SINCE 1899: THE TRACTOR

The introduction of the gasoline tractor is a development confined wholly to the period following 1899, and perhaps not yet entirely completed. The transition from steam to gasoline as a source of draft power, and the displacement of animal energy by the gasoline motor in regions in which steam had never been adopted, were matters of rather gradual change. Dates are not easy to establish. Certainly bigger and better self-propelled steam-powered combines were still being built in California as late as 1905.[33] It is possible that the internal combustion engine was not applied seriously to the combine until about 1910; its successful use in this connection in Argentina appears to have played a part in its introduction in this country. Beyond a doubt, however, the war of 1914–18 was the immediate occasion for the widespread adoption of the gasoline tractor for harvesting grain: for high grain prices accompanied by a shortage of labor led to extensive mechanization in the Great Plains wheat area. While this war-

[31] See E. P. Powell, "Farming in the Twentieth Century," *The Making of America,* Vol. V.

[32] Among the few who perhaps foresaw the new development was J. D. Lewis, writing in 1902: "It seems safe to predict, in view of the development of the automobile, that within the next decade this feature of modern invention will have found an additional application as a motive force in connection with agricultural implements of tillage, planting and harvesting. An automobile lawn mower is already meeting with considerable favor where the conditions warrant its use" ("Agricultural Implements," *Twelfth Census, Manufactures,* Vol. X, Part IV, p. 364). However, "automobile" may perhaps have been intended to cover other forms of traction besides the gasoline motor.

[33] Elwood, Arnold, Schmutz and McKibben, *Wheat and Oats,* pp. 28-29.

time mechanization meant the establishment of gasoline as a recognized form of draft power, displacing steam on the larger farms and gaining adoption in many places where steam traction had never been considered worth while, the older form of power continued for many years as the standard means of threshing where harvesting was performed by the binder and the combine was not in use.

So far as concerns the development of gasoline traction for the operation of draft machinery, the period since 1899 falls roughly into two parts, broken by the year 1924 which saw the introduction of the all-purpose tractor. The earlier tractors, both steam and gasoline, could be used for plowing, harvesting, and as a stationary source of power for threshing, but they could not be used for cultivating row crops. Naturally, therefore, they made most rapid progress on farms growing wheat and other small grains which do not require cultivation. Many notable inventions of an earlier period—the gang plow, the self-binder and the combine—had first made headway in the wheat-producing regions of Montana, the Dakotas, Nebraska, Kansas, and of course California, a state which was once a much more important source of wheat than it is today. It was in these states also that the gasoline tractor was first tried out on a large scale, and for very similar reasons—the presence of large areas devoted to a single crop, broken by few irregularities of terrain.

Probably the gasoline tractor appeared, and began to be substituted for steam power, before the market for the steam tractor was saturated. It is a safe assumption that the number of steam tractors in use would have continued to increase, and their sphere of usefulness have continued slowly to expand, even if the gasoline tractor had been stillborn. But the application of power, and especially of draft power, to agriculture would inevitably have been much slower in such a case. For the gasoline motor in its full development turned out to be much cheaper than the steam engine; it was less trouble to operate; and it could be applied to terrain and crops to which steam power was entirely unsuited. If the history of mechanical power in agriculture is not synonymous with the history of the gasoline engine, it has tended to become so as the years have passed.

It is recorded that efforts were made to apply the internal combustion engine to the solution of the problem of draft power on farms as early as 1889.[34] Certainly gasoline tractors were not entirely unknown in agriculture at the opening of our period, even if they had as yet made little or no impression upon the agricultural writers of that day. The real impact of gasoline as a source of power appears to date from the Winnipeg Exposition of 1908. On that occasion gasoline and steam tractors were pitted against each other for the first time in a series of plowing contests. It does not seem that gasoline carried off the honors in any unmistakable fashion at this meeting; probably it was still too undependable. For example Davidson and Chase, writing in the same year, do not appear to have felt that the day of gasoline traction had yet arrived. After an extended discussion of gasoline as a source of stationary power, they write of the gas tractor in the following cursory terms:

> The gasoline engine is as portable as the steam engine. As to furnishing its own traction, there are several gasoline traction engines on the market, and there is no reason why with the addition of clutches and variable-speed devices the gasoline engine cannot be made as reliable an engine as the steam traction engine. In proof of the fact that it may be made to furnish its own tractive power it is only necessary to refer to the automobile, which is made to work under great variance of speed.[35]

[34] E. G. McKibben and R. A. Griffin, *Tractors, Trucks, and Automobiles* (National Research Project, Philadelphia, 1938), p. 3.

[35] J. B. Davidson and L. W. Chase, *Farm Machinery and Farm Motors* (Zudd, New York, 1908), p. 433.

TABLE 29

TRACTORS, TRUCKS AND AUTOMOBILES: ESTIMATED NUMBER ON FARMS, 1910–42[a]

Thousands

Year	*Tractors*[b]	*Trucks*[c]	*Automobiles*[c]
1910	1	0	50
1911	4	2	100
1912	8	5	175
1913	14	10	258
1914	17	15	343
1915	25	25	472
1916	37	40	687
1917	51	60	966
1918	85	89	1,502
1919	158	111	1,760
1920	246	139	2,146
1921	343	207	2,382
1922	373	263	2,425
1923	428	316	2,618
1924	496	363	3,004
1925	549	459	3,283
1926	621	559	3,605
1927	693	662	3,820
1928	782	753	3,820
1929	827	840	3,970
1930	920	900	4,135
1931	997	920	4,077
1932	1,022	910	3,798
1933	1,019	865	3,399
1934	1,016	875	3,399
1935	1,048	890	3,642
1936	1,125	900	3,826
1937	1,230	910	4,073
1938	1,370	925	4,161
1939	1,447	925	4,101
1940	1.545	935	4,185
1941	1,665		
1942	1,800		

[a] As of January 1 of each year.

[b] Bureau of Agricultural Economics release by A. P. Brodell and R. A. Pike, "Farm Tractors: Type, Size, Age, and Life" (1942). Data for 1941 and 1942 preliminary.

[c] U. S. Department of Agriculture, *Income Parity for Agriculture* (Washington, 1940), Pt. II. Sec. 3. Data for 1939 and 1940 subject to revision.

Nevertheless it was beginning to appear that the farmer must consider in the future the possible advantages of gasoline over steam in deciding what form of power equipment to buy. Three years later, in 1911, two observers summarized their impressions of the situation at that time as follows:

> Steam engines in use for plowing undoubtedly outnumber gas tractors, even in North America, where the latter have been increasing most rapidly in numbers. But the internal combustion, or gas, tractor is coming rapidly into favor, and possibly this year, for the first time, its sale will surpass that of the steam tractor in the plowing field. The majority of the gas tractors built are now used for plowing, whereas many small steam tractors are built simply for threshing in the Central and Eastern states. The use of the electric motor for plowing is as yet confined to a few isolated localities in Europe, notably in Germany and Italy.[36]

The gasoline tractor, clearly, was coming into its own, but the concluding sentence illustrates once again the superior ability of electricity to fire the imagination of those who wrote about the problems of the farmer. The first gasoline tractors had wheel drive, were large and heavy, and looked not unlike their steam prototypes. Caterpillar treads were fitted only for special purposes, and rubber tires were still quite unknown.

When the wartime boom in grain production set in, coinciding as it did with an acute labor shortage, perhaps the most usual arrangement consisted of a gasoline tractor for plowing and a steam engine for threshing—unless indeed the farm were large and modern enough to own a combine. As the combine, whose adoption was stimulated by the wartime need to economize labor, became an increasingly commonplace piece of equipment on the Great Plains, the importance of stationary power for threshing gradually diminished.

[36] Ellis and Rumely, *Power and the Plow,* p. 14.

Meanwhile the advantage of possessing a cheap and convenient form of draft power, both for plowing and for harvesting, received more and more emphasis. The ousting of the steam engine, now proven definitely inferior for draft purposes, continued steadily.

The gasoline tractor itself was being continually improved. Ellis and Rumely, writing in 1911, do not mention any tractors lighter than two and a half tons in weight, and some of the early models apparently weighed as much as fifteen tons, which is about what a steam engine would weigh.[37] Toward 1912 the gearbox was introduced, and by 1914 crankshaft revolutions had been stepped up to 1,000 a minute from about 200 on the original models. The magneto and float-feed carburetor followed shortly thereafter, adding further to the efficiency and adaptability of gasoline.[38] Of course the tractor benefited greatly, both in design and in production, from the concurrent development of the automobile: by 1917 Ford was building tractors on the assembly line.[39] In 1918 a low-cost wheel tractor weighing only one and a half tons, but capable nonetheless of pulling a two-bottom plow, was introduced and well on the way to popularity.[40]

The problem of applying gasoline power to the cultivation of row crops had, however, still to be solved. To meet this need, a tractor which steered from the rear had been designed and manufactured on a small scale at quite an early date, but it could not perform other tasks adequately and failed to gain acceptance.[41] In 1921 it was still possible to consider that the future of the tractor lay primarily in seedbed preparation. Thus three Illinois writers of that period classified farm work as follows:

[37] *Ibid.*, p. 106.
[38] *Yearbook of Agriculture, 1932,* pp. 437-38.
[39] *The Prairie Farmer,* Jan. 11, 1941, p. 31.
[40] McKibben and Griffin, *Tractors, Trucks, and Automobiles,* pp. 6-7.
[41] Ellis and Rumely, *Power and the Plow,* p. 105.

Tractor operations—Plowing, disking, harrowing; road work.

Operations of doubtful suitability for the tractor—Drilling small grains; cutting with binder; loading hay; hauling gravel, feed and fertilizer.

Operations not suitable for the tractor—Planting, cultivating and husking corn; mowing hay; miscellaneous hauling.[42]

But in fact the tractor was already used extensively for drilling and harvesting small grains, and to some extent for mowing; the cultivation of row crops was to follow.

A true "all-purpose" tractor at last appeared in 1924. Besides being equipped for every task it could already accomplish, the tractor was now given sufficient clearance and facility of control to permit its use for row cultivation as well: in particular, the driving wheels were made to slide on their axle so that the width of the track could be adjusted according to the requirements of individual row crops. The new tractor continued to offer a power takeoff, first brought out in 1922, and a belt pulley for stationary work.[43] Once these various functions had been successfully combined, the all-purpose tractor gained rapid popularity for tasks that previous types had been unable to handle; it now invaded farming areas, especially in the East, which had been unacquainted with the advantages of mechanical power. Nearly half of all tractors at present in use, and nearly three quarters of current sales of new tractors, are of the all-purpose type.[44]

A more recent development is the mounting of tractors on rubber, a trend that has become important only during the last ten years with the manufacture of specially designed, highly serrated, low pressure pneumatic tires. The first tires for farm tractors were sold in 1932. Fourteen percent of trac-

[42] W. F. Handschin, J. B. Andrews and E. Rauchenstein, *The Horse and the Tractor,* Bulletin 231 (Illinois Agricultural Experiment Station, 1921), p. 203.

[43] *Yearbook of Agriculture, 1932,* pp. 438-39.

[44] McKibben and Griffin, *Tractors, Trucks, and Automobiles,* p. 9.

tors manufactured in 1935 had rubber tires; the proportion rose to 83 percent in 1939 and to over 90 in 1940. Tests have shown considerable fuel economy for tire-equipped tractors because the machine offers less resistance in travel; while the reduced strain to which the machine is subject has cut down the need for repairs. In addition rubber tires have the advantage that they make operation more comfortable and less fatiguing, and enable the tractor to travel at relatively high speed on an ordinary highway. With the attachment of a trailer it can be used to some extent for actual highway transportation. Rubber tires have also made possible the very small tractors and combines which have recently been placed on the market.[45]

There were about 1,800,000 tractors of all types in the United States in 1942, almost double the number reported for 1930 (Table 29). Of these about one third were in the Corn Belt, and nearly one tenth in the state of Illinois.[46] It is interesting to inquire how far the market for new machines—as distinct from replacements—should now be considered saturated. In spite of the continued development of cheap low-power machines, the market for tractors among very small farms is probably rather limited. If we confine our attention to farms of more than 100 acres, the number of tractors per farm in 1939 ranged from .78 in the North Central states to as little as .39 in the South Central and .33 in the South Atlantic states.[47] The advent of cheap and efficient mechanical power has affected the different phases of cropping in very varying degree. According to a survey made in 1939 [48] tractor power was used for breaking land on about 55 percent of the nation's crop acreage (not including acreage under hay);

[45] *Technology on the Farm,* pp. 101-03; also *The Prairie Farmer,* Jan. 11, 1941, pp 38-39.

[46] *The Prairie Farmer,* p. 32.

[47] *Technology on the Farm,* pp. 9-10.

[48] See a release by A. P. Brodell entitled "Machine and Hand Methods in Crop Production" (U. S. Department of Agriculture, 1940).

while 57 percent of the disking and 43 percent of the harrowing was performed by tractor. Manure was spread mechanically on 58 percent of all land so treated, but this may not

TABLE 30

PERCENTAGE DISTRIBUTION OF TRACTORS SOLD FOR DOMESTIC USE IN THE UNITED STATES, BY TYPE[a]

Year	*Standard Wheel*	*General Purpose*	*Track Laying*	*Garden*
1925	92.5	.9	3.8	2.8
1930	45.5	38.5	11.4	4.6
1935	18.4	68.3	10.2	3.1
1940	4.1	85.5	6.7	3.7

Source: A. P. Brodell and R. A. Pike, *Farm Tractors: Type, Size, Age, and Life* (U. S. Department of Agriculture, 1942).

[a] Includes sales to users other than farmers. According to the compilers of the table, only some 5 percent of standard wheel and general purpose tractors are bought by nonfarmers, while of the track-laying tractors not more than one third are bought by farmers.

always have involved the use of a tractor. Of the acreage of small grains, as much as 71 percent was tractor-broken; on this acreage 70 percent of the disking, 57 percent of the harrowing, 48 percent of the drilling, and 69 percent of the harvesting was performed by tractor. Cotton growing is much less highly mechanized. Tractor plowing was found on 30 percent of the cotton acreage, mostly in the newer cotton areas from Texas to California. It is in these areas also that other phases of cultivation are handled by tractor, for in the older eastern sections of the Cotton Belt tractors remain relatively scarce. These figures suggest that even on the Great Plains there is still scope for further mechanization; and a considerable increase in the use of mechanical power seems likely in the South, even in the absence of a satisfactory cotton picker. Of course the rate at which mechanical power is introduced in any area depends upon feed and other costs of maintaining work animals as well as the price of tractors and their fuel. It has been predicted that a further half million tractors will be in use by 1950.[49] The substantial proportion of horse-drawn cultivators, binders and mowers still in use suggests that this estimate may not be wide of the mark.[50]

FARM MACHINERY SINCE 1899: FIELD IMPLEMENTS

The strongest influence upon the development of field implements in recent decades has naturally been the extensive adoption of mechanical draft power. Because of the use of greater power and higher speeds, tillage implements, for example, have been redesigned, the disk has displaced the moldboard plow in many regions, and numerous implements are now attached to the tractor itself instead of being drawn through some kind of hitch. Among other advantages the latter practice allows a closer approach to fences, and adoption of a power lift for raising and lowering the implement in use. It may also economize labor, for instance in mowing, for if the mechanism is mounted on the tractor one man is sufficient, whereas if the mower is hauled through a hitch two men are required.[51] The coming of the tractor has had other effects also. The considerable investment involved in mechanical power has naturally suggested that the fullest use should be made of it. For example, a much wider range of cultivating equipment has been developed than was formerly available. Virtually all crops may be seeded or planted mechanically if appropriate attachments are used; fertilizer is often distributed simultaneously with planting. Nor have the special requirements of truck farming been forgotten.

[49] *Technology on the Farm*, p. 12.
[50] McKibben, Hopkins and Griffin, *Field Implements, passim.*
[51] F. N. G. Kranich, *Farm Equipment for Mechanical Power* (Macmillan, 1923), Ch. V.

Plowing and Seeding Equipment

The moldboard plow has become heavier, in order to cope with the increased speed of mechanical plowing: it has also been altered somewhat in shape, since the line of haul of a tractor is horizontal, and there is no tendency to pull the share out of the furrow as with the horse-drawn implement. Besides this, higher speeds require a tougher share. Most notable perhaps has been the popularity of the vertical disk plow for large scale cultivation on the Great Plains.

The disk plow was originally developed as a means of improving the efficiency of mechanical tillage. It made a heavier demand upon draft power than the moldboard plow; on the other hand it was less likely to be broken by an obstruction and so could be used at higher speeds. The disk plow is essentially a pulverizing instrument and has slight cutting action: it is therefore unsuitable for breaking virgin soil, or for use where much vegetable matter has to be plowed under. The disks in a gang were originally mounted separately, one in front of another, and of course each at an angle to the direction of travel. In 1924 the vertical disk plow, in which the disks were all mounted on a common axle, was introduced; this axle now became horizontal, and the disks were therefore vertical, instead of being tilted as in previous models. The disk plow was at one time thought to be ideally suited for shallow plowing in semi-arid regions,[52] and in fact gained rapid acceptance on the western plains.[53] Recently, however, experience has shown that where rainfall is uncertain its use leads to wind erosion, particularly if plant residue is absent from the soil. In the dry-farming areas, therefore, the tendency is now to replace the disk plow by implements like the field cultivator or the duckfoot cultivator. The majority

[52] Ellis and Rumely, *Power and the Plow,* pp. 178-82.
[53] McKibben, Hopkins and Griffin, *Field Implements,* pp. 29-31.

of disk plows sold in recent years have been of the vertical type, and practically all are designed for use with tractors. But sales of moldboard plows still outnumber the disk variety by more than five to one.[54] The advantages of the moldboard type are of course that it may be used on a wider variety of soils, and that it can be drawn by horse as well as by tractor.

Improvements in secondary tillage during the last forty years have been less sensational, but still important. For example the availability of mechanical draft power has encouraged the use of heavier harrows, often operated in tandem, and particularly of implements like the duckfoot field cultivator which require large amounts of power for their operation.[55]

The influence of the tractor upon the design of drills and other seeding implements has apparently been slight, for the amount of power they require for their operation is in general small. According to the survey conducted by the National Research Project, sowing is still carried out almost exclusively by animal power except in the Wheat Belt—and even here the horse is still largely used for this purpose.[56] The lister-planter for corn, which opens a furrow and seeds in a single operation, requires more power than the ordinary grain drill and is usually drawn by tractor; however, this implement has not yet been extensively adopted except in the West.[57] Indeed in 1939 six percent of the total acreage under corn was still planted by hand.[58] The cultivation of row crops with the all-purpose tractor has already been mentioned; it is likely to become increasingly important, especially in the case of crops like corn, which must be cultivated several times.

[54] *Ibid.,* pp. 100-01.
[55] *Ibid.,* Ch. III.
[56] *Ibid.,* Table 28.
[57] Macy, Arnold and McKibben, *Corn,* pp. 31-32, 54, 73, 88, 105.
[58] Brodell, "Machine and Hand Methods in Crop Production."

Harvesting Equipment

Harvesting equipment falls into a number of separate categories according to whether it is designed to handle (1) small grains, (2) hay and other forage crops, (3) corn, or (4) crops presenting special problems, such as cotton or potatoes. The simplest type of apparatus still commonly in use for harvesting grain is the cradle and mower; the great advantage of this combination, besides its relatively low first cost, is that the mower can be used also for cutting forage crops. According to a recent study, however, only 4 percent of the wheat acreage and 7 percent of the acreage of oats were cut in 1938 by devices other than the binder and the combine. The acreage still cut by mower and cradle must therefore be very small, for these percentages also include acreage cut by the header, a machine which clips the stalks below the heads and delivers these to wagons for subsequent threshing. During the late nineteenth century the header was very common in the Wheat Belt where the stalks were not required for fodder, but it has now been almost entirely superseded by the combine. We are safe in assuming that acreage cut by header is today smaller even than acreage harvested by mower and cradle; the latter is concentrated mainly in the eastern and southern states.[59]

[59] See A. P. Brodell, "Increasing Use of the Combine," *The Agricultural Situation*, Aug. 1939, pp. 14-16. The detailed data upon which this article is based appear in a release by the U. S. Agricultural Marketing Service, "Acreage of Wheat, Oats and Corn for Grain, Harvested by Specified Methods, and Custom Harvest and Labor Rates, 1938" (1939).

The survey did not cover the New England states or Florida. However, it appears that in 1938 West Virginia, Georgia and Alabama harvested more than 40 percent, and South Carolina as much as 30 percent, of their wheat acreage by means other than binder or combine. The percentages in the remaining states included in the survey and reporting wheat acreage were all lower than this. In the case of oats, harvesting appears to be somewhat less highly mechanized than in that of wheat; several states reported more than half, and ten states together (all in the South and East) reported more than 30 percent of their acreage of oats as harvested by methods other than binder or combine.

The binder, which developed from the reaper soon after the middle of the nineteenth century, and the combine (harvester-thresher), which appeared in 1880,[60] have evidently both been in use for many decades. Indeed among field implements these two machines are peculiar, as we have seen, in that they were already highly developed (though not widely adopted) before the advent of the tractor, in spite of the large demands they make upon the source of draft power. Combines are now almost always drawn by tractor, but binders are still most frequently horse-drawn except in the southern Wheat Belt.[61] In 1938 combines harvested 49 percent of the wheat acreage and binders 47 percent; for oats, on the other hand, only 10 percent went to the combine and 83 percent went to the binder. Farmers consider oat straw superior to other straws, and to obtain this straw a binder must be used. Broadly speaking, binders are at present by far the commonest means of harvesting small grains except in the southern Wheat Belt, in the Southwest, and on the Pacific Coast: in these areas, which of course are noted for the large size of their farms, the combine is the more important.[62]

Since 1935 the baby combine, and since 1939 the "midget" combine, have opened up the smaller farms as a potential market for mechanized harvesting equipment. In 1939, 80

[60] Twenty combines were in use in California by 1881 and 500 of them seven years later; see Brodell, "Increasing Use of the Combine."

[61] McKibben, Hopkins and Griffin, *Field Implements,* Tables 37 and 40. The horse-drawn binder appears to be steadily diminishing in importance, however. Mr. H. L. Boyle of the International Harvester Company informs us that in 1941 his company sold 12,790 binders, of which 5,629 were designed for tractor use exclusively; 4,988 were of the large 8-foot type intended primarily for use with a tractor; and only 2,173 were of the smaller sizes which are commonly horse-drawn.

[62] According to the Agricultural Marketing Service more wheat acreage was harvested in 1938 by combine than by binder in the following states: Nebraska, Kansas, Oklahoma, Texas, Montana, Colorado, New Mexico, Arizona, Nevada, Washington, Oregon and California. In all other states reporting wheat a larger acreage was harvested by binder than by combine. A larger acreage of oats was harvested by binder than by combine in all states except (curiously) Louisiana and Mississippi; the acreage of oats in these two states is very small, however.

percent of the combines sold were either of the baby or the midget class.[63]

For the harvesting of hay and alfalfa the mower is used. Like the grain binder, from which it may sometimes be converted, its demands upon draft power are not great, and it is still most commonly horse-drawn.[64] Some more complicated haying machines have indeed been developed, in combination with the tractor, but acreages of forage crops large enough to justify their use are rare. However, recent improvements in the pick-up baler have led to its adoption in some farming areas, particularly for harvesting alfalfa.[65]

The harvesting of corn has been less widely mechanized up to the present than has the harvesting of small grains.[66] In 1939, 43 percent of the total acreage cut, and about the same proportion of the acreage cut in the Corn Belt itself, were still harvested by hand; only in the Wheat Belt was the harvesting of corn fully mechanized.[67] Where mechanical harvesting is in operation the type of equipment depends upon whether or not the stalks as well as the ears are desired. If corn is grown for ensilage, and both are harvested—conditions common outside the Corn Belt—the binder is employed. This implement, which resembles a wheat binder, was already in use at the beginning of our period. Being largely confined to the dairy regions of the North and East, and requiring only moderate tractive effort, the corn binder is still

[63] *Technology on the Farm,* p. 14. For baby combines the swath is 5 to 6 feet in width; for midgets, only 40 inches.

[64] McKibben, Hopkins and Griffin, *Field Implements,* Table 47.

[65] *Ibid.,* p. 92.

[66] The estimated growth of combines from 4,000 in 1920 to 100,000 in 1938 is to be compared with about 10,000 corn pickers in 1920 and 70,000 in 1939; see A. P. Brodell, "Increasing Use of the Combine," and "Mechanizing the Corn Harvest," *The Agricultural Situation,* Sept. 1939, pp. 18-20.

[67] Brodell, "Machine and Hand Methods in Crop Production." In Iowa only one acre in ten was cut by hand, the rest being harvested mechanically; in the other corn states (Illinois, Indiana and Ohio) the proportion was much higher. In Kansas, Nebraska and the Dakotas, by contrast, the corn acreage cut by hand was negligible.

predominantly horse-drawn.[68] On the other hand, where the corn is desired for grain and not for ensilage, the corn picker is the most efficient method of harvesting. This is a heavy and elaborate piece of machinery which gathers the ears from the standing corn, husks them, and delivers them to a waiting truck, performing much the same function as the combine in the case of wheat. It is hardly ever drawn by horses.[69] Like the combine, it was invented quite early,[70] but did not come into general use in the Corn Belt until the labor shortage of 1917–18. And just as the combine is used mainly in the Wheat Belt, so the corn picker is still found principally in the Corn Belt. For the country as a whole, only about 13 percent of that part of the corn acreage which was harvested for grain was gathered by mechanical picker in 1938.[71]

Among machines for harvesting those crops which present peculiar difficulties the potato digger is noteworthy. This ingenious implement consists of a kind of large hoe mounted before a power-driven sieve, and may have a variety of different attachments for delivering the potatoes. Requiring almost as much power to operate as the corn picker, the machine is essentially a tractor-driven implement.[72] Horse-drawn potato diggers were in existence in the 1890's, but apparently were little used.[73] In 1929 an improved two-row digger appeared on the market.[74]

68 McKibben, Hopkins and Griffin, *Field Implements,* Table 42.

69 *Ibid.,* Table 44.

70 Ardrey, *American Agricultural Implements,* Ch. XII.

71 Brodell, "Mechanizing the Corn Harvest," pp. 18-20. The highest percentages for individual states were Illinois, 43, Minnesota, 35, and Iowa, 35. Corresponding percentages for the (gross) output of corn so harvested would be somewhat higher owing to the tendency for the picker to be used on farms where the yield per acre is above average: about 20 percent of all corn used for grain was produced on the acreage mentioned in the text.

72 Kranich, *Farm Equipment for Mechanical Power,* Ch. XIV.

73 Ardrey, *op. cit.,* p. 146.

74 H. E. Knowlton, R. B. Elwood and E. G. McKibben, *Potatoes* (National Research Project, Philadelphia, 1938), p. 35.

Evidently the extent of mechanization practiced at any given time has varied greatly as between farming operations, crops and regions. The earliest and most complete mechanization probably came in the seeding and harvesting of wheat, oats and other small grains in the areas which specialized in those crops. On the Great Plains wide and level areas devoted to a single crop were ideally suited to the introduction of mechanical equipment. Here harvesting was already partially mechanized even before the advent of mechanical draft power—whether steam or gasoline. Threshing was, as we have seen, one of the earliest applications of the steam engine, whereas the gasoline tractor had its first successes in seeding and harvesting the wheat fields of the West. The spread of the new implements, and of the gasoline power which normally went with them, to other crops and into other farming areas was a much slower development. It was a process which required numerous adaptations of equipment to peculiarities of task or terrain, to the needs of the fruit and the vegetable farm or of the small general farm so common in the East. Even in fields where mechanization has been most successful, the dissemination of its benefits is still far from complete. And in large measure it has passed by important areas of farming activity, such as the cultivation of cotton and tobacco.

SOME UNSOLVED HARVESTING PROBLEMS

Not all crops can be harvested mechanically at present. Several must still be picked entirely by hand, and in the case of others only a small part of the work has been mechanized. Mr. Fowler McCormick, vice-president of the International Harvester Company, summarized the situation as follows:

> At the present time, machinery is available for handling all processes in the production of hay, small grain and some row crops. On the other hand, the production of cotton, tobacco,

and vegetables can only be handled in part by machinery. It might be of interest to enumerate some of the major farm operations for which so far no satisfactory commercial machines have been developed.

A crop which badly needs mechanical assistance at present is the sugar beet crop. What is required is a machine that will pull the beet out of the ground, cut off the green top without removing a wasteful amount of the beet itself, and load the beet into a truck. Fairly successful machines can be built, but none now exists which can justify itself on a medium or small-sized farm from an investment standpoint.[75]

Existing machines for lifting and topping sugar beets perform satisfactorily only where the beets are rather uniform in size; [76] such machines were invented more than half a century ago,[77] so that advance since then seems to have been slow. Mr. McCormick continued:

Secondly, there is now a demand for a corn combine, a machine to do for corn harvesting what the combine does for wheat; that is, to pick, husk, and shell the corn in one continuous operation. The problem is not yet solved. It is not a mechanical problem, but one of the moisture content of the corn. The corn must in some way be dehydrated after shelling so that it may be safely stored in bins.[78]

It will be recalled that the corn picker described in the preceding section performs the first two of these operations, but not the third. To quote Mr. McCormick further:

Thirdly . . . there is a large demand for a sugarcane harvester. Cane presents a problem because it varies greatly in size and requires three operations by a commercially successful ma-

[75] *Investigation of Concentration of Economic Power,* Hearings, Part 30 (Temporary National Economic Committee, Washington, 1940), p. 17032.

[76] *Technology on the Farm,* p. 106.

[77] Ardrey, *American Agricultural Implements,* p. 146.

[78] Hearings, Part 30, pp. 17032-33.

> chine. The cane stalk must be cut as close as possible to the ground, the leaves must be stripped from it, and the two upper joints of the stalk, which have no sugar content, must be cut off. There is a great demand for this machine, but you might be interested to know that the problem has defied satisfactory solution so far as we are concerned for more than 35 years.
>
> Now, it is a fact that several machines have been built for these purposes, but they are very large and bulky and expensive machines, and we have never come anywhere near finding a solution to that problem mechanically and what we think is a commercial product.[79]

Some experimental sugarcane harvesters have apparently weighed as much as 20 tons.[80]

Meanwhile the harvesting of cotton still occupies 4 million pickers for a season of perhaps 40 workdays each year. Moreover, since the bolls are only one to two feet above the ground, cotton cannot be picked unless the worker stoops; harvesting is therefore exceedingly laborious. It is hardly surprising that the construction of a satisfactory mechanical cotton picker should have been a problem to puzzle the wits and fire the imagination. In fact the Patent Office is littered with abortive attempts to reach a solution. Mr. McCormick reviewed the situation as follows:

> For many years there has been a demand for a mechanical cotton picker. This was especially true during the 1920 decade when labor was fully employed and foreign migrant labor was frequently imported to pick cotton. Several machines now exist which will get the cotton off the plants in a fairly satisfactory manner provided the conditions are favorable.
>
> Our company's experimental work on cotton pickers has extended over approximately thirty years, but we are not yet really satisfied with the results and have never offered a ma-

[79] *Ibid.*, p. 17033.

[80] *Technology on the Farm*, p. 107.

> chine for sale. The necessity of leaving the cotton plant uninjured for further growth and subsequent pickings, and the great irregularities in the size of the cotton plants present difficult problems. Cotton picked with present experimental machines is usually graded down because of the presence of leaf stains and more or less trash, and the grading down means a lower price and less possibility of saving.[81]

In the semi-arid, short season, low yield, cotton areas of Texas, all the bolls, together with much of the foliage, can be stripped fairly easily with the help of a sort of large comb. Either horse or tractor power may be used, but the cotton is found to contain much trash and may require special ginning equipment. This method, by no means entirely satisfactory even in Texas, is quite unsuited to the older, more humid, cotton areas of the East, where the cotton matures over a much more extended period. Although pneumatic and electrostatic principles have been tried, the nearest approach to a successful cotton picker relies upon the rotation of a small metal spindle. These spindles engage the cotton fiber and dislodge the boll. The spindle is periodically reversed to unwind the cotton attached to it. The machines actually succeed in picking the cotton, but they also gather up a good deal of trash, as Mr. McCormick remarked; and they apparently leave some 5 percent of the crop in the field unharvested, even after three separate harvestings have taken place. This latter difficulty has suggested that mechanical picking of the major part of the crop might possibly be combined with gleaning of the remainder by hand. It appears in any case that improved ginning equipment will become necessary. These difficulties are indeed so substantial that some efforts have been made to attack the problem from the other end; that is, to adapt the cotton plant itself to the requirements of mechanical harvesting. If it were possible to breed new varieties of cotton with less foliage, bolls that open wider as they

[81] Hearings, Part 30, p. 17035.

ripen, and a shorter maturing season, the problem might be greatly simplified.[82]

CHANGES IN DAIRYING EQUIPMENT

The most important step in the mechanization of dairying was undoubtedly the introduction of the milking machine during the first decade of the present century. By 1900 numerous patents had been registered for machines using a variety of different principles,[83] and during the 1890's tests were undertaken by the experiment station at Guelph, Ontario. The first successful machine seems to have appeared in Australia in 1902,[84] and to have come on the market in this country shortly thereafter. Models using intermittent suction, which is the principle universally employed today, apparently proved their superiority at quite an early date, but the fire hazards associated with the early gasoline engines led to frequent preference for the treadmill as a source of power. For many years a prejudice existed against milking machines on the ground that they impaired the milk-producing capacity of the cow, but it has now been rather securely established that if the machine is properly used there is no ground for this notion.[85]

Besides milking machines, a number of other kinds of mechanical equipment have been more or less widely adopted on dairy farms. The declining importance of farm butter production, and the tendency for deliveries to creameries to be made in milk rather than in cream have somewhat diminished the importance of the separator as a farm implement. On the other hand a wide range of feeding equipment, auto-

[82] See R. L. Horne and E. G. McKibben, *Mechanical Cotton Picker* (National Research Project, Philadelphia, 1937).

[83] For a description of some of the early machines, see Oscar Erf, *Milking Machines,* Bulletin 140 (Kansas Agricultural Experiment Station, 1906).

[84] See G. A. Smith and H. A. Harding, *Milking Machines,* Bulletin 353 (New York State Agricultural Experiment Station, 1906), p. 329.

[85] See A. C. Dahlberg, *The Influence of Machine Milking upon Milk Production,* Bulletin 654 (New York State Agricultural Experiment Station, 1935).

matic watering equipment and litter-carrying machinery has come into use within recent years.

CHANGES IN PLANTS AND ANIMALS

Technology does not exhaust itself in the mechanics of tractors and combines or the design of improved field implements. Plant improvements, animal breeding, and the continuing wars against disease and pests are equally part of it. To the extent to which they have impinged upon bearing or producing potentialities, changes in strains of plants or animals must obviously influence agricultural productivity. They are as much part of the general picture of the output-employment relationship as are changes in working equipment.

If such innovations appear less spectacular than those introduced in the field of machinery, the reason is probably that progress in this field is slow and gradual. Moreover, the emphasis has been on maintenance rather than increase in yields, at least as far as crops are concerned. Over as long a period as 70 or 80 years available evidence reveals only isolated instances in which yields have shown any marked tendency to advance. There exists, on the other hand, a great deal of historical material which suggests that but for the timely intervention of the scientist many crops today would bring forth yields far below those actually attained.

In the case of animals, however, the weight of research has been on increasing and improving yields by breeding beasts superior in any one of a number of desired characteristics. Comparisons with past decades suffer from lack of data, but in a way the past is still with us. Even today there exist in this country dairy cows that will produce as much as 20,000 pounds of milk per year and those whose yield will measure but one tenth of this amount or less. The latter are probably as nearly representative of a past period as statistical data would be, while the dairy cow with the 20,000-pound yield points to the possibilities of purposive breeding.

Plant Breeding

Progress has taken place generally along the following lines:

(1) Introduction of new varieties.

(2) Selection of superior varieties.

(3) Crossing of existing varieties to evolve hybrids combining the desirable traits of both parents, a development which marks the transition from the art of breeding to the science of breeding.

(4) Control of pests by the institution of quarantines and eradication campaigns where the host or bearer of the pest is identified.

(5) Evolution of baits, sprays and dusts which will destroy the pest without affecting the crop.

(6) Biological control, i.e., the use of beneficial insects to suppress noxious pests.

Although up to very recently there have been few cases of substantial increase in yields,[86] we have already mentioned in passing one outstanding instance of revival through the efforts of the plant breeder after yields had dropped to a dangerously low level. We are referring, of course, to the sugar-cane growing industry of Louisiana, which was saved only through the introduction of disease-resistant strains.[87] The case of spring wheat has been similar. The varieties existing 25 years ago lacked resistance to stem rust, and heavy losses were consequently suffered in years of serious infestation. Continuous introduction of new varieties and breeding of cross strains are held responsible for a segment of between 40 and 50 million bushels which could not have been produced

[86] As noted below (pp. 278-83), potatoes are one of the exceptions.
[87] See above, pp. 92-93.

by the varieties known in 1890.[88] In an analogous way, selection of new varieties at first and hybridization later have been instrumental in maintaining yields of many other crops and in protecting them from ever-changing attack by pests and diseases.

The most spectacular example of movement toward higher yields has been the case of hybrid corn, a development of most recent origin. Planted in 1939 on roughly one fourth of the country's corn acreage, hybrid corn is estimated to return a yield from 10 to 20 percent above that of open-pollinated corn.[89] In other instances, as in tobacco growing and sugar-beet cultivation, effective control for specific diseases is still developing. Another type of problem that has still to be resolved is illustrated by the declining vigor of California's lemon trees.[90] Indications are that improved varieties may be less effective than a change in the quality of the soil. Similarly, a large number of peach trees in California have aged past peak output, challenging scientists to identify and remedy the source of declining yields.[91]

Animal Breeding

Technological changes in the field of animal husbandry may be subsumed under three headings: feeding, breeding, and combating disease. Naturally, the art of feeding did not assume its present role until the exhaustion of the free range posed the question of what to feed. Since then our knowledge of animal feeding has advanced *pari passu* with our knowledge of human nutrition and so has made rapid strides, particularly in the past quarter century. Nutritional deficiencies and their consequences have become a vast field for research

[88] *Technology on the Farm,* p. 138.
[89] *Ibid.,* pp. 135-36.
[90] *Science, Servant of Agriculture* (Agricultural Experiment Station, University of California, 1940), p. 65.
[91] *Ibid.,* p. 82.

with regard to both vitamins and minerals. To cite but one example, it has been found that the hatchability of eggs is increased more than 10 percent if an otherwise well-balanced diet is supplemented by manganese.[92] Similarly, feeds rich in riboflavin have been observed to lead to increased efficiency of feed utilization by chickens.[93] The importance of feeding practices is indicated further by an estimate that if the feeding standards of only one third of the 600,000 dairy herds containing 10 or more milking cows were raised to those prevailing among the dairy herd improvement associations, total butterfat output might be expanded some 5 percent.[94] Another branch of research has concentrated not on the general influence of various feeds on the well-being of the animal, but on the type of feed that will produce certain desired qualities, such as a given consistency of fat.

Many accounts suggest that breeding retained a great deal of its haphazard character until the practice of progeny-testing was adopted. This in turn was dependent upon a rigid system of registration. As a result of years of selection, the average herds as they existed at the end of the last century were probably superior to their ancestors fifty or more years before. Yet breeding as a science did not really begin until around 1900. It is very significant, for example, that in an article published in 1899 [95] we encounter a most severe denunciation of the technique of inbreeding, itself one of the cornerstones of modern breeding when practiced wisely.[96] Linking the spread of bovine tuberculosis with that of "incestuous" breeding, the writer of 1899 observes sternly, "Nature exacts the penalty for reversion or disobedience of

[92] *Technology on the Farm*, p. 118.
[93] *Ibid.*, p. 120.
[94] *Ibid.*, p. 121.
[95] John Clay, Jr., "Work of the Breeder in Improving Live Stock," *Yearbook of the Department of Agriculture, 1899*, pp. 627-42.
[96] G. M. Rommel, *Essentials of Animal Breeding*, Farmers' Bulletin 1167 (U. S. Department of Agriculture, 1920).

her laws."[97] This homily is in sharp contrast to modern views on inbreeding.

By far the most progressive step, as indicated above, has been progeny-testing (i.e., the empirical analysis of the transmitting abilities of sires); this originated with dairy herds which provide rather prompt and continuous material for study. The first cow-testing association was organized in 1906, and by 1940 more than 700,000 cows and close to 50,000 bulls were registered. In terms of the country's total dairy cattle force this is still only a beginning. How far the increase in average milk production per cow, which between 1909 and 1940 has amounted to more than 20 percent,[98] can be linked up with the spread of progeny-testing, it is impossible to say. On the basis of records achieved by outstanding cows and sires it is clear, however, that the possibilities for improvement are great.

Progress has been much slower with beef cattle, undoubtedly because feed utilization and rate of gain—these are the qualities to be tested—are more complicated concepts, and because beef cattle are normally difficult to keep under close observation. In the case of swine the old method of selection by individual merit still prevails, even though experiments have revealed great differences in the breeding value of outwardly similar sires.[99]

Progeny-testing is widely applied to chickens, since laying ability is a quality easily observed. The knowledge that a hen of superior laying quality is not necessarily superior in transmitting this gift to her progeny has removed a great deal of the guesswork from poultry breeding.

The most recent technological advance in breeding has

[97] Clay, *op. cit.*, p. 636.

[98] R. G. Bressler, Jr. and J. A. Hopkins, *Trends in Size and Production of the Aggregate Farm Enterprise, 1909–36* (National Research Project, Philadelphia, 1938), Tables A-95 and A-96; *Agricultural Statistics, 1941*, Table 571. See also Table 50 below.

[99] *Technology on the Farm*, pp. 130-31.

been the introduction of artificial insemination. Here too the use of the new technique has been most widespread with dairy cattle, largely because of the existence of proved sires. Its advantages are many, chief among them the extension of the services of the superior bull both in place and in time, and the elimination of various obstacles to conception which exist when natural mating is practiced.

From this brief review of the outstanding changes in agricultural technology during the present century an impression may be gained of the immense variety of ways in which an advance on the technological front may be achieved. In part mechanical, in part chemical or physical, in part biological, innovation has appeared in one guise after another. Some developments, for example the mechanical cotton picker, appeared promising at the opening of the period studied here but to this day have failed to mature; others, notably hybrid corn, came suddenly upon the scene and were widely adopted within a very few years. To assess accurately the relative importance of different innovations, or even of diverse types of technological change, is an obvious impossibility. Yet all of them have influenced, in greater or less degree, the trend of agricultural productivity, and have contributed to the rise in output per unit of input, to the measurement of which we shall now turn. Estimates of agricultural employment, which are presented in Chapter 6, are followed in Chapter 7 by measures of productivity.

Chapter 6

Employment in Agriculture

THE abundance and variety of data relating to agricultural production stand in striking contrast to the sparseness and unreliability of the material available for estimates of agricultural employment. Both because of the quantitative importance of the subject, and because of the inconsistency of existing estimates, the difficulties encountered in the measurement of employment in agriculture call for more extended discussion than is necessary when one seeks to appraise the labor force of most other segments of the national economy.

These difficulties originate in the nature of agricultural enterprise itself, and in the character of the employment to which it gives rise. In most other fields of endeavor labor input consists largely of working time remunerated by the hour, day or week. The payroll bears a close, if not always a constant, relationship to the amount of labor consumed. It is true in a general way, for such industries, to say that the compilation of payrolls involves a simultaneous compilation of numbers employed—if not indeed of days or hours worked. Statistics of labor input are therefore in a certain sense a by-product of the execution of the wage contract. In many industries, to be sure, before a complete picture can be obtained separate account must be taken of the labor of individual entrepreneurs, who in a sense employ themselves, but this qualification is seldom of great quantitative importance. Except in the professions, which, like agriculture, are peculiar in this respect, the wage contract itself remains by far the most important source of employment data.

In the case of agriculture the situation is quite different. In the first place, farmers do not normally keep payroll records of a kind that can be made to yield, through Census or other inquiry, adequate statistics of their labor purchases. But even if they did, such statistics would not go very far toward a solution of the problem. According to the Census of 1930, out of 10.5 million persons engaged in agriculture only 2.7 million, or about a quarter of the total, worked for wages. The remaining three quarters of the labor force consisted of farmers themselves (including croppers) and of unpaid family laborers. It is apparent, then, that one cannot compile reliable estimates of total labor input on an hourly, daily, or even weekly, basis. In the case of agriculture the best we can do is to attempt to measure the aggregate working population at different dates, and to treat this total as a measure of labor input. But even this is not easy to do, for the number of farm laborers, whether family or hired workers, was not reported by any Census of Agriculture prior to 1935. We are therefore forced to depend in the main upon the Census of Population, and to regard the labor force as equivalent to the number of persons reported as gainfully occupied in agriculture. This treatment is admittedly far from satisfactory: it leads to the inclusion of those who are unemployed, yet regard themselves as attached to agriculture; and it makes no distinction between a farmer who works 365 days a year and a laborer who may work only during a few weeks of peak activity.

Besides the Census of Population, there are the results of a number of sample studies of agricultural employment; of these, the Crop Reporting Board data, collected monthly since 1923, are the most important.[1] But the fact that, for years prior to 1935 at least, the Census of Population provides

[1] For a description of these data, see especially E. E. Shaw and J. A. Hopkins, *Trends in Employment in Agriculture, 1909–36* (National Research Project, Philadelphia, 1938), Appendix C. The annual series derived by Shaw and Hopkins from these data are discussed below, pp. 239-44.

the only global estimates available, is responsible for the largest part of the difficulties that have to be faced in any attempt to estimate agricultural employment.

CENSUS DATA–GAINFUL WORKERS

The Census of Population totals for all persons living on farms, and for the number "gainfully occupied" in agriculture (i.e., reporting themselves as engaged in the industry, whether or not actually employed on the date of enumeration) are shown in Table 31. However, the comparability of the original Census data for gainfully occupied is not accepted even by the Bureau of the Census itself, which has recently published the revised series shown at the foot of the table.[2] It will be observed that about one person in three living on a farm is reported as occupied in agriculture: the remainder do not work regularly, are below or above working age, or are occupied in other industries.

The revisions undertaken by the Bureau of the Census—upward in 1900 and 1920, downward in 1910—are substantial. A brief discussion of the circumstances that gave rise to the revisions illustrates well the difficulty of estimating the size of the agricultural labor force, and in addition throws some light upon the validity of the revised totals themselves.

The reasons for the upward revision in 1920 are perhaps easiest to appreciate. The Census of that year was taken in January, when agricultural employment is lower than at other seasons. Many workers who would have reported themselves as engaged in agriculture, had the Census been taken later in the year, no doubt stated that they were unoccupied or elsewhere engaged. The revised total therefore represents

[2] U. S. Bureau of the Census, "Industrial Distribution of the Nation's Labor Force: 1870 to 1930" (Press release, Oct. 23, 1938). The revision represents an attempt to place numbers reported in earlier years upon the same basis as the total reported for 1930. It was made by the Bureau in conjunction with a reclassification of the occupation statistics of Censuses from 1870 to 1920 in order to conform to the classification used in 1930: the detailed results of this reclassification have yet to be published.

TABLE 31

FARM POPULATION, AND GAINFUL WORKERS IN AGRICULTURE[a]

Thousands

	June 1 1900	*April 15 1910*	*January 1 1920*	*April 1 1930*	*April 1 1940*
Farm population	..	32,077[d]	31,614	30,445	30,547
Gainfully occupied, 10 years and over, original Census data[b]	10,249	12,388	10,666	10,472	9,163[e]
Farmers (including managers and foremen)	5,779	6,183	6,480	6,079	..
Hired laborers	2,103	2,895	2,336	2,733	..
Unpaid family workers	2,366	3,311	1,850	1,660	..
Gainfully occupied, 10 years and over, Revision by Bureau of the Census[c]	10,912	11,592	11,449	10,472[e]	9,163

[a] All data in this table are derived directly or indirectly from the Census of Population.
[b] As summarized by J. D. Black and J. C. Folsom, *Research in Farm Labor* (Social Science Research Council, 1933).
[c] U. S. Bureau of the Census, "Trends in the Proportion of the Nation's Labor Force Engaged in Agriculture: 1820 to 1940" (Press release, March 28, 1942).
[d] As estimated by Bureau of the Census; see *Agricultural Statistics, 1940* (U. S. Department of Agriculture), p. 553.
[e] May be an underestimate because of omission of workers on some small farms: see below, pp. 243-44.

the presumed result of the 1920 Census had it been taken in April rather than in January.[3]

The Census of 1910 does not differ appreciably from that of 1930 in respect of date of enumeration, but variations in the field instructions apparently led to a substantial over-count of women and children [4] among unpaid family labor in that year.[5] That the coverage of the Census was considerably more inclusive in 1910 than in other years is apparent from the data presented in Table 32.

TABLE 32

FARM LABORERS REPORTED BY THE CENSUS

	1900	*1910*	*1920*	*1930*
Farm laborers				
Total	4,469,446	6,205,434	4,186,130	4,392,764
Women	457,766	1,115,565	615,230	519,934
Children, male	851,881	1,017,438	456,175	343,100
Children, female	207,200	410,142	187,999	126,397
Farm laborers per farm				
Total	.78	.97	.65	.70
Unpaid family workers	.41	.52	.29	.26

Source: J. D. Black and J. C. Folsom, *Research in Farm Labor* (Social Science Research Council, 1933), Table 1; *Fifteenth Census (1930)*, Vol. IV, p. 85.

Both the rather constant number of women workers, and the declining trend in the number of occupied children, are sharply disturbed by the large increases in these categories reported for 1910.

[3] *Fourteenth Census (1920)*, Vol. IV, pp. 22-23.

[4] I.e., workers aged 10 to 15 inclusive.

[5] See especially *Thirteenth Census (1910)*, Vol. IV, pp. 26-29; *Fourteenth Census (1920)*, Vol. IV, pp. 18-24. If it is thought that, on the contrary, instructions in other years were insufficiently inclusive, the total for 1910 can of course be regarded as appropriate and the totals for other years considered too low. It is evident, however, that the Bureau of the Census believes that the 1910 instructions resulted in an overstatement, in relation to *any* reasonable definition of employment, and not merely in relation to the employment reported for other years. Hence the Bureau has revised the 1910 total downwards for comparability with 1930, in preference to the reverse process. It has been suggested (though not by the Bureau of the Census) that there is some undercoverage in the 1930 Census because of an undercount of small farms in that year (see below, pp. 243-44).

Since we must of necessity depend almost entirely upon the Census of Population for data concerning agricultural employment, it is worth while to consider first the metamorphosis of the instructions to enumerators since 1900. In 1900 the instruction was extremely brief: [6]

> 154. Column 19. Occupation.—This question applies to every person 10 years of age and over who is at work, that is, occupied in gainful labor, and calls for the profession, trade, or branch of work upon which each person depends chiefly for support, or in which he is engaged ordinarily during the larger part of the time.
>
> 166. . . . Enter the older children of a farmer (who work on the farm) as farm laborers. . . .

Clearly in that year the enumerator might well have felt free to leave the occupation column blank; nor was he given any encouragement to press for an occupational designation where one was not immediately disclosed. No special directions were given as to the treatment of women and children working on farms.

The instructions to enumerators in 1910 have an entirely different emphasis:

> 144. Column 18. Trade or profession.—An entry should be made in this column for *every* person enumerated. The occupation, if any, followed by a child, of any age, or by a woman is just as important, for census purposes, as the occupation followed by a man. Therefore it must never be taken for granted, without inquiry, that a woman, or child, has no occupation.
>
> 154. Women doing farm work.—A woman working regularly at outdoor farm work, even though she works on the home farm for her husband, son, or other relative and does not receive money wages, should be returned in column 18 as a *farm laborer*. . . .

[6] The quotations which follow are from the *Fourteenth Census (1920),* Vol. IV, pp. 27-30; the italics appearing therein are in the original.

> 155. Children on farms.—In the case of children who work for their own parents on a farm . . . [or] as farm laborers for others . . . the entry should be *farm laborer*.
>
> 156. Children working for parents.—Children who work for their parents at home merely on general household work, on chores, or at odd times on other work, should be reported as having no occupation. Those, however, who materially assist their parents in the performance of work other than household work should be reported as having an occupation.

The unfortunate feature of the 1910 instruction appears to have been the statement that "an entry should be made . . . for *every* person enumerated" without at the same time explicit mention (except in the case of children working for their parents) that "no occupation" would be an acceptable description. The result has undoubtedly been the inclusion as agricultural workers of many who worked only occasionally. The entirely laudable desire to prevent sex discrimination in the minds of enumerators may have had a similar influence. At any rate the Bureau of the Census believes that the instructions led to a substantial overcount of women and children occupied in agriculture in 1910.

In the Census of 1920 a valiant attempt was made to define more precisely the type of information desired, and the instructions were amended as follows:

> 152. Column 26. Trade or profession.—An entry should be made in this column for *every* person enumerated. The entry should be either (1) the occupation pursued—that is, the word or words which most accurately indicate the particular kind of work done by which the person enumerated earns money or a money equivalent, as *physician, carpenter, dressmaker, laborer, newsboy*; or (2) *none* (that is, no occupation). The entry *none* should be made in the case of all persons who follow no gainful occupation.
>
> 159. Women doing farm work.—For a woman who works *only occasionally*, or *only a short time each day* at outdoor

> farm or garden work, or in the dairy, or in caring for livestock or poultry, the return should be *none*; but for a woman who works *regularly* and *most of the time* at such work, the return should be *farm laborer* . . . Of course, a woman who herself operates or runs a farm or plantation should be reported as a *farmer* and not as a "farm laborer."
>
> 160. Children on farms.—In the case of children who work *regularly* for their own parents on a farm . . . [or] as farm laborers for others . . . the entry should be *farm laborer.*
>
> 161. Children working for parents.—Children who work for their parents at home merely on general household work, on chores, or at odd times on other work, should be reported as having no occupation. Those, however, who somewhat regularly assist their parents in the performance of work other than household work or chores should be reported as having an occupation.

As in previous Censuses, the enumerators in 1920 were instructed to include women and children occupied in agriculture: but they were now explicitly discouraged from doing so unless the persons concerned were engaged in farm work "regularly," or even "most of the time." In the opinion of the Bureau of the Census, these new qualifications appear to have met the case, for the instructions just quoted for 1920 were repeated, without material alteration, for the Census of 1930.[7] It should be added that the revision made by the Bureau in its estimate of gainfully occupied persons in 1920 (Table 31 above) is believed to have been occasioned entirely by the date of the Census, and not by any belief that the instructions to enumerators in that year were still defective.

It should now be clear why the Bureau of the Census itself regarded the Census totals for numbers occupied in agriculture in 1900, 1910 and 1920 respectively as incomparable with similar data for 1930. The revisions shown at the foot of Table 31 therefore represent an attempt by the Bureau to at-

[7] See instructions 186, 197, 199 and 200, *Fifteenth Census (1930)*, Vol. II, pp. 1400-01.

tain the presumed results of enumeration in earlier years, on the assumptions (1) that the Censuses of 1900 and 1920 had been taken in April, and not in June and January, respectively; (2) that the Censuses of 1900 and 1910 had been taken with the use of instructions to enumerators similar to those employed in 1920 and later years. It is plain that this attempt leads to a downward revision for 1910 and to an upward revision for 1920. It is less apparent, however, that it must result in an upward revision for 1900 (see Table 31). More people are employed in agriculture in June than in April, so that any revision occasioned by the date of the Census would cause a reduction in the total for 1900. On the other hand, the absence of any specific instruction concerning the occupational status of women doing farm work, and the small number of women reported as occupied in agriculture in that year (see Table 32), apparently call for an upward revision of the 1900 total which, in the view of the Bureau of the Census, more than offsets the downward revision on account of the date of enumeration.

CENSUS DATA—ALTERNATIVE SERIES

The revisions by the Bureau of the Census in the totals for persons gainfully occupied in agriculture were carried out with the help of the distribution by sex, and such distributions by age as the Census provides. The revisions are large: upward by 6.5 percent in 1900, downward by 6.4 percent in 1910, and upward by 7.3 percent in 1920. Obviously a very high degree of accuracy cannot be claimed for the resulting totals. The largest part of the variation in Census instructions, and of the consequent uncertainty in the size of the occupied population, relates to the counting of women and children. For this reason an alternative series may be constructed,[8] showing only farmers and adult male laborers (i.e.,

[8] See especially J. D. Black and Nora Boddy, "The Agricultural Situation, March, 1940," *Review of Economic Statistics,* Vol. XXII (May 1940), pp. 60-63.

TABLE 33

FARMERS AND ADULT MALE LABORERS IN AGRICULTURE

Thousands

	1900	*1910*	*1920*	*1930*
Farmers (including managers and foremen)[a]	5,779	6,183	6,480	6,079
Male farm laborers, 20 years and over[b]	2,025	2,541	2,151	2,491
Correction for date of Census, 1920[c]	..	..	215	..
Farmers plus adult male laborers	7,804	8,724	8,846	8,570

[a] From Table 31.

[b] J. D. Black and J. C. Folsom, *Research in Farm Labor* (Social Science Research Council, 1933), Table 3.

[c] Correction, one tenth of previous item, suggested by J. D. Black, "The Agricultural Situation, March, 1940," *Review of Economic Statistics,* May 1940, p. 60. E. E. Shaw and J. A. Hopkins give seasonal indexes for total employment of 81 for January 1st and 96 for April 1st; see *Trends in Employment in Agriculture, 1909–36* (National Research Project, Philadelphia, 1938), Table 2. So large a correction would be excessive, for not every worker unemployed in January will fail to report his occupation. (*Ibid.,* pp. 127-28.) An adjustment of 10 percent appears reasonable.

The index for June 1st is 116, and the 1900 Census may therefore have reported more laborers than it would have if taken in April. On the other hand such an overcount is probably compensated for by the character of the instructions to enumerators (see text); consequently no adjustment has been made in 1900 for the date of the Census.

males aged 20 years and over reporting themselves as occupied in agriculture). This series, which is not available for 1940 at the time of writing, is shown for Census years 1900 through 1930 in Table 33. While obviously less comprehensive than that developed by the Census Bureau in its revision of numbers gainfully occupied, it rests more directly upon Census data, and contains a smaller element of guesswork. It has the further advantage that farmers and adult male laborers are perhaps likely to be employed more regularly and intensively than the women and children who are now excluded. When the two series are placed on a 1930 base, the following comparison results:

TABLE 34

INDEXES OF AGRICULTURAL EMPLOYMENT

1930:100

Year	*Gainfully Occupied, 10 Years and Over*[a]	*Farmers and Adult Male Laborers*[b]
1900	104.2	91.1
1910	110.7	101.8
1920	109.3	103.2
1930	100.0	100.0
1940	87.5	..

[a] From Table 31.
[b] From Table 33.

Taking this comparison at its face value, we may say that the whole number gainfully occupied in 1900 was about the same as, and in 1910 and 1920 considerably greater than, the number in 1930, whereas farmers and adult laborers were considerably less numerous in 1900, and about the same in number in 1910 and 1920 as in 1930. In other words, the importance of women and children as a group (included in the first series but not in the second) declined, both absolutely and relatively, between 1900 and 1930. Reference to Table 32 above, which shows the numbers of occupied women and children reported by the Census, suggests (with allowance for the overcount in 1910) that this decline was concentrated among children. The number of women laborers does not seem to have changed significantly, but the number of occupied children appears to have been halved during the course of these three decades.

We have evidently to choose one of the two series—gainfully occupied, or farmers plus adult males—as a measure of the agricultural labor force. The decision should be governed, however, not merely by the appropriateness or inappropriateness of allowing for the decline in the number of child laborers. For, as the preceding discussion has emphasized, the count of occupied children, like the enumeration of women laborers, is itself subject to doubts and difficulties much more serious than in the case of farmers and adult males. This is the principal ground for preferring the second series to the first.

ANNUAL EMPLOYMENT DATA

Quite apart from uncertainties of the kind already discussed, the two series so far presented have further deficiencies. For they refer only to decennial Census years; and they measure the occupied population, i.e., the number of workers attached to agriculture, rather than the number actually employed. An attempt to overcome both these defects has been made by Eldon E. Shaw and John A. Hopkins in a series developed for the National Research Project and now continued by the Agricultural Marketing Service.[9] Such an enterprise involves two steps. First, some relation must be established between the sizes of the occupied and employed populations at Census dates. Judging that employment in April is not very far from

[9] See Shaw and Hopkins, *op. cit.*, especially Section II and Appendices A, C and D. A revision and extension of the same methods is described in A. R. Sabin, *A New Technique for the Estimation of Changes in Farm Employment* (U. S. Agricultural Marketing Service, New York, 1940).

the average for the year, the authors apparently treated the numbers reported by the Census of Population in 1910 and 1930 as "occupied in agriculture" as equivalent to "average numbers employed," the 1920 total being adjusted for the date of the Census.[10] Second, a medium for interpolation between Census dates must be obtained; for this purpose Shaw and Hopkins used the crop-reporter estimates, available monthly since October 1923, for numbers of wage workers and unpaid family laborers, respectively, employed per farm.[11] The number of farms was estimated annually by fitting curves through Census dates,[12] so that the crop-reporter data for 1925 and later years could be converted into estimates of total employment. From the description they give, it is unfortunately not clear how the authors derived their annual employment estimates for 1909–24, but it is plain that these estimates must depend heavily upon curve-fitting between Census dates.[13] The entire task was apparently carried out on a regional basis, and numerous adjustments, which it is impossible to review here, had to be made.

These annual series for farm employment, the only ones available, are reproduced in Table 35. In Chart 45 the Shaw-Hopkins total is plotted against the revised Bureau of the Census estimates already discussed; the Bureau of the Census revision was not available to Shaw and Hopkins.[14] It cannot be said that the agreement is at all satisfactory. In principle, the Bureau of the Census series, which relates to numbers engaged in April, might be expected to fall short of the Shaw-Hopkins totals, which represent annual averages.[15] On the

[10] Shaw and Hopkins, *op. cit.*, p. 128. However, in 1930, the authors made various adjustments, some of which are discussed below.

[11] *Ibid.*, Appendix C.

[12] *Ibid.*, Appendix B.

[13] *Ibid.*, Appendix A.

[14] *Ibid.*, p. 127.

[15] According to Shaw and Hopkins, April 1st employment averages 96 percent of mean annual employment (*ibid.*, Table 2). The discrepancy should be smaller than this, for not all those unemployed on the date of enumeration would fail to return themselves as engaged in agriculture.

other hand, inasmuch as the authors exclude some 100,000 wage workers (or 1 percent of the total) who reported themselves as unemployed in 1930, the Bureau of the Census data should run correspondingly higher on this account. But these sources of disagreement are quite minor in character and par-

Chart 45

AGRICULTURAL EMPLOYMENT

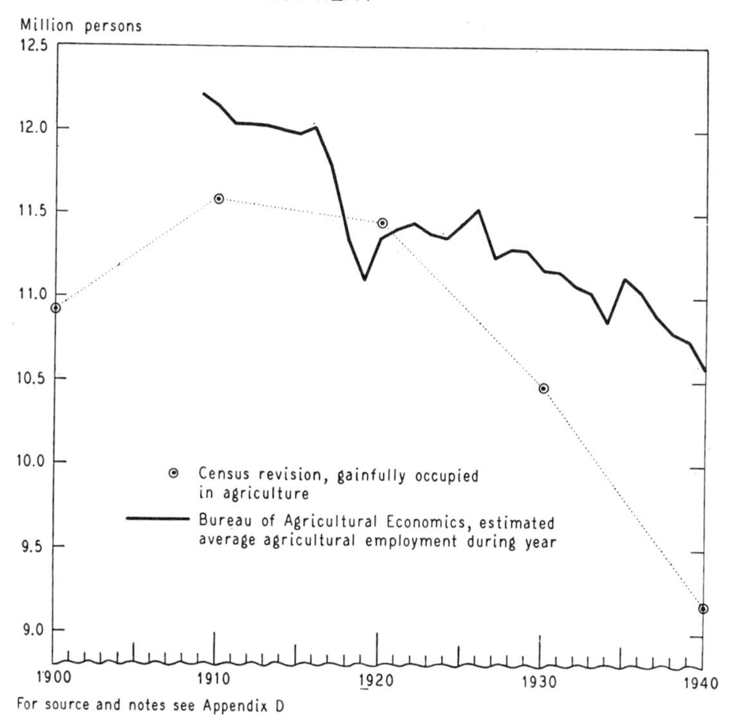

For source and notes see Appendix D

tially offset each other. In fact the Shaw-Hopkins series runs as much as 4.8 percent above the Bureau of the Census revision in 1910, 0.8 percent below in 1920, and 6.7 percent above in 1930.[16] For two series whose level is derived from

[16] See Tables 31 and 35. For 1940 the Bureau of Agricultural Economics extension of the Shaw-Hopkins data, included in Table 35, runs as much as 15.5 percent above the Census figure.

TABLE 35

AGRICULTURAL EMPLOYMENT[a]

Bureau of Agricultural Economics Estimates

Thousands

Year	*Total Employment*	*Family Workers*	*Hired Workers*
1909	12,209	9,341	2,868
1910	12,146	9,269	2,877
1911	12,042	9,172	2,870
1912	12,038	9,149	2,889
1913	12,033	9,128	2,905
1914	12,000	9,081	2,919
1915	11,981	9,047	2,934
1916	12,016	9,050	2,966
1917	11,789	8,856	2,933
1918	11,348	8,507	2,841
1919	11,106	8,322	2,784
1920	11,362	8,479	2,883
1921	11,412	8,511	2,901
1922	11,443	8,528	2,915
1923	11,385	8,491	2,894
1924	11,362	8,488	2,874
1925	11,446	8,577	2,869
1926	11,534	8,507	3,027
1927	11,246	8,296	2,950
1928	11,296	8,340	2,956
1929	11,289	8,305	2,984
1930	11,173	8,323	2,850
1931	11,159	8,469	2,690
1932	11,069	8,571	2,498
1933	11,023	8,590	2,433
1934	10,852	8,506	2,346
1935	11,131	8,702	2,429
1936	11,047	8,486	2,561
1937	10,892	8,261	2,631
1938	10,796	8,176	2,620
1939	10,740	8,145	2,595
1940	10,585	8,019	2,566
1941	10,361	7,829	2,532

[a] Average of persons employed on the first of each month. Compiled by the Agricultural Marketing Service. For 1909–34, see *Crops and Markets,* Jan. 1942, p. 5. For 1935–41, Bureau of Agricultural Economics release, April 16, 1942. The same series through 1934 may be found in E. E. Shaw and J. A. Hopkins, *Trends in Employment in Agriculture, 1909–36* (National Research Project, Philadelphia, 1938), Table 1; this table, however, contains several misprints.

common source material, these discrepancies are surprisingly large and call for comment.

It will be recalled that the Bureau of the Census made no revision of the reported total for numbers engaged in 1930. The excess of 700,000 in the Shaw-Hopkins estimate (see Chart 45) is therefore due entirely to revisions proposed by these authors. These revisions may be accounted for approximately as follows:

	(thousands)
Census total, gainfully occupied (April 1930)[17]	10,472
minus unemployed hired workers[18]	−104
plus adjustment for undercount of farms in 1930[19]	+422
plus difference between average employment for the year and employment in April[20]	+414
unaccounted for	−31
Shaw-Hopkins total for average employment in 1930[21]	11,173

The most important revision introduced by Shaw and Hopkins in 1930 therefore relates to an alleged undercount of farms. Black suggests that "150,000 or more small farms" were omitted in this Census.[22] It is true that the Census of Agriculture taken in 1935 reported half a million more farms than were found in 1930, but this is very generally regarded as an overcount. The Bureau of the Census on the other hand refrained from making any such revision in its 1930 data for numbers occupied. To the deduction for unemployment there is no objection, but the addition of 400,000, or about 4 percent, to compensate for the difference between annual average and April employment seems of doubtful validity. Such an adjustment assumes that all persons seasonally unemployed in April would report themselves as without an agricultural occupation. If required at all, the adjustment

[17] *Census of Population, 1930,* Vol. V, p. 40; see Table 31 above.

[18] *Abstract of the Fifteenth Census (1930),* p. 477.

[19] Daniel Carson, "Labor Supply and Employment" (unpublished report for the National Research Project), Table D-4a.

[20] *Trends in Employment in Agriculture, 1909–36,* Table H-1.

[21] Table 35.

[22] *Review of Economic Statistics* (May 1940), p. 60.

should be much smaller than that made by the authors. Moreover these adjustments are not made for other Census years, and are therefore not really needed in 1930 to establish comparability with earlier Censuses.

It may well be that there was some underreporting of farms in 1930 and a corresponding undercount of the working population.[23] In that case a comparable series for Census dates would, in 1930, lie somewhat above the 10,472 thousand reported for that year, and not far from the 10,912 thousand obtained by the Bureau of the Census revision for 1900. It seems safe to conclude that, if we include women and child laborers, agricultural employment in 1930 was exceedingly close to its level in 1900.

In 1920 the Shaw-Hopkins annual series is very close to the Bureau of the Census revision, the adjustment made for the date of the Census being almost the same in the two series. No special comment on this point is required. The much higher total given by Shaw and Hopkins in 1910 is attributable to the far less extensive downward revision they made (because of the overcount of women and children in that year) than was made by the Bureau of the Census. Finally, for 1940 the extension of the Shaw-Hopkins data by the Bureau of Agricultural Economics (Table 35) comes out as much as 1.4 million above the corresponding figure from the 1940 Census of Population. During recent years at any rate, the Bureau of Agricultural Economics series appears to have a substantial upward bias. For all these reasons we have preferred the Bureau of the Census revision to the Shaw-Hopkins series, and have used the latter only for purposes of interpolation.[24]

[23] For the manner in which an undercount of farms may lead to an undercount of farmers, see J. D. Black and R. H. Allen, "The Counting of Farms in the United States," *Journal of the American Statistical Association*, Vol. 32 (Sept. 1937), pp. 444-45.

[24] In the present study we have used the Bureau of Agricultural Economics employment series (Table 35) only as a means of interpolating the Bureau of the Census estimates (Table 31): see Tables 37, 38 and 45 below.

SUMMARY

Data on agricultural employment have to be derived from the number of persons reported by the Census of Population as occupied in agriculture. Because of variations of interpretation by Census enumerators, it is extremely difficult to estimate reliably the trend of agricultural employment even over a period as long as forty years. The following outline probably embodies all that can be said with any sense of security; the movements are summarized in Table 36 below.

After 1900 numbers gainfully occupied appear to have increased for about a decade, and to have reached a maximum at a level some 5 or 10 percent above that at the opening of the century. Thereafter this total declined fairly steadily: in 1930 it was about the same as, or slightly below, the figure for 1900. In 1940 persons gainfully occupied in agriculture were substantially less numerous than at the opening of the century. While the proportion of women workers did not vary greatly, these movements in the occupied population as a whole conceal a sharp decline in the relative importance of child labor.[25] The number of children occupied in 1930 was about half the number occupied in 1900.

Difficulties in the statistical treatment of women and children engaged in agriculture make it convenient to use the number of farmers plus adult male laborers as an alternative measure of agricultural employment. Because of the decline in the importance of child labor just noted, this alternative series rises by somewhat more than 10 percent between 1900 and 1910, and thereafter remains approximately stable. Both series will be used for the survey of agricultural productivity in Chapter 7.

The comparative mildness of the changes in the agricultural working population did not prevent a steady decline in the

[25] The entire occupied population includes persons 10 years of age and over: the Census defines a child as aged 10 to 15 inclusive.

TABLE 36

INDEXES OF AGRICULTURAL EMPLOYMENT, 1900–40

Year	*Gainfully Occupied, 10 Years and Over*[a]	*Farmers and Adult Male Laborers*[b]	*Gainfully Occupied in Agriculture as Percent of Gainfully Occupied, All Occupations*[c]
	(1900: 100)		
1900	100	100	37.5
1910	106.2	111.8	31.0
1920	104.9	113.4	27.0
1930	96.0[d]	109.8	21.4
1940	84.0	..	17.6

[a] Based on data in Table 31.
[b] Based on data in Table 33.
[c] Bureau of the Census releases of October 23, 1938 and March 28, 1942.
[d] May be an underestimate, owing to omission of workers on some small farms. See text.

relative importance of agriculture among occupations in general; this decline reflects, of course, the rapid rise—from 29 million in 1900 to 52 million in 1940—of the occupied population as a whole. To the general question of the position of agriculture in the national economy, and its prospects as a source of livelihood, we shall return in Chapter 8.

Chapter 7

Agricultural Productivity

THE productivity of an industry may be defined as the ratio of its output to its input. This formula is not as simple as it sounds, for meanings have to be given to both output and input, and specifications for their measurement provided. To a large extent the resulting measure of productivity will depend upon the concepts chosen. Of the two definitions required, that for output offers the least difficulty, and in fact has already been treated at length.[1] So far as possible in measuring output we have excluded the products used by farmers themselves for purposes of seed and feed, but have included agricultural commodities consumed by farm families. We have then combined the physical output of different commodities, using farm prices as weights, to yield indexes for groups as well as for agricultural output as a whole.

No such comprehensive measure will be offered here for agricultural input, which consists of labor, materials (e.g., fertilizer and feed), and the services of land and equipment. Quantities so diverse cannot readily be combined into a single physical measure, and satisfactory statistics for several of them are lacking. If, on the other hand, we relate output in turn to each kind of measurable input, we obtain indexes of productivity which have a definite meaning; but we are debarred at the same time from constructing any single index that could be treated as a *unique* measure of agricultural productivity. Such partial indexes can, however, be put to useful service, and several will be considered in this chapter.

[1] See above, pp. 12-14.

OUTPUT PER WORKER

The most interesting among the productivity concepts are probably those which relate output to the corresponding input of labor. Now labor input can be calculated in terms either of numbers employed, or of hours worked. Since each procedure has its peculiar advantages, we shall confine our attention to the former in the present section, and turn in the one to follow to an examination of data on hours worked in agriculture.

The most comprehensive measure of the agricultural labor force at our disposal is the number of persons gainfully occupied, a quantity which, though not identical with employment, serves as the nearest approximation we can make to the latter in the realm of agriculture. Persons occupied in agriculture are those who so report themselves in the Census of Population; they include farmers and laborers (family and hired), whether or not they were actually employed on the date when the enumerator called. The estimation of numbers occupied in Census years was discussed in Chapter 6 above. For convenience the data shown there (Table 36) may be roughly converted to an annual basis with the help of the Agricultural Marketing Service series for annual employment shown in Table 35. The resulting indexes of labor input and of output per worker are compared on a 1924–29 base in Table 37 with similar data compiled by the National Research Project. It will be recalled that the constituents of the NRP production series are weighted by direct labor requirements instead of by value, and that the NRP employment series pays somewhat less attention than does our own to the variation in Census instructions. In spite of these differences, the results of the two calculations agree closely. According to our own index, output per worker increased somewhat more rapidly than it did according to the NRP figures.

Both productivity indexes—our own and that of the National Research Project—shown in Table 37 are based upon estimates of the number of gainfully occupied persons 10 years of age and over. They are, therefore, open to objection, not only because they measure numbers engaged rather than employment, but for other reasons also. In the first place, as we saw in Chapter 6, these totals are somewhat precarious, since it is a difficult matter to allow for variations in Census instructions. That is to say, the coverage of the original Census totals varies markedly from one Census to

TABLE 37

INDEXES OF PRODUCTION, EMPLOYMENT AND OUTPUT PER WORKER SINCE 1909

1924–29:100

Period	*National Bureau of Economic Research*			*National Research Project*[c]		
	Production[a]	Employment[b]	Output per Worker	Production	Employment	Output per Worker
1909–13	82	106	77	86	106	81
1917–21	88	104	84	90	100	90
1922–26	96	102	94	96	101	97
1927–31	102	97	105	102	99	104
1932–36	94	92	103	93	97	96
1937–38	107	88	122	110	95	116

[a] Derived from Table 6; data are averages for years shown.
[b] Total gainfully occupied; based on data underlying Table 38 below, col. 2.
[c] J. A. Hopkins, *Changing Technology and Employment in Agriculture* (U. S. Bureau of Agricultural Economics, 1941), Table 63.

another, and we have no assurance that the correction we have chosen to apply on this account is appropriate. In the second place, even if the trend in our figures for gainfully occupied can be considered reliable, the figures clearly take no account of the changing composition of the agricultural labor force, and especially of the decline in the proportion of child workers and the increase in the proportion of adult males since the beginning of the century. It will be recalled that to meet this difficulty we have developed a series for the number of farmers plus adult male laborers. This second measure of the labor force suffers from a much smaller degree of uncertainty as to its coverage; but it neglects entirely the work performed by children, and also by women. The main reason for excluding both these categories from the alternative series presented here is to eliminate the uncertainty arising from changing Census instructions. In addition, the purpose of excluding child workers is to avoid the assumption, implicit in the former series, that the substitution of an adult male for a child leaves the labor force unaltered; to a minor degree this is also the reason for the exclusion of women, although their relative importance has not changed greatly since 1900. The second series, for farmers plus adult male laborers, therefore measures more accurately what it sets out to measure, and also represents a much more homogeneous quantity, than does the first employment series considered, i.e., for the total gainfully occupied. Like the first series, the second may be converted roughly to an annual basis with the help of the Agricultural Marketing Service employment series (Table 35).

Since year-to-year variations in our output index are mainly reflections of changes in the weather, it is best, in measuring productivity, to reduce this index to a 5-year average basis; in this manner it is shown for 1900 and annually for 1909 and following years in the first column of Table 38, the initial year being treated as the base. For the sake of comparability our two employment series, for gainfully occupied and for farmers and adult males, have also been reduced to 5-year averages, appearing in columns 2 and 3 of the same table. Because of the decline in the number of child workers (Table 32), the latter is at the same level at the end of the period as at the beginning, whereas the former shows a sizable decline over the four decades considered. These two series for labor input may be employed to indicate a trend in agricultural productivity. Thus, if we divide column 1 by columns 2 and 3, we obtain as A and B respectively in columns 4 and 5

TABLE 38

OUTPUT PER WORKER, FIVE-YEAR AVERAGES, 1900–38

1900:100

Year	*Output*	*Employment*[c]		*Output per Worker*	
		Gainfully Occupied	Farmers and Adult Male Laborers[d]	A Gainfully Occupied	B Farmers and Adult Male Laborers[d]
	(1)	(2)	(3)	(4)	(5)
1900	100	100[a]	100[a]	100	100
1909	112	107[a]	112[a]	105	100
1910	115	106[b]	112[b]	108	103
1911	116	106	112	109	103
1912	120	107	113	112	106
1913	123	107	113	115	108
1914	123	107	114	115	108
1915	123	108	115	114	107
1916	125	107	114	117	110
1917	125	106	113	118	110
1918	125	105	113	118	110
1919	124	104	113	119	110
1920	126	104	112	121	112
1921	126	104	113	122	112
1922	128	104	113	124	113
1923	130	103	113	126	115
1924	136	103	113	132	120
1925	138	102	113	136	122
1926	141	101	112	140	125
1927	142	100	112	143	127
1928	144	99	111	146	129
1929	144	97	110	149	131
1930	145	96	110	151	132
1931	144	95	109	151	132
1932	139	94	107	148	130
1933	136	93	106	147	129
1934	133	92	105	145	127
1935	135	91	104	149	130
1936	137	90	103	153	134
1937	145	89	102	164	143
1938	154[b]	87	100	176	154

[a] Actual figure for year shown.

[b] Three-year average centered on year shown.

[c] Derived from Table 36, with total employment in Table 35 used for interpolation.

[d] Data for estimating farmers and adult male laborers from the Census of 1940 are not yet available; for years after 1930 this series is computed on the basis of the preceding column.

two alternative measures of output per worker. It will be seen that series A, based on the gainfully occupied population, rises more rapidly than series B, based on farmers plus adult males. This is to be expected, for numbers occupied decline, while farmers and adult males do not change over

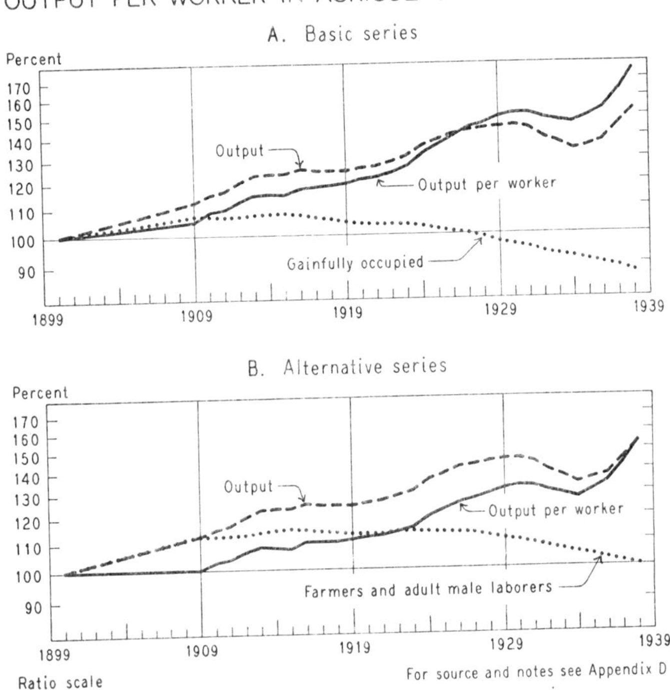

the period. Between 1900 and 1930 series A rises at a rate of somewhat over 1.5 percent per annum; while series B increases at about 1 percent per annum. After 1930 the decline in output caused by depression, drought and the Agricultural Adjustment program leads to a fall in both indexes of productivity, followed by a recovery in very recent years. In the case of both indexes the most rapid increases occur between 1922 and 1930, and during the last few years of the period.

Before we conclude our discussion of changes in output per worker, we may briefly sketch the outlines of a somewhat broader picture. The Department of Agriculture has published indexes of agricultural production which run back to

TABLE 39

OUTPUT PER WORKER, 1870–1940

1870:100

Year	*Output*[a]	*Employment*[b]	*Output per Worker*	*Percentage Change in Output per Worker in Each Decade*
1870	100	100	100	
				+20
1880	150	125	120	
				+ 9
1890	189	145	130	
				+15
1900	238	159	149	
				+ 8
1910	273	169	162	
				+11
1920	299	167	179	
				+26
1930	345	153	225	
				+26
1940	379	134	284	
			Mean:	+16

[a] For 1870 and 1940, 3-year averages centered on year indicated. For other years, 5-year averages, similarly centered. Data for 1900 through 1930 are derived from NBER index, Table 6. For years before 1900 the extrapolation is based upon the arithmetic index computed by Frederick Strauss and L. H. Bean, *Gross Farm Income and Indices of Farm Production and Prices in the United States, 1869–1937,* Technical Bulletin 703 (U. S. Department of Agriculture, 1940), Table 58. For 1940 the extrapolation is based upon the Bureau of Agricultural Economics index of agricultural production; see *The Farm Income Situation* (U. S. Bureau of Agricultural Economics, Nov. 1941), p. 10.

[b] Numbers occupied in farming as shown in U. S. Bureau of the Census, "Trends in the Proportion of the Nation's Labor Force Engaged in Agriculture: 1820 to 1940" (Press release, March 28, 1942).

1869; and since our own calculations were completed, data for 1940 and (in preliminary form) for 1941 have become available. Moreover estimates of the numbers occupied in agriculture have been made for all Census years since 1870. The indexes in Table 39, which are obtained by extrapolating the series shown in columns 1, 2 and 4 of Table 38, touch a somewhat lower level of accuracy than the material so far considered in this chapter, but they extend over a much longer period. They suggest that the increase in the effectiveness of labor engaged in farming has been continuous, but that it has varied considerably in magnitude from one decade to another. To attempt to relate differences in the rates of growth in different decades to variations in the rate of technical change is tempting. However, the margin of uncertainty surrounding the comparison of employment data drawn from successive Censuses of Population—a topic discussed at length in the preceding chapter—would make such an undertaking hazardous. Similarly, the much more rapid growth in output per worker during the last two decades of the period than in earlier decades invites comment. Here again the explanation may be statistical rather than economic or technological in character. We have already seen that the proportion of women and children in the labor force has declined rather sharply in recent decades, and this fact is responsible, in part at least, for the high rates of growth in productivity reported for the period since 1920. With these summary reflections we leave the subject of output per worker and turn to a different approach to the problem.

DIRECT LABOR REQUIREMENTS

How has the rise in productivity been distributed between different types of agricultural enterprise? This question can be answered only approximately. Despite much regional specialization, very few areas are devoted exclusively to the production of a single crop. For example, although we may speak of the "corn area" or the "cotton area," [2] these regions produce a great deal besides corn and cotton, respectively. Nor do the dairy areas produce only dairy products. The prevalence of "mixed farming" makes it impossible to impute the output of a particular product to a given set of workers. On this account the distribution of changes in agricultural productivity must be studied from an altogether different standpoint. The discussion now to be undertaken differs from that of the preceding section in two important respects. In the present section we shall consider only a few staple products and we shall be concerned with their gross rather than with their net output.

The input of labor, on any farm producing more than one crop or type of livestock, may be divided roughly into two parts, according to whether it can or cannot be imputed to the output of a particular product. Thus the labor involved in plowing, seeding, cultivating and harvesting corn is to be charged to the corn crop alone, since it does nothing to further the production of wheat. Labor that can be allocated in this fashion to the output of a particular product may be compared in a general way to the prime cost of operating a manufacturing enterprise. Such amounts, when measurable, are termed the "direct labor requirements" for the crop or kind of livestock under consideration. Perhaps half the total labor on the average farm can be imputed to some individual product in this manner. The remainder may be termed "indirect labor," and may be compared to "overhead cost" in manufacturing, for while it contributes to the production of the farm as a whole, it cannot be imputed to particular portions of the output. Such labor includes the maintenance of machinery, the care of work animals and of farm structures, fencing, drainage, and so forth.

[2] For the definition of these and other areas, see note a to Table 40 below.

Unlike the number of workers employed, which is the subject of Census inquiry, the amounts of indirect labor, and of direct labor on different crops, can be derived for agriculture as a whole only by an elaborate process of estimation. The basic materials for this purpose are output, or acreage and numbers of livestock, on the one hand, and sample data for hours required for different operations, on the other. We shall first consider the data on direct labor requirements for various products collected by the National Research Project.[3] These can be expressed in hours per unit of product, but since crop yields per acre have not changed markedly,[4] it is more convenient and only slightly less accurate to treat hours per acre. In the case of livestock we use hours per head or per thousand pounds, an arrangement which makes no allowance, however, for the increase in milk production per cow or egg production per chicken. The National Research Project data on hours per acre for five major crops and three kinds of livestock, and for truck crops, are summarized in Table 40. These products account together for about four fifths of the direct labor used by American agriculture.[5] The data in Table 40 are shown in the form of annual averages for the periods 1909–13 and 1932–36 respectively. While events before 1909 are of interest to us, no such systematic analysis of direct labor is available prior to that year: in this section therefore we shall confine attention to the period since 1909.

The figures of principal interest in Table 40 are the averages for the United States, but the areas reporting highest and lowest hours per unit respectively also are shown for

[3] The detailed data and sources will be found in individual reports prepared by the Project; they are conveniently summarized for five major crops, three kinds of livestock, and fifteen truck crops by J. A. Hopkins, *Changing Technology and Employment in Agriculture* (U. S. Bureau of Agricultural Economics, 1941), Ch. VIII, from which source Tables 40 and 41 are mainly taken.

[4] See, however, pp. 278-86 below.

[5] Hopkins, *op. cit.*, Table 54.

each period. It is evident that the regional dispersion of the data on which the averages are based is very considerable: for example, in the eastern dairy area corn requires four times as many hours per acre as it does in the small grain area.[6] This dispersion must in some degree reduce the reliability of the United States averages. Nevertheless, the changes reported over the twenty-five year period are for the most part so large that their direction and significance are scarcely affected by doubts of this nature. For each of the five major crops very marked reductions are reported in manhours per acre, ranging from 15 percent for corn and potatoes to 46 percent for wheat. This last result accords with the rapid mechanization of wheat production noted in Chapter 5. In the case of corn and potatoes the rather moderate declines in labor input per acre are probably a reflection of the greater difficulties encountered in the mechanization of these crops. Curiously enough, the largest absolute reduction in the United States average apparently occurred in the case of cotton, a crop which has perhaps resisted mechanization more than any other; in this instance, however, regional shifts in acreage were an important influence upon labor requirements. Thus the western cotton area, with hours per acre about half the level in other regions, increased the number of acres planted to cotton from 12.4 million in 1907–11 to 13.4 million in 1933–36; while over the same period the combined acreage of the other chief cotton producing areas (eastern, Delta and middle eastern) declined from 19.0 to 14.0 million.[7] This shift was responsible for a large part of the reduction in aver-

[6] In the latter area corn is cut primarily for grain, whereas in the former it is predominantly a silage crop. That this difference is responsible only in part for the regional variation in hours per acre is suggested by the very wide dispersion even among crops harvested exclusively for grain: in the eastern dairy area for the second period oats require six times as many hours per acre as they do in California.

[7] For the regional coverage of these areas, see note a to Table 40. Acreages quoted are from Hopkins, *op. cit.,* Table 43; see also W. C. Holley and L. E. Arnold, *Cotton* (National Research Project, Philadelphia, 1938), Table A-1.

TABLE 40

ANALYSIS OF CHANGE IN HOURS PER ACRE OR PER UNIT OF LIVESTOCK[a]

	Hours per Acre or per Unit of Livestock, 1909–13					Hours per Acre or per Unit of Livestock, 1932–36					Change in U. S. Average		Change in Hours Associated with:	
	Regional Averages— Highest		Regional Averages— Lowest		U. S. Average	Regional Averages— Highest		Regional Averages— Lowest		U. S. Average				
	Area	Hours	Area	Hours	Hours	Area	Hours	Area	Hours	Hours	Hours	Percent	Change in Hours per Unit[f]	Regional Shifts[f]
Corn	Eastern dairy	59.4	Small grain	12.9	28.7	Eastern dairy	46.2	Small grain	10.0	24.4	− 4.3	−15	− 5.1	+ .8
Wheat	Eastern dairy	22.7	North-western	9.4	12.7	Eastern dairy	17.2	Cali-fornia	3.2	6.8	− 5.8	−46	− 5.0	− .8
Oats	Eastern dairy	25.1	Small grain	8.8	12.5	Eastern dairy	16.7	Cali-fornia	2.8	8.6	− 3.9	−31	− 4.3	+ .4
Cotton	Middle eastern	139	Western cotton	70	105.3	Middle eastern	130	Western cotton	50	87.6	−17.6	−17	−11.4	−6.2
Potatoes[b]	Pa., N.Y., Me.	102	N.J., Va.	78	89.1	Pa., N.Y., Me.	94	Minn., Wis., Mich., N.J., Va.	65	75.8	−13.2	−15	−11.9	−1.4
Milk cows[c]	Middle eastern	175	Small grain	106	135.1	Middle eastern	174	Small grain	116	139.6	+ 4.5	+ 3	+ 5.0	− .3
Chickens[d]		..		..	..	Middle eastern	2.5	Western cotton, Calif.	1.9	2.15	..	..	..	..
Hogs[e]	Middle eastern	76.6	Corn	26.8	44.8	Middle eastern	77.6	Corn	25.3	42.1	− 2.7	− 6	− .8	−1.9
Truck crops		..		..	..	Range	145	Western dairy	61	113	..	..	..	..

[a] These data, derived by the National Research Project from a wide variety of published and unpublished sources, are taken from J. A. Hopkins, *Changing Technology and Employment in Agriculture* (U. S. Bureau of Agricultural Economics, 1941), Ch. VIII. The two areas reporting the largest and smallest estimated average number of hours per unit, respectively, for each product are shown separately in order to provide some indication of the very considerable dispersion of the averages for different areas about the U. S. averages. In computing U. S. averages for corn, wheat and oats for 1932–36, it is convenient, because of the effects of drought and of the Agricultural Adjustment program, to employ acreages for years more normal than those specified. The U. S. averages for these crops given by Hopkins for 1932–36 are based on annual average acreages for 1927–31; we have preferred to use acreage data for 1937–39, and this accounts for slight differences between the U. S. averages for these crops quoted here for 1932–36 and those given by Hopkins. Data for chickens and for truck crops are not available for the earlier period.

The data for hours per acre or per unit shown in the table for the earlier period relate to 1907–11 in the case of cotton; and for the later period relate to 1934–36 in the case of wheat, oats and potatoes, to 1933–36 in the case of cotton, and to 1933–35 in the case of chickens.

The regional classification underlying the NRP study is as follows:

Corn area: Illinois, Indiana, Iowa, Ohio.
Eastern dairy area: Connecticut, Massachusetts, New Hampshire, New York, Pennsylvania, Vermont.
Western dairy area: Michigan, Minnesota, Wisconsin.
Eastern cotton area: Alabama, Georgia, South Carolina.
Delta cotton area: Arkansas, Louisiana, Mississippi.
Western cotton area: Oklahoma, Texas.
Small grain area: Kansas, Montana, Nebraska, North Dakota, South Dakota.
Middle eastern area: Kentucky, Maryland, North Carolina, Tennessee, Virginia, West Virginia.
Range area: Arizona, Colorado, Nevada, New Mexico, Utah, Wyoming.
Northwestern area: Idaho, Oregon, Washington.
California area: California.

Six states are excluded from this classification, but figures for them are included in U. S. totals: Maine, Rhode Island, New Jersey, Delaware, Florida, Missouri.

[b] Data are available only for three regions (which do not correspond to the areas used elsewhere in the NRP study): Minnesota, Wisconsin and Michigan; Pennsylvania, New York and Maine; and New Jersey and Virginia.

[c] Hours per milk cow; no allowance is made for labor on calves, heifers or bulls. The estimates include the labor used in caring for the cows, milking, cooling, separating and hauling, feeding the cows, cleaning stables, and all work expended directly in producing milk and cream; they do not include labor used in growing feed; see R. B. Elwood, A. A. Lewis and R. A. Struble, *Dairying*, National Research Project Report A-14 (U. S. Department of Agriculture, 1941), p. 69.

[d] Hours per chicken.

[e] Hours per thousand pounds of hogs.

[f] The part of the change associated with a change in hours per unit is

$$\frac{\Sigma\,(x_2 - x_1)\,y_1}{\Sigma y_1},$$

where x denotes the hours per unit, y the number of units (acres, head of livestock, etc.), suffixes the first and second period respectively, and Σ summation over all areas. The part associated with regional shifts is

$$\frac{\Sigma x_2\left(\frac{y_2}{p} - y_1\right)}{\Sigma y_1}, \text{ where } p = \frac{\Sigma y_2}{\Sigma y_1}.$$

These results have been rounded and therefore do not agree exactly with the aggregate changes in the United States averages reported in a preceding column.

age United States hours per cotton acre. As may be seen from Table 40, regional shifts in acreage were not an important influence in reducing hours per acre for the other four crops: indeed in the case of corn and oats there appears actually to have been a slight tendency for production to move in the reverse direction, i.e., from areas with low labor requirements per acre to those with high.

The regional dispersion of unit labor input is also substantial in the case of livestock, but the trend in the United States averages is in marked contrast to that shown for crops. For chickens we have no data for the earlier period, but for milk cows and for hogs the level of direct labor requirements per unit in 1932–36 was practically the same as it had been a quarter of a century earlier.

While the small increase (3 percent) shown in the table for hours per cow may not be statistically significant, it allows us to say with confidence that no substantial decline has occurred.[8] At first sight this result is surprising. Although mechanical improvements in dairying have been slight in comparison with similar improvements in crop production, we might expect the introduction of milking machines and mechanical transportation to have had some influence upon labor requirements. In fact the amount of labor necessary in caring for milk cows depends to a large extent upon the forms in which milk is sold or otherwise distributed. The two outlets for milk which require the largest amounts of farm labor are butter production upon the farm itself and retail sales of milk and cream by the farmer. Milk fed to calves or sold through wholesale channels involves considerably less labor. The percentage of total milk production used for farm butter (including butter consumed in farm house-

[8] Since milk production per cow increased about 11 percent between 1909–13 and 1932–36 hours per pound of milk declined in spite of the apparent rise in hours per cow. See R. B. Elwood, A. A. Lewis and R. A. Struble, *Dairying*, National Research Project Report A-14 (U. S. Department of Agriculture, 1941), Table 15; also Table 50 below.

holds) declined from 31 in 1909–13 to 11 in 1932–36.[9] It is fairly certain that the fraction retailed by farmers themselves has also declined over the period.[10] On both these grounds also we should expect a decline to have occurred in average hours per cow. Nor can the absence of such a decline be explained by a shift from areas with low labor requirements to areas with high: if anything, the trend disclosed in Table 40 has been in the reverse direction.

There can be little doubt that the principal factor tending to maintain the level of hours per cow has been the increasing stringency of sanitary regulation. During the past twenty years states and municipalities have, with the encouragement of the U. S. Public Health Service, made great efforts to raise the quality of dairy products, and especially of liquid milk for human consumption. The resulting improvement has been widespread and extensive, and has obscured any decline that might otherwise have appeared in hours per cow.[11]

For truck crops satisfactory data are not available for the period 1909–13, but we may notice that between 1918–21 and 1932–36 hours per acre declined from 145 to 135 in the case of vegetables for market, and from 80 to 65 in the case of vegetables for processing.[12] The trend in labor requirements per acre for truck crops therefore appears to have been similar to that disclosed for the five major crops mentioned.

In analyzing direct labor input we have so far confined ourselves to a discussion of hours per acre or per unit of livestock. The data on which Table 40 is based allow us also to examine the trend in aggregate consumption of direct labor by each of

[9] E. E. Vial, *Production and Consumption of Manufactured Dairy Products,* Technical Bulletin 722 (U. S. Department of Agriculture, 1940), Table 5; U. S. Agricultural Marketing Service, *Farm Production, Disposition and Income from Milk, 1924–40, by States* (Washington, 1941), Table 2.

[10] See below, Appendix Table A-1, footnote 73.

[11] See especially Elwood, Lewis and Struble, *op. cit.,* pp. 61-67.

[12] Hopkins, *Changing Technology and Employment in Agriculture,* Table 45.

the major types of agricultural activity there listed. The change in this aggregate consumption is of course compounded of changes in hours per unit of the kind just discussed together with changes in the number of units (acres or amounts of livestock). For the earlier period contemporary acreages can conveniently be used, but acreages of corn, wheat and oats harvested in 1932–36 were severely reduced by drought and by the Agricultural Adjustment program. In order to obtain representative figures for aggregate labor requirements in the later period for these crops, we have used average acreages for the crop years 1937–39. The data for acreages and amounts of livestock are summarized in Table 41.

By multiplying acreages and livestock quantities, for each product and region, by corresponding labor requirements of the kind shown in Table 40 total direct labor requirements for each product may be built up. The results of this calculation are shown in Table 42. It will be seen that in the case of each of the five crops for which data appear, a substantial reduction took place in estimated total manhours required for direct labor—a reduction ranging from 35 percent for oats to 22 percent for potatoes. In Table 42 the change shown in column 3 is broken down in columns 5, 6 and 7 into three parts associated with the reduction in manhours per acre, with regional shifts in acreage between farming areas, and with the change in total United States acreage of each crop, respectively. For all crops except cotton more than half of the reduction in direct labor requirements is accounted for by the reduction in hours per acre reported in summary form in Table 40. For cotton, however, more than half the total saving in direct labor can be traced either to the over-all reduction in cotton acreage (Table 41), or to the shift in acreage from the older cotton areas toward Texas and Oklahoma where hours per acre are relatively low. In none of the other four crops did regional shifts apparently affect aggregate labor requirements in an important degree; however, reduction in total acreage led in the case of corn to a sizable decline in the amount of labor used for that crop. There were also reductions of acreage, for the United States as a whole, in oats and potatoes; but the wheat acreage was actually higher in 1937–39 than in 1909–13 (Table 41), although the increase

TABLE 41
SUMMARY OF CHANGES IN ACREAGE AND LIVESTOCK UNITS[a]

Product	*Unit of Measure*	*Period*[b]	*Annual Average*	*Period*[b]	*Annual Average*	*Percentage Change*
		(1)	(2)	(3)	(4)	(5)
Corn	mil. acres	1909–13	101.0	1937–39	91.5	− 9.4
Wheat	mil. acres	1909–13	48.1	1937–39	62.6	+30.2
Oats	mil. acres	1909–13	36.7	1937–39	34.6	− 5.7
Cotton	mil. acres	1907–11	31.8	1933–36	28.4	−10.5
Potatoes	mil. acres	1909–13	1.82	1934–36	1.68	− 7.7
Milk cows	million	1909–13	17.3	1932–36	24.2	+39.7
Chickens	million	1910	336	1932–36	420	+25.0
Hogs	bil. pounds	1909–13	11.9	1932–36	13.7	+14.7
Truck crops	mil. acres	1909–13	[c]	1932–36	3.49	[c]

[a] With the exception of the corn, wheat and oats acreages for 1937–39, all data in this table are taken from J. A. Hopkins, *Changing Technology and Employment in Agriculture* (U. S. Bureau of Agricultural Economics, 1941), Ch. VIII. The former are from *Crops and Markets,* Dec. 1940.
[b] For crops, crop years; for livestock, calendar years.
[c] Not available.

was insufficient to offset a decline in total labor requirements for other reasons (Table 42). For the five crops taken together the 25 percent decline in total labor requirements appears to have resulted from reduction in hours per acre (about two thirds), from over-all reduction in acreage (about one quarter), and from shifts from areas requiring many, to areas requiring few, hours per acre (the small remainder).

There can be little doubt that the substantial reductions observed in hours per acre have been due in the main to mechanization of the types sketched in Chapter 5. To say more is not easy, but we can perhaps suggest the extent to

TABLE 42

ANALYSIS OF CHANGE IN DIRECT LABOR REQUIREMENTS FOR MAJOR PRODUCTS[a]

Product	*Average Annual Requirements*				*Change in Requirements Associated with*		
	Approximate Period 1907–13	1932–39	Absolute Change	Percentage Change	Change in Manhours per Acre or per Unit of Livestock[g]	Regional Shifts in Acreage or Livestock[g]	Change in Aggregate Acreage or Livestock[g]
	(1)	(2)	(3)	(4)	(5)	(6)	(7)
	(million manhours)				(million manhours)		
Corn	2,898	2,231	−667	−23.0	−512	+78	−233
Wheat	609	429	−180	−29.6	−240	−39	+99
Oats	458	297	−161	−35.2	−157	+14	−20
Cotton	3,343	2,489	−854	−25.5	−364	−196	−294
Potatoes	162	127	−35	−21.6	−21	−3	−11
Total, major crops	7,470	5,573	−1,897	−25.4	−1,294	−146	−459
Milk cows[b]	2,551	3,679	+1,128	+44.2	+93	−7	+1,041
Chickens[c]	722	903	+181	+25.1	0[c]	0	+181
Hogs	535	577	+42	+7.9	−10	−22	+74
Total, livestock	3,808	5,159	+1,351	+35.5	+83	−29	+1,296
Total, major crops and livestock	11,278	10,732	−546	−4.8	−1,211	−175	+837
Truck crops[d]	200	394	+194	+97.0	..	..	..
Total, major products	11,478[e]	11,126[f]	−352	−3.1	..	..	..

[a] The figures in this table are obtained by multiplying estimated hours per acre or per unit of livestock, by areas, by acreage harvested or amount of livestock maintained. With the exception of the corn, wheat and oats acreages for 1932–39, this table is based entirely upon data to be found in J. A. Hopkins, *Changing Technology and Employment in Agriculture* (U. S. Bureau of Agricultural Economics, 1941), Ch. VIII. The hours per acre and per livestock unit for each area are annual averages for the periods shown in Table 40. The acreages and livestock units for each area are annual averages for the periods shown in Table 41. The items (other than truck crops) in-

which the economy of labor has been associated with the adoption of gasoline power on the farm. The National Research Project has indicated that by 1935 the direct saving of labor in field operations through the adoption of the tractor must have been about 165 million hours per year.

> If it is assumed (conservatively) that there were 1.1 million tractors on farms in 1935, that they were operated on the average thirty 10-hour days per year, and that their use resulted in an average increase in effective capacity of 50 percent per operator over the units replaced, the reduction in labor requirements would have amounted to 150 manhours per tractor, or a total of 165 million manhours.[13]

[13] E. G. McKibben and R. A. Griffin, *Tractors, Trucks and Automobiles* (National Research Project, Philadelphia, 1938), p. 36.

---

cluded in this table accounted in 1924–29 for about 76 percent of the gross product of the agriculture of the United States (*ibid.*, Table 54).

[b] Includes labor expended on raising calves and heifers and on the care of bulls; *ibid.*, Table 47.

[c] No data are available on the change in hours per chicken between 1910 and 1933–35, and the labor requirements for this product are therefore computed by using the 1933–35 data for both periods.

[d] Data for hours per acre on truck crops are not available by areas for the earlier period.

[e] This total differs slightly from that provided by Hopkins (11,486 million hours; *ibid.*, Table 54) because we have used the data for cows given by him in Table 47; these data do not check exactly with the summary figures in his Table 54.

[f] This total differs slightly from that given by Hopkins (11,128 million hours; *ibid.*, Table 54) owing to our use of acreage data for 1937–39 instead of 1927–31 in the case of corn, wheat and oats.

[g] The part of the change associated with a change in hours per unit (summed over all areas) is

$$\Sigma y_1(x_2 - x_1),$$

where x denotes the hours per unit, y the number of units (acres, head of livestock, etc.), and the suffixes the first and second periods respectively. The part associated with regional shifts is

$$\Sigma x_2 \left(\frac{y_2}{p} - y_1\right),$$

where $p = \frac{\Sigma y_2}{\Sigma y_1}$. The part associated with the change in acreage or units of livestock is $\frac{p-1}{p}(\Sigma x_2 y_2)$.

Undoubtedly the five major crops, for which changes in labor requirements are analyzed in Table 42, are not the only ones to have benefited immediately from the spread of tractor cultivation. We may note, however, that the saving in direct labor associated with a reduction of hours per acre for these five crops amounted to about 1,300 million hours, or close to eight times the estimated direct savings attributable to the advent of the tractor for agriculture as a whole. It is probable, for this reason, that the large reductions in hours per acre have resulted directly from the tractor only to a minor degree, and are to be credited mainly to other influences, notably the improvement in agricultural implements. To the extent that these implements are too heavy or complicated to be used with horses, their very introduction may of course have been conditioned by the tractor. And in this sense a much more substantial fraction of the saving in hours per acre may be traceable to the advent and general adoption of tractor cultivation. Again, the substitution of the tractor for the horse has economized labor, also indirectly, through the decline in the demand for horse feed. To some extent such savings of labor have been offset by an increase in labor devoted to producing and distributing gasoline, but this aspect of the question is not relevant here. The saving of labor in the production of feed for horses has been estimated by the National Research Project at 380 million manhours, broken down as follows: [14]

	(million hours)
Corn	207
Oats	53
Hay	121
TOTAL	381

[14] *Ibid.*, p. 67. It is assumed that 28, 9 and 12 manhours were required per acre in 1936 for producing corn, oats and hay respectively; these rates are applied to the estimated reductions between 1909 and 1936 in acreage required for horse feed shown in *ibid.*, Table D-4. They make no allowance for saving in labor through the abandonment of 4½ million acres of pasture.

It will be seen that this estimate accounts for practically the whole reduction in labor requirements in corn cultivation, and in the case of oats for the entire reduction, associated with decreases in acreage, reported in Table 42.

In contrast to experience with the five major crops listed, the three principal kinds of livestock each absorbed more labor in the later than in the earlier period. For cows the increase was 44 percent, for chickens 25 percent,[15] and for hogs 8 percent. To a slight extent the increase in labor on cows is accounted for by an actual rise in hours per cow (Table 40). By far the most important source of the increase in total labor on cows, however, was the expansion in their number; the same is true of hogs, and probably also of chickens.

In the case of truck crops a sizable increase in total labor requirements is reported. The increment cannot, however, be imputed to various types of change as it can with the other products shown.

The combined result of these differing trends, for all the products indicated, is a net decline of about 3 percent in total hours worked. To summarize broadly: for major crops, a small decline in acreage and a large decline in hours per acre together cut total labor requirements by 25 percent; for livestock a large increase in numbers and a small increase in hours per head together raised labor requirements by 35 percent. Truck crops, which now consume more labor than either oats or potatoes and almost as much as wheat, doubled their combined labor input. Close to 2 billion manhours used annually for crop raising in 1907–13 were no longer needed for this purpose in 1932–39. More than two thirds of the labor so displaced was absorbed by the increasing de-

[15] The estimates are of course confined to chickens on farms. No data are available for hours per chicken in the earlier period, and this percentage is computed on the assumption that such hours underwent no change. Even if hours per chicken have in fact declined, it is highly unlikely that any reduction has been of sufficient magnitude to upset the conclusion that total hours on chickens increased over the quarter of a century considered.

mands of livestock production, and one tenth was transferred to the cultivation of truck crops; the remaining fifth of the labor displaced by major crops represented a net reduction in combined labor requirements for all the various products shown, a reduction equal to about 3 percent of the total.

TOTAL LABOR INPUT

In the preceding sections of this chapter we have approached the problem of measuring the labor input of agriculture from two altogether different angles: on the one hand, the use of numbers gainfully occupied as a reflection of total employment, and on the other, the examination of hours of direct labor required for the gross output of different products. At this point we are prompted to inquire whether there is any way in which we can integrate these two approaches.

The problem may be sketched in the following terms. Given total hours of direct labor for all products, and given also some measure of the hours spent for indirect or "overhead" labor, we could arrive at a figure for total annual labor input measured in hours. Dividing this by the number of workers, we should obtain as a result an estimate of the average number of hours worked per year per worker. This would be one possible procedure. As an alternative, given average hours worked per year and multiplying by employment, we could again estimate total annual labor input in hours. Deducting total hours of direct labor (which we can approximate), we should then obtain an estimate for the input of indirect labor. Unfortunately we have reliable information neither about the ratio of direct to indirect labor in agriculture, nor about the average number of hours worked on farms. It might seem the part of wisdom, therefore, to abandon the attempt to relate our data for numbers occupied to our data for direct labor required by specific products. Nevertheless, the question has seemed of sufficient interest to warrant a hypothetical calculation, wherein plausible assumptions must do duty where necessary for information that is not available.

In this highly tentative reconstruction, it seems best to begin with hours worked per year, for which scattered data have been summarized in Table 43. We know, for example, that average annual hours per worker are highest where livestock has to be cared for, i.e., in the corn and dairy areas; and lowest where there is little livestock but marked seasonal variation in the demand for labor on crops, i.e., in the cotton areas.[16] The evidence in Table 43 has been assembled from a large number of different studies, and the data are doubtless not fully comparable. It suggests that in spite of the probable increase in 1917–18, hours worked per year have been subject to a declining trend over the past thirty years and may perhaps have been significantly lower in 1932–36 than in 1909–13. This decline might well have been more pronounced were it not for the increased attention given to livestock in conformity with more stringent sanitary regulations.[17] Nevertheless, the decline in hours worked per year, when averaged over the entire occupied population (Chapter 6), must have been very slight, for two factors have operated to eliminate workers with very low hours per year. First, among those reported as gainfully occupied a marked decline has occurred in the proportion of children, who presumably work fewer hours per year than adults. Second, mechanization has caused a reduction in peak labor requirements at harvest time, thus probably eliminating some casual laborers, reported as occupied but working few hours per year. It is quite unlikely that the effects of these two factors are properly represented in the data of Table 43, which should be regarded rather as average hours worked by "full-time adults."

The considerations advanced in the preceding paragraph

[16] Hopkins, *Changing Technology and Employment in Agriculture,* p. 148.
[17] *Ibid.,* p. 26. See also p. 261 above.

Table 43

HOURS WORKED PER YEAR[a]

Region	Years	Type of Farm	Number of Cases	Annual Hours per Worker
Corn Area				
Northern Ohio	1923	General	17	3,283
Southern Ohio	1923	"	20	3,027
Marshall County, Iowa	1922–24	"	34	2,880
Shelby County, Iowa	1922–24	"	36	2,950
Iowa County, Iowa	1925–27	"	62	3,237
Hancock County, Ill.	1914–16	"	23	2,985
"	1920–22	"	26	3,162
Champaign-Piatt Counties, Ill.	1920–22	"	26	2,884
"	1923–27	"	58	2,847
"	1928–30	"	52	2,834
"	1931–35	"	112	2,754
Western Dairy Area				
Northfield, Minn.[b]	1905–12	"	64	3,453
Marshall, Minn.[b]	1905–11	"	41	3,311
Halstad, Minn.[b]	1905–12	"	58	3,410
Wisconsin	1922	Dairy	23	3,405
Northern Minnesota	1925	"	29	3,242
Southern Minnesota	1923	General	23	3,224
Eastern Dairy Area				
Seneca County, N. Y.	1919	Dairy	218	3,370
New York	1914–20	"	229	3,055
"	1921–25	"	156	3,138
"	1926–30	"	326	2,989
"	1931–35	"	396	2,981
Small Grain Area				
South Dakota	1925	Small grain	19	3,098
North Dakota	1925	"	22	3,076
Kansas	1925	"	21	3,273
Montana	1920	Irrigated crops	16	2,831
Range Area				
Colorado	1924	"	21	2,590
Middle Eastern Area				
North Carolina	1925	Tobacco and livestock	20	2,781
Western Cotton Area				
Texas	1925	Cotton	19	2,024
Other States				
Missouri	1912–14	General	28	3,020

[a] Except where otherwise stated, all data in this table are from J. A. Hopkins, *Changing Technology and Employment in Agriculture* (U. S. Bureau of Agricultural Economics, 1941), Table 14. The composition of the areas will be found in note a to Table 40.

[b] T. P. Cooper, F. W. Peck and Andrew Boss, *Labor Requirements of Crop Production,* Bulletin 157 (Minnesota Agricultural Experiment Station, 1916), Tables III and IX.

have suggested as a working basis the hours per year shown in Table 44. For the reasons given we may doubt whether there has been any actual decline in the averages if these could be computed for all occupied persons. We have therefore preferred to make alternative assumptions: (1) that hours per year were 5 percent higher in 1909–13 than in 1932–36; (2) that hours per year were the same in the earlier as in the later period. Next, we may estimate the average number of workers, by areas (Table 45). These figures lead, on the basis of

TABLE 44

ASSUMED AVERAGE ANNUAL HOURS PER WORKER GAINFULLY OCCUPIED, BY AREAS[a]

Area	*1909–13*		*1932–36*
	(1)	(2)	
Corn and dairy	3,150	3,000	3,000
Small grain	3,045	2,900	2,900
Cotton	2,205	2,100	2,100
Other	2,730	2,600	2,600

[a] These annual averages are roughly based on material in Table 43 and upon considerations advanced in the text. They are necessarily highly speculative and are intended only as rough approximations for use in the tentative reconstruction of total labor input undertaken on the following pages. For 1909–13 two alternative assumptions are made: estimate (1) implies that hours per year were 5 percent higher in 1909–13 than in 1932–36; estimate (2) assumes hours per year were the same in 1909–13 as in 1932–36.

TABLE 45

AVERAGE NUMBER OF WORKERS GAINFULLY OCCUPIED, BY AREAS[a]

Thousands

Area	*1909–13*	*1932–36*
Corn and dairy	3,339	2,635
Small grain	763	686
Cotton	4,129	3,540
Other	3,387	3,156
United States	11,619	10,017

[a] The data in this table are obtained by adjusting the series for total employment in Table 35 to conform to the level of the Census year estimates in the last line of Table 31. The required breakdown of the former series will be found in J. A. Hopkins, *Changing Technology and Employment in Agriculture* (U. S. Bureau of Agricultural Economics, 1941), Table 11.

the hypothetical annual hours per worker of Table 44, to tentative estimates for total labor input in manhours (Table 46). How much of these totals can we account for in terms of measurable direct labor requirements? The data on direct labor summarized in Table 42 cover only the products shown

TABLE 46

AVERAGE ANNUAL LABOR INPUT, BY AREAS[a]

Billion manhours

Area	*1909–13*		*1932–36*
	(1)	(2)	
Corn and dairy	10.5	10.0	7.9
Small grain	2.3	2.2	2.0
Cotton	9.1	8.7	7.4
Other	9.2	8.8	8.2
United States	31.2	29.7	25.5

Source: Tables 44 and 45.
[a] On basis of hours assumed in Table 44.

there—five major crops, three kinds of livestock, and truck crops. However, we have rough values for the percentages of major crops and livestock, in terms of direct labor requirements, to total agricultural production. Thus the coverage of the data in Table 42 (not including truck crops) ranges by areas from 32 percent in California to 86 percent in the Delta cotton area.[18] Taking the data in Table 42 by areas, and adjusting for coverage with the help of these percentages, we may obtain rough totals for direct labor on all products (Table 47).

The precarious nature of the results shown in Tables 46 and 47 has already been emphasized. Even the estimates for direct labor, which have been taken from studies by the National Research Project, are surrounded by a substantial margin of uncertainty. The figures for total labor input measured

[18] Hopkins, *op. cit.*, Table 54.

TABLE 47

DIRECT LABOR, AND ITS RATIO TO ANNUAL LABOR INPUT, BY AREAS[a]

Area	*1909–13* Average Annual Direct Labor	Percent of Average Annual Input[b]		*1932–36* Average Annual Direct Labor	Percent of Average Annual Input
	(billion manhours)	(1)	(2)	(billion manhours)	
Corn and dairy	4.7	45	47	4.9	62
Small grain	1.2	50	53	1.3	64
Cotton	5.3	58	61	4.3	57
Other	3.6	39	41	3.7	45
United States	14.8	48	50	14.1	55

[a] The estimates for direct labor are obtained by applying coverage adjustments, by areas, to the data in Table 42. The percentages are obtained by expressing these estimates for direct labor in terms of the figures for total labor input shown in Table 46.

[b] Estimate (1) assumes hours per year 5 percent greater in 1909–13 than in 1932–36; (2) assumes hours per year the same in 1909–13 as in 1932–36. See Table 46 above and discussion in text.

in manhours, although plausible enough, are in reality little more than guesswork. If, however, these results are even roughly correct, it would appear that while the input of direct labor (measured in hours) declined about 5 percent, total labor input (also measured in hours) fell by some 15 or 20 percent (Table 46). As a consequence, the share of direct labor in total labor input appears to have increased from about 50 to about 55 percent (Table 47). We have assumed that hours worked per year remained constant or declined; only if average annual hours per gainfully occupied worker actually rose between 1909–13 and 1932–36 could the conclusion reached be readily upset.

How is such a result to be interpreted? So far as crops are concerned, it is probable on a priori grounds that the considerable economy in direct labor suggested by Table 42 has been accompanied also by some savings of indirect labor, for it may be supposed that gasoline power units require less time for maintenance than do work animals. One estimate puts the reduction in overhead labor due to this cause at half a billion manhours.[19] On our assumptions the aggregate decline in overhead labor appears to have been much greater than this, and if estimate (1) is adopted, nine or ten times as great. Consequently there seem to have been other economies in overhead labor besides those attributable to the reduction in the burden of caring for work animals. Some of these no doubt arise indirectly from the introduction of gasoline power: trucking, for example, takes less time than animal transportation.

Although there has been a substantial reduction in direct labor on crops, the economy in direct labor as a whole has of course been very slight—apparently less than a billion manhours annually, or perhaps 5 percent. The explanation for this small saving is to be found in the fact that the substantial reduction in hours per acre in the case of staple crops has been largely offset by the growth in the importance of livestock and to a lesser extent of truck crops (Table 42). Consequently for agriculture as a whole the reduction we report for overhead labor is, over the quarter of a century considered, very much larger than the reduction in direct labor requirements. To summarize: for the United States as a whole, it seems fairly certain that direct labor has increased in importance relatively to total labor input, despite the sharp reductions which have occurred in hours per acre for practically all crops.

While the ratio of direct to total labor appears to have risen only moderately for the United States as a whole, it seems to have gone up rather sharply in the corn, dairy and

[19] E. G. McKibben and R. A. Griffin, *Tractors, Trucks and Automobiles* (National Research Project, Philadelphia, 1938), Sec. VI. The estimate quoted is built up as follows: economy in caring for work horses displaced, 280 million hours; in caring for horses retained, 160 million hours; and in growing young stock, 50 million hours.

small grain areas, and to have fallen slightly in the cotton areas. Because of the uncertainty concerning the assumptions underlying Table 47, these conclusions cannot be regarded as positively established, but they are at least suggestive, and it is worth while to inquire whether they are plausible. Changes in the ratio of direct to total labor appear to be associated with corresponding changes in the distribution of activity between crops and livestock. We presented in Table 42 evi-

TABLE 48

SHIFTS IN DIRECT LABOR, BY AREAS[a]

Million manhours

Area	*Five Major Crops*			*Livestock (Cattle, Hogs, Chickens)*		
	1909–13	1932–36	Change	1909–13	1932–36	Change
Corn and dairy	1,662	1,191	−471	1,848	2,420	+572
Small grain	524	299	−225	330	529	+199
Cotton	3,964	2,943	−1,021	541	759	+218
Other	1,320	1,139	−181	1,097	1,451	+354
United States	7,470	5,573	−1,897	3,816	5,159	+1,343

[a] The data shown in this table provide a partial breakdown of, and are derived in the same manner as, the material in Table 42 above; except for crops in 1932–36 they will be found in Hopkins, *op. cit.*, Table 54. The U. S. total for livestock in 1909–13 differs slightly from that shown in Table 42 above (3,808 million hours) because the latter is derived from Hopkins' Table 47: see footnote e to Table 42 above.

dence of a substantial shift in direct labor from crops toward livestock. In Table 48 this shift is broken down by areas. The decline in direct labor for crop production and the increased requirements for livestock apparently occurred in all four major regions shown in that table, but the incidence of the shift varied considerably. This variation is apparent from the percentages in Table 49, which gives the ratio of direct labor on crops to direct labor on crops and livestock in each region at the two dates. In both the corn and dairy areas and the small grain area, where the ratio of direct to total labor has risen appreciably, the shift appears to have been largest: the percentage of direct labor engaged in crop production declined by 14 and 25 percentage points respectively. In "other areas," where the ratio of direct to total labor seems to have increased only slightly, the shift from crops to livestock was apparently more moderate: labor on crops declined by 11

TABLE 49

PERCENTAGES OF DIRECT LABOR ENGAGED IN CROP PRODUCTION, BY AREAS[a]

Area	*1909–13*	*1932–36*
Corn and dairy	47	33
Small grain	61	36
Cotton	88	79
Other	55	44
United States	66	52

[a] Percentages shown in this table are computed from the data in Table 48, and cover five major crops and three livestock enterprises only.

percentage points. Finally in the cotton area, where the ratio of direct to total labor appears to have remained unchanged or to have fallen slightly, the shift from crops to livestock was comparatively slight: 9 points.

These results suggest that a shift toward livestock production tends to increase the ratio of direct to total labor. And if this is so, it might be thought that those areas (notably corn and dairy) where livestock is most important should show a higher value for this ratio than the areas (such as cotton) where comparatively little livestock is raised. In Table 47, however, either our measures are too rough, or the areas in question are too dissimilar in character for such a relationship to emerge at all clearly. True, the relative importance of direct labor in the corn and dairy areas had become, in 1932–36, greater than that in the cotton areas, but it was still no greater than in the small grain area.

It is nonetheless a plausible assumption that an increase in the relative importance of livestock production should raise the ratio of direct to total labor. For livestock must be tended, and must therefore absorb direct labor, all the year round; at the same time the demands of livestock upon machinery and work animals, whose maintenance requires overhead labor, are limited. Crops, on the other hand, require direct labor only at certain seasons of the year, but impose substantial demands for overhead labor for the maintenance of work animals and machinery. It seems probable that technological changes have reduced the direct labor requirements of crop production in larger measure than they have lessened the need for overhead labor: reductions in hours per acre for the five major crops have resulted in an economy of about a billion and a quarter hours of direct labor (Table 42), while the saving in overhead labor through the supersession of work animals by tractors has been put at only half a billion hours.[20] Presumably then, in the absence of a shift toward livestock production, there would have appeared a general fall in the ratio of direct to total labor for agriculture as a whole. The effect of the increased share of labor devoted to livestock may therefore be viewed as a factor which has more than outweighed the decline in the ratio of direct to total labor attributable to technological changes in crop production. In the corn and dairy areas the shift toward livestock appears to have been more than sufficient to offset this decline, and to have led to an actual increase in the relative importance of direct labor. In the cotton areas, on the other hand, factors making for a decline in the ratio of direct to total labor appear to have been in the ascendant; among these may be mentioned the migration of cotton production to Texas and Oklahoma where direct labor requirements per acre are much below those still prevailing in the older cotton areas.[21]

[20] See above, footnote 19.
[21] See above, p. 262.

YIELDS PER ACRE AND PER LIVESTOCK UNIT

It will be recalled that the discussion of labor requirements in the second section of this chapter was confined on grounds of convenience to a treatment of hours per acre and per livestock unit, and was limited to the period following 1909 because data on direct labor for earlier periods are lacking. We are more interested, however, in output of product than in acres cultivated, and the discussion in that section must now be supplemented by some consideration of the trend in yield per acre and per unit of livestock. Moreover, since much of the data is available for long periods of years we need not restrict ourselves here to the period since 1909.

Crop yields fluctuate with great violence from one year to another, and on this account the data in Table 50 and Chart 47 are shown in the form of 5-year averages. It will be seen from Table 50, which shows the trend in crop yields since the turn of the century, that few substantial changes have occurred. Most of what was said above concerning the trend in hours per acre holds also, therefore, for hours per physical unit of gross product. Yet there are some notable exceptions to this generalization, for marked increases have appeared, particularly in very recent years, in the yields of cotton and potatoes, and also of rice and tobacco—crops whose labor requirements were not treated separately above. In these cases, of course, hours of direct labor per bushel have fallen even more than hours per acre.

Crop yields are influenced by a wide variety of factors besides weather: particularly by the extent to which the application of fertilizer or of improved methods of cultivation offsets erosion and the natural exhaustion of the soil; by the development of new and more productive seed varieties; and by the appearance of fresh pests or improvements in the control of existing ones. Moreover, the United States averages quoted here may quite possibly conceal the effects of shifts

Table 50

CHANGES IN YIELD PER ACRE AND PER LIVESTOCK UNIT[a]

Averages for years indicated

Product	*Unit of Measure*	*1897–1901*	*1907–11*	*1917–21*	*1927–31*	*1937–40*
Major crops						
Corn	bushels	25.3	26.5	27.2	24.7	28.4
Wheat	bushels	13.8	14.0	13.4	14.7	14.0
Oats	bushels	29.2	26.1	30.5	29.8	31.7
Cotton	pounds	196	186	164	171	250
Potatoes	bushels	81	95	99	114	125
Other crops						
Barley	bushels	24.1	21.1	21.7	22.6	22.7
Rye	bushels	13.0	13.3	12.1	12.2	12.4
Buckwheat	bushels	16.1	17.2	16.0	15.1	15.5
Rice	bushels	27.0	36.5	38.4	45.4	49.9
Flaxseed	bushels	8.4	7.8	6.1	6.4	9.1
Tame hay	tons	1.27	1.27	1.30	1.31	1.37
Sweetpotatoes	bushels	84	95	96	90	85
Tobacco	pounds	784	827	785	771	927
Sugarcane[b]	tons	[d]	17.0[e]	15.4	14.9	20.5
Sugar beets	tons	[d]	[d]	9.5	11.1	12.3
Vegetables[c]	tons	[d]	[d]	4.0[f]	3.4	3.4
Livestock						
Milk	pounds per milk cow	[d]	3,779[e]	3,781	4,510	4,497
Eggs	per laying chicken	[d]	85[e]	88	93	102

[a] Acres refer to acreage harvested. Data are taken from *Agricultural Statistics, 1941.* For milk, additional data are from R. G. Bressler, Jr. and J. A. Hopkins, *Trends in Size and Production of the Aggregate Farm Enterprise, 1909–36* (National Research Project, Philadelphia, 1938), Tables A-95 and A-96. Data for vegetables from *Crops and Markets,* December 1940.

[b] Sugarcane for sugar and for seed.

[c] Asparagus, snap beans, cabbage, cantaloups, carrots, cauliflower, celery, sweet corn, cucumbers, lettuce, onions, peas, spinach, tomatoes, watermelons. The coverage, even of these items, is not complete.

[d] Not available.

[e] Average 1909–11.

[f] Average 1919–21.

between regions with differing yield levels. While we have not investigated this question in detail, we have thought it worth while to test the trend in the yield of a number of important crops for which data are readily available since 1866. The average annual change computed by least squares is shown for six such crops in Table 51. The figures in the column called "fiducial level" measure the expectation that the value shown for the annual change in yield would be obtained by chance if the true trend were perfectly horizontal. It is evident that the trends reported, small even in the case of potatoes, must be considered significant in all cases except corn.

The absence of any upward trend in the yield of corn suggests that, at least until very recently, it has been fighting a losing battle against pests and soil depletion. Moreover there has been a slight shift in acreage away from the high-yielding regions of the corn area toward lower-yielding dairy states. The commercial development of hybrid corn in the middle 1930's is likely in time to reverse this situation, perhaps very shortly. Yields per acre of hybrid corn apparently run up to 35 percent above corresponding yields of open-pollinated varieties formerly in use.[22] Hybrid corn was first introduced commercially in the early 1930's, and employed in 1939 to plant about one quarter of the entire corn acreage; it gained most rapid acceptance in the Corn Belt itself. The increase in yield obtained by its use—from 10 to 20 percent—is apparently much the same in regions with a low yield as in regions with a high yield per acre.[23]

The slow increase in the yield of wheat—0.15 percent per annum over the last three quarters of a century—is the outcome of a conflict between improved techniques, on the one

[22] L. K. Macy, L. E. Arnold and E. G. McKibben, *Corn* (National Research Project, Philadelphia, 1938), p. 16.

[23] U. S. Department of Agriculture, *Technology on the Farm* (Washington, 1940), pp. 21-22; A. A. Dowell and O. B. Jesness, "Economic Aspects of Hybrid Corn," *Journal of Farm Economics*, Vol. XXI (May 1939), pp. 479-88.

Chart 47
CROP YIELDS
Five-Year Averages, 1869 - 1939

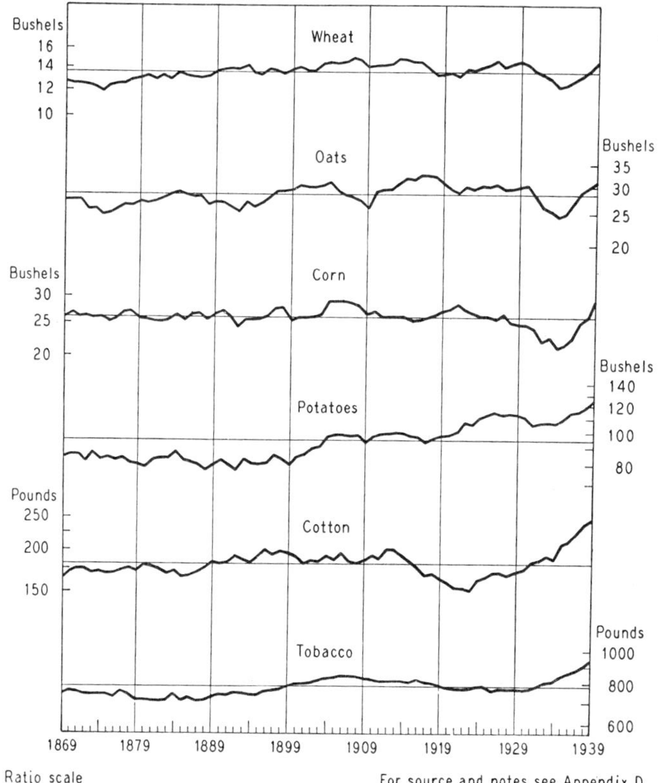

hand, and the exhaustion of the soil and shifts toward climatically less favored areas, on the other. The introduction of new varieties has been slowly gaining over rust and insect pests, while irrigation and crop rotation have helped to compensate for the irregularity of precipitation in some of the newer wheat areas.[24] In particular it has been found useful

[24] R. B. Elwood, L. E. Arnold, D. C. Schmutz and E. G. McKibben, *Wheat and Oats* (National Research Project, Philadelphia, 1939), Ch. V.

in the dry areas to leave the land fallow. Nevertheless, yields have actually declined in the range area of the western plains, whereas in California diminishing acreage has been accompanied by higher yields on the acres remaining.[25] The average annual percentage increase in the yield of oats has been about the same as for wheat, and the crop has been subject to much the same influences, although losses due to infection have been somewhat less serious. Except in areas of extremely low or uncertain rainfall, rust in one form or another is the main

TABLE 51
ANALYSIS OF CHANGE IN YIELD PER ACRE
Selected Crops, 1866–1940

Crop	*Unit of Measure*	*Mean Annual Change in Yield per Acre*	*Ratio of Mean to Its Standard Error*	*Fiducial Level*	*Mean Annual Percentage Change in Yield per Acre*
Corn	bushels	−.0084	.50	.6	0
Wheat	bushels	+.0199	2.64	.01	+.15
Oats	bushels	+.0427	2.20	.03	+.15
Cotton	pounds	+.4344	3.21	<.01	+.24
Potatoes	bushels	+.5277	9.07	<.01	+.56
Tobacco	pounds	+1.5994	5.42	<.01	+.21

obstacle faced by both these crops. Sprays have been developed; and since 1936 a campaign has been undertaken for the destruction of the buckthorn and barberry bushes of the Great Plains which act as intermediate hosts to the fungus. It seems most likely, however, that the problem will eventually be solved through the medium of improved varieties, both of wheat and of oats.[26]

The average annual increase in the yield of cotton is about one-quarter percent—greater than that shown by either wheat or oats. Here again new varieties have played their part, par-

[25] *Ibid.*, pp. 6-7.
[26] *Ibid.*, Ch. V.

ticularly in resisting the attacks of the boll weevil. The problem has been to produce varieties that mature early enough to escape the ravages of the weevil, and yet offer a reasonably long staple. This problem has not yet reached its solution. It seems certain that cotton yields would have increased very much more rapidly but for this form of infestation, and the primary influence in rising yields must probably be credited to improvements of fertilizers and their increasing use. No doubt the average yield for the United States as a whole also would have risen more rapidly but for the shift of production toward the western cotton area, Texas and Oklahoma, in which appreciable amounts of fertilizer are not used, the farmers being content with comparatively low yields per acre.[27]

The greatly augmented yield of potatoes—more than 0.5 percent per annum on the average—is attributable largely to the importance of three states—Maine, Idaho and Colorado. The yield per acre is well above the national average in these states, and is still increasing; moreover there have been decided acreage shifts in their favor. Concentration upon the potato in each of them has apparently made profitable extensive use of commercial fertilizer and pest control.[28] New varieties also have played their part. Potatoes show a wider regional disparity in yield than do most other crops: for example, Maine, Idaho and California each had an average yield of more than 250 bushels an acre in 1937–40, compared with less than 100 bushels in Minnesota, North Dakota and several other important potato-producing states. These differences do not seem to be traceable to climatic or soil conditions; and it is clear that an improvement in cultural practices in the less efficient regions would have a marked effect upon average yields from year to year in the nation as a whole.

[27] Holley and Arnold, *Cotton,* Sec. IV.

[28] H. E. Knowlton, R. B. Elwood and E. G. McKibben, *Potatoes* (National Research Project, Philadelphia, 1938), Sec. III.

Tobacco yields have probably been increased as a result of more intensive cultivation in response to acreage restrictions under the AAA, and especially to the Kerr-Smith Act of 1934. But the rise in yields antedates these restrictions, and is to be traced also to the growing importance, ever since the early 1920's, of flue-cured cigarette tobacco in North Carolina: both yields and acreage have swelled in this state.

Among other crops, the figures in Table 50 suggest a rising trend in the yield of sugar beets. This results largely from sharply increased yields in California during the past fifteen years; in that state the crop was introduced into especially suitable areas and disease-resistant varieties were selected for cultivation.[29]

Yields of vegetables, although data are available only since 1919, appear to show a downward trend. Reasons for this have been summarized as follows:

> The effect of new varieties on yields . . . has been obscured by many other factors which have tended, on the whole, to decrease yields. It is quite generally believed among horticulturalists that diseases and insect pests take a heavier toll than they did in former years. A relative shift of vegetable acreage to poorer lands and the decline in fertility of much of the irrigated land through the accumulation of deposited salts have tended further to reduce yields. With the great increase in vegetable production, and particularly during the depression, many farmers entered into vegetable production without previous experience and sufficient knowledge to obtain high yields. The ever-increasing emphasis on quality has also probably affected yields through closer culling and by causing vegetables to be harvested at smaller sizes when the quality is choicer.[30]

[29] L. K. Macy, L. E. Arnold, E. G. McKibben and E. J. Stone, *Sugar Beets* (National Research Project, Philadelphia, 1937), p. 11.

[30] J. C. Schilletter, R. B. Elwood and H. E. Knowlton, *Vegetables* (National Research Project, Philadelphia, 1939), p. 17.

The data summarized in Chart 36 (Chapter 3) suggest, however, that the downward trend in the yields of these crops may have been arrested.

In Table 52 the material in Table 50 has been used for the construction of indexes of yield per acre and per livestock unit, as a further aid to the examination of the trend in these data. It will be seen that in 1927–31 crop yields were not on the average significantly different from the level prevailing three decades previously; but that during the most recent decade a rise of 15 to 20 percent apparently took place. We cannot be certain, of course, how far this increase has been attributable to the particular circumstances of individual crops, and how far to more intensive cultivation or

TABLE 52

INDEXES OF YIELD PER ACRE AND PER LIVESTOCK UNIT[a]

1907–11:100

Product	*1897–1901*	*1907–11*	*1917–31*	*1927–31*	*1937–40*
Five major crops[b]	100.0	100.0	95.4	99.9	120.0 103.3[f]
Fifteen crops[c]	100.3	100.0	95.8	99.8	118.5 103.9[g]
Milk and eggs[d]	..	100.0	101.2	116.7	119.0
Combined index[e]	..	100.0	97.5	105.7	116.5 108.6[g]

[a] These indexes are based upon the data given in Table 50; the yields shown in that table have been weighted by the product of price and acreage required for net output (or number of animals) for 1899, 1909, 1919, 1929 and 1937 with the use of the Edgeworth formula. Figures are averages for years indicated.

[b] Corn, wheat, oats, cotton and potatoes.

[c] These comprise the various crops in Table 50 with the exception of truck crops.

[d] Eggs per laying chicken; milk per milk cow.

[e] Data for fifteen crops; and for milk and eggs.

[f] Excluding cotton for the comparison of 1937–40 with 1927–31.

[g] Excluding cotton and tobacco for the comparison of 1937–40 with 1927–31.

the selection of the better soils as a result of acreage restrictions associated with Agricultural Adjustment. To what extent the increase will prove permanent it is still more difficult to say. Acreage restrictions have probably played a part in the case of cotton and tobacco, and perhaps also in that of wheat. Although we have no data for milk cows and chickens before 1909, it seems clear that the increase in their productivity is more marked and of longer standing than that of crop acres.

CONCLUSION

From the results cited here it is evident that during the forty years under review the trend in the yield of crops per acre has had very little effect upon agricultural productivity as a whole, except for very recent years. The series for output per worker in Table 38 were probably depressed somewhat during the middle of the period by low yields, especially for cotton. But if yields per acre of all crops had remained constant throughout, it is unlikely that these indexes of productivity would have been changed, except for the last two or three years of the period, by more than a point or two. In these most recent years, by contrast, yields exercise an important influence. The rise in output per worker reported for 1937 and 1938 (Table 38)—a rise which is all the more striking if one considers that the indexes are 5-year averages—must be ascribed largely to the sharp upswing in yields per acre, particularly of cotton and tobacco.

If the increase in productivity between 1900 and 1930—a rise of about 30 percent in output per adult male—is due not at all to changes in yield per acre, to what can it be attributed? So far as crops are concerned, it must be credited entirely to reductions in hours per acre, and in associated indirect labor. These reductions were, as we have seen, substantial. In the case of livestock, on the other hand, there was no economy in hours of direct labor per animal, but milk per cow and eggs per chicken were already increasing steadily before 1930. There may also have been a shift toward more economical feeds or methods of feeding, but we can say little on that point. Meanwhile livestock benefited indirectly through economies in the labor needed to raise feed crops. Since we cannot divide the labor supply between crop production on the one hand and livestock raising on the other, we are unable to distribute the increase of productivity accurately between these two sectors of the industry. Nevertheless, the foregoing discussion lends support to the view that the largest part of the measurable gain in output per worker since 1900 is associated with crop rather than with livestock production. This is not to imply that the greatest scope for further increase of efficiency is to be found in the latter rather than in the former kind of activity. Yet it is true that mechanization has been the largest single influence in reducing labor input per unit of product; and it is true also that mechanization has lagged notably in livestock production. Whether this lag is to prove permanent or will be overcome in the years to follow, only the future can disclose.

Part Four

Summary and Conclusions

Chapter 8

Agriculture in the Nation's Economy *

WE HAVE now to summarize the results set forth in preceding chapters and to consider their implications. Over the four decades since 1899 the output of farm products increased by about 50 percent, or at a somewhat slower rate than population.[1] Changes in the composition of this output were reviewed in detail in Chapters 2 and 3; here the briefest recapitulation must suffice. Citrus fruit increased in output more than tenfold; the production of sugar, vegetable oils, milk products and poultry doubled; potatoes and tobacco rose a little more than 50 percent. Cotton and livestock expanded less than 50 percent; grain production was about the same at the end of the period as at the beginning; and the net output of hay fell sharply over the four decades. These movements may be observed in comparative form in Chart 3.

In interpreting the behavior of the production data we found (Chapter 3) that the contraction of exports (in absolute terms and relative to farm output) has played an especially important part in moderating the expansion in the output of the grains, of cotton, and of livestock products. Tobacco, on the other hand, has been much better able to maintain its position in export markets, and its production

* A note on this chapter, by C. Reinold Noyes, Director, appears on pp. 316-21.

[1] Deficient coverage in early years is probably responsible for some downward bias in our index of output, i.e. it does not rise quite as rapidly as it should. On the most extreme assumption possible, i.e. that the output of every product omitted in 1899 was zero in that year, the rise in an index which included these items for the entire period would still be less than 60 percent (see Appendix A). Population rose by 75 percent between 1899 and 1939.

has been hampered to a smaller extent by the decline in foreign trade. To what is the decline in agricultural exports to be attributed? Among various causes the tariff policy of the United States itself is sometimes cited. Certainly the Fordney-McCumber Act of 1922 and the Smoot-Hawley Act of 1930 raised tariff rates on manufactured goods, on many minerals, and on some few farm products that are imported, to levels not previously attained. The consequent discouragement of imports might conceivably react upon farm exports in two principal ways. A rise in the price of manufactures, for example of farm machinery, might raise the costs of farming, and so both diminish the supply of farm products and push their prices to a level at which exportation became unprofitable. But this line of reasoning is tenuous, and seems to have had little applicability during our period of study. In fact the agricultural staples that are commonly exported were in ample supply in most years, and there is little to suggest that their prices were pushed up by high farming costs. The other principal way in which tariff policy may have reacted upon farm exports is through the diminution of the supply of dollars available to our customers who were unable to make sales in the United States. This approach perhaps affords a more promising method of tying up the observed reduction of agricultural exports with domestic tariff policy. At the same time, however, one must recall that for a considerable part of the period under observation exports were to a large extent financed by foreign lending or by the import of gold, so that the connection between total United States imports and total exports from this country must have been a somewhat loose one.

In the future there may possibly arise situations in which the volume of farm exports is immediately related to the level of the tariff. We cannot doubt that in the long run our tariff policy is one of the determinants of the total volume of our exports, for anything which restricts imports must eventually restrict exports also. But since the beginning of the century it would seem likely that other factors in the situation were of more immediate importance, at any rate in reducing the volume of *farm* exports. We have already referred, for instance, to the trend toward agricultural protection in Europe, a trend with many different elements, and one which may be explained only to a minor degree, if at all, by the tariff policy of this country. Partly because of this, but partly also as a result of progress in the art of manufacturing, the character of American exports has undergone a drastic change. For example, around 1900 about two fifths of American exports (in value terms) consisted of foodstuffs; in recent years, before the outbreak of the present war, foods comprised only about one tenth of all our exports. In part at least, the decline in farm exports is the obverse of the increased contribution to total exports by the products of manufacturing industry—a shift which would naturally occur as the nation became more highly industrialized.

Whatever its causes, the decline in the share of farm produce absorbed by overseas markets has substantially increased the influence of the domestic consumer in determining the output of agriculture as a whole, and of individual farm products, from one period to another. The fact that some 85 percent of net farm output is destined for human food, most of which is consumed domestically, prompted us to examine, in Chapter 4, the character of the nation's food supply. The main findings of that inquiry were a rather steady decline in per capita intake of calories, and a tendency toward expansion in the consumption of milk products and fresh fruit and vegetables. Such an increased use of the "protective foods" is in accordance with the recommendations of dietary science. On the other hand, both the tentative estimates we have been able to make for per capita consumption of several vitamins and minerals, and the results of other recent studies, suggest that there are still serious nutritional deficiencies in the diet of a large part of the population. Accordingly, the principal scope for the expansion of agricultural output in the future appears to be in the production of larger quantities of the "protective foods." This seems likely to come about partly by spontaneous assimilation, through rising living standards, of lower-income-bracket diets to those already common in the upper income brackets; and partly through the more general dissemination of recent advances in nutritional knowledge. A greatly increased demand in the future for the older staple foodstuffs, for textile fibers, or for tobacco, appears, especially in view of the slowing down of population growth, to be much more problematical.

So much for trends in output. What is to be said concerning agricultural productivity?

In spite of the difficulty of measuring agricultural employment, we can say at least that it was no higher, and probably that it was somewhat lower, in 1939 than in 1899. Total numbers occupied (including women, and children 10 years of age and over) reached a peak some time between 1910 and 1920, and in 1930 stood 3 or 4 percent lower than in 1900; but this movement concealed an increase of about 10 percent in farmers plus adult male laborers (Table 36). It may be supposed that on the average women and children work less hard and less continuously than do adult males. Clearly an index of labor input which took proper account of such differences would move somewhere between the indexes just quoted, and would reveal little change between 1900 and 1930. Data for computing the number of farmers and adult male laborers from the 1940 Census have not yet been released; but in 1940 total numbers occupied fell sharply to a point 16 percent below their level at the turn of the century. It seems probable that other measures of labor input also would be lower in 1940 than in 1900 if we could compute them. Thus, farmers and adult male laborers began to decline after 1920, and in 1940 must have numbered about the same as in 1900. If suitable account is taken of women and child workers, therefore, employment in 1940 would measure perhaps 5 or 10 percent, but not as much as 16 percent, below its level at the beginning of the century. And if labor input was lower at the end of the forty-year period covered by this study than it was at the beginning, production per worker must have increased somewhat more rapidly than total output, i.e., by more than 50 percent (Table 38). Put otherwise, labor input per unit of output must have declined by at least one third.

If we take a somewhat longer view and carry our indexes back to 1870, we find that output almost quadrupled, while the labor force increased during the seven decades considered by about one third (without regard to changes in its composition). As a result, output per worker nearly tripled, increasing at an average rate of about 16 percent per decade (Table 39). The gain in productivity seems to have been particularly rapid since 1920, but this may result from the increasing proportion of adult males in the labor force.

The prevalence of mixed farming, and the impossibility of obtaining comprehensive data for the labor input associated with individual products, prevent us from accurately distributing these gains in efficiency among different kinds of output or varieties of farming enterprise. But the discussion in the preceding chapter suggests that productivity has increased more rapidly in crop production than it has in dairying or the raising of livestock. Nor is such a result surprising, in the light of the advances in agricultural technology described in Chapter 5. It is plain that in this field the outstanding development of the last forty years has been the exploitation of the gasoline tractor; and it is easy to see that economies in crop labor attributable to the tractor must have far outweighed similar economies in the raising of livestock or the care of milk cows. Moreover, although the mechanization of dairying is capable of lightening in marked degree the burden of caring for milk cows, the evidence adduced in Chapter 7 suggests that up to the present such effects have been largely offset by more stringent sanitary regulation of the dairy industry. Indirectly the tractor has aided dairying by improving the availability of feed. And it is possible that in the future improved breeding methods, and the more general application of mechanical power (e.g.) to milking, may lead to gains in the efficiency of dairying comparable to those already achieved in the production of staple crops.

Trends in output, employment and output per worker in agriculture are in marked contrast to analogous trends in manufacturing industry. Compared with a 50 percent increase in farm production, the physical output of manufactured goods in 1939 was some four times its volume at the beginning of the century. Whereas the output of farm products barely kept pace with population growth, that of manufactures grew far more rapidly. Moreover, while farm employment in 1940 was the same as, or somewhat smaller than, it had been in 1900, employment in manufacturing nearly doubled in four decades. The contrast in the behavior of output per worker is somewhat less striking but still significant: for agriculture the index rose by about 50 percent, while for manufacturing it doubled. If we could compare changes in output per manhour in the two branches of activity a sharper contrast would probably result, for data considered in Chapter 7 suggest that the reduction in the hours of agricultural labor (per week or per year) have been slight, whereas similar reductions in manufacturing are known to have been substantial.

The stationary level of employment and the comparatively mild expansion in output shown by agriculture would probably contrast markedly with experience in several other segments of industry besides manufacturing, were comparable data available. But since we seek to observe the change in the status of agriculture in the economy of the nation as a whole, our purpose should be to compare farming, not with this or that activity selected at random, but rather with all other industries combined. This can be done only for characteristics that are measurable over the entire economy. For physical output no such comprehensive data are available, but we do have estimates for the total number of gainful workers, and for national income, for the United States as a whole at different dates. The position of agriculture in the economy is illustrated in terms of these measures in Tables 53 and 54. The estimates for the share of income accruing to agriculture are probably subject to a rather wide margin of error in early years, but it has seemed preferable nevertheless to present data for as long a period as possible.

TABLE 53

PERCENTAGE SHARES OF AGRICULTURE AND MANUFACTURING IN REALIZED INCOME, 1799-1937[a]

Year	*Agriculture*	*Manufacturing*	*Other Activities*
1799	39.5	4.8	55.7
1809	34.0	6.1	59.9
1819	34.4	7.5	58.1
1829	34.7	10.3	55.0
1839	34.6	10.3	55.1
1849	31.7	12.5	55.8
1859	30.8	12.1	57.1
1869	24.1	15.9	60.0
1879	20.7	14.5	64.8
1889	15.8	21.1	63.1
1899	21.2	19.6	59.2
1909	22.1	20.1	57.8
1919	22.9	25.8	51.3
1929	12.7	26.2	61.1
1937	12.3	30.3	57.4

[a] R. F. Martin, *National Income in the United States, 1799–1938* (National Industrial Conference Board, 1939), Table 17. Data for 1937 exclude benefit payments. The income totals on which these percentages are based include neither corporate savings nor income produced by government. On this account the percentages shown above for agriculture and for manufacturing run somewhat higher than those given by Simon Kuznets, *National Income and Its Composition, 1919–1938* (National Bureau of Economic Research, 1941), Table 12.

It will be seen that the farmer's share in national income has followed a downward trend for at least a century; by contrast the fraction of income accruing to manufacturing industry exhibits a rising tendency. To a large extent these two movements have been complementary, the expansion of manufacturing being but the obverse of the relative stagnation of agriculture. The percentage of income accruing to "other activities" in Table 53 has not altered greatly.

Figures for recent years compiled at the National Bureau by Simon Kuznets suggest that within the past decade the downward trend in the percentage of income accruing to agriculture may have been arrested, at least temporarily.[2] For example, according to Dr. Kuznets' data, which include benefit payments in agricultural income and differ in scope from the figures in Table 53 in other respects also, no decline occurred between 1929 and 1937 in agriculture's share of the income of the nation. In what measure the recovery of agriculture's share from an all-time low in 1932 is to be attributed to the Agricultural Adjustment program it is impossible to say.

For the distribution of gainfully occupied workers we have estimates by the Bureau of the Census which begin in 1820 and tell a similar story. Here again (Table 54) the share of agriculture has declined and the share of manufacturing has risen. In 1870 more than half the occupied population was engaged in agriculture; in 1940 little more than one sixth.[3] Half the occupied population is now engaged in activ-

[2] Simon Kuznets, *National Income and Its Composition, 1919–1938* (National Bureau of Economic Research, 1941), Table 12, p. 164.

[3] In respect of income shares "other activities" appear not to have altered their importance appreciably (Table 53); whereas it would seem that agriculture has lost workers (relatively speaking) not only to manufacturing but to other occupations also, and the latter change appears to be the larger. As a means of judging shifting importance, Table 54 probably gives the more accurate picture, for the income data we have quoted (Table 53) take no account of income produced by governmental activity, increasingly important in recent decades.

ities other than farming and manufacturing, and the increases have been largest in clerical occupations and in the professions.

The striking decline in the relative importance of agriculture in the economy of the nation must undoubtedly be attributed to the superior attractiveness of other occupations. At the same time one must avoid the conclusion that

TABLE 54
PERCENTAGE SHARES OF AGRICULTURE AND MANUFACTURING IN THE GAINFULLY OCCUPIED POPULATION, 1820–1940

Year	*Agriculture*	*Manufacturing and Mechanical Industries*	*Other Activities*[a]
1820	71.8	28.2	
1830	70.5	29.5	
1840	68.6	31.4	
1850	63.7	36.3	
1860	58.9	41.1	
1870	53.0	20.5	26.5
1880	49.4	22.1	28.5
1890	42.6	23.7	33.7
1900	37.5	24.8	37.7
1910	31.0	28.5	40.5
1920	27.0	30.3	42.7
1930	21.4	28.9	49.7
1940	17.6	82.4	

Source: U. S. Bureau of the Census, "Industrial Distribution of the Nation's Labor Force: 1870 to 1930," and "Trends in the Proportion of the Nation's Labor Force Engaged in Agriculture: 1820 to 1940" (press releases, Oct. 23, 1938 and March 28, 1942 respectively).
[a] Includes government.

since the share of farming in the national income has been consistently smaller than its share in numbers engaged (see Tables 53 and 54) it therefore provides us with a measure of the unattractiveness of agriculture. This is certainly not the case. During the first half of the nineteenth century, at a time when farming did not yet suffer in any important degree from the competition of manufacturing in attracting resources, agriculture's share of the national income was only about one third, despite the fact that it provided a living for more than half of the occupied population. In the case of farming, measurable income per occupied person has probably been below the national average since very early times, yet this state of affairs does not indicate an inferior position in the competition for the economic resources of the nation. Such statistics understate the net advantages of farming for several reasons. First, we cannot take adequate account of income produced in kind. Second, rural occupations probably have a superior appeal for many persons. Third, capital employed in agriculture tends to be owned by those who are themselves engaged in farming, so that the fraction of income accruing to those who do not report themselves as occupied in the industry is smaller in agriculture than it is elsewhere. Finally, agriculture bulks large in several southern states where income per person occupied (in all industries together) is much below the national average.

> Farming has a powerful attraction for large numbers of people, in spite of the risks and hardships associated with it, and the low financial return that it yields to the capital and labor employed. It commonly assures at least a minimum living at moderate cost. It is easy to enter, though for certain types considerable capital is essential. It does not require extensive training, though specialized education and experience both contribute to efficiency and pecuniary success. Children of farmers particularly find it easy to stay on the farm, and adults established in farming often find it difficult to quit. Many like not only to live but to work in the open country, and get very real satisfaction out of cooperating with Nature in making plants and animals grow. Farming is the principal remaining field of independent enterprise other than retail-store keeping, and that freedom is cherished in spite of its practical limitations. Many who have tried urban occupations

> and residence find that these have drawbacks not apparent at first sight. Moreover, developments of recent years have made available to farmers in some countries, at a cost within reach of large numbers, such additions to their traditional standards of living as electricity, the telephone, automobile, and radio, and have lightened their drudgery with mechanical devices for farming and the farm household.[4]

For all these reasons, the fact that measurable income per head is lower in farming than elsewhere can in no wise be taken as proof of the inferior attractiveness of agriculture as a form of economic activity.[5] Nevertheless, although it cannot be demonstrated statistically, we may be reasonably certain that the real return to farming has lagged in competition with other types of activity. Only on the assumption that this is so can we explain, in a system of free enterprise and choice of occupation, the apparently continuous decline in the importance of farming in the economy as a whole.

An agriculture which expands less rapidly than other forms of activity, or which shows actual contraction, has, with only temporary exceptions, been a characteristic of the industrialization of most if not all western countries. In Britain, for example, those engaged in agriculture represented 12.5 percent of all gainfully occupied in 1881, 5.7 percent in 1931. In Germany the corresponding percentage declined from 41.5 in 1882 to 33.7 in 1933. Similar results could be quoted for other European and probably also for some Asiatic countries. It may be objected that in Europe the trend was magnified through the substitution of imported foodstuffs and textile materials for the products of domestic agriculture; in the United States the substitution of imported

[4] J. S. Davis, *On Agricultural Policy, 1926–1938* (Food Research Institute, Stanford University, 1939), pp. 34-35.

[5] Agriculture's smaller share in income than in numbers has also been noted in Germany. See Wilhelm Bauer and Peter Dehen, "Landwirtschaft und Volkseinkommen," *Vierteljahrshefte zur Wirtschaftsforschung, 1938–39,* pp. 411-32.

for domestic foods and fibers has played but a microscopic role in retarding the growth of farming. But it is doubtful if, even in Europe, except perhaps in Britain, the substitution of imported for domestic farm products has been the most important factor in the growth of nonagricultural occupations at the expense of farming. Nor can the drop in the exports of American farm products explain the decline in the relative importance of agriculture in this country, for the latter antedates the former. Declining exports, like the disappearance of the urban demand for horse feed, have intensified a trend which began many decades earlier.

To discover the factors chiefly responsible for the declining relative importance of agriculture as a source of livelihood we must look elsewhere. In the first place, farmers are now relieved of many of the functions which they once performed. The manufacture of butter and cheese and the slaughtering of animals have been largely transferred, within the last hundred years, to nonagricultural establishments. Even more important in recent decades has been the substitution of mechanical for animal power. Time was when the farmer raised both his own horses and the materials with which to feed them: now he buys tractors, gasoline and oil. These transfers of function—mainly from farming to manufacturing—have diminished the number of *agricultural* workers needed to produce a unit of farm output. But we should beware of assuming, merely on this account, that the total number of persons—farmers and nonfarmers—engaged in producing a given product has diminished.[6]

[6] The transfer of cheesemaking from the farm to the factory had been practically completed by 1899. Some slaughtering is still performed on farms, but the majority of animals were already being killed at the factory when our period opened. The production of farm butter has been diminishing, but it is still important: our indexes of output and productivity are so constructed that they take this change into account. In Chapter 7 estimates were given for the saving of labor occasioned by the tractor in the raising and feeding of work animals, but no allowance for this saving has been made in computing our indexes, and in this respect they overstate the rise in agricultural productivity.

When all necessary allowance has been made, however, for qualifications of this sort, it still appears to be true that the proportion of the labor force engaged in agricultural pursuits has declined rather steadily. Now, we should expect those branches of activity in which technological development is most rapid to lose labor, as the years go by, to other branches whose techniques of production have progressed little or not at all—unless indeed products of the one group can be substituted for products of the other group easily enough to prevent this from happening.[7] Prominent among the first group are most of the commodity-producing industries; among the second, those types of endeavor whose business it is to furnish services. In a rough kind of way we may identify the latter group with the "other activities" of Table 54. As employers of labor these activities—and especially educational, medical, distributive and governmental services—have become steadily more important. Data for 1940 have not yet been released: but we may note that although the fraction of the labor force engaged in manufacturing and mechanical industries was higher in 1920 than it had been at any previous Census, by 1930 these occupations also had begun to lose adherents to "other activities." In large part such developments must be viewed as the natural outcome of differing rates of technological advance.

But technological change is not the whole story. It seems likely that agriculture's share of the working population has

[7] Alfred Marshall, *Principles of Economics* (8th ed. Macmillan, 1920), pp. 274-77. However, there is evidence that an opposite relation holds among individual manufacturing industries. For these industries changes in output per worker and in employment appear to be positively correlated. (See Solomon Fabricant, *The Relation Between Factory Employment and Output Since 1899,* Occasional Paper 4, National Bureau of Economic Research, 1941, pp. 16-20; the matter is discussed further in the same author's *Employment in Manufacturing, 1899–1939,* National Bureau of Economic Research, 1942.) No doubt the substitutability among manufactured products is greater than that between such products and other types of good. If the demand for the product of an industry is sufficiently elastic, its employment may clearly increase even in the face of very rapid technological change.

declined for other reasons also. We have seen that among farm products foodstuffs are easily first in quantitative importance. In the United States, judged by value, about 85 percent of net farm output consists of food for human consumption. For purely physiological reasons there is a rather rigid limit to per capita consumption of food in terms of weight, calories and other constituents. For a population with a given age distribution, therefore, we should expect the demand for food to be inelastic, when related to real income, once this limit is approached.[8] The results of family budget studies suggest that this is the case, i.e. that the elasticity in question is positive but less than unity.[9] As long as the elasticity is positive, we would expect some increase in consumer expenditure on food to accompany an increase in real income. But it is not so certain that higher living standards must also involve increased expenditure upon the output of foodstuffs by farmers. For increased expenditure on food by consumers may mean merely that the packaging or processing of the foodstuffs in question has become more elaborate, or it may reflect the purchase of increased amounts of the services associated with food consumption—for example, of restaurants. The tendency for increased food expenditures to take this form suggests that the elasticity of demand for the raw foodstuffs produced by agriculture must be significantly less than the corresponding elasticity as measured by consumer expenditures.

The elasticity which is relevant to the demand for agricultural output is of course one which measures the increase in the consumption of raw foodstuffs, rather than the increase

[8] Elasticity of demand in terms of income is measured approximately by the percentage increase in consumption associated with a 1 percent increase in income.

[9] For example, data collected by the National Resources Committee for 1935–36 yield an indicated elasticity of demand for food, in terms of income, of about 0.5 for the population as a whole (National Resources Planning Board, *Consumer Expenditures in the United States,* Washington, 1939, Tables 19A and 20A).

in consumer expenditures for food, which occurs as the real income of the community rises. We may first of all consider the consumption of such foodstuffs by weight or in terms of calories. In the case of the United States, as we have seen in Chapter 4, rising living standards [10] have been accompanied by an actual reduction in per capita consumption of calories. We should hesitate to conclude on this account that the elasticity of the demand for food, even when expressed in calories, in terms of real income, is actually less than zero, for concurrent changes have also taken place in the occupations and habits of the population, changes related only very indirectly to the increase in per capita real income as this concept is ordinarily understood. Moreover, there probably still exist in the United States some rather restricted groups of people who consume substantially less than their physiological requirements, not of this or that food element, but of food in general, whether measured in pounds or in calories. Yet when all necessary qualifications have been made, it seems an inevitable conclusion that the income elasticity of demand for food in general—in this sense—cannot be significantly positive in the United States today. We may expect, in other words, that a further rise in the standard of living will indeed lead to larger (though not proportionately larger) consumer expenditures on food, but will fail to lead to any appreciable increase in food consumption per capita, measured in physical terms, even if important changes should occur in the character of the food supply. But elasticity of demand is not the only consideration. As the average age of the population continues to rise and occupations become more sedentary, it is likely that we shall see a continuation of the tendency for per capita consumption of food, in terms

[10] Per capita income payments, in constant prices, increased about 10 percent between 1909–13 and 1934–38 (Simon Kuznets, *National Income and Its Composition, 1919–38,* National Bureau of Economic Research, 1941), Table 11.

of calories, to decrease. Similar conclusions would probably hold for other western countries.

Once per capita intake of food approaches its physiological optimum (or maximum)—and we must suppose that for the bulk of the population in the United States this stage was reached many decades ago—we should expect a decline in the fraction of the community's resources devoted to producing food. Only if there were marked changes in the composition of the food supply, or an entire absence of technical progress in agriculture, would this expectation be unfulfilled. But we know that in fact continual advance has characterized agricultural technology; while crop yields per acre have increased only slowly, substantial increments have occurred in output per worker engaged. To be sure, the decline in labor per unit of product has been more rapid in many other sectors of the economy than it has in agriculture; but where the income elasticity of demand for the product of an industry is zero, *any* increase in labor productivity must lead to a decline in its percentage share of occupied population. In the past the farmer has chiefly sold calories, the elasticity of demand for which is low. This goes far to explain the decline in the relative importance of farming that has already occurred. Unless other factors intervene, moreover, the further advances that may be anticipated in agricultural technique appear to insure that the secular decline in the fraction of the nation's human resources engaged in farming will continue.

Unless other factors intervene: but what are the other factors that must be considered in this connection? One has already been suggested—the possibility of a change in the character of the food supply. The rather rigid limitation imposed by physiological considerations upon food intake in terms of pounds or calories does not rule out a shift toward more expensive foodstuffs—those which use up a larger quantity of agricultural resources per pound or calorie. Man does not live by calories alone, and both the foods richest in vitamins and minerals and those of superior flavor require in general a larger expenditure of resources per calorie or per pound of nutrient than do the traditional staples in the diet of our ancestors. It is probable that a continued upward tendency in real income per capita will lead to a diversification of diet of this character. We can hardly hope to determine to what extent such a change can be expected to result from advances in nutritional education or medical propaganda, and to what extent it may eventually come about through the reconciliation of diets characteristic of the lower income brackets with those common in the upper brackets. But that such a change is already under way may be seen from the evidence presented in Chapter 4, and especially from the persistent decline in the per capita consumption of cereals.

It was suggested in Chapters 5 and 7 that technical progress has been slower in the production of dairy products and vegetables than in that of crops, and it may well be that the provision of a given supply of calories in the first form requires more labor than in the second. But there are already indications that this backwardness in technique may be remedied before long, perhaps through wider use of milking machines and advances in breeding in the case of dairying, and the all-purpose tractor and the selection of seed in the raising of vegetables. The tendency for dairy and other livestock products to expand faster than crop production, a tendency which, we saw in Chapter 2, dates from about 30 years ago, is likely enough to continue. Yet it does not seem probable that this trend can do more than mitigate in some degree the decline to be expected for other reasons in the demand for the services of agriculturalists.[11]

[11] It has been suggested (J. P. Cavin, H. K. Stiebeling and Marius Farioletti, "Agricultural Surpluses and Nutritional Deficits," *Yearbook of Agriculture, 1940,* p. 334) that raising the American diet to the level designated by the Bureau of Home Economics as "expensive good diet" would call into production some 30 to 40 million acres; such a quantity would constitute a substantial compensation for acreage taken out of producing staples and might be capable of absorbing a sizable fraction of the present surplus farm popula-

A second possible development that might check the secular decline in the relative importance of agriculture is an expansion in the demand for industrial raw materials. The chief industries using farm products are those processing tobacco, cotton and wool; industries making or using starches and oils; and industries manufacturing wine, beer and distilled spirits. The demand by these industries for the products of domestic agriculture depends partly upon the availability of similar materials from abroad, and partly upon the competition of substances not of agricultural origin. The principal domestic products subject to competition from imports are vegetable oils, wool and hides—and among the foodstuffs, sugar. In the case of at least two of these—wool and sugar—domestic output has been powerfully influenced by the availability of imported supplies.[12] The competition of nonagricultural products is felt mainly in respect to fibers; there can be little doubt that rayon has diminished the demand for cotton and possibly, to a minor extent, for wool also. But apart from substitutions of this sort, the elasticity of demand, in terms of real income, for textile products in general is probably not very great, even if it considerably exceeds the very low elasticity we associate with foodstuffs.

---

tion. The assumption is not, however, too realistic. At manhours prevailing in 1932–36—as estimated in various National Research Project studies—a raising of our diet to not quite as high a level, namely that designated "good" (see Chapter 2 above) would, according to estimates made by the authors, call for an additional expenditure of 2.8 billion manhours, or 900,000 manyears at 3,000 hours per man per year. This calculation rests on the assumptions (1) that no compensating reductions in output occur in other parts of agriculture, i.e., that the additions suggested above are *net;* (2) that the proposed changes are accomplished in a comparatively short time interval so that their effect in providing additional labor opportunities will not be seriously impaired by technological advances in just those expanding fields. Furthermore, the conversion of manhours into manyears rests on the questionable ratio of 3,000 hours per year and assumes that none of the additional labor could be performed by agriculturalists not now fully employed. However rough the nature of these computations, they indicate that not too much can be expected from shifts in diet.

[12] See Chapter 3 above.

National Resources Committee data for 1935–36 indicate an elasticity of about 0.9 for clothing, which suggests increased purchases slightly less than proportionate to any rise of income which may occur. It is unlikely, however, that the income elasticity of demand for raw fibers to be used for clothes is as high as this; for we must suppose that increased expenditures for clothing result, in part at least, from a higher degree of fabrication of the article concerned.

To be sure, a large amount of attention has been devoted to the question of new uses for cotton—for example as a base for plastics and even as road material. Indeed it seems obvious that any substantial expansion in the use of farm products as industrial materials must come as a result of technical changes outside agriculture. The more extended use of vegetable oils and of a wide range of corn and soybean by-products by the chemical and allied industries must wait upon the progress of manufacturing technology. Most agricultural products can be converted into industrial alcohol; large quantities of grain will undoubtedly be used for the purpose during the present war. Attempts to manufacture paper from cornstalks have been a failure commercially, whereas the use of flaxstraw in making carpets has apparently succeeded.[13] But there is little sign that potential uses of this kind for farm products offer a field in which they can effectively compete with much cheaper substances derived from other sources. It is possible therefore, though it seems unlikely, that developments of the kind mentioned will arrest the transfer of labor from agriculture to other occupations.

Thirdly, the downward trend in the relative importance of agriculture may conceivably be halted through a revival of foreign trade. As long as the present war lasts, the volume of farm exports will be determined mainly by the size and scope of lend-lease shipments. To date, so far as concerns agricul-

[13] H. E. Barnard, "Prospects for Industrial Uses for Farm Products," *Journal of Farm Economics*, Vol. XX (Feb. 1938), pp. 119-33.

tural commodities, these shipments have consisted largely of food products of animal origin. The export of such staples as cotton and tobacco has fallen to a low level. After the war is over, large quantities of American farm products will probably be sent to Europe and elsewhere during the process of reconstruction. But the question considered here concerns a rather longer view. What are the prospects for agricultural exports in the post-war world? Certainly, with the possible exception of tobacco, the trend in farm exports has been downward for at least two decades.[14] A reversal of this trend has frequently been held to depend on the inauguration of a regime of freer international trade. There can be no doubt that the reduction of barriers, especially by nations that are potentially food-importing, would measurably increase the volume of international trade in agricultural products. The question still remains, how much of these overseas markets would accrue to the American, and how much to the Argentine, the Egyptian, or the Australian farmer? For, by and large, if the tariff barriers of importing nations fall, they will fall for others besides ourselves. It is not certain that the comparative advantage of the United States in respect to the things which it exports, as that phrase is used by students of international trade, is as great as it was formerly; or even, in the case of some products (possibly including wheat) that it still exists. If the advantage of the United States in exporting farm products has declined, such a decline must, like the fall in relative numbers engaged in agriculture, be viewed as the obverse of the growth of manufacturing and of other activities. But this possibility suggests that, even if tariff barriers are substantially reduced upon the return of peace, the revival of farm exports by this country may well be on a rather modest scale.

There remain two other influences to consider—government policies initiated during the past decade, and the demand created by the present war. Since 1933 the original

[14] The evidence on this point was discussed in Chapters 2 and 3 above.

Agricultural Adjustment Act and its successors have applied acreage and marketing restrictions to numerous crops and have distributed substantial Federal appropriations to farmers in return for soil conservation and for other purposes. These measures appear to have raised farm income significantly above the level it would otherwise have reached. However, they have not prevented agricultural output from attaining record levels, nor have they brought to a halt the steady decline in the relative number of persons engaged in farming. There are two ways—and only two ways—in which government policy might conceivably prevent a further decline in agriculture's share of the working population. One is by promoting a still more rapid expansion of output; the other is by halting the rise in output per worker.

Current agricultural policy affects the demand for farm products by promoting research, particularly toward new uses for fibers; by diverting surplus commodities toward, or subsidizing consumption by, lower income groups; and by subsidizing the export of farm products. Within recent years the Department of Agriculture has been active in all three directions. Of these, only the development of new uses for farm products could permanently check the drift away from the land, and few such uses are yet in sight. The diversion of surpluses toward lower income groups, especially under the food stamp plan, is a venture of appreciable size, but its effect upon output is ultimately limited by the potential disappearance of the undernourished. Export subsidies have still more obvious limitations so far as long term expansion is concerned. To date the adjustment programs have tended to emphasize the restriction of output, at least so far as increased farm income might encourage the expansion of staple crops. Even if, as many consider, Agricultural Adjustment has come to stay, its probable effects upon the long term level of agricultural output appear distinctly limited.

It hardly seems possible that our current agricultural

policies will halt the rising trend in output per worker. Whether or not the farmer continues to have a motive for improving his methods and increasing the productivity of his enterprise depends very much upon the mechanism by which his activities are controlled. Under the original Agricultural Adjustment Act of 1933 and under the Soil Conservation and Domestic Allotment Act of 1936 the chief emphasis lay upon acreage reduction, and where this is the principal form of control a strong motive remains for the improvement of yield per acre. It has been argued that some of the early programs "tended to subsidize inefficient and high-cost farming to a significant extent." [15] And on the other side it has been claimed that the more recent soil conservation plans, besides encouraging soil-building and the concentration of crops on the best land, have had some effect in hastening the adoption of superior techniques at other points also.[16] In the cotton and tobacco acts of 1934 control shifted to the marketing quota, and in the Agricultural Adjustment Act of 1938 provision for marketing restrictions was extended to wheat, corn and rice. The same method of control has been applied also to a number of minor crops, particularly fruit and vegetables. Where marketing quotas are in force the advantage of obtaining a higher yield per acre is diminished, but other forms of cost reduction may still appear worth striving for. Evidently, technological advance may continue. In fact there is little reason to suppose that government policy will prevent further increases in output per worker.

We may conclude that the number of persons likely to be engaged in farming in the future is not subject to any appreciable influence by present government policies. Increased rewards to agriculturalists may slow down the drift from the soil, but we may still expect that, as opportunities for em-

[15] E. G. Nourse, J. S. Davis and J. D. Black, *Three Years of the Agricultural Adjustment Administration* (Brookings, 1937), p. 374.

[16] T. W. Schultz, "Economic Effects of Agricultural Programs," *American Economic Review*, Vol. XXX, No. 5 (Feb. 1941), p. 139.

ployment in nonagricultural occupations expand, the fraction of the working population engaged in farming will continue to diminish.

In spite of its obvious current importance, it seems difficult to believe that the present war can have much influence upon the long-term tendencies we have examined. During the first World War the output of many farm products went to record levels. It was a substantial undertaking to feed and clothe large armies and to supply our allies. Today, too, outlets exist (with few exceptions) for all the produce our farms can furnish. Increase in food exports, coupled with decline in imports (starch and sugar), and expanded demand for materials (especially fibers and oils) by industry will insure record agricultural output and income as long as hostilities continue. And when the present war is over, food may be needed by starving populations on the continent of Europe. For a time shortages of fertilizers and machinery, and even of labor, may be expected to restrict farm output in Europe and perhaps in other parts of the world as well, and thus temporarily maintain a high level of exports by the United States. But it seems reasonably certain that within a very few years after the advent of peace the trends discussed in this chapter will reassert themselves. There appear to be no reasons for supposing that current and prospective high levels of farm output will prove any more permanent than did similar levels occasioned by the first World War. The present war may perhaps retard, but it can hardly prevent, further reductions in the fraction of the community's human resources devoted to farming.

Up to this point the distribution of resources between agricultural and other kinds of employment has been considered mainly in relative terms. We have discussed the factors that might be expected to influence the percentage of the occupied population attached to agriculture from one period to another. The trend in this percentage, in the United States as in most other western countries, has been observed to be a downward one. We have seen that historically the trend is of long duration, and have suggested that—partly for physiological, partly for technological, reasons—it is likely to continue. On the other hand until very recently this downward trend did not imply any absolute reduction in the number of farmers. That peak employment in agriculture is already past seems fairly well established from the data in Chapter 6: between 1920 and 1940 the number of persons occupied in farming apparently fell by about 2 million. If the decline in the rate of population growth continues, and especially if two or three decades hence population increase ceases altogether, a further decline in agriculture's fraction of the labor force seems likely to involve further reductions in the absolute number of persons or families engaged in farming.

In an economy where choice of occupation is free, a reduction in the number of persons attached to agriculture can come about, in the ordinary course of events, only through a decline in its net advantages relative to those of other occupations. During the nineteenth century it was undoubtedly the comparative unattractiveness of farming which prevented the absolute number of those engaged in it from rising as rapidly as those engaged in manufacturing. Governmental policy has tended to raise farm incomes during the past decade; yet the absolute number of persons engaged in farming already shows a marked decline. It is the *relative* advantages that count, and if other occupations were sufficiently attractive even "parity incomes" might not prevent a decline in the number of farmers.

We conclude, then, that the pressure to reduce the fraction of the community's efforts devoted to farming, and thereby also the absolute number of agriculturalists, must reassert itself before the cessation of hostilities has receded very far into the past. Only factors of a rather long range character are capable of alleviating this pressure and obviating the need for a continued downward adjustment in the scale of domestic agriculture, when this is measured in terms of persons occupied in farming. Possible influences of this sort have already been enumerated: a cessation of technical advance in farming; a substantial shift in dietary habits in the direction of more expensive foodstuffs; entirely new uses for industrial purposes of fibers or other farm products. It is unlikely that technical improvements in agriculture have exhausted their scope, or that further declines in labor per unit of output should not be anticipated. Further diversification in diet appears quite probable, but the possible increase on this score in the demand for farmers' services appears to be somewhat limited. Some alleviation of the downward pressure upon the scale of agriculture may indeed be anticipated from changes in dietary habits, but their influence is hardly likely to be decisive and will probably be felt principally rather in shifts from one type of farming to another than in any increase in aggregate employment in the industry. Some new industrial applications of farm products were noticed in Chapter 3, but the outlook here is too uncertain for accurate appraisal.

As our study progressed, certain long range factors emerged even more clearly from the agricultural picture. Among these factors technical progress, the slowing down of population growth and the inelasticity of the demand for foodstuffs perhaps stand out most clearly. Like other industries, agriculture has been forced to adapt itself to a changing environment. This adaptation has involved a cessation of growth or actual reduction in the output of some products, rapid expansion in the production of others. It has affected diverse farming areas in very different fashion. While agricultural output as a whole is still tending upward, the past four decades have seen farm employment reach a peak and begin to decline. Changes such as these are a measure of adaptation already achieved. The extent to which further adaptation will be required in the future depends primarily upon the course of long range factors of the kind we have discussed.

Note by C. Reinold Noyes, Director—The first seven chapters of *American Agriculture, 1899-1939,* consist of a somewhat detailed study of the available statistics on the following subjects:

(1) Output of the chief agricultural commodities, together with a chapter on the nation's changing food requirements.

(2) Employment on farms (including self-employment) together with a chapter on changes in technology, farm machinery, etc. The comparison of employment with output figures yields estimates of changed output per worker.

From this very restricted basis the authors then launch into a final chapter which attempts to deal with the vast subject of "Agriculture in the Nation's Economy."

The general conclusion appears to be that aggregate agricultural output will shortly cease to increase and that the trend of the past 20 years toward an absolute reduction in those gainfully occupied in agriculture will continue. The first part of this conclusion is not based on present trends in output, which are still generally upward, but on the expected influence of several trends in demand—first, the recent trend toward the loss of foreign markets; second, the trend in births over deaths pointing toward a stationary population; and third, the recent trend toward the consumption of "protective" instead of basic foods. With regard to basic foods the existing income elasticity of demand is assumed to be zero or negative. The second part of the general conclusion is based on one trend appearing for the first time in the last 20 years—the absolute decline in farm workers—and on another and longer one—improvements in technique permitting fewer workers for a given output. This part is also supported by *a priori* reasoning from, or interpretation in the light of, theory—the theory of "relative advantages"—and by analogy with Western Europe where the authors have detected a "diversion of resources" from agriculture to industry.

This conclusion takes a very positive position on a vital question which has been exercising this country, politically and socially, for the past twenty years. It lends support to the policy of "letting nature take its course" or to the more humane forms of the same policy—the limitation of agricultural production and the facilitation of transfer of superfluous farm population to other pursuits. Moreover, the fact that these arguments and conclusions, while not in themselves novel, are ostensibly the result of a piece of purely scientific analysis might well increase the weight of this support. The question of their validity is therefore one of more than usual importance.

My judgment is that the last chapter of this book—the argument and conclusions—is subject to three serious kinds of weakness in respect of scientific method. In what follows I am concerned, first, with the validity of the methods used by these authors in deriving their conclusions and, second, with the presentation of a different approach, of apparently equal propriety, which leads to precisely the opposite conclusions. In the light of the first I conclude that the conclusions presented in the last chapter are opinions rather than scientific forecasts; in the light of the second I conclude that one opinion is as good as the other.

The three types of weakness in method may be described as follows:

1. It seems inappropriate to proceed on the assumption that the brief trends described in this report are secular and can therefore be used to extrapolate the future. These trends may be no more than swings in long cycles or even parts of movements in historical processes that will shortly come to an end.

2. It seems improper:
   a. To draw conclusions with regard to a large and complex subject from the examination of one sector of that subject only.
   b. To draw conclusions not implicit in the data studied, with the aid of imported assumptions or considerations not examined as to their validity; or, conversely, to omit other conclusions which are implicit in the data but not consistent with those presented.
   c. To treat as trends the net change accomplished by two opposite movements occurring in succession.

3. It seems undesirable to approach empirical studies such as this with preconceived theories, into the framework of which the facts are forced. This is apt to lead to distortion of the facts and to their misinterpretation.

Under 1, above, it should be noted that all of the influences given weight in determining the general conclusion are treated as trends, though several of those which are not given weight are treated as temporary only. Upon what basis is this discrimination made? Is it sound? Under 2a, I would point to the fact that the other two factors in agricultural production, land and capital, are excluded from consideration in the "distribution of resources" to agriculture and, therefore, their influence, if any, is not appraised; furthermore, the period examined is but a small portion of a long historical process in which this temporal sector may play but an inconsiderable part. Under 2b, I would cite first the importation of the population trend, without discussion, and the dismissal of agricultural policy without previous examination. Under 2b, also, two contrary conclusions appear to have deserved consideration, or more than they get, because they are implicit in the data.

The trends of output are still upward, particularly if the influence of the long period of drought years on grains is discounted. It appears that the long drought in the Middle West showed lowered grain yields (Chart 47, p. 281) and some loss of animals in all the years from 1931 to 1937 inclusive. Perhaps to determine the true trend these years should have been passed over and 1940–42 added. The output of grains in 1938 was the fourth highest and of meats in 1939 the highest ever (Table 5, pp. 42-43, above). Perhaps the special effect of the drought years vitiates conclusions based on 5-year averages and ending on the average around 1937. If this trend had been considered, remarks on demand (pp. 291-93) could not have been interpreted as "trends in output" (p. 294). These features of demand may affect output. But since they have not done so as yet it is improper to telescope the two. Again, in view of the food trend (Chapter 4) to products requiring a much larger input of labor (Chapter 7), the three lines (Chapter 8, p. 307) in which this is dismissed as an influence seem to be inadequate consideration. Under 2c, I cite p. 294. In spite of the fact that there was an increase in agricultural employment from 1899 to about 1920 and that the decline since, though slightly greater, has only lasted for about 20 years, there is constant reference to the process, as if it had been going on for a long time.

Thus "drift from the soil" (Chapter 8, p. 312), "the transfer of labor from agriculture to other occupations" (p. 309), the "downward adjustment in the scale of domestic agriculture" and in the "absolute number of agriculturalists" (pp. 314 and 315). Under 3, I refer to the whole view that the "relative attractiveness" of agriculture and industry has determined their respective rates of growth. "The striking decline in the relative importance of agriculture in the economy of the nation must undoubtedly be attributed to the superior attractiveness of other occupations" (p. 299; see also p. 301, end of paragraph, and p. 314). It is that view which leads to all the emphasis on the "relative" measures of agricultural employment, income, etc., in this final chapter, so much of which is meaningless in the light of the actual historical process. It is, of course, true that a nation is well off in inverse proportion to the percentage of its population required to produce its food. That is equally true in regard to all its other requirements—shoes and ships and sealing-wax. But because such economizings are to be welcomed is no reason why they should be expected or treated as a law of nature. Moreover, in the actual historical process, changes in the ratios between agriculture and industry—of output, employment, income, etc.—are largely accidental, due to the fact that the two developments take place under different limiting conditions and are almost wholly independent of each other.

Because it lies behind much of my criticism, and because it has a strong bearing on the conclusions advanced in this study and still more so on the most important "agricultural problem," it may be well to elaborate on this matter of historical process—the other approach referred to above. Growth seems to be taken as a matter of course by our generation. As a matter of fact, in the socio-economic field, it is almost an abnormality. In most periods of history population has been limited by the food supply and the food supply has been limited by available land—except as occasional improvements in technique have increased the yield per acre. When available land was fixed, the food supply (with the above exception) and consequently the population were also approximately fixed. Correspondingly, in most periods of history all other (industrial) production has been fixed, chiefly by the limits of technique (output per worker) and only slightly by the availability of raw materials. Against this background the economic development of the United States appears as an exception to the rule. Here, economic growth has been, in its two chief aspects, the result of two almost unique historical processes stemming from the same root but thereafter almost wholly independent of each other.

These two processes were, or are, the settlement of the United States and its industrialization (Industrial Revolution). The first movement began, on a continental scale, after the Revolutionary War and continued in the agricultural sphere until about 1920, when it appears to have been practically completed—i.e. the frontier disappeared. This movement is ignored entirely in this study, though some trends are shown from 1799 and though the process continued through about half the period under review—that is, from 1899 to 1919. The second movement, industrialization, can hardly be dated, but its most notable effects appeared after 1870, say, and it is continuing today. This movement is referred to occasionally in this study, but its fundamental effects on these trends are not mentioned. There is room in what follows for only a few rough and general statements on these matters.

The development of agriculture in the United States up to 1920 was in large part determined by the unique historical process of settlement. The settlement of a new country consists first—always and necessarily—of settlement on the land to raise food. The analogy of a flow of water over the land is appropriate. The water tends to cover the land before it begins to grow deep. So agriculture covers the land first before other pursuits follow. But some other pursuits (e.g. trade and transportation) tend to follow almost immediately. It is doubtful if the thirteen colonies, or any subsequent settlements, ever showed more than 60 to 70 percent of employed engaged in agriculture. Since agriculture still accounted for 53 percent of the gainfully employed in 1870 it is clear that most of the increase in gainfully employed up to that time was due to settlement of new land. But the rate of settlement was largely governed by acquisition and opening up of new territory, and by extension of transportation facilities, all within the limits made possible by growth of population. In 1850, when the acquisition of new territory was completed, only 15 percent of the land area was in farms as against 50 percent by 1920. As far as the Great West was concerned the process of opening up the new territory only began after the Civil War and was not completed until after 1900. As far as the limitation set by population growth is concerned it would have required the entire population increase from 1790 up to 1870 or even 1880 to settle the enlarged area with the same ratio employed on the farm as at the beginning. It was these delaying factors which made the movement extend over more than 130 years, and only gradually permitted the increase of land in farms from probably less than 95 million acres (present acreage of thirteen colonies) in 1790 to about ten times that in 1920.

The rate of growth in agriculture (acreage, output and employment) was almost uniquely determined by the rate of settlement of new land. Therefore, the rate was almost completely independent of the rate of industrialization and had no connection with trends abroad where settlement was already complete long before industrialization really commenced. It is to be assumed that this growth so far as acreage is concerned will now stop, since settlement is complete. For land is limited in a sense that labor and capital are not. The absolute limit may have been reached in 1920. By reason of the substitution of capital for labor increased productivity per worker might theoretically continue. But, up to 1920, this process involved more land per worker, not more product per acre. Roughly speaking, from 1890 to 1920 acreage per gainfully employed increased from 63 to 85. Page 286 above shows that the increase per manhour, even up to 1930, was all in the form of fewer hours per acre and none in greater yield per acre. The latter changed little until very lately (p. 285). This trend, then, up to 1920 or 1930, represented a movement toward more *extensive* culture—and the added land per worker was new land. How can that continue, if the limit of land has been reached? Will it be reversed? Any further increase in output would appear to require the substitution of *intensive* for *extensive* agriculture, a process which, in most lines, has not yet appeared in this country. Where it obtains it always involves more labor per acre. Can the substitution of capital for labor operate in intensive culture? If it cannot, then any further increase in output will doubtless reverse the past and present trend in output per worker, and therefore necessitate an increase in absolute employment in agriculture, as it has elsewhere, thus reversing also the recent trend in absolute employment. Hence the historical viewpoint leads to a forecast precisely the opposite of our authors' conclusions, if an increase in output is needed. Whether that does become necessary depends, of course, on whether there is to be *any* future increase in population. That is anybody's guess. On the face of the matter, however, a condition under which the world's richest area, in point of natural resources, continued to maintain a population with a density only from one-half to one-tenth that of the other chief areas that are well endowed, would appear to be a condition of unstable equilibrium. Such a continuance may be very desirable. Whether it is probable or even possible is another question.

During the period of growth of acreage (settlement) increase of major food crops was always possible, but the rate was usually governed by the character of the new land and by the process of settlement itself. For instance, from 1850 to 1890 land in farms increased about 112 percent; but wheat acreage increased about 275 percent. On the other hand, from 1890 to 1920 wheat acreage increased at about the same rate as land in farms—that is, about 14 percent. Again, as other population followed along after the first settlers, subdivision of farms took place and the character of local demand changed. This tended to displace grains and meat in the old sections. The same tendency was enhanced by rapid exhaustion of the soil by "soil-robbers" (e.g. New England and New York). Thus the process of settlement seems to have accounted for much of the changes in the composition of output, until recently, and for the fact that these changes have exhibited no single long-term trend.

The second historical process referred to above, the industrial development of the United States, has been chiefly determined by the equally unique but different movement called the Industrial Revolution. Because developments in the two fields, agriculture and industry, have been principally the results of these two almost entirely independent processes there is no *a priori* reason to expect that the rate of growth should have been similar in both. Comparisons of such rates are therefore almost meaningless, in any scientific sense. They are ratios between two independent variables.

These two movements were also entirely separate in their influence on growth and allocation of population. Settlement without the Industrial Revolution might have increased the population from 4 to 40 million, as noted above. The Industrial Revolution appears to have been responsible for the other two thirds of the increase to 1940. And this accords with the figures for Western Europe where, in the most intense period of industrialization (1810–1910, say) the population increased to about 3 times (200 percent) its former level, although, there, no opportunity for further settlement on the land existed. (Neither was there "diversion of human resources" on any extensive scale abroad. Approximately the same population remained on the land. It was the increase that went into industry.) Thus, after this form of industrialization, countries generally seem to show about one third the proportion of population on the land that existed before. Taking the broad view, it was the process of settlement, which occurred only here, that determined the expansion of agriculture and the growth of population on the land; it was the independent process of the Industrial Revolution that determined the change, here and abroad (Western Europe), from the old to a new ratio of population on the land to total population. Settlement is now probably complete; industrialization may not be; if industrialization continues to develop, population will probably continue to increase; therefore this one factor in the ratio will probably determine the trend in ratio of population on the land to total population. But whether or not such future industrialization will occur cannot be determined by extrapolation of past time series even of the very recent past.

Of the total increase of population nearly one third was due to immigration in the nineteenth and twentieth centuries. Of this number—some 38 million in all—all but 7 million came over after 1870. Therefore, though immigrants did participate in the settlement process, both before and after 1870, they came chiefly for industrial employment in the period after our industrialization had really got going. The relation of that portion of our growth of population to industrialization was a direct one. The growth was in response to demand for industrial labor and was the chief limiting factor upon the rate of industrialization. However, that immigration for industrial employment was largely responsible for the change in the relative figures between 1870 and 1920. There was no drift away from the land; there was a drift of foreign population to industry. The significance to both agriculture and industry of the reduction of this immigration in 1924 and its near cessation in 1930 has not yet been appraised.

Besides facilitating the process of settlement in many ways (e.g. transportation) and making possible some industrialization of the farm (e.g. power and machinery) the Industrial Revolution relieved the farming population of much manufacturing and, on the other hand, it concentrated almost all agricultural production on the farm. On both sides the last process represents a change in product rather than a change in productivity and should modify estimates of changes in productivity, even after 1899, to a very considerable extent.

From this more inclusive and more fundamental viewpoint the authors' choice of the period to be studied—doubtless on account of availability of statistics—seems unfortunate. Their forty years divides itself into two halves, which in certain respects are in marked contrast to one another. The first half appears to represent the last two decades of the process of settlement. The peak of acreage so far was in 1920; that of employment of males so far was also in 1920. The second half may possibly represent new trends—drift from the farm, etc. But twenty years of troublous times are not enough to settle that question. So far the signs of drift are only marked in the last decade (1930–40) which included the prolonged depression and the prolonged drought. At any rate, from this standpoint it appears clearly unsafe to hitch together trends prior to, and trends after, 1920. The forty years represents a mixture in which the trends in certain respects are in opposite directions. Even though the direction may seem to be the same in some cases, the causes may be quite different. Finally, if there is any chance that these recent trends merely represent swings, or temporary processes, it is clearly unsafe to let them delude us into dismantling any part of our agricultural economy or allowing it to run down. And, on the chance that the Malthusian "law" is still operating under our noses, it may be wiser to tide over, by artificial measures, what may prove to be only an interim period before the pressure of population on the food supply will again begin to be felt.

Appendix A

The Net Output of Agriculture

Appendix A

The Net Output of Agriculture

THIS appendix describes the construction, and offers some notes on the coverage, of the indexes of agricultural output appearing in Chapters 2 and 3. In Table A-1 will be found the entire body of basic data underlying the computation of these indexes; sources of material are indicated in detail in notes following the table. Table A-2 shows the farm value of net output for each product in selected years. Table A-3 contains the indexes of net output of crops and livestock products, respectively, mentioned in Chapter 2. In Table A-4 will be found continuous series for milk production, in original units which, while not used directly in the construction of the indexes, afford a basis for Chart 30 in Chapter 3.

Gross and Net Output

The gross output of crops is the amount harvested, of dairy products the total amount produced, and of livestock the number or weight sold plus or minus additions to or deductions from inventory. As explained in Chapter 1, an index of agricultural output computed from the gross output of individual products would involve duplication, since it would include commodities that never leave agriculture but are used up in the productive process itself. From the data for gross output we therefore deducted in the case of each product the amounts used for further production, i.e. crops used for seed and feed and, in the case of milk, the amount fed to calves. For many commodities these deductions are small, or do not have to be made at all: as noted in Chapter 3, they are most important in the case of the grains and hay. In Table A-1, which contains the basic data underlying our group and combined indexes, deductions for seed and feed have been made wherever necessary. The quantity data in that table therefore relate to net output rather than to gross output. For recent years the disposition studies of the Department of Agriculture make the transition from gross output to net output a comparatively simple matter. For early years we had to construct what appeared to us as the best estimates of seed and feed requirements that could be devised. The sources of the original data and the adjustments made are indicated in footnotes to the table.

Method of Construction of the Output Indexes

As in Solomon Fabricant's *The Output of Manufacturing Industries, 1899–1937* (National Bureau of Economic Research, 1940), the first report in this series, the standard basis of comparison adopted was that usually known as the Edgeworth formula:

$$\frac{\Sigma q_1 (p_0 + p_1)}{\Sigma + q_0 (p_0 + p_1)}$$

where the q's refer to quantities, the p's to prices,[1] and the suffixes identify the years to be compared. This is equivalent to the ratio of the values of the outputs in the two years, these values being computed in constant prices: for each commodity the price chosen is its mean for the two years considered. The formula has the advantage that the weighting system is revised for each new comparison and, when computed for successive pairs of years, additional commodities can be included as data become available. The index takes the form of a chain of such comparisons. However, it may readily be shown that a series of successive year-to-year comparisons between, say, 1899 and 1939, may offer a result which differs significantly from that obtained in a single direct comparison between the years in question. At different points in this study we have been interested both in year-to-year changes and in long term trends. Some form of compromise had therefore to be adopted. In fact the construction of each of our

[1] So far as possible average prices received by farmers during the crop year or marketing season were used.

indexes involved the following steps. First, comparisons were made between 1899 and 1909, 1909 and 1919, 1919 and 1929, and 1929 and 1937.[2] Second, a chain index was computed for the entire period 1897 [3] to 1939, and this annual series was then fitted into the framework provided by the four comparisons just mentioned. That is, for the years 1899–1909 we adjusted the chain index by distributing the discrepancy between it and the direct comparison 1899–1909 in an even fashion over the decade in question. For 1897 and 1898 and for 1938 and 1939 the chain comparisons were left undisturbed. In this way the comparison between 1899 and 1937 as reported by the index involves four links only; that between 1899 and 1939 involves six links. The comparison between, say, 1909 and 1921, is made in three links, two of which (1919–20 and 1920–21) involve a small adjustment of the type mentioned.

As a check upon the results a value for the combined index was also computed with the use of a single direct comparison between five-year averages centered upon 1899 and 1937 respectively. Thus the standard method of construction described above and used in computing the data in Tables 1, 5 and 6 leads to a rise of 47.7 percent between 1897–1901 and 1935–39, whereas according to a direct Edgeworth comparison between the two periods the expansion of output was 42.1 percent. The latter calculation omits some products, data for which are not available in 1897–1901. The output of these products (especially truck crops) expanded rather rapidly, and this explains why the direct comparison reports a smaller rise in farm output over forty years than does our basic index.

Coverage of the Basic Index

The most convenient way of assessing the coverage of our basic index of agricultural output is to measure it against the United

[2] Except for 1937 these are Census years. The year 1937 was selected instead of 1939 because many calculations had to be made before data for the latter year were available.

[3] The calculations were carried back to 1897 in order that five-year averages might go back to 1899.

States Department of Agriculture estimates of gross farm income. This is preferable to a comparison with Census data, since the latter are expressed in terms of gross rather than of net output. As explained in Chapter 1, gross income is comparable with net rather than with gross output.

To carry out such a comparison for 1937, the most recent year in our chain of decennial Edgeworth comparisons, it would be simplest to compute the total value of those products included in our index by multiplying 1937 net output by 1937 farm price (as is done in Table A-2), and then to express this total as a percentage of gross farm income. However, since gross income is reported for calendar years, while our output data relate partly to crop years, such a comparison could not be made. We circumvented this difficulty by summating instead the official (calendar-year) income estimates for all products included in our index, and expressed the aggregate as a percentage of gross farm income as a whole. The result indicates that in 1937 our index covers 93 percent of agricultural production as defined in the gross income estimates of the Department of Agriculture.[4]

For earlier years the coverage is naturally lower, but it cannot be computed accurately owing to the absence of detailed estimates of farm income. We can, however, gauge approximately the limits of the error to which our output index is subject on account of changing coverage. This may be done as follows. Let us assume that the output of the products omitted in any given year (say 1919) was actually zero in the preceding Edgeworth comparison year (1909), but that the prices were the same in both years. We can then compute an index—for 1909—whose coverage includes the omitted products. The assumption is the most extreme it is possible to make, for we know that most of the omitted products, although produced in smaller quantities, were available; and the output of some may actually have been as large or larger in the year for which data are not available.

The computation was carried out for the links 1919–29, 1909–19 and 1899–1909, with the following results (1929: 100):

[4] The most important items omitted are forest products, nursery products, the output of farm gardens, seeds, and horses and mules.

For 1919 the index is lowered from 87.1 to 86.6
" 1909 " " " " " 77.4 " 76.0
" 1899 " " " " " 69.5 " 67.4

The error is of course cumulative, since we are working with a chain of several Edgeworth comparisons. If we consider only two Edgeworth years at a time, we find that the change is about the same in 1899 as in 1909, and smallest in 1919.

We can now make our assumption somewhat more realistic, restricting our computation to the 1909–19 comparison. For most of the crops which are excluded from the comparison between these two years we have Census value figures. The total value of these crops amounts to $105 million in 1909, as against roughly $290 million in 1919. When we take into account the unusually high price level which obtained in 1919, it seems fair to say that the output of omitted products in 1909 must have been at least 50 percent of the output of these same products in 1919. On this assumption we obtain an index for 1909 (1919: 100) of 88.4, which is only half a point below the value computed for our basic index. There can be little doubt that this represents the maximum degree of upward bias present in our index for the decade in question. In the same manner we can allow for the possibility of downward bias. Assume that the output of omitted items fell as much as 50 percent between two reference years, say 1909 and 1919. This is a violent assumption, which is no doubt far from the truth. It yields an index for 1909 (1919: 100) of 90.5 compared with 88.9 for our basic index unadjusted for omitted items.

We can conclude, at least for the period since 1909, that changes in coverage do not affect our basic index by more than about one percentage point per decade in either direction.

Crop Years

The production and price data in Table A-1, and the various indexes of output computed from them, relate to crop years in the case of crops, and to calendar years in the case of livestock and livestock products. The crop year corresponds to the marketing season. "Crop year 1935" normally means a twelve-month period starting some time in 1935 and ending some time in 1936.

The following information was taken from *Crops and Markets*, November 1937, and *Farm Production, Disposition and Value of Principal Crops, 1938–40* (U. S. Agricultural Marketing Service, 1941); the reader is referred to these publications for further details. The months given are in each case the first month of the crop year or marketing season; marketing usually extends over twelve months, although in the case of some products the season is shorter. Thus "crop year 1935" for wheat extends from July 1, 1935 to June 30, 1936; for corn from October 1, 1935 to September 30, 1936; and so forth. In the case of fruits and vegetables the crop year given is for fresh consumption; production for canning or processing sometimes has a different marketing season. In the case of many products, a few states have a slightly different crop year from that shown. For a number of items no single crop year can be given, since the marketing season varies with the variety or the region; these exceptions are rice, potatoes, peanuts, tobacco, apples, snap beans, beets, cabbage, celery, peppers.

February—Asparagus.

March—Maple sugar and sirup, California Valencia oranges

April—Cantaloups, sweet corn, onions

May—Apricots, peaches, plums, prunes, watermelons

June—Figs, grapes, pears

July—Wheat, oats, barley, rye, flaxseed, sweetpotatoes, sorgo sirup, broomcorn, hay

August—Cotton, cottonseed, almonds

September—Buckwheat, dry edible beans, sugar beets, hops, cranberries, Florida oranges, grapefruit

October—Corn, sugarcane, soybeans, olives, California navel oranges, walnuts, pecans

November—Lemons, carrots, cauliflower, cucumbers, eggplant, lettuce, peas, spinach, tomatoes

December—Strawberries

Composition of Combined and Group Indexes

The combined (or basic) index for the net output of agriculture, shown in Tables 1, 5 and 6, and Chart 1, includes for all or part of the period all products shown in Table A-1. In any particular year, it includes all products for which both quantities and prices are given in that table.

As explained in the text, the groups shown in Tables 5 and 6 and Charts 3 and 5 are neither exhaustive nor free from duplication. The composition of these groups is as follows:

Grains—Wheat, corn, oats, rye, barley, rice, buckwheat, flaxseed

Potatoes and related products—Potatoes, sweetpotatoes, dry edible beans

Hay—Hay

Cotton—Cotton, cottonseed

Tobacco—Tobacco

Sugar crops—Sugar beets, sugarcane, sugarcane sirup, sorgo sirup, maple sirup, maple sugar

Wool—Wool, mohair

Meat animals—Cattle, calves, sheep and lambs, hogs

Poultry and eggs—Chickens, eggs

Milk and milk products—Whole milk, butter, butterfat

Fruit, noncitrus—Apples, apricots, figs, grapes, peaches, pears, plums, prunes, cranberries, strawberries

Fruit, citrus—Oranges, lemons, grapefruit

Oil crops—Flaxseed, peanuts, soybeans, cottonseed

Truck crops—Artichokes, asparagus, snap beans, beets, cabbage, cantaloups, carrots, cauliflower, celery, sweet corn, cucumbers, eggplant, lettuce, onions, peas, peppers, spinach, tomatoes, watermelons

Tree nuts—Almonds, pecans, walnuts

TABLE A-1

PHYSICAL OUTPUT AND FARM PRICE OF INDIVIDUAL PRODUCTS, 1897–1939

A general note appears at the end of this table, followed by specific notes numbered in the same manner as the columns to which they refer.

	(1) Wheat		(2) Corn		(3) Oats		(4) Barley		(5) Rice	
	Net Output	*Price*	*Net Output*	*Price*	*Net Output*	*Price*	*Net Output*	*Price*	*Net Output*	*Price*
Year	Mil. bu.	¢ per bu.	Mil. bu.	¢ per bu.	Mil. bu.	¢ per bu.	Mil. bu.	¢ per bu.	Mil. bu.	¢ per bu.
1897	576.1	80.9	457.5	26.0	248.9	21.0	51.3	34.3	5.91	73
1898	714.9	57.9	470.3	28.5	252.7	25.1	49.1	38.9	7.28	82
1899	574.1	58.8	529.2	29.8	281.2	24.5	59.1	38.8	7.86	82
1900	531.3	62.1	532.4	35.0	283.6	25.3	48.3	40.7	8.54	74
1901	704.4	63.1	343.2	60.0	239.9	39.7	61.9	45.4	11.11	74
1902	630.2	63.0	554.8	40.1	323.1	30.5	73.1	45.3	12.84	76
1903	585.4	69.3	503.0	41.9	265.6	33.7	74.7	44.7	17.33	77
1904	484.5	92.6	537.3	43.6	303.5	30.9	83.1	41.2	17.69	65
1905	627.0	74.7	590.8	40.6	331.3	28.8	85.8	39.4	14.52	94
1906	662.5	66.0	606.6	39.1	306.8	31.7	89.6	41.8	16.09	90
1907	542.1	86.6	522.8	50.5	240.3	44.4	75.3	66.5	18.94	85
1908	561.6	96.7	513.3	65.0	248.8	49.2	85.4	56.6	20.41	81
1909	614.9	99.1	574.6	61.6	331.3	42.8	90.1	55.8	21.48	79
1910	560.4	90.8	599.7	51.6	335.2	35.6	73.9	60.7	22.69	67
1911	507.7	86.9	487.9	68.0	245.3	44.9	81.0	82.5	20.51	80
1912	633.6	80.7	589.3	55.3	400.1	33.7	103.7	50.9	21.37	93
1913	639.1	79.4	393.4	70.4	280.4	38.6	77.4	52.5	22.09	86
1914	788.9	97.4	488.5	70.8	314.1	43.9	85.5	53.7	21.16	92
1915	900.3	96.1	546.4	68.0	412.2	38.3	94.1	52.0	23.54	90
1916	517.3	143.4	452.5	116.6	318.2	48.7	69.2	80.4	36.66	88
1917	501.9	204.7	653.9	145.9	447.1	70.1	75.1	123.2	31.43	189
1918	769.9	205.0	419.1	152.2	386.7	68.5	89.2	95.1	36.69	191
1919	825.3	216.3	510.1	151.3	292.8	76.7	49.7	124.4	39.12	266
1920	734.1	182.6	741.9	61.8	431.7	53.8	68.5	84.4	48.68	118
1921	697.8	103.0	639.1	52.3	265.1	32.2	53.1	47.8	36.18	94
1922	712.2	96.6	533.7	74.5	300.0	37.4	61.7	49.9	39.01	92
1923	615.7	92.6	621.0	82.5	324.9	40.7	62.8	54.6	30.69	110
1924	706.0	124.7	450.4	106.1	412.3	47.8	68.9	74.2	30.07	134
1925	561.7	143.7	619.8	69.9	373.6	38.9	74.2	61.4	30.07	148
1926	714.7	121.7	498.5	74.5	272.7	40.0	50.9	57.9	39.06	113
1927	740.7	119.0	537.6	85.0	230.1	47.1	79.5	68.9	41.68	90
1928	774.1	99.8	567.0	84.0	290.1	40.7	108.7	56.8	41.26	91
1929	681.1	103.6	490.1	79.9	228.3	41.8	76.7	53.9	36.69	99
1930	648.4	67.1	358.0	59.6	215.1	32.2	79.6	40.5	42.05	78
1931	687.6	39.0	470.7	32.0	190.0	21.3	36.8	32.8	41.99	48
1932	548.5	38.2	587.2	31.9	210.1	15.7	75.0	22.1	39.09	41
1933	401.6	74.4	437.0	52.2	96.6	33.5	45.4	43.5	35.07	77
1934	360.1	84.8	170.1	81.5	58.9	48.0	39.8	68.6	36.49	79
1935	455.6	83.2	409.5	65.5	203.7	26.3	98.6	37.8	36.52	77
1936	441.9	102.6	245.1	104.4	120.7	44.9	52.3	78.4	46.60	83
1937	668.3	96.3	595.0	51.8	224.4	30.1	87.7	54.0	50.22	65
1938	730.3	56.1	629.6	50.0	175.8	23.7	96.3	36.6	49.46	64
1939	585.1	69.1	704.7	56.7	154.3	31.1	106.5	40.3	50.44	72

TABLE A-1—INDIVIDUAL PRODUCTS (continued)

Year	(6) RYE Net Output Mil. bu.	(6) RYE Price ¢ per bu.	(7) FLAXSEED Net Output Mil. bu.	(7) FLAXSEED Price ¢ per bu.	(8) BUCKWHEAT Net Output Mil. bu.	(8) BUCKWHEAT Price ¢ per bu.	(9) POTATOES Net Output Mil. bu.	(9) POTATOES Price ¢ per bu.	(10) SWEETPOTATOES Net Output Mil. bu.	(10) SWEETPOTATOES Price ¢ per bu.
1897	22.1	42.6	12.20	78	9.23	41.9	166.5	49.8	34.1	53.5
1898	20.6	44.1	17.36	90	7.73	44.8	201.9	38.0	41.6	(55.0)
1899	17.8	49.5	18.45	98	7.05	56.1	229.0	36.1	34.7	58.1
1900	18.5	50.1	14.27	146	7.39	55.8	218.1	38.7	37.5	55.6
1901	21.3	55.0	25.47	133	9.79	56.3	174.2	69.0	39.5	63.1
1902	24.3	50.0	34.33	105	8.66	59.5	249.1	42.7	40.2	63.6
1903	20.2	53.5	24.21	81	9.15	60.8	232.1	55.1	43.4	64.0
1904	19.6	69.2	21.28	99	10.02	62.5	293.6	40.8	45.5	66.4
1905	22.2	60.3	27.28	84	10.38	58.3	252.6	55.1	48.0	63.8
1906	21.0	58.5	26.15	102	9.53	59.4	286.8	45.6	47.4	68.3
1907	19.8	72.6	22.50	96	9.12	69.9	279.8	54.7	47.0	77.7
1908	19.9	72.8	19.48	116	9.40	77.7	256.4	67.8	51.1	73.2
1909	19.9	73.0	18.14	142	9.10	72.3	326.6	56.8	48.4	76.2
1910	18.6	72.9	9.94	228	8.68	67.5	289.9	58.8	49.5	78.9
1911	19.7	80.7	17.01	197	8.04	75.8	254.0	94.3	45.3	92.0
1912	25.4	65.0	27.11	129	8.59	67.8	336.0	55.7	46.5	86.8
1913	26.5	61.0	14.28	123	5.67	76.2	280.9	68.2	45.9	83.7
1914	28.6	82.3	12.36	131	6.91	80.6	302.0	55.9	44.4	85.2
1915	32.8	84.0	10.60	168	6.56	81.6	285.9	68.1	51.9	76.1
1916	26.1	112.4	10.75	231	5.33	126.6	224.4	152.8	50.5	96.6
1917	39.8	173.4	7.48	311	6.93	167.1	333.0	125.5	59.7	128.2
1918	59.7	149.6	11.97	358	7.47	163.9	296.1	118.8	56.3	151.5
1919	58.6	145.9	5.86	442	6.14	158.7	251.8	193.6	64.2	169.0
1920	45.0	146.4	10.27	233	5.72	125.4	304.1	125.3	63.2	141.7
1921	40.0	84.0	7.51	165	5.16	87.9	270.6	113.3	60.5	113.1
1922	78.8	63.9	9.44	208	4.99	89.5	332.4	65.9	64.3	100.4
1923	36.5	59.3	14.70	212	4.59	95.8	309.5	92.5	52.4	120.6
1924	43.7	95.3	29.59	218	4.43	107.4	321.3	68.6	36.8	149.6
1925	30.5	79.0	20.78	226	4.54	87.2	254.6	170.5	41.1	165.1
1926	21.9	83.0	17.04	203	4.80	87.1	273.0	131.4	51.9	117.4
1927	38.3	83.5	23.74	192	5.09	86.9	315.4	101.9	58.2	109.0
1928	25.5	83.6	17.38	194	4.65	89.9	341.7	52.3	48.5	118.0
1929	20.6	85.7	13.61	281	4.13	96.3	284.4	131.6	53.3	117.1
1930	18.5	44.5	19.71	161	3.53	78.9	288.4	91.4	44.6	108.2
1931	10.8	34.1	10.33	117	3.29	42.3	318.6	45.9	54.8	72.7
1932	14.2	28.1	10.52	88	3.01	43.4	311.8	37.7	70.9	54.2
1933	6.0	62.7	6.03	163	3.06	55.8	287.6	82.3	61.7	69.5
1934	1.4	71.8	4.38	170	3.01	58.6	326.5	44.6	63.6	79.8
1935	28.6	39.5	13.15	142	3.20	55.0	319.0	59.2	68.2	70.4
1936	4.9	80.9	4.54	190	2.58	85.2	280.5	114.0	52.6	93.2
1937	24.1	68.6	6.49	187	2.74	66.9	333.9	52.8	61.6	82.5
1938	25.8	33.8	6.79	159	2.60	54.4	312.9	55.8	62.9	73.3
1939	15.8	44.0	18.25	146	2.35	62.8	307.2	68.7	59.6	74.9

TABLE A-1—INDIVIDUAL PRODUCTS (continued)

Year	(11) Dry Edible Beans: Net Output, Mil. bags	(11) Dry Edible Beans: Price, $ per bag	(12) Sugar Beets: Net Output, Th. s.t.	(12) Sugar Beets: Price, $ per s.t.	(13) Sugarcane: Net Output, Th. s.t.	(13) Sugarcane: Price, $ per s.t.	(14) Sugarcane Sirup: Net Output, Mil. gal.	(14) Sugarcane Sirup: Price, ¢ per gal.	(15) Sorgo Sirup: Net Output, Mil. gal.	(15) Sorgo Sirup: Pric[illegible], ¢ per gal.
1897	2.46	..	410	(4.19)	4,384	3.60	..	..	..	..
1898	2.58	..	360	(4.19)	4,361	4.20	..	..	..	..
1899	2.70	2.52	835	(4.19)	2,138	4.40	..	..	..	..
1900	3.04	..	853	(4.19)	4,561	4.60	..	..	..	..
1901	3.37	..	1,770	4.50	4,550	4.00	..	..	..	..
1902	3.70	..	1,991	5.03	5,222	3.50	..	..	..	..
1903	4.03	..	2,180	4.97	3,892	3.70	..	..	..	..
1904	4.36	..	2,176	4.95	5,810	4.00	..	..	..	..
1905	4.69	..	2,799	5.00	5,474	4.30	..	..	..	..
1906	5.03	..	4,448	5.10	3,808	3.70	..	..	..	..
1907	5.36	..	3,956	5.20	5,516	3.80	..	..	..	..
1908	5.69	..	3,586	5.35	5,796	4.10	..	..	..	..
1909	6.02	3.30	4,285	5.06	4,389	3.83	21.6	46.3	..	..
1910	5.57	3.44	4,249	5.45	5,222	3.69	24.2	47.2	..	..
1911	6.16	3.57	5,315	5.50	6,010	4.29	25.1	46.6	..	..
1912	6.25	3.44	5,648	5.82	2,292	3.73	26.3	44.6	..	..
1913	5.56	3.40	5,886	5.69	4,326	3.13	26.6	45.5	..	..
1914	6.64	4.00	5,585	5.45	3,256	3.75	24.4	45.0	..	..
1915	6.56	4.86	6,511	5.67	2,034	4.55	24.9	49.4	..	..
1916	5.46	9.32	6,228	6.12	4,171	5.29	27.9	58.6	..	..
1917	8.17	10.02	5,980	7.39	3,845	7.10	29.1	64.4	..	..
1918	8.78	7.30	5,949	10.00	4,220	7.28	33.4	79.4	..	..
1919	7.38	7.19	6,421	11.74	1,899	14.00	23.1	108.4	30.95	108.7
1920	5.41	4.23	8,538	11.63	2,593	5.76	23.1	103.5	32.90	106.7
1921	5.20	4.78	7,782	6.35	4,228	3.63	23.3	47.6	28.80	60.8
1922	6.70	5.99	5,183	7.91	3,787	5.83	22.7	54.4	18.85	70.0
1923	8.18	5.53	7,006	8.99	2,427	7.09	19.3	71.4	14.76	83.3
1924	7.63	6.07	7,508	7.95	1,228	5.58	17.9	69.7	12.13	93.8
1925	9.90	5.00	7,381	6.39	2,644	4.05	15.7	76.9	10.71	93.1
1926	8.97	4.70	7,223	7.61	864	4.92	16.8	72.9	14.88	83.2
1927	8.37	5.78	7,753	7.67	962	4.61	17.0	75.6	12.05	83.7
1928	9.12	7.74	7,101	7.11	1,873	3.85	18.3	69.3	10.68	90.3
1929	10.62	6.83	7,315	7.08	3,120	3.73	19.7	71.7	9.38	89.[illegible]
1930	12.46	4.04	9,199	7.14	2,910	3.31	17.4	58.0	8.88	78.[illegible]
1931	11.33	2.08	7,903	5.94	2,524	3.21	15.2	50.3	17.89	42.8
1932	9.68	1.98	9,070	5.26	3,307	2.98	18.4	40.1	15.51	37.8
1933	11.26	2.78	11,030	5.13	3,069	3.18	22.0	45.8	15.87	47.9
1934	9.79	3.51	7,519	5.16	3,403	2.33	25.6	45.5	14.52	50.[illegible]
1935	12.55	2.94	7,908	5.76	4,573	3.15	26.0	42.4	13.35	54.9
1936	9.54	5.38	9,028	6.05	5,419	3.67	22.7	42.8	11.89	56.8
1937	13.96	3.08	8,784	5.27	5,892	2.90	25.1	44.4	11.92	56.[illegible]
1938	13.35	2.54	11,615	4.65	6,741	2.70	22.2	44.4	11.40	55.[illegible]
1939	12.77	3.24	10,781	4.76	5,783	2.84	24.9	42.9	10.23	58.[illegible]

TABLE A-1—INDIVIDUAL PRODUCTS (continued)

Year	(16) MAPLE SIRUP Net Output Mil. gal.	(16) MAPLE SIRUP Price $ per gal.	(17) MAPLE SUGAR Net Output Th. lb.	(17) MAPLE SUGAR Price ¢ per lb.	(18) PEANUTS Net Output Mil. lb.	(18) PEANUTS Price ¢ per lb.	(19) SOYBEANS Used for Crushing Th. bu.	(19) SOYBEANS Price $ per bu.	(20) HOPS Net Output Mil. lb.	(20) HOPS Price ¢ per lb.
1897	..	..	..	..	198	3.2	..	..	43.1	9.3
1898	..	..	..	..	223	3.8	..	..	41.1	13.0
1899	..	..	..	..	252	3.5	..	..	49.2	8.2
1900	..	..	..	..	270	3.2	..	..	45.0	12.0
1901	..	..	..	..	285	3.8	..	..	39.9	12.3
1902	..	..	..	..	301	4.0	..	..	38.8	22.9
1903	..	..	..	..	318	5.1	..	..	39.0	22.9
1904	..	..	..	..	337	4.5	..	..	44.3	27.2
1905	..	..	..	..	356	4.4	..	..	49.1	14.9
1906	..	..	..	..	376	4.9	..	..	60.3	11.4
1907	..	..	..	..	399	4.1	..	..	54.0	9.9
1908	..	..	..	..	423	4.4	..	..	39.0	10.9
1909	..	..	..	..	449	4.9	..	..	40.0	22.2
1910	..	..	..	..	472	4.7	..	..	44.0	15.8
1911	..	..	..	..	494	4.6	..	..	51.7	41.8
1912	..	..	..	..	516	4.7	..	..	53.4	18.3
1913	..	..	..	..	538	4.7	..	..	62.9	22.8
1914	..	..	..	..	561	4.4	..	..	43.4	14.9
1915	..	..	..	..	583	4.3	..	..	53.0	11.7
1916	..	..	..	..	606	4.65	..	..	50.6	12.0
1917	4.26	..	10,525	..	927	7.12	..	..	29.4	33.3
1918	4.86	..	12,944	..	821	6.45	..	..	21.5	19.3
1919	3.26	2.63	9,541	32.5	615	9.40	..	..	28.3	77.4
1920	3.13	..	6,928	..	622	4.82	..	..	33.6	35.7
1921	2.15	..	4,699	..	611	3.86	..	..	29.3	24.1
1922	3.37	..	5,227	..	459	5.37	159	2.01	27.7	8.6
1923	3.26	..	4,656	..	491	6.48	102	2.28	19.8	18.8
1924	3.57	2.00	4,096	26.0	636	5.81	307	2.47	27.7	10.3
1925	2.82	2.08	3,238	26.9	652	4.50	351	2.34	28.6	21.8
1926	3.50	2.12	3,585	29.3	583	4.83	335	2.00	31.5	23.1
1927	3.43	2.05	3,183	28.7	759	5.12	559	1.83	30.7	22.9
1928	2.78	2.02	2,189	28.6	752	4.96	883	1.90	32.9	19.3
1929	2.36	2.03	1,362	30.0	814	3.75	1,666	1.87	33.2	11.4
1930	3.64	2.03	2,370	30.1	599	3.58	4,069	1.32	23.4	14.8
1931	2.21	1.72	1,646	25.7	947	2.02	4,725	.48	26.4	13.8
1932	2.41	1.51	1,623	24.5	844	1.54	3,470	.56	24.1	17.5
1933	2.19	1.18	1,288	20.8	712	2.84	3,054	.99	40.0	30.4
1934	2.40	1.33	1,271	24.7	904	3.32	9,105	1.01	43.2	14.5
1935	3.38	1.42	1,704	26.5	1,033	3.14	25,181	.79	42.3	9.8
1936	2.40	1.44	985	26.7	1,142	3.74	20,618	1.28	25.2	27.6
1937	2.51	1.60	1,047	29.0	1,112	3.31	30,310	.84	39.5	16.2
1938	2.77	1.61	1,078	28.3	1,193	3.28	44,648	.68	29.6	19.7
1939	2.52	1.71	760	29.3	1,076	3.39	57,072	.77	31.5	27.8

TABLE A-1—INDIVIDUAL PRODUCTS (continued)

	(21) Broomcorn		(22) Hay		(23) Cotton		(24) Cottonseed		(25) Tobacco	
	Net Output	*Price*	*Sales off Farms*	*Price*	*Net Output*	*Price*	*Net Output*	*Price*	*Net Output*	*Price*
Year	Th. s.t.	$ per s.t.	Mil. s.t.	$ per s.t.	Mil. bales	$ per bale	Mil. s.t.	$ per s.t.	Mil. lb.	¢ per lb.
1897	..	..	11.4	7.21	10.99	33.40	2.10	9.5	703	7.4
1898	..	..	12.4	6.52	11.53	28.65	2.35	9.7	909	6.1
1899	..	..	11.1	8.20	9.35	34.90	2.48	13.3	870	7.1
1900	..	..	10.6	9.78	10.12	45.75	2.42	13.6	852	6.7
1901	..	..	10.5	9.88	9.51	35.15	3.15	16.6	886	7.2
1902	..	..	11.4	9.05	10.63	38.00	3.27	16.2	960	6.9
1903	..	..	12.2	9.18	9.85	52.45	3.24	14.0	976	6.7
1904	..	..	12.6	8.82	13.44	44.90	3.34	10.8	857	7.8
1905	..	..	12.8	8.49	10.58	53.90	3.13	13.1	939	8.2
1906	..	..	11.7	10.40	13.27	47.90	3.84	18.5	973	9.6
1907	..	..	12.6	11.60	11.11	51.80	2.56	18.0	886	10.0
1908	..	..	13.4	9.47	13.24	45.05	3.67	16.2	836	10.2
1909	..	..	13.0	10.58	10.00	67.60	3.27	24.15	1,054	10.1
1910	..	..	12.0	11.54	11.61	69.80	4.11	25.99	1,142	9.3
1911	..	..	9.8	14.32	15.70	48.25	4.92	17.15	941	9.3
1912	..	..	12.3	11.17	13.70	57.50	4.58	18.33	1,117	10.7
1913	..	..	10.6	11.49	14.15	62.35	4.85	21.90	992	12.8
1914	..	..	10.7	10.92	16.11	36.75	5.77	15.46	1,037	9.7
1915	..	..	10.8	10.34	11.17	56.10	4.19	30.13	1,157	9.0
1916	..	..	11.0	11.21	11.45	86.80	4.50	45.70	1,207	14.8
1917	..	..	9.1	16.60	11.28	135.45	4.26	64.30	1,326	24.0
1918	..	..	8.4	19.88	12.02	144.40	4.46	65.16	1,445	27.9
1919	54.6	155.0	8.7	21.00	11.41	176.70	3.99	65.59	1,444	31.2
1920	37.8	127.5	8.0	16.46	13.43	79.45	4.10	25.65	1,509	17.3
1921	39.2	71.6	6.8	11.63	7.94	85.00	2.90	29.07	1,005	19.5
1922	38.2	219.3	7.0	11.64	9.76	114.40	3.22	30.33	1,254	22.8
1923	81.4	160.2	6.7	13.08	10.14	143.45	3.28	41.20	1,518	19.0
1924	77.0	96.1	6.1	12.66	13.63	114.55	4.59	33.25	1,245	19.0
1925	31.0	142.9	5.2	12.77	16.10	98.05	5.52	31.69	1,376	16.8
1926	54.2	79.2	4.4	13.24	17.98	62.35	6.36	22.08	1,289	17.9
1927	40.1	103.0	4.4	10.29	12.96	100.95	4.59	34.86	1,211	20.7
1928	52.6	97.4	3.5	11.22	14.48	89.95	5.08	34.15	1,373	20.0
1929	47.3	114.5	3.0	10.90	14.82	83.95	5.02	30.94	1,533	18.3
1930	51.1	66.3	2.2	11.06	13.93	47.30	4.69	22.09	1,648	12.8
1931	49.3	44.8	2.3	8.69	17.10	28.30	5.62	8.97	1,564	8.2
1932	40.9	37.0	2.4	6.22	13.00	32.60	4.54	10.30	1,017	10.5
1933	30.0	102.0	2.3	8.12	13.05	50.85	4.16	12.88	1,371	13.0
1934	28.7	164.4	1.9	13.28	9.64	61.80	3.42	33.10	1,082	21.3
1935	61.3	73.9	2.3	7.51	10.64	55.45	3.75	30.51	1,297	18.4
1936	38.0	117.0	1.9	11.04	12.40	61.65	4.52	33.27	1,155	23.6
1937	45.5	70.3	2.2	8.69	18.95	42.05	6.62	19.51	1,563	20.4
1938	37.0	62.9	2.4	6.82	11.94	43.00	4.26	21.79	1,376	19.7
1939	30.3	107.1	2.3	7.08	11.82	45.45	4.16	21.15	1,849	15.4

TABLE A-1—INDIVIDUAL PRODUCTS (continued)

Year	(26) Apples		(27) Apricots		(28) Figs, Fresh and Canned		(29) Figs, Dried		(30) Grapes	
	Net Output Mil. bu.	*Price* $ per bu.	*Net Output* Th. s.t.	*Price* $ per s.t.	*Net Output* Th. s.t.	*Price* $ per s.t.	*Net Output* Th. s.t.	*Price* $ per s.t.	*Net Output* Th. s.t.	*Price* $ per s.t.
1897	163.7	.73	99	..	..	..	..	..	650	(22.0)
1898	118.1	.98	36	..	..	..	..	..	660	(22.0)
1899	175.4	.70	52	31	..	..	..	..	671	21.7
1900	205.9	.68	97	..	..	..	..	..	737	22.8
1901	135.5	.86	57	..	..	..	..	..	670	29.3
1902	212.3	.50	121	..	..	..	..	..	908	30.1
1903	195.7	.59	80	..	..	..	..	..	811	26.7
1904	233.6	.56	67	27	..	..	..	..	775	22.7
1905	136.2	.96	28	..	..	..	..	..	737	28.9
1906	216.7	.76	27	..	..	..	..	..	872	31.2
1907	119.6	.78	15	..	..	..	..	..	1,016	34.3
1908	148.9	.88	141	..	..	..	..	..	976	23.9
1909	145.4	.85	97	29.9	..	..	..	..	1,099	19.5
1910	141.6	.87	109	29.6	..	..	..	..	967	22.3
1911	214.0	.77	85	49.1	..	..	..	..	1,172	21.1
1912	235.2	.66	137	29.3	..	..	..	..	1,198	20.7
1913	145.4	.92	81	44.0	..	..	..	..	984	26.4
1914	253.2	.62	148	36.3	..	..	..	..	1,255	21.5
1915	230.0	.70	130	25.3	..	..	..	..	1,216	24.9
1916	193.9	.89	88	46.8	..	..	..	..	1,274	28.6
1917	166.7	1.15	133	56.6	..	..	..	..	1,441	33.3
1918	169.6	1.38	128	55.1	..	..	..	..	1,325	46.9
1919	140.6	1.75	172	87.1	.9	..	12.0	150	1,575	65.4
1920	206.7	1.22	108	87.4	1.2	..	12.3	90	1,521	77.4
1921	95.6	1.64	100	56.5	1.6	..	9.6	145	1,220	73.8
1922	189.4	1.02	163	76.5	2.6	..	11.0	120	1,985	48.8
1923	180.9	1.13	210	31.8	3.3	..	9.5	90	2,250	26.5
1924	160.2	1.21	142	52.3	2.2	104	8.5	100	1,775	39.2
1925	152.4	1.25	150	61.8	3.1	100	9.6	110	2,062	32.2
1926	222.3	.89	176	68.0	5.1	112	11.4	95	2,429	27.0
1927	115.7	1.40	210	57.3	5.4	100	12.0	45	2,450	26.9
1928	177.8	1.08	179	51.4	6.1	87	11.5	45	2,501	20.1
1929	135.1	1.39	221	64.4	7.3	100	17.0	90	2,085	27.3
1930	156.6	1.02	195	40.3	7.7	90	21.0	48	2,339	19.5
1931	203.3	.66	279	30.1	6.3	74	17.0	37	1,636	22.6
1932	142.6	.60	262	18.9	6.5	36.5	19.0	25.5	2,077	13.4
1933	144.1	.78	270	30.1	5.9	50.5	21.5	43.8	1,936	18.0
1934	125.7	.89	149	55.0	9.0	51.8	22.9	59.3	1,958	19.7
1935	173.9	.72	223	46.3	10.2	56.5	24.0	43.0	2,488	14.9
1936	117.5	1.05	254	38.3	11.0	54.0	20.0	77.0	1,916	21.6
1937	198.3	.67	321	37.6	12.0	70.3	28.7	68.0	2,767	20.7
1938	127.4	.83	176	36.6	11.0	56.5	31.5	65.1	2,704	14.8
1939	171.7	.64	315	33.7	12.0	50.4	25.0	77.8	2,471	16.4

TABLE A-1—INDIVIDUAL PRODUCTS (continued)

Year	(31) OLIVES Net Output Th. s.t.	(31) OLIVES Price $ per s.t.	(32) PEACHES Net Output Mil. bu.	(32) PEACHES Price $ per bu.	(33) PEARS Net Output Mil. bu.	(33) PEARS Price $ per bu.	(34) PLUMS, FRESH AND FOR CANNING Net Output Th. s.t.	(34) PLUMS, FRESH AND FOR CANNING Price $ per s.t.	(35) PRUNES, CANNED Net Output Th. s.t.	(35) PRUNES, CANNED Price $ per s.t.
1897	..	..	48.4	..	7.87	..	11.8	..	..	..
1898	..	..	50.9	..	7.80	..	8.6	..	..	..
1899	..	..	15.4	..	6.62	..	13.9	..	..	..
1900	..	..	49.4	..	9.32	..	18.2	..	..	..
1901	..	..	46.4	..	8.35	..	14.9	..	..	..
1902	..	..	37.8	..	9.87	..	23.3	..	..	..
1903	..	..	28.8	..	7.62	..	18.1	..	..	..
1904	..	..	41.1	..	10.02	..	16.7	..	..	..
1905	..	..	36.6	..	9.04	..	22.1	..	..	..
1906	..	..	44.1	..	11.18	..	20.5	..	..	..
1907	..	..	22.5	..	6.85	..	17.0	..	..	..
1908	..	..	48.1	..	11.64	..	28.7	..	..	..
1909	..	..	35.3	.83	9.12	.89	22.2	42.4	..	..
1910	..	..	43.7	1.00	10.75	1.01	22.4	42.3	..	..
1911	..	..	32.7	1.18	12.15	.85	23.4	58.2	..	..
1912	..	..	49.4	.94	12.77	.79	29.6	50.2	..	..
1913	..	..	41.7	1.04	10.91	.93	25.6	55.1	..	..
1914	..	..	52.3	1.02	13.24	.78	30.1	41.0	..	..
1915	..	..	60.4	.82	12.56	.90	34.0	30.3	..	..
1916	..	..	37.5	1.08	12.59	.93	30.5	52.8	..	..
1917	..	..	47.5	1.34	13.93	1.16	43.6	48.5	..	..
1918	..	..	37.9	1.67	13.59	1.38	38.8	65.4	..	..
1919	8.8	131.6	51.9	1.89	14.89	1.84	47.7	64.55	2.3	97.8
1920	8.0	78.5	44.7	2.21	17.43	1.68	42.3	82.74	1.7	41.8
1921	8.5	69.2	33.1	1.55	11.56	1.69	44.7	54.88	1.7	41.2
1922	9.7	88.7	57.7	1.41	20.49	1.09	56.1	47.40	4.2	35.5
1923	17.0	83.1	45.1	1.51	17.29	1.24	73.5	30.56	4.1	23.9
1924	6.5	72.1	52.0	1.32	18.72	1.43	44.8	43.06	2.1	22.4
1925	15.0	55.8	45.8	1.58	20.23	1.44	54.7	39.80	4.5	34.4
1926	12.2	92.2	65.3	1.07	24.84	.90	79.4	23.00	7.5	18.5
1927	20.8	85.3	40.8	1.26	18.25	1.34	60.9	44.75	6.9	19.7
1928	22.0	80.0	62.1	1.03	23.95	1.05	72.9	37.00	10.0	31.1
1929	21.0	66.9	44.7	1.51	21.60	1.45	44.4	85.95	16.1	25.8
1930	20.0	62.7	51.1	1.02	25.73	.76	89.4	35.08	13.3	18.3
1931	15.5	39.4	72.5	.60	24.42	.63	65.0	24.11	13.7	12.0
1932	16.8	32.0	35.6	.62	20.61	.42	64.2	17.52	10.2	9.4
1933	14.0	58.3	43.1	.82	21.08	.58	54.4	25.15	14.9	16.9
1934	17.7	85.3	45.3	.88	27.06	.70	67.5	32.79	18.8	17.1
1935	32.0	45.4	54.7	.90	25.30	.64	54.0	36.41	28.0	13.5
1936	27.0	62.5	47.5	1.01	27.16	.79	68.3	30.40	31.0	17.3
1937	28.0	67.6	59.7	1.02	28.58	.69	71.8	41.80	28.6	22.2
1938	41.0	46.9	50.8	.78	29.63	.52	65.9	29.03	15.3	9.8
1939	22.0	75.9	60.4	.80	29.85	.62	70.3	31.55	31.5	8.5

TABLE A-1—INDIVIDUAL PRODUCTS (continued)

Year	(36) PRUNES, DRIED		(37) PRUNES, FRESH		(38) CRANBERRIES		(39) STRAWBERRIES	
	Net Output	*Price*	*Net Output*	*Price*	*Net Output*	*Price*	*Net Output*	*Price*
	Th. s.t.	$ per s.t.	Th. s.t.	$ per s.t.	Th. bbl.	$ per bbl.	Mil. crates	$ per crate
1897	54.2	..	..	..	..	..	..	..
1898	53.7	..	..	..	..	..	..	..
1899	58.6	64.9	..	..	..	..	..	..
1900	92.0	..	..	..	318	6.61	..	..
1901	52.8	..	..	..	414	5.68	..	..
1902	105.0	..	..	..	317	6.33	..	..
1903	97.5	..	..	..	419	6.21	..	..
1904	71.5	47.6	..	..	385	5.18	..	..
1905	36.8	..	..	..	271	7.62	..	..
1906	100.0	..	..	..	412	6.50	..	..
1907	65.0	..	..	..	452	6.45	..	..
1908	36.5	..	..	..	344	7.62	..	..
1909	90.0	62.9	..	..	601	5.46	..	..
1910	50.0	..	..	..	569	5.85	..	..
1911	107.0	..	..	..	473	7.13	..	..
1912	106.5	..	..	..	512	6.64	..	..
1913	62.0	..	..	..	498	6.48	..	..
1914	61.2	110.0	..	..	664	4.02	..	..
1915	101.8	..	..	..	476	6.55	..	..
1916	99.8	..	..	..	571	6.59	..	..
1917	120.5	..	..	..	293	10.39	..	..
1918	75.5	..	..	..	375	8.72	6.25	4.45
1919	158.8	253.3	27.1	69.04	590	7.89	6.66	4.79
1920	116.9	146.3	25.5	51.92	472	10.42	6.46	4.87
1921	113.7	138.4	41.2	46.63	397	13.44	7.84	4.63
1922	147.0	144.1	27.6	42.50	597	10.49	10.72	3.39
1923	158.0	104.8	54.0	5.87	686	7.96	10.75	3.64
1924	164.0	116.5	25.9	57.72	610	9.97	12.24	3.37
1925	161.5	112.9	29.0	37.34	609	11.23	8.91	4.18
1926	192.5	104.8	44.4	18.58	762	7.14	10.20	4.16
1927	248.8	72.1	45.4	26.89	512	12.95	12.55	3.61
1928	228.9	101.8	56.2	14.11	559	14.35	12.86	3.34
1929	160.1	135.3	69.9	20.93	570	13.49	12.45	3.23
1930	285.2	57.1	57.4	17.26	584	10.83	9.08	4.00
1931	242.4	56.6	43.5	21.33	654	6.55	11.28	3.29
1932	194.5	55.5	47.5	12.59	580	7.79	12.66	1.94
1933	205.5	81.2	37.6	18.75	699	6.41	12.06	1.74
1934	201.1	65.9	49.1	15.42	445	11.58	10.00	2.02
1935	297.3	56.7	49.3	28.40	516	12.13	10.98	2.31
1936	184.3	78.0	46.2	24.72	504	13.58	9.45	2.81
1937	255.7	54.6	36.8	28.42	877	8.75	11.79	2.92
1938	238.3	42.2	48.5	15.01	476	10.98	11.26	2.68
1939	213.4	65.8	54.9	12.57	671	10.30	13.60	2.39

TABLE A-1—INDIVIDUAL PRODUCTS (continued)

Year	(40) Citrus Fruit, California: (A) and (B) Oranges and Lemons — Net Output Mil. boxes	(A) and (B) Oranges and Lemons — Price $ per box	(A) Oranges — Net Output Mil. boxes	(A) Oranges — Price $ per box	(B) Lemons — Net Output Mil. boxes	(B) Lemons — Price $ per box	(C) Grapefruit — Net Output Th. boxes	(C) Grapefruit — Price $ per box
1897	6.50	.64	..	..	..	..	0	..
1898	4.43	1.03	..	..	..	..	0	..
1899	7.63	1.11	..	..	..	..	0	..
1900	10.23	.66	..	..	..	..	0	..
1901	8.62	1.02	..	..	..	..	0	..
1902	9.89	.62	..	..	..	..	0	..
1903	12.33	.53	..	..	..	..	0	..
1904	11.81	.87	..	..	..	..	0	..
1905	..	..	9.97	1.51	1.28	2.11	0	..
1906	..	..	11.43	1.36	1.19	2.41	0	..
1907	..	..	11.94	1.27	1.72	1.22	0	..
1908	..	..	14.94	1.07	2.18	1.28	0	..
1909	..	..	12.24	1.33	1.75	2.57	19	(2.00)
1910	..	..	17.46	1.29	2.45	2.03	36	(2.00)
1911	..	..	15.31	1.10	2.28	2.03	64	2.13
1912	..	..	6.87	1.89	.97	4.39	85	2.05
1913	..	..	20.12	.94	1.30	2.58	107	1.44
1914	..	..	17.74	1.32	2.75	.66	139	1.16
1915	..	..	16.99	1.60	2.90	2.28	159	1.33
1916	..	..	21.53	1.34	3.21	2.32	188	1.41
1917	..	..	7.92	3.97	2.68	4.32	227	1.70
1918	..	..	17.93	2.88	4.45	2.59	380	2.24
1919	..	..	17.07	3.38	4.53	1.76	363	1.73
1920	..	..	22.55	2.20	5.64	3.18	395	1.87
1921	..	..	13.92	3.31	4.38	2.77	360	2.67
1922	..	..	21.29	1.87	3.78	3.51	394	1.79
1923	..	..	24.32	1.86	6.43	1.77	363	1.97
1924	..	..	18.54	3.36	5.30	3.65	387	3.55
1925	..	..	24.20	2.68	7.32	2.26	600	2.84
1926	..	..	28.17	3.05	7.45	2.75	672	2.35
1927	..	..	22.74	4.22	5.42	3.97	720	3.80
1928	..	..	38.99	2.09	7.62	3.28	972	2.50
1929	..	..	21.48	4.22	6.11	4.35	1,000	2.65
1930	..	..	35.47	1.72	7.95	2.83	1,290	1.25
1931	..	..	34.90	1.30	7.70	2.23	1,431	1.00
1932	..	..	34.26	1.09	6.70	2.66	1,350	.85
1933	..	..	27.46	1.73	7.30	2.85	1,713	1.10
1934	..	..	43.65	1.43	10.75	1.97	2,167	1.00
1935	..	..	32.20	1.80	7.79	3.29	2,267	.97
1936	..	..	28.80	2.22	7.58	3.43	1,310	1.14
1937	..	..	44.71	.91	9.36	2.60	1,943	.58
1938	..	..	38.47	.96	11.11	2.00	1,744	.48
1939	..	..	43.40	1.36	11.96	(2.00)	1,975	.50

ABLE A-1—INDIVIDUAL PRODUCTS (continued)

	(41) Citrus Fruit, Florida				(42) Citrus Fruit, Other					
	(A) Oranges		(B) Grapefruit		(A) Oranges		(B) Grapefruit, Texas		(C) Grapefruit, Arizona	
	Net Output	*Price*	*Net Output*	*Price*	*Net Output*	*Price*	*Net Output*	*Price*	*Net Output*	*Price*
ar	Mil. boxes	$ per box	Mil. boxes	$ per box	Th. boxes	$ per box	Th. boxes	$ per box	Th. boxes	$ per box
97	.395	(1.50)	0	..	..	..	..	..	..	..
98	.277	(1.50)	0	..	..	..	..	..	..	..
99	.301	(1.50)	0	..	..	..	..	..	..	..
00	.310	(1.50)	.075	(2.00)	..	..	..	..	..	..
01	.857	(1.50)	.205	(2.00)	..	..	..	..	..	..
02	1.01	(1.50)	.240	(2.00)	..	..	..	..	..	..
03	1.72	(1.50)	.411	(2.00)	..	..	..	..	..	..
04	2.61	(1.50)	.622	(2.00)	..	..	..	..	..	..
05	3.34	(1.50)	.797	(2.00)	..	..	..	..	..	..
06	3.34	(1.50)	.798	(2.00)	..	..	..	..	..	..
07	2.87	(1.50)	.677	(2.00)	..	..	..	..	..	..
08	4.08	(1.50)	.973	(2.00)	..	..	..	..	..	..
09	5.33	.89	1.41	1.82	..	..	..	..	..	..
10	3.35	1.25	1.71	1.65	..	..	..	..	..	..
11	4.13	1.60	1.12	2.94	..	..	..	..	..	..
12	6.29	1.47	2.52	1.61	..	..	..	..	..	..
13	6.28	1.38	2.35	2.01	..	..	..	..	..	..
14	6.51	1.14	3.97	.92	..	..	..	..	..	..
15	6.06	1.59	3.00	1.58	..	..	..	..	..	..
16	5.24	1.62	3.03	1.81	..	..	..	..	..	..
17	3.66	3.02	2.37	2.20	..	..	..	..	..	..
18	6.18	2.75	3.31	2.43	..	..	..	..	..	..
19	7.53	2.96	5.90	2.05	..	..	3	..	29	..
20	9.46	2.04	6.14	2.06	..	..	5	..	34	..
21	8.37	2.77	6.64	1.96	..	..	8	..	35	..
22	10.90	2.32	7.77	1.81	..	..	35	..	60	..
23	13.72	1.48	8.94	1.19	..	..	65	..	95	..
24	11.64	2.39	9.18	1.49	154	2.71	301	2.00	105	3.50
25	10.04	2.66	7.66	2.32	353	2.90	200	2.50	150	3.00
26	11.51	2.15	8.69	1.99	383	2.81	361	2.50	120	2.50
27	9.49	3.27	8.16	2.63	484	3.70	524	1.90	176	3.80
28	15.59	1.76	11.31	1.76	549	2.75	753	1.60	211	3.50
29	10.30	2.49	8.27	2.49	834	2.79	1,530	2.15	365	2.50
30	19.21	1.76	16.11	1.22	681	1.75	1,135	1.15	400	1.50
31	14.22	1.84	10.79	1.13	1,044	1.33	2,480	.55	450	.90
32	16.20	1.20	11.80	.88	950	1.31	1,385	1.10	614	.75
33	18.10	1.28	10.70	1.09	835	1.08	1,140	.90	800	.80
34	17.60	1.37	15.20	.91	1,341	1.27	2,760	1.00	1,240	.85
35	18.00	1.64	11.50	1.35	1,264	1.53	2,762	1.04	1,800	1.08
36	22.50	1.84	18.10	1.05	2,611	1.76	9,630	.68	1,400	1.12
37	26.70	1.32	14.60	1.04	2,171	1.13	11,800	.57	2,750	.62
38	33.90	.93	23.60	.54	3,811	.87	15,670	.31	2,700	.20
39	28.00	.97	15.90	1.01	3,242	1.20	13,900	.38	2,900	.42

TABLE A-1—INDIVIDUAL PRODUCTS (continued)

	(43) ALMONDS		(44) PECANS		(45) WALNUTS		(46) ARTICHOKES For Market		(47) ASPARAGUS (A) For Market	
	Net Output	*Price*	*Net Output*	*Price*	*Net Output*	*Price*	*Net Output*	*Price*	*Net Output*	*Pr*[illegible]
Year	Th. s.t.	$ per s.t.	Mil. lb.	¢ per lb.	Th. s.t.	$ per s.t.	Th. boxes	$ per box	Mil. crates	$ pe[illegible] crat[illegible]
1897	..	..	..	..	..	..	..	..	..	..
1898	..	..	..	..	..	..	..	..	..	..
1899	..	..	..	..	5.33	..	..	..	..	..
1900	2.9	..	..	..	5.86	..	..	..	..	..
1901	1.6	..	..	..	7.45	..	..	..	..	..
1902	3.4	..	..	..	9.26	..	..	..	..	..
1903	3.4	..	..	..	5.94	..	..	..	..	..
1904	.8	..	..	..	8.20	..	..	..	..	..
1905	2.2	..	..	..	6.91	..	..	..	..	..
1906	.8	..	..	..	7.56	..	..	..	..	..
1907	.8	..	..	..	7.99	..	..	..	..	..
1908	3.0	..	..	..	9.94	..	..	..	..	..
1909	1.6	..	..	..	10.10	..	..	..	..	..
1910	3.5	..	..	..	10.37	..	..	..	..	..
1911	1.5	..	..	..	13.50	..	..	..	..	..
1912	3.2	..	..	..	12.15	..	..	..	..	..
1913	1.2	..	..	..	12.26	..	..	..	..	..
1914	2.4	..	..	..	9.61	..	..	..	..	..
1915	3.7	..	..	..	16.0	..	..	..	..	..
1916	3.6	..	..	..	15.8	..	..	..	..	..
1917	4.2	..	..	..	17.8	..	..	..	..	..
1918	5.4	..	..	..	21.5	..	..	..	1.42	2.2[illegible]
1919	7.9	440	69	19.5	30.2	550	..	..	1.13	2.4[illegible]
1920	6.0	360	10	25.7	23.0	400	..	..	1.26	2.5[illegible]
1921	6.2	320	48	17.6	23.3	400	..	..	1.16	2.6[illegible]
1922	9.0	290	11	26.5	29.4	360	..	..	1.12	2.8[illegible]
1923	11.0	260	58	19.3	27.0	400	..	..	1.45	2.8[illegible]
1924	8.0	300	38	23.4	24.6	460	..	..	2.08	2.6[illegible]
1925	7.5	400	52	22.1	36.6	441	1,266	1.01	2.74	2.4[illegible]
1926	16.0	300	96	15.6	15.9	481	1,470	1.77	3.49	2.[illegible]
1927	12.0	320	37	20.6	52.1	331	1,272	2.02	3.59	2.0[illegible]
1928	14.0	340	69	16.6	27.4	421	978	1.97	4.24	2.4[illegible]
1929	4.7	480	51	15.0	43.2	321	988	2.36	3.70	2.[illegible]
1930	13.5	200	52	15.2	29.8	410	1,011	1.50	4.68	2.[illegible]
1931	14.8	176	84	7.8	34.0	236	818	1.70	5.12	1.9[illegible]
1932	14.0	165	59	5.8	48.5	178	570	2.10	5.90	1.4[illegible]
1933	12.9	186	69	7.8	33.0	224	743	1.24	5.22	1.2[illegible]
1934	10.9	180	46	12.5	45.8	191	1,060	1.00	5.91	1.2[illegible]
1935	9.3	280	106	6.3	55.2	204	1,017	1.70	5.00	1.4[illegible]
1936	7.6	402	40	12.0	43.3	217	864	2.00	6.21	1.4[illegible]
1937	20.0	275	77	7.3	60.1	181	808	2.35	5.98	1.5[illegible]
1938	15.0	258	50	8.8	50.8	221	873	2.15	6.10	1.[illegible]
1939	19.2	209	62	9.4	57.3	173	1,122	1.80	6.89	1.4[illegible]

TABLE A-1—INDIVIDUAL PRODUCTS (continued)

Year	(47) Asparagus (B) For Manufacture Net Output Th. s.t.	Price $ per s.t.	(48) Snap Beans (A) For Market Net Output Mil. bu.	Price $ per bu.	(B) For Manufacture Net Output Mil. s.t.	Price $ per s.t.	(49) Beets (A) For Market Net Output Th. bu.	Price $ per bu.	(B) For Manufacture Net Output Th. s.t.	Price $ per s.t.
1897	..	..	..	..	..	..	..	..	..	..
1898	..	..	..	..	..	..	..	..	..	..
1899	..	..	..	..	..	..	..	..	..	..
1900	..	..	..	..	..	..	..	..	..	..
1901	..	..	..	..	..	..	..	..	..	..
1902	..	..	..	..	..	..	..	..	..	..
1903	..	..	..	..	..	..	..	..	..	..
1904	..	..	..	..	..	..	..	..	..	..
1905	..	..	..	..	..	..	..	..	..	..
1906	..	..	..	..	..	..	..	..	..	..
1907	..	..	..	..	..	..	..	..	..	..
1908	..	..	..	..	..	..	..	..	..	..
1909	..	..	..	..	..	..	..	..	..	..
1910	..	..	..	..	..	..	..	..	..	..
1911	..	..	..	..	..	..	..	..	..	..
1912	..	..	..	..	..	..	..	..	..	..
1913	..	..	..	..	..	..	..	..	..	..
1914	..	..	..	..	..	..	..	..	..	..
1915	..	..	..	..	..	..	..	..	..	..
1916	..	..	..	..	..	..	..	..	..	..
1917	..	..	..	..	..	..	..	..	..	..
1918	22.6	65	3.32	1.39	33.6	56.9	..	..	..	..
1919	25.7	85	3.42	1.76	39.5	55.3	..	..	..	..
1920	25.5	110	3.65	1.74	23.7	62.9	..	..	..	..
1921	22.2	70	4.05	1.79	20.3	60.8	..	..	..	..
1922	31.0	85	4.13	1.95	29.3	58.7	..	..	..	..
1923	38.0	100	4.90	2.19	34.3	64.3	165	.40	..	..
1924	44.8	100	6.05	1.94	44.3	66.0	597	.64	..	..
1925	43.4	78	6.27	1.88	73.8	63.5	586	.51	..	..
1926	55.8	66	6.15	1.80	48.1	60.3	530	.56	..	..
1927	52.6	70	6.54	1.77	54.1	62.5	1,194	.77	..	..
1928	58.6	79	7.42	1.72	70.2	61.5	1,560	.69	..	..
1929	66.8	82	8.96	1.63	92.3	62.7	1,819	.66	36.0	17.39
1930	66.8	81	9.95	1.40	90.4	62.1	1,994	.62	55.9	15.40
1931	43.8	75	9.83	1.29	68.7	53.0	1,826	.43	30.1	11.76
1932	35.3	51	11.28	.98	43.9	38.0	1,682	.42	21.6	8.56
1933	54.2	46	11.14	.92	60.2	38.6	1,781	.48	24.8	9.72
1934	50.0	67	14.32	.84	66.1	41.4	2,382	.44	40.1	10.47
1935	56.7	76	12.92	1.02	81.5	43.1	1,779	.54	47.6	10.21
1936	59.1	79	11.88	1.20	76.5	44.5	1,728	.47	47.1	12.42
1937	51.2	91	12.54	1.24	105.3	47.8	1,716	.53	62.6	11.80
1938	44.7	71	15.03	.92	128.4	44.8	1,966	.38	70.8	9.79
1939	47.6	73	16.15	.90	90.7	43.4	2,021	.41	38.7	10.87

TABLE A-1—INDIVIDUAL PRODUCTS (continued)

	(50) CABBAGE				(51) CANTALOUPS AND OTHER MUSKMELONS		(52) CARROTS		(53) CAULIFLOWE	
	(A) For Market		(B) For Manufacture				For Market		For Marke	
	Net Output	*Price*	*Net Output*	*Price*	*Net Output*	*Price*	*Net Output*	*Price*	*Net Output*	*Pr*
Year	Th. s.t.	$ per s.t.	Th. s.t.	$ per s.t.	Mil. crates	$ per crate	Mil. bu.	$ per bu.	Mil. crates	$ pe crat
1897	..	..	..	..	..	..	..	..	..	..
1898	..	..	..	..	..	..	..	..	..	..
1899	..	..	..	..	..	..	..	..	..	..
1900	..	..	..	..	..	..	..	..	..	..
1901	..	..	..	..	..	..	..	..	..	..
1902	..	..	..	..	..	..	..	..	..	..
1903	..	..	..	..	..	..	..	..	..	..
1904	..	..	..	..	..	..	..	..	..	..
1905	..	..	..	..	..	..	..	..	..	..
1906	..	..	..	..	..	..	..	..	..	..
1907	..	..	..	..	..	..	..	..	..	..
1908	..	..	..	..	..	..	..	..	..	..
1909	..	..	..	..	..	..	..	..	..	..
1910	..	..	..	..	..	..	..	..	..	..
1911	..	..	..	..	..	..	..	..	..	..
1912	..	..	..	..	..	..	..	..	..	..
1913	..	..	..	..	..	..	..	..	..	..
1914	..	..	..	..	..	..	..	..	..	..
1915	..	..	..	..	..	..	..	..	..	..
1916	..	..	..	..	..	..	..	..	..	..
1917	..	..	..	..	..	..	..	..	..	..
1918	752	24.30	116	10.79	7.85	1.92	..	..	1.95	1.[illegible]
1919	584	26.50	48	11.26	9.86	1.52	..	..	1.97	1.[illegible]
1920	1,014	17.99	67	9.46	10.48	1.59	..	..	2.46	1.[illegible]
1921	625	25.75	65	13.50	11.30	1.37	..	..	2.39	1.[illegible]
1922	918	13.23	161	6.60	12.73	1.82	..	..	2.75	1.[illegible]
1923	666	24.98	167	9.50	11.16	1.95	2.58	.90	3.23	1.[illegible]
1924	956	17.20	122	7.09	13.33	1.44	3.77	.83	2.94	1.[illegible]
1925	897	18.04	90	7.44	14.01	1.49	4.08	.63	3.48	1.[illegible]
1926	938	18.05	117	6.65	14.28	1.31	5.05	.60	5.90	.[illegible]
1927	1,008	15.82	157	6.68	14.93	1.48	6.24	.57	4.48	1.[illegible]
1928	819	23.59	153	9.54	15.69	1.32	6.34	.70	5.49	.[illegible]
1929	882	20.04	173	10.22	17.24	1.31	10.35	.58	6.85	.[illegible]
1930	801	22.57	214	7.74	15.76	1.21	10.76	.58	6.03	.[illegible]
1931	871	11.13	136	6.03	17.32	1.00	10.77	.48	7.19	.[illegible]
1932	847	13.40	152	4.11	13.83	.83	10.43	.61	7.55	.[illegible]
1933	748	18.53	95	11.21	12.05	.79	10.74	.47	6.84	.[illegible]
1934	1,131	9.19	216	6.35	12.20	1.09	12.99	.50	6.60	.[illegible]
1935	980	13.85	135	5.17	13.10	.91	13.27	.56	6.99	.[illegible]
1936	926	21.26	115	13.17	13.00	1.02	13.43	.57	7.60	.[illegible]
1937	997	14.31	149	9.68	14.27	1.12	14.18	.59	8.32	.[illegible]
1938	1,214	9.61	195	5.29	12.81	1.03	15.99	.52	8.40	.[illegible]
1939	940	16.26	147	7.62	14.40	.98	16.06	.59	8.42	.[illegible]

TABLE A-1—INDIVIDUAL PRODUCTS (continued)

	(54) Celery		(55) Sweet Corn				(56) Cucumbers			
	For Market		(A) For Market		(B) For Manufacture		(A) For Market		(B) For Pickles	
Year	*Net Output* Mil. crates	*Price* $ per crate	*Net Output, New Jersey only* Mil. ears	*Price* $ per th. ears	*Net Output* Th. s.t.	*Price* $ per s.t.	*Net Output* Mil. bu.	*Price* $ per bu.	*Net Output* Mil. bu.	*Price* $ per bu.
1897	..	..	..	..	..	..	..	..	..	..
1898	..	..	..	..	..	..	..	..	..	..
1899	..	..	..	..	..	..	..	..	..	..
1900	..	..	..	..	..	..	..	..	..	..
1901	..	..	..	..	..	..	..	..	..	..
1902	..	..	..	..	..	..	..	..	..	..
1903	..	..	..	..	..	..	..	..	..	..
1904	..	..	..	..	..	..	..	..	..	..
1905	..	..	..	..	..	..	..	..	..	..
1906	..	..	..	..	..	..	..	..	..	..
1907	..	..	..	..	..	..	..	..	..	..
1908	..	..	..	..	..	..	..	..	..	..
1909	..	..	..	..	..	..	..	..	..	..
1910	..	..	..	..	..	..	..	..	..	..
1911	..	..	..	..	..	..	..	..	..	..
1912	..	..	..	..	..	..	..	..	..	..
1913	..	..	..	..	..	..	..	..	..	..
1914	..	..	..	..	..	..	..	..	..	..
1915	..	..	..	..	..	..	..	..	..	..
1916	..	..	..	..	..	..	..	..	..	..
1917	..	..	..	..	..	..	..	..	..	..
1918	3.86	1.86	..	..	536	17.99	1.90	2.53	3.70	.86
1919	3.90	2.65	..	..	588	17.69	2.43	2.19	3.08	.89
1920	4.20	2.09	..	..	595	19.32	2.27	1.82	2.06	.99
1921	4.79	2.21	..	..	361	13.50	2.61	1.60	4.66	1.04
1922	4.71	2.05	..	..	475	10.99	3.65	1.34	2.81	.93
1923	5.60	1.92	..	..	603	12.54	3.40	2.12	3.52	1.15
1924	6.20	2.04	117	24.4	528	14.17	4.41	1.63	2.90	1.15
1925	6.67	1.88	128	12.0	1,014	15.04	4.87	1.33	7.22	1.02
1926	6.09	2.08	119	14.5	816	13.24	4.42	1.38	4.07	.95
1927	7.65	1.76	95	21.5	416	11.96	4.54	1.28	3.02	.95
1928	7.85	1.86	111	19.5	600	12.64	4.41	1.28	4.93	.84
1929	9.02	1.60	99	17.0	707	13.09	4.57	1.71	4.16	.82
1930	9.88	1.59	101	15.3	661	13.22	4.44	1.10	7.78	.79
1931	9.22	1.84	92	11.5	785	11.06	4.44	.77	6.11	.70
1932	9.64	1.17	110	10.2	387	7.50	3.12	.74	1.88	.51
1933	8.49	1.28	120	11.4	394	8.01	2.89	.79	3.74	.45
1934	8.70	1.22	151	9.7	498	8.46	3.65	.85	4.40	.47
1935	8.35	1.80	134	9.0	860	9.31	4.21	.77	5.04	.52
1936	9.38	1.78	122	10.5	608	10.21	3.76	1.00	6.33	.57
1937	10.27	1.73	120	12.0	978	11.56	3.75	1.10	8.05	.59
1938	11.61	1.34	110	12.5	883	9.98	4.59	.80	6.11	.59
1939	11.53	1.58	114	10.0	648	8.41	4.56	.96	3.86	.58

Table A-1—INDIVIDUAL PRODUCTS (continued)

Year	(57) Eggplant For Market Net Output Th. bu.	Price $ per bu.	(58) Lettuce For Market Net Output Mil. crates	Price $ per crate	(59) Onions For Market Net Output Mil. sacks	Price $ per sack	(60) Peas (A) For Market Net Output Th. bu.	Price $ per bu.	(60) Peas (B) For Manufacture Net Output Th. s.t.	Price $ per s.t.
1897	..	..	..	..	..	..	..	..	..	..
1898	..	..	..	..	..	..	..	..	..	..
1899	..	..	..	..	..	..	..	..	..	..
1900	..	..	..	..	..	..	..	..	..	..
1901	..	..	..	..	..	..	..	..	..	..
1902	..	..	..	..	..	..	..	..	..	..
1903	..	..	..	..	..	..	..	..	..	..
1904	..	..	..	..	..	..	..	..	..	..
1905	..	..	..	..	..	..	..	..	..	..
1906	..	..	..	..	..	..	..	..	..	..
1907	..	..	..	..	..	..	..	..	..	..
1908	..	..	..	..	..	..	..	..	..	..
1909	..	..	..	..	..	..	..	..	..	..
1910	..	..	..	..	..	..	..	..	..	..
1911	..	..	..	..	..	..	..	..	..	..
1912	..	..	..	..	..	..	..	..	..	..
1913	..	..	..	..	..	..	..	..	..	..
1914	..	..	..	..	..	..	..	..	..	..
1915	..	..	..	..	..	..	..	..	..	..
1916	..	..	..	..	..	..	..	..	..	..
1917	..	..	..	..	..	..	..	..	..	..
1918	..	..	3.79	1.63	10.85	1.81	604	2.17	152	61.2
1919	..	..	4.33	1.91	8.17	3.04	650	2.33	112	62.0
1920	..	..	7.70	1.53	11.87	1.44	697	2.26	155	66.7
1921	882	1.45	7.21	1.89	7.91	2.80	933	2.17	115	58.2
1922	856	1.52	9.29	1.88	10.48	1.77	1,305	1.95	164	57.0
1923	850	2.12	10.37	1.60	9.79	2.26	1,685	1.93	161	59.6
1924	723	1.25	12.42	1.60	10.81	1.92	2,028	1.80	244	59.3
1925	738	1.07	13.70	1.45	11.00	2.20	2,724	1.97	207	59.0
1926	657	1.21	15.10	1.66	12.24	1.68	3,269	1.77	215	58.2
1927	655	.94	16.98	1.35	13.38	1.68	5,170	1.81	159	56.4
1928	754	.86	18.65	1.70	11.35	2.29	5.200	1.72	198	56.8
1929	688	1.57	19.97	1.81	13.96	1.47	5,520	1.67	204	57.8
1930	798	.89	19.77	1.71	14.67	.97	6,741	1.44	244	57.6
1931	811	.74	19.61	1.48	10.33	1.85	6,015	1.43	147	54.5
1932	809	.64	17.31	1.26	14.91	.81	7,023	1.27	117	43.9
1933	910	.54	17.28	1.27	12.18	1.27	8,395	.93	137	42.5
1934	791	.59	18.94	1.36	12.71	1.34	7,607	1.38	165	50.1
1935	707	.63	19.41	1.44	14.18	1.42	8,130	1.12	268	51.8
1936	820	.60	20.90	1.45	16.29	.85	9,449	1.17	188	51.6
1937	921	.69	20.92	1.57	14.65	1.31	9,081	1.12	268	52.7
1938	961	.62	19.40	1.50	14.40	1.12	8,505	1.21	303	52.8
1939	1,092	.65	22.95	1.40	17.16	.82	9,592	1.16	194	45.8

Table A-1—INDIVIDUAL PRODUCTS (continued)

	(61) Peppers		(62) Spinach				(63) Tomatoes			
	For Market		(A) For Market		(B) For Manufacture		(A) For Market		(B) For Manufacture	
	Net Output	*Price*	*Net Output*	*Price*	*Net Output*	*Price*	*Net Output*	*Price*	*Net Output*	*Price*
Year	Mil. bu.	$ per bu.	Mil. bu.	$ per bu.	Th. s.t.	$ per s.t.	Mil. bu.	$ per bu.	Th. s.t.	$ per s.t.
1897	..	..	..	..	..	..	..	..	..	..
1898	..	..	..	..	..	..	..	..	..	..
1899	..	..	..	..	..	..	..	..	..	..
1900	..	..	..	..	..	..	..	..	..	..
1901	..	..	..	..	..	..	..	..	..	..
1902	..	..	..	..	..	..	..	..	..	..
1903	..	..	..	..	..	..	..	..	..	..
1904	..	..	..	..	..	..	..	..	..	..
1905	..	..	..	..	..	..	..	..	..	..
1906	..	..	..	..	..	..	..	..	..	..
1907	..	..	..	..	..	..	..	..	..	..
1908	..	..	..	..	..	..	..	..	..	..
1909	..	..	..	..	..	..	..	..	..	..
1910	..	..	..	..	..	..	..	..	..	..
1911	..	..	..	..	..	..	..	..	..	..
1912	..	..	..	..	..	..	..	..	..	..
1913	..	..	..	..	..	..	..	..	..	..
1914	..	..	..	..	..	..	..	..	..	..
1915	..	..	..	..	..	..	..	..	..	..
1916	..	..	..	..	..	..	..	..	..	..
1917	..	..	..	..	..	..	..	..	..	..
1918	..	..	2.44	.65	..	..	10.5	1.48	1,566	21.7
1919	..	..	3.42	.72	18.6	24.8	10.7	1.51	1,111	18.5
1920	..	..	3.93	.68	22.2	31.8	11.6	1.63	1,100	19.8
1921	2.69	1.59	5.17	.62	30.3	22.9	10.2	1.77	457	11.6
1922	2.66	1.68	5.92	.68	39.1	24.0	14.2	1.96	1,199	12.6
1923	2.84	1.63	7.39	.57	54.8	22.5	13.4	2.31	1,165	13.6
1924	3.32	1.25	8.52	.62	48.8	22.2	15.4	2.19	1,190	15.7
1925	3.05	1.40	10.06	.63	35.3	21.1	16.9	2.08	1,809	14.8
1926	3.18	1.28	9.90	.53	52.9	18.0	13.6	2.06	999	14.7
1927	3.19	1.19	10.31	.53	57.1	16.3	16.5	1.62	1,196	14.3
1928	3.89	.98	11.25	.60	73.2	17.5	15.9	1.80	997	14.2
1929	3.34	1.13	12.12	.47	96.9	16.8	18.2	1.77	1,535	15.2
1930	3.65	1.07	11.34	.54	38.4	14.8	17.3	1.61	1,758	15.0
1931	4.38	.77	13.51	.39	34.7	12.8	16.8	1.10	976	11.8
1932	3.89	.71	11.79	.46	20.5	13.0	17.9	1.03	1,199	10.1
1933	4.23	.48	11.55	.37	36.0	12.0	16.3	1.14	1,081	11.4
1934	3.79	.75	11.52	.40	41.3	11.9	20.3	1.21	1,426	12.0
1935	3.57	.67	10.19	.56	53.3	12.3	20.8	1.14	1,700	11.7
1936	4.03	.67	13.13	.39	63.4	13.3	20.8	1.30	1,988	12.6
1937	4.83	.72	15.08	.36	64.8	14.2	21.5	1.29	1,926	13.1
1938	4.97	.66	12.56	.36	38.6	13.9	24.5	1.07	1,743	12.4
1939	5.07	.85	13.33	.35	47.2	14.6	24.6	1.37	1,926	12.3

TABLE A-1—INDIVIDUAL PRODUCTS (continued)

	(64) Watermelons		(65) Peppermint Oil		(66) Cattle		(67) Calves		(68) Hogs	
					Net Output, Live Weight	*Price*	*Net Output, Live Weight*	*Price*	*Net Output, Live Weight*	*Price*
	Net Output	*Price*	*Net Output*	*Price*						
Year	Mil.	$ per th.	Th. lb.	$ per lb.	Bil. lb.	$ per cwt.	Mil. lb.	$ per cwt.	Bil. lb.	$ per cwt.
1897	..	..	..	..	10.93	3.42	677	3.89	11.89	3.32
1898	..	..	..	..	11.36	3.52	699	4.39	11.77	3.50
1899	..	..	..	..	13.48	3.70	808	4.62	11.32	3.69
1900	..	..	..	..	12.98	3.85	790	4.49	11.39	4.60
1901	..	..	..	..	12.75	3.84	799	4.28	11.06	5.32
1902	..	..	..	..	12.21	3.94	885	4.44	10.64	6.23
1903	..	..	..	..	12.66	3.63	872	4.55	11.37	5.46
1904	..	..	..	..	12.13	3.39	844	4.17	11.70	4.69
1905	..	..	..	..	12.24	3.49	930	4.46	12.04	4.78
1906	..	..	..	..	12.20	3.52	999	4.72	12.58	5.69
1907	..	..	..	..	11.90	3.64	1,027	4.87	12.92	5.55
1908	..	..	..	..	12.15	3.73	1,067	4.90	12.61	5.19
1909	..	..	..	..	12.17	4.13	1,092	5.44	11.04	6.69
1910	..	..	..	..	11.74	4.78	1,104	6.42	12.04	8.11
1911	..	..	..	..	11.73	4.46	1,106	6.02	12.53	6.23
1912	..	..	..	..	12.64	5.12	1,189	6.44	11.95	6.62
1913	..	..	..	..	13.74	5.90	1,164	7.47	12.23	7.45
1914	..	..	..	..	14.40	6.23	1,150	7.81	12.60	7.48
1915	..	..	..	..	14.03	6.00	1,154	7.61	13.95	6.53
1916	..	..	..	..	14.74	6.47	1,271	8.35	13.59	8.09
1917	..	..	..	..	15.34	8.17	1,383	10.54	12.94	13.19
1918	29.5	154	..	..	14.43	9.44	1,300	11.93	14.80	15.82
1919	42.4	170	..	..	11.75	9.59	1,445	12.76	14.00	16.01
1920	58.9	185	..	..	11.26	8.42	1,383	11.86	13.54	12.88
1921	62.9	177	..	..	11.29	5.50	1,510	7.85	14.15	7.82
1922	72.5	155	..	..	12.41	5.43	1,335	7.69	16.53	8.34
1923	43.9	252	..	..	12.39	5.58	1,419	7.99	17.02	7.10
1924	58.3	162	..	..	11.52	5.84	1,597	7.83	15.35	7.34
1925	56.1	236	..	..	11.63	6.53	1,592	8.59	14.15	10.91
1926	71.3	146	..	..	11.85	6.75	1,567	9.34	15.04	11.79
1927	57.5	185	..	..	11.16	7.62	1,565	10.14	16.26	9.64
1928	63.4	170	..	..	11.71	9.52	1,473	11.75	16.07	8.54
1929	71.0	170	1,073	3.19	12.14	9.47	1,470	12.16	15.77	9.42
1930	77.8	116	1,103	1.93	12.71	7.71	1,382	9.68	15.23	8.84
1931	75.4	101	683	1.19	12.45	5.53	1,603	6.95	16.48	5.73
1932	55.2	80	421	1.41	12.96	4.25	1,696	4.95	16.57	3.34
1933	55.5	93	503	1.78	14.40	3.75	1,704	4.64	16.10	3.53
1934	60.2	105	873	2.39	9.91	4.13	1,548	4.92	11.89	4.14
1935	64.1	97	1,352	1.67	12.59	6.06	1,739	7.20	10.97	8.63
1936	63.4	129	957	1.93	13.42	5.82	1,886	7.22	13.10	9.30
1937	71.0	106	885	1.99	12.70	7.01	1,860	8.10	12.28	9.48
1938	68.2	108	890	1.99	12.92	6.56	1,853	7.86	14.29	7.74
1939	65.3	117	843	1.91	14.26	7.03	1,753	8.42	16.69	6.23

Table A-1—INDIVIDUAL PRODUCTS (continued)

Year	(69) Sheep and Lambs		(70) Eggs		(71) Chickens		(72) Turkeys	
	Net Output, Live Weight Mil. lb.	*Price* $ per cwt.	*Net Output* Bil. doz.	*Price* ¢ per doz.	*Net Output* Mil.	*Price* ¢ per head	*Net Output* Mil. head	*Price* $ per head
1897	1,164	3.71	1.42	11	332	29.6	..	..
1898	1,211	4.13	1.45	12	332	29.2	..	..
1899	1,231	4.27	1.45	13	363	31.6	..	..
1900	1,131	4.66	1.57	13	382	30.0	..	..
1901	1,160	3.95	1.66	14	353	31.0	..	..
1902	1,008	4.53	1.55	17	395	36.2	..	..
1903	966	4.54	1.71	16	400	38.7	..	..
1904	963	4.54	1.74	18	405	38.4	..	..
1905	1,274	5.81	1.76	18	454	37.7	..	..
1906	1,301	5.83	1.96	17	508	38.2	..	..
1907	1,245	5.88	2.19	18	459	40.6	..	..
1908	1,421	5.20	2.02	19	463	38.7	..	..
1909	1,206	5.90	2.02	20.0	498	41.4	..	..
1910	1,271	6.27	2.15	20.9	543	44.8	..	..
1911	1,167	5.19	2.35	17.5	517	41.4	..	..
1912	1,199	5.57	2.26	20.2	513	41.8	..	..
1913	1,307	5.91	2.25	19.4	514	46.7	..	..
1914	1,176	6.25	2.22	20.5	531	47.9	..	..
1915	1,204	6.81	2.39	19.4	514	44.8	..	..
1916	1,109	8.07	2.30	22.1	501	51.3	..	..
1917	1,059	12.45	2.21	31.8	509	64.2	..	..
1918	1,288	13.48	2.24	36.0	543	82.5	..	..
1919	1,131	12.26	2.45	41.3	527	93.5	..	..
1920	990	10.97	2.39	43.5	514	99.9	..	..
1921	1,090	6.56	2.48	28.3	556	79.4	..	..
1922	1,146	9.28	2.66	25.0	585	73.0	..	..
1923	1,261	9.60	2.82	26.5	610	72.6	..	..
1924	1,397	9.99	2.80	26.7	605	74.0	..	..
1925	1,448	11.52	2.83	30.4	626	78.0	..	..
1926	1,559	10.88	3.02	28.9	665	84.1	..	..
1927	1,587	10.72	3.13	25.1	694	76.3	..	..
1928	1,715	11.50	3.14	28.1	640	80.5	..	..
1929	1,755	11.13	3.08	29.8	692	85.6	16.5	3.25
1930	1,915	7.40	3.18	23.7	714	68.1	16.3	2.76
1931	1,938	5.39	3.14	17.6	647	60.1	17.5	2.61
1932	1,790	4.29	2.95	14.2	673	45.3	21.9	1.77
1933	1,872	4.83	2.89	13.8	685	36.4	22.8	1.63
1934	1,550	5.62	2.81	17.1	605	42.6	21.3	2.14
1935	1,843	6.76	2.72	23.4	632	56.6	20.3	2.91
1936	1,894	7.33	2.77	21.8	703	60.4	27.4	2.32
1937	1,858	8.19	3.09	21.3	578	63.5	25.3	2.70
1938	2,021	6.59	3.03	20.3	645	59.0	25.9	2.67
1939	1,934	7.28	3.14	17.4	694	52.2	32.4	2.41

TABLE A-1—INDIVIDUAL PRODUCTS (continued)

(73)
MILK AND MILK PRODUCTS
(A) BUTTER

Year	(A₁) and (A₂) Total Butter		(A₁) Farm Butter		(A₂) Factory Butter		(A₃) Farm Butter		(A₄) Butterfat	
	Net Output Mil. lb.	*Price* ¢ per lb.	*Net Output* Mil. lb.	*Price* ¢ per lb.	*Net Output* Mil. lb.	*Price* ¢ per lb.	*Sales off Farms* Mil. lb.	*Price* ¢ per lb.	*Sales off Farms* Mil. lb.	*Price* ¢ per lb.
1897	1,533	13.0	..	..	..	..	..	..	..	..
1898	1,473	13.0	..	..	..	..	..	..	..	..
1899	1,493	14.0	..	..	..	..	..	..	..	..
1900	1,540	15.8	..	..	..	..	..	..	..	..
1901	1,575	15.8	..	..	..	..	..	..	..	..
1902	1,401	17.7	..	..	..	..	..	..	..	..
1903	1,485	16.7	..	..	..	..	..	..	..	..
1904	1,540	15.8	..	..	..	..	..	..	..	..
1905	1,667	17.7	..	..	..	..	..	..	..	..
1906	1,545	17.7	..	..	..	..	..	..	..	..
1907	1,537	19.5	..	..	..	..	..	..	..	..
1908	1,763	20.5	..	..	..	..	..	..	..	..
1909	1,622	22.3	..	..	..	..	..	..	..	..
1910	1,706	24.2	1,073	25.5	633	20.8	..	..	..	..
1911	..	..	1,069	22.9	692	18.3	..	..	..	..
1912	..	..	870	25.7	722	21.1	..	..	..	..
1913	..	..	841	26.7	767	21.6	..	..	..	..
1914	..	..	899	25.1	786	20.1	..	..	..	..
1915	..	..	971	25.7	780	20.4	..	..	..	..
1916	..	..	968	28.0	825	23.2	..	..	..	..
1917	..	..	810	35.9	838	30.0	..	..	..	..
1918	..	..	632	42.7	832	35.8	..	..	..	..
1919	..	..	708	50.3	939	42.1	..	..	..	..
1920	..	..	637	54.3	929	43.8	..	..	..	..
1921	..	..	610	37.0	1,132	29.2	..	..	..	..
1922	..	..	644	35.3	1,227	28.3	..	..	..	..
1923	..	..	666	40.4	1,320	33.3	..	..	..	..
1924	..	..	645	39.4	1,425	30.4	..	..	..	..
1925	..	..	564	40.7	1,440	32.0	..	..	..	..
1926	..	..	493	41.1	1,522	31.5	..	..	..	..
1927	..	..	514	42.3	1,551	33.3	..	..	..	..
1928	..	..	529	43.3	1,522	34.8	..	..	..	..
1929	..	..	544	43.0	1,585	34.5	..	..	..	..
1930	..	..	524	36.3	1,584	26.3	..	..	..	..
1931	..	..	547	27.3	1,653	18.9	..	..	..	..
1932	..	..	589	20.8	1,677	13.7	..	..	..	..
1933	..	..	587	20.2	1,745	14.3	..	..	..	..
1934	..	..	559	22.7	1,676	17.3	109	22.7	1,272	22[illegible]
1935	..	..	..	..	..	..	111	26.7	1,228	28[illegible]
1936	..	..	..	..	..	..	103	28.9	1,212	3[illegible]
1937	..	..	..	..	..	..	99	29.7	1,171	3[illegible]
1938	..	..	..	..	..	..	95	26.7	1,262	2[illegible]
1939	..	..	..	..	..	..	90	25.1	1,278	2[illegible]

TABLE A-1—INDIVIDUAL PRODUCTS (continued)

(73)

MILK AND MILK PRODUCTS (concluded)

(B) MILK, WHOLE

Year	(B₁) Total Milk Output Mainly for Fluid Consumption		(B₂) Total Milk Output Mainly for Fluid Consumption		(B₃) Milk, Whole, Sold Wholesale Sales off Farms		(B₄) Milk, Whole, and Cream, Sold Retail, Milk Equivalents Sales off Farms		(B₅) Milk Consumed on Farms in All Forms, Milk Equivalents	
	Bil. lb.	Price ¢ per lb.	Bil. lb.	Price ¢ per lb.	Bil. lb.	Price ¢ per lb.	Mil. quart	Price ¢ per quart	Bil. lb.	¢ per lb.
97	21.2	1.21	..	..	..	..	..	..	..	..
98	23.3	1.21	..	..	..	..	..	..	..	..
99	23.4	1.24	..	..	..	..	..	..	..	..
00	23.1	1.33	..	..	..	..	..	..	..	..
01	23.4	1.36	..	..	..	..	..	..	..	..
02	22.0	1.40	..	..	..	..	..	..	..	..
03	26.6	1.51	..	..	..	..	..	..	..	..
04	26.2	1.50	..	..	..	..	..	..	..	..
05	24.0	1.49	..	..	..	..	..	..	..	..
06	27.1	1.55	..	..	..	..	..	..	..	..
07	27.8	1.70	..	..	..	..	..	..	..	..
08	24.1	1.78	..	..	..	..	..	..	..	..
09	28.3	1.75	..	..	..	..	..	..	..	..
10	27.3	1.90	27.3	1.87	..	..	..	..	..	..
11	..	..	26.9	1.83	..	..	..	..	..	..
12	..	..	31.2	1.90	..	..	..	..	..	..
13	..	..	31.9	1.93	..	..	..	..	..	..
14	..	..	32.1	1.93	..	..	..	..	..	..
15	..	..	32.1	1.90	..	..	..	..	..	..
16	..	..	32.5	2.05	..	..	..	..	..	..
17	..	..	36.6	2.71	..	..	..	..	..	..
18	..	..	40.9	3.33	..	..	..	..	..	..
19	..	..	37.0	3.71	..	..	..	..	..	..
20	..	..	40.6	3.71	..	..	..	..	..	..
21	..	..	39.1	2.82	..	..	..	..	..	..
22	..	..	39.5	2.58	..	..	..	..	..	..
23	..	..	39.6	2.94	..	..	..	..	..	..
24	..	..	42.9	2.72	..	..	..	..	..	..
25	..	..	45.4	2.87	..	..	..	..	..	..
26	..	..	48.4	2.87	..	..	..	..	..	..
27	..	..	49.6	2.96	..	..	..	..	..	..
28	..	..	51.4	2.98	..	..	..	..	..	..
29	..	..	52.7	3.00	..	..	..	..	..	..
30	..	..	54.4	2.71	..	..	..	..	..	..
31	..	..	55.4	2.19	..	..	..	..	..	..
32	..	..	55.0	1.74	..	..	..	..	..	..
33	..	..	54.5	1.75	..	..	..	..	..	..
34	..	..	53.5	2.00	33.8	1.55	3,293	9.4	21.9	1.49
35	..	..	..	..	35.1	1.71	3,294	9.8	21.6	1.68
36	..	..	..	..	38.0	1.87	3,260	10.1	21.0	1.84
37	..	..	..	..	39.2	1.97	3,270	10.5	20.9	1.93
38	..	..	..	..	40.9	1.72	3,266	10.3	20.9	1.67
39	..	..	..	..	42.0	1.68	3,156	10.2	20.9	1.60

TABLE A-1—INDIVIDUAL PRODUCTS (concluded)

	(74) Wool		(75) Mohair	
Year	*Net Output Shorn Wool (grease basis)* Mil. lb.	*Price* ¢ per lb.	*Net Output* Mil. lb.	*Price* ¢ per lb.
1897	237	13.7	..	..
1898	248	14.9	..	..
1899	257	15.9	..	..
1900	281	16.8	..	..
1901	287	14.3	..	..
1902	296	15.2	..	..
1903	265	16.8	..	..
1904	270	17.7	..	..
1905	274	21.4	..	..
1906	277	21.4	..	..
1907	277	21.4	..	..
1908	292	18.6	..	..
1909	310	22.2	6	22.6
1910	306	21.7	6	26.5
1911	302	15.8	6	30.2
1912	278	17.3	6	29.5
1913	266	16.7	7	28.5
1914	251	16.6	7	26.7
1915	241	22.1	7	30.4
1916	244	26.1	7	44.9
1917	237	41.6	7	44.0
1918	254	57.7	8	58.4
1919	270	49.5	8	52.0
1920	251	45.5	9	24.1
1921	242	17.3	9	19.4
1922	228	27.1	9	43.1
1923	230	39.4	9	46.5
1924	238	36.6	10	65.4
1925	253	39.5	11	55.8
1926	269	34.0	13	60.7
1927	289	30.3	14	56.1
1928	315	36.2	16	70.1
1929	328	30.2	17	47.0
1930	352	19.5	18	33.5
1931	376	13.6	19	16.6
1932	351	8.6	17	9.0
1933	374	20.6	17	29.2
1934	370	21.9	16	18.8
1935	365	19.2	16	36.3
1936	360	26.9	16	54.1
1937	367	32.0	16	54.1
1938	372	19.1	17	34.8
1939	377	22.3	19	47.3

General Note to Table A-1

Net output of crops represents the harvested portion exclusive of the amount used for seed and the part that is fed to livestock on the farms where the crops are grown. Usually, additional amounts are used for seed or feed on farms other than the place of origin, but frequently those portions, becoming the subject of commercial transactions, cannot be separated from sales consummated for other purposes. Net output, therefore, sometimes includes portions of varying magnitude, which are consumed as seed or feed.

The sources of seed and feed allowances, as a rule, are United States Department of Agriculture data, recently made available, covering the years following 1909; for years prior to 1909 we have had to work out estimates of our own based on the records of succeeding years. In some cases our estimates have had to cover a longer span than the period prior to 1909. Neither seed nor feed deductions are shown in the table. However, the source or the factors used are supplied in footnotes, so that the figures may easily be reconstructed by the interested reader.

Ripened but unharvested portions, when known, are excluded (largely in fruit and vegetables), and a note is made of the deduction.

Except where otherwise indicated, prices are season average prices received by farmers. Very few price series are available on an annual basis throughout the entire period. Generally, prior to the second decade of the century, December 1 prices replace annual prices. To test the importance of this break in comparability, with a view to possible adjustment, we consulted the correlation coefficients between December and annual prices as worked out for a number of crops by Henry Schultz[a] and also compared the absolute levels of the two prices in the years closest to the one in which the break occurs. On this basis it was found necessary only rarely to adjust the December or other monthly price to an annual basis. In such cases the method used is specified in a footnote. In all other cases only the year of the break is noted. In years in which output is available but no price is shown, data for the commodity in question were not used in the construction of the indexes. Where prices could be estimated only roughly, but such estimates were used in the computations, they are shown in parentheses.

The reference to *Agricultural Statistics* (abbreviated as *Agr. Stat.*) applies to the 1940 edition, except in special cases of which note is taken.

Data for 1938 and 1939, unless otherwise noted, are based on *Farm Production, Farm Disposition, and Value of Principal Crops, 1938–1940* (U. S. Agricultural Marketing Service, 1941) for output, and on *Crops and Markets*, December 1940, for prices.

The following abbreviations are used in the table.

Doz. dozen
Th. thousand
Mil. million
Bil. billion (thousand million)
Bu. bushel
S.t. short ton (2,000 lb.)
Gal. gallon
Bbl. barrel
Cwt. hundredweight (100 lb.)

[a] *Theory and Measurement of Demand* (University of Chicago Press, 1938).

Footnotes to Table A-1 continued on next page.

Footnotes to Table A-1, continued.

(1) Wheat (1 bu. = 60 lb.):

1897–1910: harvested production from "Wheat Acreage and Production in the United States Since 1866," *Wheat Studies*, Vol. II (Food Research Institute, Stanford University, June 1926), pp. 260-61; seed allowance based on 1.48 bu. per acre harvested from same source, and feed disappearance estimated at 4 percent of gross output, except for 1901, for which year 6 percent was deducted, in view of the high corn-wheat ratio of that year.

1911–37: net output based on *Agr. Stat.*, Table 9.

Prices from *Agr. Stat.*, Table 1.

1938–39: see *general note* above.

Prior to 1908 prices relate to December 1.

(2) Corn (1 bu. = 56 lb. shelled):

1897–1908: corn grown for all purposes, from *Agr. Stat.*, Table 45; seed and feed used on farms where grown were estimated to have absorbed 80 percent of the crop each year.

1909–37: net output based on *Agr. Stat.*, Table 49.

Prices from *Agr. Stat.*, Table 45.

1938–39: see *general note* above.

Prior to 1908 prices relate to December 1.

(3) Oats (1 bu. = 32 lb.):

1897–1908: harvested production from *Agr. Stat.*, Table 69; seed and feed used on farms where grown were estimated to have absorbed 70 percent of gross output each year.

1909–37: net output based on *Agr. Stat.*, Table 74.

Prices from *Agr. Stat.*, Table 69.

1938–39: see *general note* above.

Prior to 1908 prices relate to December 1.

(4) Barley (1 bu. = 48 lb.):

1897–1908: harvested production from *Agr. Stat.*, Table 86; seed and feed used on farms where grown were estimated to have absorbed 50 percent of gross output each year.

1909–37: net output based on *Agr. Stat.*, Table 90.

Prices from *Agr. Stat.*, Table 86.

1938–39: see *general note* above.

Prior to 1908 prices relate to December 1.

(5) Rice (1 bu. = 45 lb.):

1897–1908: harvested production from *Agr. Stat.*, Table 116; seed use of 2.1 bu. per acre based on individual state seed requirements data, given in *Disposition of Rice* (U. S. Bureau of Agricultural Economics, 1939), p. 1; feed use estimated at 1 bu. per acre. In this connection a suggestion by Mr. John S. Dennee, of the Bureau of Agricultural Economics, proved very helpful.

1909–37: net output based on *Agr. Stat.*, Table 116, and data on feed and seed in *Disposition of Rice.*

Prior to 1924 prices relate to December 1. For 1899 price is based on the 1900 Census of Agriculture. For 1897–98 and 1900–03 prices are those given in Frederick Strauss and L. H. Bean, *Gross Farm Income and Indices of Farm Production and Prices in the United States, 1869–1937*, Technical Bulletin

703 (U. S. Department of Agriculture, 1940), Table 28. For 1904–37 prices are from *Agr. Stat.,* Table 116.
1938–39: see *general note* above.

(6) Rye (1 bu. = 56 lb.):
1897–1908: harvested production from *Agr. Stat.,* Table 31. Seed use on all farms estimated at 2 bu. per acre; feed consumed on farms where grown assumed to have accounted for 15 percent of gross output.
1909–37: net output based on *Agr. Stat.,* Table 35.
Prices from *Agr. Stat.,* Table 31.
1938–39: see *general note* above.
Prior to 1908 prices relate to December 1.

(7) Flaxseed (1 bu. = 56 lb.):
1897–1908: harvested production from *Agr. Stat.,* Table 99. Flax used for seed on all farms estimated at .55 bu. per acre.
1909–37: net output from *Agr. Stat.,* Table 103.
1938–39: see *general note* above.
Prior to 1908 prices relate to December 1. For 1899 price was derived from 1900 Census of Agriculture material as published in the 1910 Census. Prices for 1897–98 and 1900–01 were obtained from Strauss and Bean, *op. cit.,* Table 23. Prices for 1902–37 from *Agr. Stat.,* Table 99.

(8) Buckwheat (1 bu. = 48 to 52 lb.):
1897–1908: harvested production from *Agr. Stat.,* Table 127. Seed use on all farms estimated at 1 bu. per acre; feed consumed on farms where grown assumed to have accounted for 30 percent of gross output.
1909–37: net output based on *Agr. Stat.,* Table 129.
Prices from *Agr. Stat.,* Table 127.
1938–39: see *general note* above.
Prior to 1908 prices relate to December 1.

(9) Potatoes (1 bu. = 60 lb.):
1897–1908: harvested production and prices from *Agr. Stat.,* Table 343; net output estimated at 84 percent of gross output.
1909–37: net output based on *Disposition of Potatoes, Crop Years, 1909–1937* (U. S. Agricultural Marketing Service, 1939), p. 7.
Prices from *Agr. Stat.,* Table 343.
1938–39: see *general note* above.
Prior to 1908 December 1 prices were adjusted downward 10 percent to represent season average.

(10) Sweetpotatoes (1 bu. = 55 lb.):
No disposition data on a crop-year basis have been made available up to this time. The disposition data published as part of the *Income Parity* series of the Department of Agriculture were therefore used as a guide for the entire period. Net output was thus estimated at roughly 82 percent of gross output, as given in *Agr. Stat.,* Table 358. Prices were taken from the same source.
Prior to 1910, December 1 prices were raised 10 percent to represent the season average. The price for 1898 was estimated from the prices for adjoining years.

Footnotes to Table A-1 continued on next page.

Footnotes to Table A-1, continued.

(11) Dry edible beans (1 bag = 100 lb.):

1909–37: prices and net output, the latter defined as output of cleaned beans excluding the amount of beans used for seed on all farms, are based on *Production, Farm Disposition, and Value of Beans, Crop Years, 1909–1937* (U. S. Agricultural Marketing Service, 1940), pp. 6-7.

Prior to 1909 the only available output data are those collected for Census years by the Bureau of the Census. From 1909 on, the relationship of these data to the estimated net output of the AMS disposition study was found to be sufficiently constant to permit us to adjust the Census figures for 1899 to the AMS level by the ratio of the two figures in 1909. The years 1900–08 were then estimated by straight-line interpolation; for 1897 and 1898 we used the figures estimated by Strauss, *op. cit.*, p. 73, after we had adjusted them to the level of our series by the same ratio by which we adjusted the 1899 Census figure. It will be noted that no deductions are made for feed, as it is assumed that only uncleaned beans are fed to livestock.

1938–39: see *general note* above.

No price data are available prior to 1909, but for 1909, 1919 and 1929 Census values per unit agree well enough with AMS prices to permit us to use the 1899 Census value per unit in our computations.

(12) Sugar beets:

The output series is made up of a number of segments. The longest extends from 1913 to 1938 and is based on *Agr. Stat.*, Table 182, which also contains prices for the same years. An apparently comparable figure for 1912 was found in the *Yearbook of Agriculture, 1933,* Table 127. The 1911 figure in the same table was, however, rejected as not comparable; instead, we estimated production for the period 1901–11 from data on beets sliced, as found in the *Yearbook of Agriculture, 1913,* Table 115, raising the figures found there by 5 percent to represent production. The same procedure was followed for the years 1897, 1899 and 1900, for which data on "beets used" were found in F. R. Rutter, *International Sugar Situation,* Bureau of Statistics, Bulletin 30 (U. S. Department of Agriculture, 1904), p. 94. Data for 1901–13 given in this source agree within 1 to 2 percent with data for "beets sliced" as given in the 1913 *Yearbook.* Finally, the 1898 figure was derived from the output of refined beet sugar (*Yearbook of Agriculture, 1923,* Table 359), on the assumption of a requirement ratio of 10 tons of beets per ton of sugar.

1939 data: see *general note* above.

Prices for the years 1901–08, 1911 and 1912 are from *Yearbook of Agriculture, 1913,* p. 447; for 1909 and 1910 from a release, "Midmonth Local Market Price Report" (U. S. Agricultural Marketing Service, Dec. 30, 1940), p. 30. Price for 1899 is taken from *Abstract of the Thirteenth Census, 1910,* p. 407, and this price is used also in 1897, 1898 and 1900.

(13) Sugarcane:

Consistent output and price series on sugarcane used for sugar are now available from 1909 to 1938 in *Agr. Stat.*, Table 195. The output series was extended back to 1902 on the basis of cane sugar production as given in the *Yearbook of Agriculture, 1923,* Table 359, by assuming a requirement ratio of 14 tons of cane to one ton of raw sugar. To complete the series, data for 1897 to 1901 were derived from sugarcane crushed as given by Rutter, *op. cit.*, p. 93.

The price series was extended back to 1897 on the basis of the price of raw sugar. The relationship of the two, except for abnormal years like 1917–20, is rather steady; it was therefore assumed that on a per ton basis the price of sugarcane amounts to 5 percent of the price of raw sugar. The latter is the price as determined by the U. S. Bureau of Labor Statistics.

1939: see *general note* above.

(14) Sugarcane sirup (1 gal. = 11.25 lb.):

Agr. Stat., Table 206. Prices relate to December 1 throughout the period.

(15) Sorgo sirup (1 gal. = 11.4 lb.):

Agr. Stat., Table 208. Prices relate to December 1 throughout the period.

(16) Maple sirup (1 gal. = 11 lb.):

Agr. Stat., Table 210. The 1919 price was derived from the *Fourteenth Census, 1920,* Vol. V, p. 847.

(17) Maple sugar:

Same as (16).

(18) Peanuts:

Net output represents that part of peanut production which results in the emergence of threshed nuts either sold or consumed in the farm household. This is a slightly wider concept than commercial production, defined in the AMS disposition study of May 1939 as "Farmers' stock peanuts consumed by mills in the production of cleaned and shelled peanuts and crude peanut oil."

Net output for 1919–37 is based on *Agr. Stat.,* Table 437; for 1916–18 the production figures as published in *ibid.,* Table 435, were first lowered 9 percent in order that they might be adjusted downward by the same amount by which output data from 1919 on were lowered between the 1939 and 1940 issues of *Agr. Stat.* A second adjustment—a decrease of 10 percent—was then made to exclude feed use.

For years prior to 1916 we accepted Strauss and Bean data (*op. cit.*), which are based on Census returns linked by straight-line interpolation, but adjusted them to our 1916 estimate and lowered them 10 percent to take account of feed use.

Season average prices are taken from *Agr. Stat.,* Table 435, for 1916–38, and from *Crops and Markets,* Dec. 1935, for 1909–1915. For the period 1897–1908 Strauss and Bean data (*op. cit.*) were used, and it was assumed that the crop-year price was equivalent to the calendar-year price corresponding to the second half of the crop year.

1938–39: See *general note* above.

In 1909 the price is based on data for 8 months only.

(19) Soybeans (1 bu. = 60 lb.):

Net output is here considered to comprise only the amounts processed for oil. No data are available prior to 1922, and it can safely be assumed that little crushing was performed before that date. The source for our output data for 1922 and 1923 is *Fats, Oils, and Oleaginous Raw Materials,* Statistical Bulletin 59 (U. S. Department of Agriculture, 1937), p. 55; for 1924–28 for both output and price the source is *Feed Grains, Fats and Oils, Agricul-*

Footnotes to Table A-1 continued on next page.

Footnotes to Table A-1, continued.

tural Outlook Charts, 1941 (U. S. Department of Agriculture, 1940), p. 16; for 1929–38, *Agr. Stat.,* Tables 405 and 408.

For 1939, quarterly reports of the Bureau of the Census were consulted.

Prices for 1922 and 1923 taken from *Crops and Markets,* Dec. 1935; for 1939, *Crops and Markets,* Dec. 1940.

(20) Hops:

Data on hop production are rather scattered. Our sources were *Agr. Stat.,* Table 431, for 1915–38; a communication from Mr. R. E. Fore of Oregon State College, for 1911–14; the *Yearbook of Agriculture, 1910,* p. 597, for 1906–10; and E. Merritt, *Hops in Principal Countries,* Bureau of Statistics, Bulletin 50 (U. S. Department of Agriculture, 1907), p. 9, for the years 1897–1905. We have made every effort to ensure year-to-year comparability of these data, but some doubt remains as to the period 1911–14, for which the data may represent commercial shipments rather than production.

1939: See *general note* above.

The price as given in *Agr. Stat.,* Table 431, refers to December 1 from 1915 to 1931. For 1911–14 no United States price is available, so that we have substituted the Oregon farm price which usually bears a close resemblance to the United States price; data from George L. Sulerud, *An Economic Study of the Hop Industry in Oregon,* Station Bulletin 288 (Oregon Agricultural Experiment Station, 1931), p. 48. For the remaining years the price is taken from G. K. Holmes, *Hop Crop of the United States, 1790–1911,* Bureau of Statistics, Circular 35 (U. S. Department of Agriculture, 1912), pp. 6-7; whether the price for this early period also refers to December 1 or represents a season average is unknown.

(21) Broomcorn:

Agr. Stat., Table 418.

For 1919–24, prices relate to November 15; for 1925 and 1926 to December 1.

1939: See *general note,* above.

(22) Hay:

Net output data for 1897–1937 are those given in Strauss and Bean, *op. cit.,* p. 62. Data for 1938 and 1939 were derived as follows: their ratio for production entering into gross income for 1936–37 (3 percent) was applied to the production of tame hay as given in *Agr. Stat.,* Table 420. (It is assumed that wild hay is not sold off farms, and that its net output is zero.)

The price series for 1897–1907 is from *Agr. Stat.,* Table 420; for 1908–28 from *Crops and Markets,* Dec. 1935; and for the balance of the period from *Crops and Markets,* Dec. 1940.

(23) Cotton (1 bale = 478 lb.):

Output data for 1899 and subsequent years from *Agr. Stat.,* Table 141. Figures for 1897 and 1898 in terms of 500-pound gross-weight bales were found in G. K. Holmes, *Cotton Crop of the United States, 1790–1911,* Bureau of Statistics, Circular 32 (U. S. Department of Agriculture, 1912), p. 8. Price data from *Agr. Stat.,* Table 141, for the entire period.

Prior to 1908 prices relate to December 1.

(24) Cottonseed:

From 1909 on, the series entitled "Delivered to mills," *Agr. Stat.,* Table 173, furnished our net output and price data. There is ground for legitimate doubt as to whether the amount exchanged for meal should not have been excluded, since it provides livestock feed. Nevertheless, we have made no attempt to exclude other types of commercial feed, and no adjustment has been made on this account.

For years prior to 1909 our source was a series on crushings from *Fats, Oils and Oleaginous Raw Materials,* Table 40. For overlapping years, this series is practically identical with that more recently published, and cited above.

Price and production for 1909–38 are not exactly comparable, as the former is a weighted price based on state production rather than state sales. Years for which both production-weighted and sales-weighted prices are available indicate that the discrepancy is relatively unimportant.

The price series was carried back to 1897 by use of the average spot price of prime summer yellow cottonseed oil at New York, given in *ibid.,* Table 115.

(25) Tobacco:

Agr. Stat., Table 213. Prior to 1919 prices relate to December 1.

(26) Apples (1 bu. = 48 lb.):

Output data for 1897–1909 from *Yearbook of Agriculture, 1928,* Table 128; for 1910–18 from *Fruits and Nuts, Agricultural Outlook Charts, 1940,* pp. 12, 18; and from 1919 on from *Agr. Stat.,* Table 224. All data are exclusive of fruit not harvested. Beginning in 1939 commercial production is reported in place of total production. To preserve comparability we have estimated total production in 1939 as 120 percent of commercial production; for source of the latter see *general note,* above.

The source for the price series from 1910–38 is the *Outlook Chart,* cited above. A comparable price for the period 1897–1909 has been derived from an average New York wholesale price of six varieties, to be found in a release by M. D. Woodin, entitled "Changes in Apple Prices," (N. Y. State College of Agriculture, February 1941).

(27) Apricots:

Our data are based on unpublished material, except for the period beginning in 1919 for which data are available in *Agr. Stat.,* Table 233, and for 1938–39 in the source indicated in the *general note.* However, for 1927 and later years we added the output of Washington to that of California, the only state represented up to 1927. The Washington data were supplied to us by Mr. Reginald Royston, of the Agricultural Marketing Service.

Estimates for the period 1909–18 were made available by Professor S. W. Shear, University of California, who also directed our attention to estimates for earlier years made by O. E. Baker, of the Bureau of Agricultural Economics. Both sets of estimates were made in the early 1930's and were of a tentative nature. Moreover, they were devised before the BAE had begun its revision of historical series. Dr. Baker permitted us to use his estimates which were largely based on the work of Professor Shear and his associates at the University of California. Shear's data for 1909–18 do not include consumption of fresh apricots within California; Baker's data for 1897–1908 presumably do. In view of the approximate character of the data prior to 1919 we made no attempt to adjust the different series for comparability in overlapping years.

Footnotes to Table A-1 continued on next page.

Footnotes to Table A-1, continued.

Prices for 1909–38 are taken from "Midmonth Local Market Price Report" (U. S. Agricultural Marketing Service, Aug. 29, 1940), p. 28. Prices for 1899 and 1904 are estimates based on unit values of dried apricots as collected by the Bureau of the Census and given in Solomon Fabricant, *The Output of Manufacturing Industries, 1899–1937* (National Bureau of Economic Research, 1940), p. 400.

(28) Figs, fresh and canned (fresh basis) and

(29) Figs, dried (dry basis):

Output and prices from *Agr. Stat.,* Table 296. California only: Texas production is omitted.

(30) Grapes:

Output data for the period 1899–1918 were supplied to us by Professor S. W. Shear, University of California; from 1919 on data were taken from *Agr. Stat.,* Table 300. The two sets appear to be directly comparable. The series was completed for 1897 and 1898 from the estimates made by Strauss and Bean, *op. cit.,* p. 87. After 1919 amounts neither sold nor harvested are excluded.

The construction of the price series for the years prior to 1924, when U. S. farm prices become available (*Agr. Stat.,* Table 300), involved a great many adjustments and assumptions which space limitations do not permit us to describe in detail. Suffice it to say that the basic data from 1899 to 1919 were annual prices of different varieties of California and New York grapes, again supplied by Professor Shear. These prices were combined into a weighted average and were adjusted to the level of Census of Agriculture unit values in 1899, 1909 and (after slight adjustment) 1919. Prices for 1920–23 are based on California prices as given in *Fruits and Nuts, Agricultural Outlook Charts, 1940,* adjusted to the corrected Census value per unit in 1919. In 1897 and 1898 prices are arbitrary estimates, based on the prices of 1899 and 1900.

(31) Olives:

All data based on *Agr. Stat.,* Table 310.

(32) Peaches (1 bu. = 48 lb.):

From 1909 on the output data are taken from *Peaches: Production, Disposition, and Value, 1909–1938* (U. S. Agricultural Marketing Service, 1940). Table 153 of the *Yearbook of Agriculture, 1927* contains estimates of production from 1899 on; although the figures for 1909 and later years as published in the above study differ by an average 5 percent in either direction from these earlier estimates, the latter were used without adjustment, since no rational basis for an adjustment could be found. To complete the series for 1897 and 1898 we accepted the estimates made by O. E. Baker; see footnote (27) on Apricots.

Prices are taken from *Agr. Stat.,* Table 316, beginning with 1919, and for 1909–18 are derived from value and size of total production as given in the AMS release mentioned above. Prices found in the release apply to sales only, and were therefore considered unacceptable. No prices are available for years prior to 1909.

(33) Pears (1 bu. = 50 lb.):

To complete the series for which *Agr. Stat.,* Table 321, supplies output and price data from 1919 on, we turned again to estimates made by O. E. Baker for 1897–1908 and by S. W. Shear for 1909–18; see footnote (27) on Apricots. Shear's data were converted from pounds to bushels on the assumption of a constant ratio of 48 pounds per bushel.

Prices for 1918 are from *Yearbook of Agriculture, 1928,* Table 157, and for 1910–17 from *Yearbook of Agriculture, 1925,* Table 210. These are unrevised prices; no revisions could be located and comparisons between unrevised and revised prices for years for which both are available indicate close resemblance. The 1909 price is derived from the Census of Agriculture for that year. All prices for years prior to 1925, except that for 1909, refer to November 15.

(34) Plums (California and Michigan only):
To obtain production estimates of fresh and canned plums for the years preceding 1919, recourse was had to a number of assumptions and estimates whose exact nature it would occupy too much space to describe. The basic data used were California shipments of fresh plums back to 1897 and of canned plums back to 1906. Both are given in E. Rauchenstein, *Economic Aspects of the Fresh Plum Industry,* Bulletin 459 (University of California Agricultural Experiment Station, 1928), pp. 12 and 18 respectively. The assumptions basic to an estimate of total plum production from these data involved conversion factors from carlots and cases to tons, average relationship between California output and Michigan output (the only other state represented in plum statistics, beginning in 1919), and average relationship between fresh and canned plums. Production and price from 1919 on are based on *Agr. Stat.,* Table 338. The price series was extended back to 1909 on the basis of a California price series published in "Midmonth Local Market Price Report" (U. S. Agricultural Marketing Service, Sept. 30, 1940), p. 27.

(35) Prunes, canned (Oregon and Washington only):
Based on *Agr. Stat.,* Table 340. It proved impossible to extend the series backward or to exclude nonharvested portions.

(36) Prunes, dried (California, Oregon and Washington only):
The output series for 1919–38, based on *Agr. Stat.,* Table 340, was carried back to 1897 by the use of data given in S. W. Shear, *Prune Supply and Price Situation,* Bulletin 462 (University of California Agricultural Experiment Station, 1928), pp. 31, 50. Nonharvested portions could not be excluded. Prices for 1919–38 from the same source as output. Prices for 1899, 1904, 1909 and 1914 derived from the Census of Manufactures; see Fabricant, *op. cit.,* p. 400.

(37) Prunes, fresh (Idaho, Oregon and Washington only):
Same as (35).

(38) Cranberries (1 bbl. = 100 lb.):
Agr. Stat., Table 286.

(39) Strawberries (1 crate = 36 lb.):
Agr. Stat., Table 366.

(40)-(42) Citrus fruit:
Unfortunately, the official estimates of both output and price of citrus fruit, as published in *Production, Disposition, and Value of Citrus Fruits, Crop Sea-*

Footnotes to Table A-1 continued on next page.

Footnotes to Table A-1, continued.
sons 1909–10 to 1938–39 (U. S. Agricultural Marketing Service, 1941), reached us at a time when complete substitution of those data for our estimates, described below, would have involved an inordinate amount of recomputation, with the final results probably little changed. The reader is advised, however, to use these new official data rather than our estimates where citrus fruit are the subject of special study. In particular, our price estimates, due to the multitude of price series available—f.o.b., on tree, at packinghouse door, all methods of sale, etc.—are to be treated with caution. Comparison with the newly released series indicates that we overstated Florida prices for both oranges and grapefruit, that our lemon price estimates are fairly accurate, and that up to 1929 we more often exaggerated than underestimated California grapefruit prices. Our estimated California orange prices are surprisingly similar to the official series.

As to the prices of citrus fruit produced outside California and Florida, the figures listed by us are the most reliable available at the time of writing. The above-mentioned study, however, contains data which should be substituted for those given here.

(40) Citrus fruit, California:

Separate data for grapefruit, lemons, and oranges, prior to 1905, are available for output, but not for prices. From 1897 to 1904 we therefore present a combined series. The constituents of the output series have, however, been computed on the same principle as the data after 1905, and are dealt with in the section on lemons and oranges respectively. The derivation of the combined price is treated immediately after the description of the derivation of the price of oranges.

(A) Oranges (in California, 1 box = 70 lb.):

Output, excluding fruit lost on the tree or donated to charity, is based, for 1909–37, on a release, "California Citrus Crops Production and Utilization Estimates, 1909–10 to 1937–38" (California Cooperative Crop Reporting Service, Sacramento, 1939); for 1938–39 on *The Fruit Situation* (U. S. Bureau of Agricultural Economics, Dec. 1940), p. 25; and for 1897–1909 on interstate shipments. The latter were taken, for 1902–08, from H. R. Wellman and E. W. Braun, *Oranges,* Bulletin 457 (University of California Agricultural Experiment Station, 1928), p. 54, and assumed, on the basis of the relationship between shipments and production 1909–14, to be 90 percent of production. For 1897–1901 the source is *Annual Statistical Report, 1921* (California State Board of Agriculture), p. 237. These data as published exclude the northern California output and were accordingly marked up 5 percent to compensate for this deficiency. To convert carlots to boxes a factor of 374 boxes per car was assumed, in accordance with data given in the 1911 report, p. 139, of the above-mentioned agency. The estimated boxes were assumed to constitute 90 percent of output and were raised to represent 100 percent.

Prices for 1909–33 are our own estimates, derived in a way analogous to that described for (B) Lemons. The source for prices was a release, "Average Prices Received by Farmers for Farm Products: August 15, 1935, With Comparisons" (Crop Reporting Board, Aug. 29, 1935), pp. 12, 13. Prices for 1905–08 are f.o.b.; these were supplied by Professor H. R. Wellman of the University of California; they were reduced to a packinghouse-door basis (i.e., including cost of harvesting, but not of packing) by deduction of 45 cents a case each year, an amount that seemed reasonable in view of later records as published in Bulletin 457. For 1934–39 prices as given in *Agr. Stat.*, Table 269, were raised 10 percent to render them comparable with our estimates from 1909 to 1933. It should be mentioned that these price estimates agree well with the latest official data (see general note on Citrus fruit above).

The only price available prior to 1905 is an f.o.b. price for all citrus fruit sold, which was derived from R. M. MacCurdy, *The History of the California Fruit Growers Exchange* (G. Rice and Sons, Los Angeles, 1925), p. 70. To obtain this price, Exchange returns were raised to returns for all citrus sales by using the published annual percentages of Exchange sales to total sales. Total returns were then divided by total boxes produced and the resulting price per box was assumed to be the f.o.b. price for the entire citrus industry. From 1904 on, an f.o.b. price for all citrus fruit—based on Fruit Growers Exchange returns—is available in *Fifty-ninth Annual Report, 1912* (California State Board of Agriculture), p. 130; this price was found to be directly comparable with our estimates prior to 1905. Consequently, we used the relationship of this f.o.b. price to the average packinghouse-door price from 1905 on to convert the f.o.b. price prior to 1905 to a packinghouse-door basis. It was found that a deduction of 50 cents a case would reduce the f.o.b. price to a packinghouse-door level.

(B) Lemons (1 box = 76 lb.):

Net output for 1909–37 from same source as grapefruit (see below). Prior to 1909 shipment data—as given in H. R. Wellman and E. W. Braun, *Lemons*, Bulletin 460 (University of California Agricultural Experiment Station, 1928), pp. 9, 10, 35, for 1907 and 1908; and from *Annual Statistical Report, 1921* (California State Board of Agriculture), p. 237 for preceding years—were marked up 8 percent to represent production. The percentage is based on the average relationship of shipments and output in 1909–15. Prior to 1907 shipments are given in carlots; these have been converted to boxes by a factor of 313 boxes per car up to 1904 and 336 boxes for 1905 and 1906 (1911 report, p. 139).

Prices from 1909–34 represent our own estimates, derived from records of monthly shipments and monthly packinghouse-door prices. The former, for the years 1917 to 1939, were kindly sent to us by Mr. A. R. Spiker of the Agricultural Marketing Service; monthly prices were taken from *Crops and Markets*, December 1935. The price series was completed up to 1938 from *Agr. Stat.*, Table 274, while for 1905 to 1908 f.o.b. prices supplied to us by Professor H. R. Wellman were reduced by 80 cents to convert them to a packinghouse-door basis.

(C) Grapefruit (in California, 1 box = 60 lb.):

The source for net output data, excluding fruit lost or donated to charity, is U. S. Agricultural Marketing Service, *Production, Disposition and Value of Citrus Fruits, Crop Seasons 1909–10 to 1938–39, by States* (Washington, 1941). It was assumed that production prior to 1909 was negligible. The source for 1938 and 1939 was *The Fruit Situation*, Dec. 1940, p. 25.

Prices for 1924–34 are taken from *Agr. Stat.*, 1937, p. 156, and thereafter from *Agr. Stat.*, Table 269. The two series do not quite agree in overlapping years. Prices from 1911 to 1923 are f.o.b. prices, reduced by 50 cents each year to account for packing and selling charges; the source of the price series is

Footnotes to Table A-1 continued on next page.

Footnotes to Table A-1, continued.
H. R. Wellman and E. W. Braun, *Grapefruit,* Bulletin 463 (University of California Agricultural Experiment Station, 1928), p. 33.
Prices in 1909 and 1910 are arbitrary estimates.

(41) Citrus fruit, Florida:
(A) Oranges, including Tangerines (in Florida, 1 box = 90 lb.):
Output for 1919–39: from *Statistical Bulletin, Season 1939–40* (Florida Citrus Exchange, 1940), p. 21; 1897–1918: shipments, *ibid.,* pp. 11, 16, raised 10 percent to represent output.
Prices refer to oranges only; we have estimated that the inclusion of tangerine prices would usually raise the price by only a few cents; the largest difference, appearing in 1920, amounted to not more than 18 cents.
Prices for 1909–34 estimated from monthly shipments and prices; see note on California orange prices. For 1935–39: *Agr. Stat.,* Table 269, raised 10 percent for the sake of comparability with our own estimates. No prices are available for years preceding 1909, but a price of $1.50 a case was assumed.
(B) Grapefruit (in Florida, 1 box = 80 lb.):
Output in 1919–39 based on same source as oranges. For 1900–18 we marked up shipment data (*Statistical Bulletin,* p. 16) by not more than 5 percent to represent output, since in the earlier years most fruit seems to have been shipped out of the state.
Prices for 1909–34 were estimated from monthly prices and shipments; see note on California orange prices. From 1934 on we used the f.o.b. price (*ibid.,* p. 8), deducting 50 cents per case for packing and selling charges each year. No price could be estimated for years prior to 1909, but a price of $2.00 a case was assumed.

(42) Citrus fruit, other states:
(A) Oranges (1 box = 70 to 90 lb.):
Data from *Agr. Stat., 1937,* Table 198; *1938,* Table 227; *1940,* Table 269.
(B) Grapefruit, Texas (1 box = 80 lb.):
Data up to and including 1934 from *Agr. Stat., 1937,* Table 198; thereafter from *Agr. Stat.,* Table 269.
(C) Grapefruit, Arizona (1 box = 60 lb.):
Same as (B).

(43) Almonds:
Output for the years 1900–18 based on tabulation in *Yearbook of Agriculture, 1925,* p. 285. These figures were raised 5 percent in order to ensure comparability with the revised data from 1919 and later years as shown in *Agr. Stat.,* Table 223. The percentage was derived from a comparison for 1919–22 of the latter with the unrevised data as published in *Yearbook of Agriculture, 1928,* Table 165. Price data are not available prior to 1919; from 1919 on they were taken from *Agr. Stat.,* Table 223.

(44) Pecans:
From *Agr. Stat.,* Table 331. The price refers to November 1 for 1922, and to December 1 for the years 1923 to 1936.

(45) Walnuts:
The output series which from 1919 on, together with the price series, was taken from *Agr. Stat.,* Table 376, was carried back to 1900 by the use of esti-

mates of California production as given in *Yearbook of Agriculture, 1925*, p. 285. To adjust the earlier segment to the level of the revised estimates from 1919 on, California production was marked up 8 percent each year. For 1899 we used the Census figure, since for 1919 the revised estimate is practically identical with the 1919 Census figure.

Prior to 1919, data relate to California only; Oregon production at that time was negligible.

(46)-(64) Truck crops:

artichokes (1 box = 40 lb.)
asparagus (1 crate = 24 lb.)
snap beans (1 bu. = 30 lb.)
beets (1 bu. = 52 lb.)
cabbage
cantaloups (1 crate = 60 lb.)
carrots (1 bu. = 50 lb.)
cauliflower (1 crate = 37 lb.)
celery (1 crate = 90 lb.)
sweet corn
cucumbers (1 bu. = 48 lb.)
eggplant (1 bu. = 33 lb.)
lettuce (1 crate = 70 lb.)
onions (1 sack = 100 lb.)
peas (1 bu. = 30 lb.)
peppers (1 bu. = 25 lb.)
spinach (1 bu. = 18 lb.)
tomatoes (1 bu. = 53 lb.)
watermelons

Data from *Agr. Stat.*, Tables 234, 235, 241, 246, 250, 253, 256, 259, 262, 281, 289, 293, 307, 312, 326, 333, 363, 371, 377.

Quantities not marketed are excluded in all cases.

(65) Peppermint oil:

From *Agr. Stat.*, Table 461.

(66)-(69) Livestock:

Net output is defined as the combined liveweight poundage of animals slaughtered and of changes in number on hand. Two separate series, therefore, had to be constructed, but the same price was applied to both, since it is practically impossible to find any price that can be matched with changes in inventory (see pp. 95-96 above).

(66)-(67) Cattle and Calves:

Since neither of the two series can be discussed without reference to the other, the two are taken up jointly. The data shown for output are based on estimates of the composition of animals on farms January 1 for each year prior to 1920. It was found that between 1921 and 1934—a complete cattle cycle—the relationship between calves on hand and cattle on hand Jan. 1 (U. S. Agricultural Marketing Service, *Livestock, Meats, and Wool Market Statistics and Related Data, 1940*, Washington, 1941, p. 7) was extremely steady, deviating not more than 7 percent in either direction from the average for the period. We therefore used this average to estimate separately the number of calves and cattle on farms back to 1897. The proportions used were 22.6 percent for calves, and 77.4 percent for cattle. Although it is dangerous to project such a relationship back over a period of almost 25 years, it is unlikely that major changes in this relationship took place during the period, though no accuracy is claimed for the estimate in any given year.

Once this breakdown had been performed, number slaughtered—*Agr. Stat.*, Table 475—and change in inventory were summed for either category, and each sum was then multiplied by an estimated liveweight per head, derived

Footnotes to Table A-1 continued on next page.

Footnotes to Table A-1, continued.
from the total liveweight of all slaughter of cattle and calves respectively, as estimated by C. A. Burmeister of the Bureau of Agricultural Economics.

In order to eliminate the error introduced by applying the average liveweight of animals slaughtered to the change in inventory, we compared the inventory change for cattle and calves combined, each computed as described above, with the poundage derived from number on hand and average liveweight per head of animals on hand, the latter copied from the files of C. L. Harlan of the Agricultural Marketing Service. The comparison, made for a number of years between 1920 and 1930, revealed that by using slaughter weights we were overstating inventory weights some 7 percent. However, it was impossible to determine whether the overstatement occurred in the cattle or calves series. Consequently, for each year, we reduced or increased both the cattle and the calves series by 7 percent of the inventory changes. To the cattle series was further added the total liveweight of live cattle exported; the number exported was taken from Strauss and Bean, *op. cit.*, Table 49, for 1897–1913; from John Roberts, *Food Animals and Meat Consumption in the United States*, Department Circular 241 (U. S. Department of Agriculture, 1922; revised 1924), Table 10, for 1914–19, and from *Beef Cattle, Agricultural Outlook Charts, 1940* (U. S. Bureau of Agricultural Economics), p. 14, for 1920–38. Exports of calves were not included. Liveweight per head was assumed to be 1,250 lbs.; this high figure, used by Strauss and Bean, *op. cit.*, p. 107, is explained by the facts that the destination for most of the live steers exported has been England, which prefers heavy steers, and that transport charges are computed per animal rather than per pound. Imports do not have to be deducted, since they consist mostly of lean animals driven in from Mexico and Canada for feeding.

Prices are those given in *Livestock, Meats, and Wool Market Statistics*, p. 74, for 1910–39, supplemented for 1897–1909 by the series given by Strauss and Bean, *op. cit.*, Tables 48, 51.

For cattle in 1897 and 1898, total slaughter was estimated as 183 percent of federally inspected slaughter. This ratio was based on data for later years as given in *Livestock, Meats, and Wool Market Statistics*, p. 31. Together with the inventory change, it was then converted into pounds by multiplying by average liveweight (950 lbs.) as estimated by Strauss and Bean, *op. cit.*, p. 106.

For calves in 1897 and 1898, slaughter was estimated as .3757 of cattle slaughtered in same year, based on recorded experience of 1899 and 1900. This was combined with inventory change, and multiplied by average liveweight of 170 lbs. as derived from record of later years. For 1939 inventory changes were derived from *The Livestock Situation* (U. S. Bureau of Agricultural Economics, March 1941), p. 19.

(68) Hogs:

Slaughter figures, in terms of pounds, for 1899–1938, were made available to us by C. A. Burmeister; see note on (66)-(67).

Changes in inventory poundage for 1909–23 were provided by C. L. Harlan; see note on (66)-(67). These data were supplemented for the missing years by our own estimates based on essentially the same methods as those used by Mr. Harlan, who supplied us with estimates which he has made for the average weight per head for the period 1924–33, by states; these average weights we applied, state by state, to changes in number on hand between successive

January 1's as given on a state basis in *Livestock on Farms, January 1, 1867–1935* (U. S. Bureau of Agricultural Economics, 1938). The state figures were then aggregated into a United States total. This method allows for differences in weight between states and the changing importance of various states in total hog production. When compared to estimates based on change in the country as a whole it is found that our method yields larger results in both directions, since states having heavier hogs also predominate in magnitude of change.

The price series consists of two segments. Farm prices per cwt. liveweight are available back to 1910 in *Livestock, Meats, and Wool Market Statistics,* p. 75. Prior to 1910 we used the Chicago price (*ibid.,* p. 68), lowering it 9 percent to adjust it to the farm price. This adjustment was derived from the 1910–29 record.

For 1897 and 1898 estimates of output were based on number slaughtered, in turn derived as a percentage of number on hand January 1 (*Agr. Stat.,* Table 484) and average liveweight per animal slaughtered, derived as an average quotient over a number of years from our poundage figures and number killed (*Agr. Stat.,* Table 498). The ratio of slaughter to inventory was found to be quite constant, averaging 1.024 over the period 1899–1910, while average liveweight per animal slaughtered varied within even narrower limits.

For 1939 output was derived from number slaughtered—*Agr. Stat.,* Table 498—multiplied by liveweight per head of 230 pounds, plus change in inventory, based on *ibid.,* Table 484.

(69) Sheep and lambs:

For source of slaughter poundage, 1899–1938, see note on Hogs (68). Slaughter in 1897 and 1898 based on number slaughtered under federal inspection multiplied by 1.33, which is the average ratio of total to inspected slaughter for the years 1900–01 (*Livestock, Meats, and Wool Market Statistics,* p. 36). This estimate was then multiplied by the estimated average liveweight per animal slaughtered—85 pounds—as derived for 1899–1906 from Burmeister's poundage figures divided by number slaughtered, *Agr. Stat.,* Table 533.

Inventory changes were estimated by assuming a constant weight of 100 lb. per head for all years. Though the 1924–33 weight by states, as copied from Mr. Harlan's files—see note on Hogs (68)—ranges from 76 lb. (Alabama) to 119 lb. (New Jersey), the majority of the states show weights close to 100. Moreover, data for feeder sheep, which form part of our analysis, are not available on a state basis prior to 1925, whereas state weights include the weight of feeder sheep. It appeared, therefore, that little would be gained by computing inventory changes on a state basis, as was done in the case of hogs, and a test computation we made bore out this conjecture.

The only price for sheep and lambs combined is available in the Income Parity Study (U. S. Department of Agriculture, *Income Parity for Agriculture,* Washington, 1940, Pt. 1, Sec. 6) beginning in 1909. It includes, however, the interstate sales of sheep, for feeding and breeding, and was used only prior to 1923, since from 1923 on we were able to construct our own average price, based upon the relative number of sheep and lambs slaughtered (*Livestock, Meats, and Wool Market Statistics,* p. 50). In order to take into account the

Footnotes to Table A-1 continued on next page.

Footnotes to Table A-1, continued.
heavier weight of sheep, the percentage of sheep slaughtered was given a weight of 2 as against 1 for the lamb percentage. The average price thus estimated from the two separate prices (*ibid.*, pp. 74-75) closely resembles the *Income Parity* price.

The price series was completed to 1897 with the help of a series on cost to wholesale packers (*Agr. Stat.*, Table 557). This series exceeds the farm price but parallels its movements closely for years for which both series are available. Consequently we lowered it 5 percent to bring about a rough adjustment to the farm price level in 1909. For 1939 output was obtained from number slaughtered, *Agr. Stat.*, Table 533, multiplied by assumed weight of 86 lbs. per head.

(70) Eggs:

Net output, consisting of eggs produced adjusted to exclude eggs used for hatching, and price, 1909–39, from *Agr. Stat.*, Table 639.

The output series was completed with the help of a corrected 1899 Census figure (Strauss and Bean, *op. cit.*, Table 46) and a series on shipments to six cities which was made available to us by Mr. W. H. Shaw, formerly of the National Bureau of Economic Research and now at the Department of Commerce. The shipment series covering about 20 percent of total output was raised to the level shown by the 1899 and 1909 estimates by straight-line interpolations of ratios between the two years. Similarly, 1897 and 1898 were estimated from shipments by straight-line interpolated ratios between 1899 and a corrected Census figure for 1889 (Strauss and Bean, *loc. cit.*). Prices were also taken from *ibid.*

(71) Chickens:

From 1909–39, net output, consisting of chickens produced, and prices were taken from *Agr. Stat.*, Table 624. In making estimates for the preceding years we attempted to follow the procedure outlined in *Farm Production and Disposition, Chickens and Eggs, 1909–1924* (U. S. Bureau of Agricultural Economics, 1939), p. 1. We first estimated chickens on hand, January 1, on the basis of eggs produced (see series on eggs), using the 1910 BAE figure and a corrected 1900 Census figure as basic data between which we interpolated ratios of chickens on hand to eggs produced. These ratios multiplied by eggs produced yielded chickens on hand. The process was carried out for 1897 and 1898 by extrapolating the ratio for those two years. Next, chickens lost were estimated at 12 percent of chickens on hand; see S. A. Jones, "Poultry and Eggs," *Farm Value, Gross Income, and Cash Income from Farm Production,* Pt. II (U. S. Bureau of Agricultural Economics, 1930), p. 19.

Chickens raised were estimated as a constant ratio (.25) of eggs produced the following year. The ratio was computed for each year 1909–20, and turned out to be markedly constant.

Finally, chickens produced were computed as the difference between chickens raised and chickens lost.

The price series was completed with the help of Strauss and Bean, *op. cit.*, Table 45. The prices there published were converted to a per-head basis by estimated weight per head as supplied by Mr. Strauss.

(72) Turkeys:

From *Agr. Stat.*, Table 635.

(73) Milk and milk products (1 quart of milk = 2.15 lb.):

It is impossible to describe here in complete detail the complex procedure we found it necessary to use in estimating output and prices of milk and derived products. A great deal of widely scattered material was supplemented by returns to a special questionnaire sent out by us to all Agricultural Experiment Stations. Various assumptions and simplifications had to be introduced, so that the resulting series must be viewed as first approximations in a largely unexplored field.

Since we used data for recent years as our point of departure, we shall describe our methods in chronologically reverse order.

For the years 1934–39 data have recently become available which give output and prices in terms of disposition; this is the ideal form of presentation for our purposes. The source is *Farm Production and Income from Milk, by States, 1938–1939* (U. S. Agricultural Marketing Service, 1940). A continuation of these data back to 1924 has since appeared, unfortunately too late for inclusion in this study. However, our own estimates resemble these latest official data well enough to justify our results.

From 1910 to 1933 we relied on three series, viz. farm butter, creamery butter, and milk disposed of in fluid form. The choice of these three series was conditioned by the availability of separate price series matching, more or less, those categories. Prices are from releases by R. F. Hale and J. B. Shepard, "U. S. Average Farm Prices of Dairy Products, 1910–1934" (U. S. Department of Agriculture, 1934), and R. E. Johnson, "Wholesale Prices Received by Farmers for Whole Milk, 1909–1936" (U. S. Department of Agriculture, 1937).

Output data were derived from estimates of total milk produced. Such estimates are available from 1924 in *Agr. Stat.*, Table 572, and were extended back to 1909 with the help of data from R. G. Bressler, Jr., and J. A. Hopkins, *Trends in Size and Production of the Aggregate Farm Enterprise, 1909–36* (National Research Project, Philadelphia, 1938), p. 227. The latter series was raised to the level of the official data in 1924. From this series was excluded the amount fed to calves, from *Agr. Stat.*, Table 581, back to 1924, and estimated as 3 percent of the total prior to that date. This net output series was then split up in the following way: farm butter output for 1924 and later years, given in *Agr. Stat.*, Table 581, was converted to butter equivalents by a factor of 20.3 lbs. of milk per lb. of butter. Prior to 1924 data are derived from E. E. Vial, *Production and Consumption of Manufactured Dairy Products*, Technical Bulletin 722 (U. S. Department of Agriculture, 1940), Table 5. The two series are directly comparable.

Creamery butter is based on the same sources as farm butter, but from 1909–23 includes whey butter. This is an error of negligible proportions.

In order to apply to the creamery butter series the price of butterfat, we had to assume (1) that all creamery butter is made from milk sold as butterfat and (2) that no butterfat is sold for purposes other than the manufacture of creamery butter. Needless to say neither assumption is strictly justified. Nonetheless, we accumulated sufficient evidence, both statistical and general, to convince ourselves that the two assumptions yield a fair approximation.

In order to make the butterfat price technically applicable to the output of creamery butter—the finished product—two ratios must be assumed:

Footnotes to Table A-1 continued on next page.

Footnotes to Table A-1, continued.

(1) For the period 1924–34, 20.3 lb. of milk = 1 lb. of butter; the ratio becomes 21 prior to 1924. The change in the conversion factor constitutes a break, though not a serious one, in continuity.

(2) To sell 1 lb. of butterfat the farmer has to sell 26.6 lb. of milk.

These factors are based on data available from 1924 and 1934 respectively. The butterfat price multiplied by the ratio under (1) above, and divided by the ratio under (2), thus represents the price the farmer obtains for the amount of fluid milk he has to sell to result in the output of one pound of creamery butter, and is therefore directly comparable to the output of creamery butter.

Finally, the amount of fluid milk sold as such off farms or consumed in farm households was obtained as the difference between total milk output and the combined output, in terms of milk equivalents, of farm and creamery butter. The source of the latter two series has already been quoted; and it remains to be mentioned that prior to 1924 conversion from butter to milk was based on a factor of 21 lb. of milk per lb. of butter.

The price applied to fluid milk output was a weighted average of the wholesale price, and the price received for retail sales by farmers, of fluid milk. On the basis of statistical evidence obtained from the period 1929–39, and as a result of both general considerations and returns to the questionnaire mentioned above, the wholesale price was given a weight of 5 from 1928 to 1933 and of 4 in 1909. Between 1909 and 1928 the weight was increased by one tenth every other year, on the assumption that there has been a gradual decline in the relative importance of farmers' retail sales.

From 1897 to 1909 total production was obtained from Strauss and Bean, *op. cit.*, Table 43, by splicing the series to our 1909 estimate; 3 percent was again deducted for milk fed to calves, and the balance separated into butter and fluid milk by using total butter production as given in Vial, *op. cit.*, Table 5. The subdivision into factory and farm butter was used only to convert the farm butter price (Strauss and Bean, *op. cit.*, Table 40) into a price representing both farm and factory butter. This was achieved on the basis of the known relationship between farm butter and butterfat prices after 1910, when it was found that the price of milk sold as butterfat averaged 81 percent of the price of the identical unit of milk turned into farm butter. Farm butter was taken to have constituted 65 percent of all butter over the entire period, year-to-year fluctuations as shown in Vial, *op. cit.*, Table 5, not being considered sufficiently important and reliable to justify the use of changing ratios. Thus, the average price of all milk going into butter was obtained as the sum of the farm butter price weighted by 65, and 81 percent of the farm butter price weighted by 35; this sum equals 93 percent of the farm butter price. The resulting price was found to check closely with one derived from a Wisconsin butterfat price series given by W. P. Mortenson, H. H. Erdman and J. H. Draxler, *Wisconsin Farm Prices, 1841 to 1933,* Research Bulletin 119 (Wisconsin Agricultural Experiment Station, 1933), p. 42.

Milk disposed of in fluid form was obtained as the difference between total milk, exclusive of amount fed to calves, and the milk equivalent—based on a factor of 21—of all butter. To the resulting output series was applied a price based mainly on estimates made for New York by S. E. Ronk, *Prices of Farm Products in N. Y. State, 1841 to 1935*, Bulletin 643 (Cornell University Agricultural Experiment Station, 1936); by Leland Spencer, "A Revised Series of Milk Prices for New York," *Farm Economics*, No. 111 (Cornell University, Feb. 1939), pp. 2707-10; and by Johnson, *op. cit.* A continuous New York state price series obtained from the above three sources was adjusted somewhat to conform to the level of the United States price for fluid milk already obtained for the period after 1909. Finally, in order to take into account farmers' retail sales, the series was raised 20 percent, this being the average 1910–15 excess of our estimated wholesale-retail price over the wholesale price.

(74) Wool:

Output refers to wool shorn only, and excludes wool pulled. The series, for which output data from 1909 on were obtained from *Agr. Stat.*, Table 539, was completed with the help of estimates made by P. T. Cherington, "Wool Growing in the United States," *Bulletin* of the National Association of Wool Manufacturers, Vol. LII (July 1922), pp. 327-44; this series runs consistently below the *Agr. Stat.* data which were revised to their present level between the publication of the 1938 and 1939 issues of *Agr. Stat.* Consequently we raised the pre-1909 segment to the level of the revised series by a uniform ratio of 1.08.

The price series consists of two segments: the basic one, from 1909 to 1938, was taken from the *Income Parity* report on wool—see note on (69)—whereas prices for the earlier period are based on a series of the average wholesale price of four grades, given in the *Bulletin* of the National Association of Wool Manufacturers, Vol. LXVI (1936), p. 163; this series was adjusted to the level of the former by a uniform ratio of .305, based on the relationship of the two series for 1909–29. The 1939 price is taken from *Crops and Markets*, February 1940.

(75) Mohair:

Up to 1937 both production and price are taken from an *Income Parity* report—see note on (69)—and completed for 1938–39 from *Agr. Stat.*, Table 549, for production, and from *Crops and Markets*, March 1940 and 1941 for price.

No earlier data are available, but there is evidence that by 1899 production cannot have exceeded 1 million pounds; see G. F. Thompson, *The Angora Goat*, Bulletin 27 (U. S. Bureau of Animal Industry, 1901), p. 82.

Table A-2

VALUE OF AGRICULTURAL PRODUCTS

Million dollars

This table, based on Table A-1, shows the value in farm prices of the net output of all products included in our index of agricultural output. Where no data are shown, they could not be computed, or are not available in comparable form. Data relate to crop years in the case of crops, calender years in the case of livestock and livestock products.

Product	*1899*	*1909*	*1919*	*1929*	*1937*
Wheat	337.6	608.8	1,785.2	705.6	643.6
Corn	157.7	354.0	771.8	391.6	308.2
Oats	68.9	141.8	224.6	95.4	67.6
Barley	22.9	50.3	61.8	41.4	47.3
Rice	6.4	17.1	104.1	36.6	33.0
Rye	8.8	14.5	85.5	17.7	16.6
Flaxseed	18.1	25.8	25.9	38.2	12.1
Buckwheat	4.0	6.6	9.7	4.0	1.8
Potatoes	82.7	185.5	487.5	374.3	176.3
Sweetpotatoes	20.1	36.9	108.5	62.4	50.8
Dry edible beans	6.8	19.9	53.0	72.6	43.0
Sugar beets	3.5	21.7	75.4	51.8	46.3
Sugarcane	9.4	16.8	26.6	11.6	17.1
Sugarcane sirup	..	10.0	25.1	14.1	11.2
Sorgo sirup	..	..	33.6	8.4	6.7
Maple sirup	..	..	8.6	4.8	4.0
Maple sugar	..	..	3.1	4.1	3.0
Peanuts	8.8	22.0	57.8	30.5	36.8
Soybeans	..	..	..	3.1	25.5
Hops	4.0	8.9	21.9	3.8	6.4
Broomcorn	..	..	8.5	5.4	3.2
Hay	91.0	137.5	182.7	32.7	19.1
Cotton	326.2	676.3	2,016.3	1,244.6	796.7
Cottonseed	33.0	70.6	268.4	152.8	129.2
Tobacco	61.8	106.4	450.6	280.5	318.8
Apples	122.8	123.6	246.1	187.8	132.8
Apricots	1.6	2.9	15.0	14.2	12.1
Figs, fresh and for canning	..	..	..	.7	.8
Figs, dried	..	..	1.8	1.5	2.0
Grapes	14.6	21.4	103.0	56.9	57.2
Olives	..	..	1.2	1.4	1.9
Peaches	..	29.3	98.0	67.6	60.9
Pears	..	8.1	27.4	31.3	19.7
Plums, fresh and for canning	..	.9	3.1	3.8	3.0
Prunes, canned	..	..	.2	.4	.6
Prunes, dried	3.8	5.7	40.2	21.7	14.0
Prunes, fresh	..	..	1.9	1.5	1.0
Cranberries	..	3.3	4.7	7.7	7.7
Strawberries	..	..	31.9	40.2	34.4

TABLE A-2—VALUE OF PRODUCTS (concluded)

Product	*1899*	*1909*	*1919*	*1929*	*1937*
Citrus fruit, California					
Oranges	8.5	16.3	57.7	90.7	40.7
Lemons	..	4.5	8.0	26.6	24.3
Grapefruit	0	[a]	.6	2.6	1.1
Citrus fruit, Florida					
Oranges	.5	4.7	22.3	25.7	35.2
Grapefruit	0	2.6	12.1	20.6	15.2
Citrus fruit, other states					
Oranges	..	..	..	2.3	2.5
Grapefruit	..	..	.1[b]	4.2	8.4
Almonds	..	..	3.5	2.3	5.5
Pecans	..	..	13.5	7.6	5.6
Walnuts	..	..	16.6	13.9	10.9
Artichokes	..	..	..	2.3	1.9
Asparagus	..	..	5.0	14.1	14.2
Snap beans	..	..	8.2	20.4	20.6
Beets	..	..	..	1.8	1.6
Cabbage	..	..	16.0	19.4	15.7
Cantaloups and other muskmelons	..	..	15.0	22.6	16.0
Carrots	..	..	..	6.0	8.4
Cauliflower	..	..	2.3	5.6	7.2
Celery	..	..	10.3	14.4	17.8
Sweet corn	..	..	10.4[c]	10.9	12.7
Cucumbers	..	..	8.1	11.2	8.9
Eggplant	..	..	..	1.1	.6
Lettuce	..	..	8.3	36.1	32.8
Onions	..	..	24.8	20.5	19.2
Peas	..	..	8.5	21.0	24.3
Peppers	..	..	..	3.8	3.5
Spinach	..	..	2.9	7.3	6.4
Tomatoes	..	..	36.7	55.7	52.9
Watermelons	..	..	7.2	12.1	7.5
Peppermint oil	..	..	..	3.4	1.8
Cattle	498.8	502.5	1,126.9	1,149.7	890.0
Calves	37.3	59.4	184.4	178.8	150.7
Hogs	417.9	738.4	2,240.8	1,485.2	1,164.3
Sheep and lambs	52.6	71.2	138.7	195.3	152.2
Eggs	188.6	403.0	1,011.0	916.9	658.2
Chickens	114.7	206.2	492.7	592.4	367.0
Turkeys	..	..	..	53.7	68.3
Milk and milk products	486.9	841.3	2,126.1	2,360.7	1,937.1
Wool	40.9	68.8	133.6	99.1	117.4
Mohair	..	1.4	4.2	8.0	8.7
TOTAL	..	..	..	11,650.8	9,109.7

[a] Less than $50,000. [b] At $3.00 per box. [c] For manufacture only.

TABLE A-3

NET OUTPUT OF CROPS AND LIVESTOCK PRODUCTS, 1897–1939[a]

1929 : 100

Year	*Crops*	*Livestock Products*	*Year*	*Crops*	*Livestock Products*
1897	71.8	61.5	1919	93.2	82.1
1898	78.1	62.9	1920	101.6	81.0
1899	73.7	65.8	1921	79.5	83.1
1900	74.9	66.1	1922	91.1	89.3
1901	72.3	65.8	1923	91.7	91.9
1902	83.9	62.9	1924	99.0	91.2
1903	78.5	67.6	1925	102.1	90.7
1904	85.7	67.8	1926	109.5	95.0
1905	82.9	69.4	1927	98.4	97.8
1906	93.3	72.7	1928	108.0	98.4
1907	79.2	73.7	1929	100.0	100.0
1908	84.8	72.6	1930	99.3	101.2
1909	84.7	71.5	1931	106.9	102.8
1910	86.2	73.9	1932	94.5	103.2
1911	89.2	75.3	1933	87.0	104.4
1912	97.9	75.9	1934	72.8	91.2
1913	88.4	78.0	1935	90.6	93.3
1914	102.8	79.7	1936	83.0	100.1
1915	100.0	82.1	1937	121.3	97.4
1916	83.0	82.4	1938	108.4	102.8
1917	90.2	82.5	1939	111.1	109.4
1918	95.1	86.4			

[a] The two series in this table afford a breakdown of the combined index shown in Tables 1 and 5. Unlike the partial indexes in Table 5, the series printed here furnish a breakdown which is both exhaustive and free from duplication: "crops" include items (1) to (65), "livestock products" items (66) to (75) in Table A-1. The former relates to crop years, the latter to calendar years. This table is reproduced in five-year average form in Table 3, p. 31 above.

TABLE A-4

NET OUTPUT OF MILK, AND OF MILK PRODUCTS IN TERMS OF MILK, 1897–1939[a]

Million pounds

Year	*Fluid Milk*	*Farm and Creamery Butter (milk equivalent)*	*Total*	*Year*	*Fluid Milk*	*Farm and Creamery Butter (milk equivalent)*	*Total*
1897	21.2	32.2	53.4	1919	37.0	34.6	71.6
1898	23.3	30.9	54.2	1920	40.6	32.9	73.5
1899	23.4	31.3	54.7	1921	39.1	36.6	75.7
1900	23.1	32.3	55.5	1922	39.5	39.3	78.8
1901	23.4	33.1	56.5	1923	39.6	41.7	81.3
1902	22.0	29.4	51.4	1924	42.9	42.0	84.9
1903	26.6	31.2	57.8	1925	45.4	40.7	86.1
1904	26.2	32.3	58.5	1926	48.4	40.9	89.3
1905	24.0	35.0	59.0	1927	49.6	41.9	91.6
1906	27.1	32.4	59.6	1928	51.4	41.6	93.0
1907	27.8	32.3	60.0	1929	52.7	43.2	96.0
1908	24.1	37.0	61.2	1930	54.4	42.8	97.2
1909	28.3	34.1	62.3	1931	55.4	44.7	100.1
1910	27.3	35.8	63.1	1932	55.0	46.0	101.0
1911	26.9	37.0	63.9	1933	54.5	47.4	101.9
1912	31.2	33.4	64.6	1934	53.6	45.2	98.8
1913	31.9	33.8	65.7	1935	54.9	43.9	98.7
1914	32.1	35.4	67.5	1936	57.5	42.9	100.4
1915	32.1	36.8	68.9	1937	58.9	41.5	100.4
1916	32.5	37.7	70.1	1938	60.7	43.7	104.4
1917	36.6	34.6	71.2	1939	61.7	43.9	105.5
1918	40.9	30.7	71.7				

[a] Net output excludes milk fed to calves. This table is based on data in Table A-1, and constitutes the material from which Chart 30 is drawn. Data are for calendar years.

Appendix B

The Statistics of Food Consumption

Appendix B

The Statistics of Food Consumption

THIS appendix consists of six tables which contain basic data underlying Chapter 4. Table B-1 shows the consumption of all important foodstuffs in original units. Table B-2 gives the factors we have used to convert these foodstuffs into proteins, fats and carbohydrates. Similar factors for the vitamin and mineral content of foods will be found in Table B-3. Table B-4 shows for various foods the deductions we made to take account of inedible refuse. In Table B-5 Pearl's estimates for total calorie consumption are compared with our own. Table B-6 gives the population estimates upon which we based our per capita data.

The consumption estimates in Table B-1 are mostly obtained by correcting output for imports, exports, changes in stocks and nonfood use; see Bureau of Agricultural Economics release "Consumption of Agricultural Products" (1941). In a few cases, as indicated in footnotes, we have made adjustments to these figures, or computed data of our own. The conversion factors in Table B-2 are single-valued, and for calories are based on ratios of 4 calories per gram of protein and carbohydrate, and 9 calories per gram of fat (see p. 153). The factors in this table make partial allowance for the exclusion of inedible portions of foodstuffs shown in Table B-1. The factors for minerals in Table B-3 are also single-valued, but for vitamins we felt it necessary to indicate a range rather than a single figure. For this reason the consumption estimates for vitamins in Table 25 (p. 174) also take the form of a range of values. The percentages by which the crude food consumption data in Table B-3 were subsequently reduced to allow for inedible refuse are shown in Table B-4. These percentages make no allowance for losses of edible food in processing or transportation, in the kitchen or on the table. Except where otherwise stated, all data in this Appendix refer to calendar years.

TABLE B-1

AGGREGATE CONSUMPTION OF INDIVIDUAL FOODS, AVERAGE 1897–1901, AND ANNUALLY 1909–1939

Year	(1) *Wheat*	(2) *Corn* (a) *Dry Milling*	(2) *Corn* (b) *Wet Milling*	(3) *Oatmeal*	(4) *Rice, Milled*	(5) *Rye*	(6) *Sugar, Cane and Beet, Refined*
	mil. bu.	mil. bu.	mil. bu.	mil. lb.	mil. lb.		th. s. t.
1897–1901	407.8	249	8	370	307		2,170
1909	450.7	187	13	442	609		3,423
1910	467.4	185	17	449	683		3,564
1911	463.2	183	17	456	610		3,779
1912	480.0	179	17	480	667		3,696
1913	478.9	177	17	490	768		4,173
1914	489.6	175	12	499	555		3,949
1915	467.7	172	21	507	634		3,963
1916	498.5	168	36	533	908		3,863
1917	490.6	164	38	540	1,024		3,972
1918	402.9	159.9	53.9	546	596		4,071
1919	485.4	90.8	53.4	549	358		4,581
1920	465.0	91.5	54.7	576	555		4,767
1921	447.3	108.7	37.7	587	489		5,224
1922	478.4	103.5	53.6	595	584		5,548
1923	466.9	103.3	52.3	626	594		5,232
1924	474.3	95.3	59.4	617	628		5,916
1925	489.9	91.2	53.8	647	615		6.003
1926	499.7	89.5	65.4	656	670		6,291
1927	497.0	91.1	64.8	686	739		5,768
1928	511.5	95.4	69.6	694	699		6,516
1929	506.7	99.2	68.9	724	646		6,182
1930	502.7	93.1	63.2	709	714		6,039
1931	491.7	88.2	52.5	737	670		6,306
1932	475.2	86.9	49.3	765	762		6,012
1933	464.0	83.9	56.7	642	566		5,870
1934	468.7	81.1	55.7	588	734		6,304
1935	465.5	78.3	43.7	517	688		6,269
1936	486.3	78.8	59.9	517	770		6,203
1937	476.4	77.1	52.8	499	800		5,658
1938	484.2	78.4	56.6	517	754		5,967
1939	485.7	81.8	59.7	517	787		6,671

(7) *Potatoes* mil. bu.	(8) *Sweet-potatoes* mil. bu.	(9) *Beans, Dry Edible* th. bags	(10) *Vegetables, Other* mil. lb.	(11) *Cocoa* mil. lb.	(12) *Fats and Oils, Edible (excl. lard)* mil. lb.	(13) *Apples* mil. lb.
199.3	37.5	2,831	20,833	40.0	480	6,667
326.0	48.4	7,721	23,675	117.7	934	5,802
287.7	49.5	6,376	23,589	110.9	1,109	5,610
266.3	45.3	6,400	23,018	130.0	1,231	6,302
334.3	46.5	6,912	24,938	146.7	1,281	7,250
282.2	45.9	6,457	25,012	149.0	1,374	6,374
299.1	44.4	6,893	25,091	164.0	1,795	6,427
282.1	51.9	6,280	26,207	187.7	1,403	7,256
225.0	50.5	5,758	25,716	232.3	1,746	6,666
330.7	59.7	8,535	26,346	377.2	1,906	6,106
295.9	56.3	8,629	27,238	345.8	2,110	5,790
255.0	64.2	7,314	27,230	365.4	1,927	5,427
302.7	63.2	6,634	30,051	309.5	1,425	5,987
270.4	60.5	5,376	27,518	291.8	1,431	5,275
330.0	64.3	6,313	30,802	331.5	1,445	5,229
307.0	52.4	8,333	28,702	393.8	1,453	6,550
318.1	36.8	8,307	31,053	377.9	1,557	6,023
258.2	41.1	9,469	31,675	362.7	1,997	5,675
277.2	51.9	9,739	32,081	420.5	2,068	6,429
316.7	58.2	9,310	32,220	397.0	2,062	5,711
341.2	48.5	10,092	31,169	348.5	2,081	5,106
287.9	53.3	11,029	33,121	478.7	2,262	5,429
292.6	44.6	12,895	33,837	370.8	2,235	5,097
319.2	54.8	12,412	33,300	419.5	2,021	5,893
311.3	70.9	10,689	33,513	403.3	1,796	5,666
289.0	61.7	10,865	31,661	435.4	1,912	4,751
325.8	63.6	10,870	33,521	439.6	2,182	4,625
318.1	68.2	11,928	36,156	608.6	2,390	5,247
280.6	52.6	11,388	35,779	646.6	2,480	5,104
332.5	61.6	12,810	38,483	513.6	2,740	5,606
311.2	62.9	13,926	40,823	459.3	2,687	5,706
306.1	59.6	12,740	39,693	619.7	2,552	5,350

TABLE B-1—CONSUMPTION OF FOODS (concluded)

Year	(14) *Citrus Fruit* mil. lb.	(15) *Fruit, Other* mil. lb.	(16) *Beef* mil. lb.	(17) *Veal* mil. lb.	(18) *Pork (incl. lard)* mil. lb.	(19) *Lamb and Mutton* mil. lb.
1897–1901	524	5,400	5,133	402	6,410	509
1909	1,658	7,268	6,713	660	7,175	606
1910	1,730	7,296	6,508	667	6,898	595
1911	1,816	7,689	6,426	666	7,601	690
1912	1,714	8,318	6,153	662	7,440	730
1913	1,881	7,795	6,157	608	7,554	701
1914	2,341	8,848	6,143	572	7,525	708
1915	2,308	9,333	5,669	591	7,867	612
1916	2,326	7,904	6,004	656	8,245	595
1917	1,985	8,715	6,687	745	7,170	463
1918	1,837	8,333	7,167	761	7,658	499
1919	2,468	9,309	6,462	824	7,869	598
1920	2,977	9,813	6,294	852	8,069	579
1921	3,095	8,840	6,025	825	8,240	661
1922	3,103	10,545	6,502	858	8,722	564
1923	3,663	10,490	6,671	919	9,927	593
1924	3,879	10,996	6,785	977	10,089	596
1925	3,547	11,213	6,888	993	9,166	605
1926	3,697	12,889	7,074	958	8,972	637
1927	3,859	11,860	6,485	875	9,576	631
1928	4,242	13,286	5,872	782	10,144	664
1929	4,417	12,575	6,048	767	10,055	685
1930	4,662	11,891	6,021	794	9,803	824
1931	5,151	12,968	6,026	823	10,156	886
1932	5,081	10,735	5,830	822	10,613	883
1933	5,009	10,387	6,469	891	10,540	849
1934	5,071	11,427	7,066	1,065	9,755	796
1935	5,362	12,782	6,827	1,023	7,424	884
1936	5,683	12,969	7,551	1,098	8,584	858
1937	5,966	14,949	7,143	1,096	8,566	869
1938	7,325	13,801	7,092	985	9,019	899
1939	8,185	15,412	7,149	961	10,073	872

(20) *Chickens*	(21) *Eggs*	(22) *Milk and Milk Products* (a) *Milk, Whole*	(b) *Milk, Evap. and Condensed*	(c) *Butter*	(d) *Cheese*
mil. lb.	millions	mil. lb.	mil. lb.	mil. lb.	mil. lb.
1,284	19,945	19,312	208	1,501	284
1,775	26,496	23,969	496	1,618	354
1,905	28,329	22,440	536	1,702	405
1,956	30,900	21,932	600	1,754	387
1,897	29,637	26,239	674	1,584	382
1,886	29,483	26,427	774	1,606	427
1,909	29,268	26,293	884	1,686	437
1,929	31,456	25,253	959	1,731	432
1,879	30,506	25,473	982	1,766	410
1,834	29,095	28,649	980	1,633	437
1,865	29,707	33,295	1,077	1,443	402
1,988	31,850	28,056	985	1,608	442
1,945	31,886	33,154	917	1,577	444
1,934	32,520	31,932	1,068	1,757	450
2,079	34,773	32,283	1,197	1,884	472
2,174	36,554	31,556	1,282	1,995	489
2,197	37,001	34,831	1,349	2,053	522
2,287	36,842	37,052	1,353	2,029	537
2,328	39,749	40,487	1,388	2,044	549
2,489	40,715	41,688	1,385	2,065	530
2,423	40,753	43,035	1,472	2,063	535
2,429	40,721	43,802	1,656	2,117	562
2,643	40,787	45,535	1,673	2,134	568
2,425	41,271	46,776	1,665	2,247	555
2,461	39,095	46,228	1,745	2,282	546
2,561	37,253	44,920	1,737	2,254	565
2,364	36,469	43,490	1,895	2,312	613
2,310	35,571	44,191	2,056	2,207	669
2,482	36,968	46,067	2,036	2,135	688
2,409	39,679	47,738	2,155	2,156	712
2,299	40,294	48,290	2,241	2,194	759
2,544	40,978	49,655	2,334	2,323	749

For notes to Table B-1 see following pages.

General Note to Table B-1

Unless otherwise specified, the data presented for the years 1909–39 in Table B-1 are from a Bureau of Agricultural Economics release, "Consumption of Agricultural Products" (1941), hereafter referred to as BAE consumption study, series, or data. Estimates for the period 1897–1901 are our own, based on whatever evidence is available concerning consumption, production, foreign trade, and stocks. Whereas the BAE data refer to calendar years, our own estimates sometimes refer to crop years. Though this may introduce slight incomparabilities from year to year, the effect over any length of time will be negligible, the more so since for only 5 out of a total of 26 series do we use other than calendar-year data. As to coverage, the main item not included is seafood. Production data for fish are poor and extremely scanty, while consumption data are not available at all. Also omitted are such miscellaneous items as tree nuts, peanuts (other than those used for oil), barley (used both as pearl barley and as malt for purposes other than fermented beverages) and buckwheat. Though the quantitative result of these omissions cannot be gauged exactly, it is unlikely that the general trends are in any way affected.

The following notes, numbered in the same manner as the columns to which they refer, give definition, source, and basis of adjustment, if any, of the series. The net output data mentioned will be found in Table A-1 above.

(1) Wheat:

Only wheat used in flour production is included. For 1897–1901, "Statistics of American Wheat Milling and Flour Disposition Since 1879," *Wheat Studies,* Vol. IV (Food Research Institute, Stanford University, Dec. 1927), Appendix Table I, p. 101.

(2) Corn:

According to a communication received from Miss Elna Anderson of the Bureau of Agricultural Economics the corn consumption estimates of that Bureau include products derived in the wet-milling process which are not consumed as food, as well as corn consumed in the manufacture of fermented malt liquors. Furthermore, the composition of dry-milled corn products differs from that of wet-milled products in that the former possesses both protein and fat in addition to the carbohydrate which is the sole constituent of wet-milled products. It was therefore necessary to separate total corn consumption, as reported by the BAE, into dry-milled and wet-milled corn and to exclude from the latter such fractions as are utilized in nonfood industries. This can be accomplished with relatively little difficulty for recent years, but requires various assumptions as we approach the more remote years.

The procedure we finally adopted is as follows:

(I) BAE data converted from pounds into bushels: 56 lbs. = 1 bu.

(II) For crop years (beginning October) 1926–27 to 1939–40 corn going into dry milling is given in *Feed Statistics,* Supplement to the 1941 issues of *The Feed Situation* (U. S. Bureau of Agricultural Economics, 1941), p. 15.

(III) Corn going into wet-milled products is given in *ibid.,* p. 26, for crop years 1917–18 to 1939–40.

(IV) Comparison of (II) + (III) with (I) in such a way as to consider the crop year 1926–27 equivalent to the calendar-year 1927, etc., shows the two series to be very similar until 1933, in which year the calendar-year data exceed the sum of (II) and (III) by 6 to 7 million bushels. According to *ibid.*, Table 21, this amount is accounted for by corn used in the production of fermented malt liquors. The two series, (I) and (II) + (III) respectively, may therefore be considered as equivalent. Consequently corn going into dry milling is estimated as the difference between total corn consumed (I) and corn used in wet milling, the crop year being considered to refer to the second calendar year, i.e., 1917–18 = 1918. For 1918 and 1919 we deduct 7 million bushels from the total as going into beer production.

(V) Our estimates for 1909 to 1917 are based on per capita consumption of cornmeal products as estimated for 1909 in Holbrook Working, "The Decline in Per Capita Consumption of Flour in the United States," *Wheat Studies*, Vol. II (July 1926), p. 279, plus an allowance for the production of hominy and grits, derived from the 1909 Census of Manufactures. The figure thus obtained, and converted to aggregate consumption in terms of bushels of corn, was then linked to the comparable estimate for 1918, derived as described above, by straight-line interpolation. These estimates we deduct from BAE totals (I), the latter being reduced by 7 million bushels each year to adjust for the amount used in beer manufacture. We thus obtain estimates of corn entering the wet-milling process.

(VI) From utilization data of wet-milled products for recent years, such as those given in a mimeographed release of the U. S. Bureau of Agricultural Chemistry and Engineering, May 1940, and in a paper presented at the Program on Grain Marketing, University of Illinois, Jan. 9, 1940, by F. J. Hosking, of the Corn Industries Research Foundation, entitled "Merchandising Corn Products at Home and Abroad," we have estimated that the following fractions are used for food:

	Percent
Starch	33
Sirup	96
Sugar	100
Oil	90

No allowance for corn oil need be made at this point, since it is included in (12) Fats and Oils. For the other three products, it was assumed that 1 bushel (56 lb.) of corn will yield (alternatively) 34.5 lb. of starch, 38.1 lb. of corn sirup, or 36.4 lb. of corn sugar (80 percent reducible sugars). This information is given in *Starches, Dextrines and Related Products*, Report 138, Second Series (U. S. Tariff Commission, 1940?), p. 37. According to the abovementioned release of the Bureau of Agricultural Engineering and Chemistry, average sales for 1928–37 were as follows: starch, 722 mil. lb.; sirup, 1,010 mil. lb.; sugar, 697 mil. lb. Combining all these data, we concluded that about 21 percent of all corn utilized in the wet-milling industry is used for nonfood purposes. Accordingly, we reduced our estimates for wet-milled corn (V) by 21 percent each year. The rough nature of the above estimates is obvious.

Footnotes to Table B-1 continued on next page.

Footnotes to Table B-1, continued.

(vii) The estimate of dry-milled corn for 1897–1901 represents production of cornmeal and hominy as given in the 1899 Census of Manufactures; that of wet-milled corn is based on the trend shown by the data of the succeeding decade.

(3) Oatmeal:

Estimates for crop years from 1909–10 to 1932–33 are based on per capita consumption as given by N. L. Gold, *Agricultural Land Requirements and Available Resources,* Part III of the Supplementary Report of the Land Planning Committee of the National Resources Board (Washington, 1935), p. 5. Oats were converted into oatmeal by a factor of 1 bu. oats = 18 lb. meal. For 1933–39, calendar-year data are available in a release on "The National Food Situation" (U. S. Bureau of Agricultural Economics, Dec. 1941), Table 7. The two series were joined without adjustment, and it was also assumed that all oats for human consumption are used as oatmeal; this assumption probably does not involve a major error. Per capita consumption in 1897–1901 was estimated to have been equal to that of 1909–10 to 1911–12.

(4) Rice:

Estimates for crop years 1909–10 to 1917–18 from Gold, *op. cit.;* see note (3). Beginning in 1918–19, official estimates are available (*Agricultural Statistics, 1940,* Table 122). Consumption in 1939–40 was assumed to have been the same as that of the preceding year. The 1897–1901 estimate refers to 1899 only and is taken from *Apparent Per Capita Consumption of Principal Foodstuffs in the United States,* Domestic Commerce Series No. 38 (U. S. Department of Commerce, 1930), p. 10.

(5) Rye:

Annual consumption data are not available except for Census years (*ibid.,* p. 12). These figures indicate that aggregate consumption has not changed appreciably over the period under investigation; see also "Rye in its Relations to Wheat," *Wheat Studies,* Vol. IV (March 1928), pp. 196-98. We therefore estimated consumption for the entire period at 307 million lb. per annum.

(6) Sugar:

Refined sugar available for human consumption. For 1897–1921: *Agr. Stat., 1940,* Table 197; 1 ton raw sugar was assumed to equal .9369 tons refined sugar. For 1922–37: *Agr. Stat., 1939,* Table 181; for 1938: *Agr. Stat., 1940,* Table 197; for 1939: *Agr. Stat., 1941,* Table 206. Raw sugar for the last two years was converted into refined sugar on the basis of the two per capita consumption figures given in adjoining columns of the same tables.

(7) Potatoes:

Since BAE consumption data are not adjusted for seed use of potatoes, we used our estimates of net output for crop years, adjusted for exports and imports. Potatoes used in starch manufacture cannot be excluded, but in the light of Census data on starch manufacture they appear to account for less than 1 percent of total output.

(8) Sweetpotatoes:

BAE data run consistently higher than our net output estimates, suggesting that they represent gross output. Consequently, we substituted our net output estimates, on a crop-year basis. No adjustments for stock changes or foreign trade were made.

(9) Beans, dry edible:
Estimate for 1897–1901 is based on our net output data for crop years, unadjusted for stock changes or foreign trade.

(10) Vegetables, other:
BAE consumption data for all vegetables minus output of potatoes, sweet-potatoes, and dry edible beans. Since canned vegetables are given in terms of their fresh equivalent, this presentation overstates the total poundage to some extent. However, calorie values of canned vegetables seem to run slightly higher than those of fresh vegetables (see *Canned Food Reference Manual,* American Can Company, New York, 1939) so that the net overstatement, in terms of nutrients, is likely to be small. An alternative method would have been to use per capita consumption data as supplied annually in *Agricultural Statistics.* However, the coverage of those data is far less satisfactory, and no data are available prior to 1919. The figure for 1897–1901 represents an arbitrary estimate.

(11) Cocoa:
The 1897–1901 figure represents the best estimate that may be derived from import figures for the years in question.

(12) Fats and Oils, edible, excluding lard:
The 1897–1901 figure represents an estimate based upon average cotton-seed oil disappearance during the years 1897–1901, as given in *Fats, Oils and Oleaginous Raw Materials,* Statistical Bulletin 59 (U. S. Department of Agriculture, 1937), Table 38. The basis for this procedure lies in the similarity of the data for oil and fat consumption and cottonseed oil disappearance during the years 1909–13.

(13) Apples, fresh:
For 1897–1901 we used our net output estimates, reduced by 1 billion pounds each year to adjust for fruit going into drying, canning and export.

(14) Fruit, citrus:
For 1897–1901 we used our output estimates, adjusting roughly for imports and exports.

(15) Fruit, other:
BAE consumption data for all fruit, reduced by apples and citrus fruit. This includes the fresh-fruit equivalent of canned and dried fruit, and fruit juices. The effect may be to overstate somewhat the absolute amounts. The estimate for 1897–1901 was based on such fruit production and import figures as were available, roughly adjusted to the 1909 coverage. The resulting figure is not significant in itself, but probably introduces only a minor error into aggregate food consumption.

(16)-(19) Beef, Veal, Pork (incl. lard), Mutton and Lamb:
Data are for dressed weight, from *Livestock, Meats, and Wool Market Statistics and Related Data, 1940* (U. S. Agricultural Marketing Service, 1941), p. 100. The figure for 1897–1901 is a 3-year average of 1899–1901 only.

Footnotes to Table B-1 continued on next page.

Footnotes to Table B-1, concluded.

(20) Chickens (dressed weight):

For 1897–1901 we used our net output estimates adjusted to the level of the BAE consumption series by the average relationship existing between the two series in 1909–14.

(21) Eggs:

Revised BAE consumption data were used from 1909 on; see *The Poultry and Egg Situation* (U. S. Bureau of Agricultural Economics, April 1942), p. 13. For 1897–1901 we used our own net output data, allowing a 10 percent increase for off-farm production.

(22) Milk and Milk Products:

Since the composition of milk varies according to utilization, we are here presenting more detailed data than we do in the case of production. Though a still finer breakdown is possible, little increased accuracy would result, because of the relatively small amounts of the several manufactured dairy products.

(a) Milk, whole:

Our estimates for output of fluid milk, Table A-4 above, reduced by milk-equivalents of cheese production (1 lb. cheese = 10 lb. milk) and evaporated milk production (1 lb. evaporated milk = 2.2 lb. milk). For source of evaporated milk and cheese data see (b) and (d).

(b) Milk, evaporated:

For 1909–1938: E. E. Vial, *Production and Consumption of Manufactured Dairy Products,* Technical Bulletin 722 (U. S. Department of Agriculture, 1940).

For 1939: Based on *Dairy Situation,* BAE, Feb. 21, 1940.

For 1897–1901: Based on data for 1899, 1900, 1901 and estimated data for 1897–98.

(c) Butter:

Sources same as (b).

(d) Cheese:

Sources same as (b).

TABLE B-2

COMPOSITION OF FOODS

Food	Unit	Protein	Fat	Carbohydrate	Source
		to convert into short tons multiply by			
Wheat	Mil. bu.	2,377	208	15,659	Atwater[a]
Corn, dry	" "	1,518	314	12,441	[b]
Corn, wet	" "	..	..	15,910	[c]
Oatmeal	" lb.	80.5	36	338	Atwater
Rice, milled	" "	40	1.5	395	"
Rye	" "	34	4.5	394	"
Sugar, refined	Th. s. t.	..	..	1,000	Pearl
Potatoes	Mil. bu.	510	30	4,800	U.S.D.A., Circ. 146
Sweetpotatoes	" "	412	165	6,628	" " " " " "
Beans, dry edible	Th. bags	1.4	.15	2.85	" " " " " "
Vegetables, other	Mil. lb.	5.75	1.2	24.45	[d]
Cocoa	" "	108	145	189	Atwater
Fats and oils	" "	..	490	..	Pearl
Apples	" "	1.5	2.0	65.0	U.S.D.A., Circ. 50
Citrus fruit	" "	.3	.05	3.8	[e]
Fruit, other	" "	4	2	66	[f]
Beef	" "	76	77	..	Pearl
Veal	" "	78	31	..	"
Pork	" "	41	274	..	"
Mutton and lamb	" "	65	120	..	"
Chickens	" "	67	46	..	"
Eggs	Millions	8.17	5.83	..	"
Milk, whole	Mil. lb.	16.5	20	25	Atwater
Milk, evap.	" "	48	46	56	"
Butter	" "	5	425	..	"
Cheese	" "	148	192	..	"

General Note to Table B-2

All factors refer to the food *as purchased* and thus make partial allowance for inedible portions, but not for waste. To convert to calories, use these factors: 1 short ton = 2,000 lb.; 1 lb. = 453.6 grams; each gram of protein or carbohydrate yields 4 calories; each gram of fat yields 9 calories.

Sources: Raymond Pearl, *The Nation's Food* (W. B. Saunders, Philadelphia, 1920); W. O. Atwater and A. P. Bryant, *The Chemical Composition of American Food Materials,* Experiment Station Bulletin 28 (U. S. Department of Agriculture, 1896; reprinted 1906); Charlotte Chatfield and L. I. McLaughlin, *Proximate Composition of Fresh Fruits,* Circular 50 (U. S. Department of Agriculture, 1928); Charlotte Chatfield and Georgian Adams, *Proximate Composition of Fresh Vegetables,* Circular 146 (U. S. Department of Agriculture, 1931).

[a] We rejected Pearl's factors and went back to Atwater's original tables because it appears from Pearl's data that he converted bushels of wheat into barrels of flour on the basis of 4.5 bu. = 1 bbl. This conversion factor is appropriate for 1918 and 1919, but too low for all other years. The factors we used are taken from the table of official conversion factors given in *Agricultural Statistics, 1940,* p. 8, footnote 30.

[b] These factors are derived from Atwater's composition of "cornmeal, granular," on the assumption that 1 bu. of corn = 33 lb. of cornmeal.

[c] The factor is a weighted average of the carbohydrate content of starch, sugar and sirup, as given by Pearl for the first two items; sirup was assumed to be equivalent to sugar. The weighted content is 86 percent. Similarly, a weighted average conversion factor was computed to convert pounds of starch, sugar and sirup into bushels of corn. This factor is 37 lb. Consequently, 1 million bushels of corn will yield 15,910 short tons of carbohydrate. Corn oil is included under fats and oils.

[d] The factors are weighted averages; the individual factors, taken from Circular 146, have been weighted by their estimated relative consumption in 1929.

[e] The factors are weighted averages; the individual factors, taken from Circular 50, have been weighted by their estimated relative consumption, averaged over the period 1909–37. Differences in weight per box as between California and Florida were taken into account.

[f] The factors are weighted averages; the individual factors, taken from Circular 50, have been weighted by their estimated average relative consumption during the entire period.

TABLE B-3

AVERAGE PER CAPITA CONSUMPTION, 1935-39, AND VITAMIN AND MINERAL CONTENT OF INDIVIDUAL FOODS

Food	Average Annual Consumption, 1935–39 (100 grams)	Vitamin A (international units per 100 grams)	Vitamin B_1 (thiamin) (international units per 100 grams)	Vitamin B_2 (riboflavin) (micrograms per 100 grams)	Calcium (percent)	Phosphorus (percent)	Iron (percent)
Cereals							
Flour, wheat, white[a]	700.3		4– 33	40	.015	.101	.0013
Flour, wheat, whole[a]	14.3		110–167	100–200	.035	.300	.0040
Flour, rye	11.4		55– 73	60	.018	.278	.0013
Cornmeal[b]	45.9		17–100	80	.016	.152	.0009
Oatmeal	18.2		60–257	100–200	.081	.365	.0052
Rice	27.5		10– 13		.009	.092	.0007
Dairy products[c]							
Milk, whole	1,655.6	160– 252	13– 22	195–240	.118	.093	.0002
Milk, evaporated[d]	67.2	300– 775	17– 27	330	.236	.186	.0004
Butter	77.1	1,000–8,500			.016	.016	.0002
Cheese	24.5	1,200–4,000	13– 17	450–600	.873	.610	.0010
Eggs[h]	170.1[e]	1,000–4,500	25– 60	280–420	.058	.224	.0031
Meat, lean[f]							
Beef	143.1	10– 105	25–100	180–260	.013	.204	.0030
Veal	20.7	10– 105	25–100	180–260	.012	.221	.0024
Mutton and lamb	13.8		67–100	280	.015	.208	.0030
Pork	92.0		25–300	200	.010	.215	.0020
Chicken	84.4		30–150	100–200	.016	.218	.0019
Turkey	11.9				.023	.320	.0038

TABLE B-3—(continued)

Food	Average Annual Consumption, 1935–39 (100 grams)	Vitamin A (international units per 100 grams)	Vitamin B_1 (thiamin) (international units per 100 grams)	Vitamin B_2 (riboflavin) (micrograms per 100 grams)	Calcium (percent)	Phosphorus (percent)	Iron (percent)
Meat, organs[g]							
Liver	9.1	5,000–10,000	100–140	1,800–2,600	.008	.373	.0121
Kidney	3.3	500– 1,000	133–167	1,700–2,200	.016	.287	.0065
Fruit, fresh[h]							
Apples	185.5	40– 100	5– 40		.007	.011	.0003
Apricots	1.4	3,000– 8,000	8– 15	105	.015	.024	.0005
Bananas	92.5	160– 400	15– 60	45– 80	.008	.028	.0006
Cherries	6.4	35– 1,150	17		.017	.022	.0005
Cranberries	2.3	10– 28			.014	.011	.0006
Figs	.9	60– 90	12– 33	82	.050	.035	.0007
Grapes	95.3	15– 90	10– 20		.017	.021	.0006
Grapefruit	50.8	21	10– 33	20–100	.017	.018	.0003
Lemons	21.3		10– 30		.021	.012	.0003
Oranges	147.4	50– 400	10– 48	28– 90	.025	.019	.0003
Peaches	50.8	250– 2,800	7– 23	45	.009	.018	.0003
Pears	26.8	8– 125	10– 32	20–150	.013	.016	.0003
Pineapple	4.5	40– 200	25– 42	50– 80	.016	.011	.0003
Plums and prunes	4.5	200	16– 67		.017	.020	.0005
Strawberries	14.1	60– 90	5		.022	.022	.0009

TABLE B-3—(continued)

Food	Average Annual Consumption, 1935–39	Vitamin A	Vitamin B_1 (thiamin)	Vitamin B_2 (riboflavin)	Calcium	Phosphorus	Iron
	(100 grams)	(international units per 100 grams)		(micrograms per 100 grams)		(percent)	
Fruit, dried[h]							
Apricots	1.0	6,000–15,000	20– 40	240–300	.071	.113	.0076
Currants	.2				.075	.138	.0027
Dates	2.0	60– 300	10– 33		.072	.060	.0021
Figs	2.0	50– 100	25–100	85–125	.223	.104	.0031
Peaches	1.4	1,500– 6,300	10– 15	150–250	.025	.050	.0009
Prunes	9.6	400– 3,500	58– 90	50–650	.062	.093	.0035
Raisins	10.5	10– 100	0– 67	125	.055	.110	.0030
Fruit, canned[i]							
Applesauce	5.1	40– 100	5– 40				
Apricots	4.2	3,000– 8,000	8– 15	105	.015	.024	.0005
Cherries	3.5	35– 1,150	15				
Grapefruit	10.8	21	10– 30	20–100	.017	.018	.0003
Peaches	15.6	250– 2,800	7– 23	45	.009	.018	.0003
Pears	5.5	8– 125	10				
Pineapple	18.1	20– 60	21	20– 30	.016	.011	.0003
Plums	2.7	200	16– 67				
Vegetables, fresh[h]							
Asparagus	9.1	300– 980	45–135		.021	.052	.0012
Beans, dry edible	44.0	400	52–160	250	.031	.112	.0023
Beans, snap	31.8	600– 1,800	18– 32	65–150	.065	.044	.0011
Beets	12.2		5– 70	70–120	.026	.039	.0009
Cabbage	117.9	30– 90	20– 80	65–135	.045	.028	.0004

TABLE B-3—(concluded)

Food	Average Annual Consumption, 1935–39 (100 grams)	Vitamin A (international units per 100 grams)	Vitamin B_1 (thiamin) (international units per 100 grams)	Vitamin B_2 (riboflavin) (micrograms per 100 grams)	Calcium (percent)	Phosphorus (percent)	Iron (percent)
Vegetables, fresh (cont.)[h]							
Carrots	39.5	1,800– 7,700	20– 60	75–125	.042	.040	.0007
Cauliflower	12.7	35– 70	43–110	150–220	.025	.065	.0009
Celery	44.0	5– 50	7– 17	30– 55	.072	.046	.0007
Corn, sweet	39.9		40– 50		.009	.120	.0005
Lettuce	63.1	70– 700	10– 90	100–240	.054	.031	.0011
Onions	75.3	40	8– 40	28– 62	.032	.044	.0005
Peas	7.7	500– 3,000	25–165	200–250	.022	.122	.0019
Potatoes	581.1	30– 50	10– 55	40– 80	.013	.053	.0011
Spinach	15.0	13,000–35,000	20– 70	250–400		.048	.0034
Sweetpotatoes	104.8	1,000– 7,000	10– 45	80–100	.033	.052	.0008
Tomatoes	79.4	550– 2,100	10– 40	37– 63	.011	.027	.0006
Vegetables, canned[i]							
Asparagus	2.3	300– 980	50– 60				
Beans, snap	9.1	600– 1,800	11	65–150	.065	.044	.0011
Beets	2.9		8– 32	70–120	.026	.039	.0009
Corn, sweet	19.3		33				
Peas	22.2	80–200	67–100	200–250	.022	.122	.0019
Spinach	4.1	4,000–10,000	6				
Tomatoes	25.9	4,000	33 }	37– 63	.011	.027	.0006
Tomato juice	16.1	825	23– 38 }				
Pumpkin	2.1	84					
Cocoa	20.0				.112	.709	.0027

Source: For all items, except where otherwise noted, the source is that given for the identical item in the notes to Table B-1. Consumption for all fruit and vegetables is taken from *Agricultural Statistics, 1941,* Tables 378-82.

The following publications served as sources from which the range of vitamin contents was established:

E. V. McCollum, Elsa Orent-Keiles, and H. G. Day, *The Newer Knowledge of Nutrition* (5th ed.; Macmillan, 1939).

H. C. Sherman, *Chemistry of Food and Nutrition* (6th ed.; Macmillan, 1941).

M. A. B. Fixsen and M. H. Roscoe, "Tables of the Vitamin Content of Human and Animal Foods," *Nutrition Abstracts and Reviews,* Vol. 7 (Aberdeen University Press, April 1938), pp. 823-67.

For calcium, phosphorus and iron the source was Sherman, *op. cit.,* pp. 562-65.

Coverage: Though coverage is not complete, the omissions—caused by lack of data—do not seriously impair the significance of our findings, since none of the omitted items is consumed in quantities that could be termed large relative to the items covered. Fish is probably the most important omission. However, since its contribution is largely confined to vitamin A, consumption of which appears most satisfactory in any case, and vitamin D, consumption of which we have not attempted to estimate, the omission, even if it were quantitatively important, leaves our conclusions unaffected. Another food—peanuts—contributes to B_1 and B_2 consumption, it is true, but although peanuts rank high in content per unit of weight, aggregate consumption does not appear to result in daily per capita consumption of more than 9 units of B_1 and between 10 and 20 micrograms of B_2.

Contributions from tree nuts and a number of green vegetables are smaller than those mentioned above, even though contents per unit of weight are high.

Blanks do not necessarily denote absence of vitamin content, but may also signify that the value has not thus far been established experimentally. Since it is often impossible from the published material to say which situation prevails, we have made no attempt to indicate reasons for omitting entries.

[a] No data are available on relative consumption of white and whole wheat flour. Total wheat flour consumption was therefore roughly apportioned between the two on the basis of flour production as reported in the Census of Manufactures, 1935, 1937 and 1939.

[b] Based on data for dry-process products as given in *Feed Statistics,* Supplement to the 1941 issues of *The Feed Situation* (U. S. Bureau of Agricultural Economics), p. 15.

[c] Data are for 4-year average 1935–38, as given in *The Dairy Situation,* BAE, Feb. 21, 1940. Data for 1939 have since become available (*Agr. Stat.,* 1941, Table 588). Their inclusion would raise butter consumption by 0.7 percent; cheese by 3.7 percent; evaporated milk by 1.9 percent.

[d] Case goods, unskimmed.

[e] One egg = 2 oz., or 56.7 grams.

[f] The only type of meat for which the authors were able to locate sufficient

Footnotes to Table B-3 continued on next page.

data to enable them to determine approximately the percentage of lean meat was beef. This was set at 57 percent, on the basis of data in W. H. Tomhave, *Meats and Meat Products* (Lippincott, 1925) and L. D. Hall and A. D. Emmett, *Relative Economy, Composition and Nutritive Value of the Various Cuts of Beef,* Bulletin 158 (Illinois Agricultural Experiment Station, 1912). The same percentage was used for veal, while for mutton and lamb 40 percent and for hogs 30 percent were assumed to be lean meat. These percentages were applied to meat consumption for 1935–39. No deductions were made for fat or waste material in the case of chicken and turkey, and this undoubtedly results in an overstatement.

[g] Both liver and kidney consumption were determined separately for each of the four types of animal, and then aggregated. The estimates were based on scattered data pertaining to average weight of the organ and average dressed weight of the whole carcass, yielding percentages of dressed weight represented by each organ. These percentages are:

	Beef	*Veal*	*Mutton and Lamb*	*Pork*
Liver	1.0	2.0	4.0	1.5
Kidney	.5	1.0	.5	.5

The sources are:

(1) P. I. Aldrich, *The Packers' Encyclopedia* (The National Provisioner, Chicago, 1922).

(2) Arnold C. Schueren, *Meat Retailing* (Vaughan, Chicago, 1927).

(3) A written communication from Miss Elna Anderson of the Bureau of Agricultural Economics based in turn on data provided by the Division of Livestock, Meats, and Wool of the Agricultural Marketing Service.

There is no doubt that some portion of this meat is not designed for human consumption, since considerable portions of it go into animal feed. The degree of overstatement is unknown. The vitamin values are based on Sherman only.

[h] Consumption data include inedible refuse. Correction for this is made, in accordance with Table B-4, in the final values.

[i] For those of the canned goods for which no specific data are available, vitamin and mineral content was assumed to equal that of the fresh fruit or vegetable. No refuse factors were applied to the quantities listed under average annual consumption.

TABLE B-4

PERCENTAGE OF INEDIBLE REFUSE IN SPECIFIED FOODS

Food	*Percent*
Vegetables	
Beans, lima	55
Beans, snap	7
Beets	20
Cabbage	15
Carrots	20
Celery	20
Lettuce	15
Onions	10
Peas	45
Potatoes	20
Sweetpotatoes	20
Fruits	
Apples	25
Apricots	6
Bananas	35
Cherries	5
Grapefruit	30[a]
Grapes	25
Lemons	30
Oranges	27
Peaches	18
Pears	10
Plums	5
Prunes	6
Strawberries	5
Dates	10
Prunes, dried	15
Raisins	10
Other	
Eggs	11

Source: Atwater and Bryant, *op. cit.*
[a] Estimated.

TABLE B-5

COMPARISON OF PEARL'S ESTIMATES WITH THOSE OF THE NATIONAL BUREAU FOR ANNUAL CALORIE CONSUMPTION IN THE UNITED STATES, 1911–16[a]

Billion calories

Groups	*Pearl*	*NBER*
Grains	45,057	45,192
Meats	28,104	25,048
Dairy products	19,834	15,299
Sugars	17,197	14,166
Oils and nuts[d]	6,812[b]	6,268[c]
Fruit and vegetables[e]	9,773	13,869
Poultry and eggs	2,620	3,311
Fish	535	..
TOTAL	129,931	123,153

[a] Raymond Pearl, *op. cit.*, p. 229; average for fiscal years July of year shown to June of year following. NBER data, average for calendar years shown.

[b] Includes oleomargarine.

[c] Excludes peanuts.

[d] Includes cocoa.

[e] Coverage differs considerably.

General Note to Table B-5

As mentioned in the text of Chapter 4, two previous investigations were made in this field, one by Raymond Pearl (1920, referred to above) and one by Holbrook Working[1] who extended Pearl's estimates (in less detailed form) through 1924–25. Though we have relied heavily upon Pearl's work as far as conversion factors are concerned, the consumption data at our disposal represent great improvements over those available twenty years ago. A first glance at Table B-5 suggests that the use of a different set of consumption figures, and slightly lower calorie values, has had little effect on the results. This, however, is true only with regard to the total, and is attributable to the fact that large differences in the estimates for individual items tend to cancel one another in the aggregate.

A group-by-group comparison for the average of the six years 1911–12 to 1916–17[2] reveals that our estimates exceed Pearl's for fruits and vegetables, and eggs and poultry, whereas for meats, sugar, oils and dairy products, Pearl's estimates exceed ours. For cereals the two estimates are practically identical. In the grand total the excess of Pearl's estimate over our own amounts to about 5½ percent.

Working's continuation of, and improvement upon, Pearl's work is notable for the fact that although written at a time when current statistics suggested that the tendencies at work up to 1921 had apparently approached and even passed a turning point, it nonetheless forecast a further decrease in per capita food consumption, a forecast fully borne out during recent years. Another tentative suggestion made by Working, namely that sugar consumption would expand further at the cost of flour, has not been realized.

[1] "The Decline in Per Capita Consumption of Flour in the United States," *Wheat Studies*, Vol. II (July 1926).

[2] Since Pearl's data refer to a greater degree to crop years than do ours, we prefer to use a 6-year average that will render the two sets more comparable by partially obliterating the differences due to this fact.

Table B-6

POPULATION ESTIMATES, 1897–1941[a]

Year	A	Midyear Estimates B	C	D	Index (1929:100)
		(thousands)			
1897	72,189	..	..	..	59.2
1898	73,494	..	..	..	60.2
1899	74,799	..	..	..	61.3
1900	76,129	76,110	..	..	62.4
1901	..	77,273	..	..	63.4
1902	..	78,601	..	..	64.5
1903	..	80,143	..	..	65.7
1904	..	81,493	..	..	66.8
1905	..	83,150	..	..	68.2
1906	..	85,041	..	..	69.7
1907	..	87,198	..	..	71.5
1908	..	88,587	..	..	72.6
1909	..	90,508	..	..	74.2
1910	..	92,422	92,331	..	75.8
1911	..	..	93,812	..	77.0
1912	..	..	95,290	..	78.2
1913	..	..	97,198	..	79.8
1914	..	..	99,102	..	81.3
1915	..	..	100,579	..	82.6
1916	..	..	102,021	..	83.7
1917	..	..	103,467	..	84.9
1918	..	..	104,595	..	85.9
1919	..	..	105,159	..	86.3
1920	..	..	106,641	..	87.5
1921	..	..	108,716	..	89.2
1922	..	..	110,229	..	90.5
1923	..	..	112,109	..	92.0
1924	..	..	114,250	..	93.8
1925	..	..	115,953	..	95.2
1926	..	..	117,507	..	96.5
1927	..	..	119,125	..	97.8
1928	..	..	120,557	..	99.0
1929	..	..	121,832	..	100.0

TABLE B-6 (concluded)

Year	*A*	*B*	*Midyear Estimates* *C*	*D*	*Index (1929:100)*
			(Thousands)		
1930	..	..	123,091	123,077	101.0
1931	..	..	..	124,039	101.8
1932	..	..	..	124,840	102.5
1933	..	..	..	125,578	103.1
1934	..	..	..	126,373	103.7
1935	..	..	..	127,249	104.5
1936	..	..	..	128,052	105.1
1937	..	..	..	128,823	105.8
1938	..	..	..	129,823	106.6
1939	..	..	..	130,878	107.4
1940	..	..	..	131,956	108.3
1941	..	..	..	133,039	109.2

(A): *Statistical Abstract of the United States.*
(B): National Bureau, unpublished.
(C): BAE, "Consumption of Agricultural Products," March 1941.
(D): Bureau of the Census releases, March 15, 1941, and June 11, 1942.

[a] The figures in this table represent the best population estimates we were able to assemble, and were used in computing per capita consumption data for various foods. Figures apply to the continental United States.

Appendix C

Comparison with Other Indexes of Output

Appendix C

Comparison with Other Indexes of Output

IN ADDITION to the index presented in this volume (Tables 1 and 5), three other indexes of agricultural output have been published for recent years: by the Bureau of Agricultural Economics; by Frederick Strauss and L. H. Bean of the Department of Agriculture; and by the National Research Project. These indexes are compared with our own, on a 1929 base, in Table C-1. The four indexes resemble each other closely in general movement. Two of them—the BAE index and the Strauss-Bean index —attempt to measure net output (i.e., exclude crops used for seed and feed, and milk fed to calves) and use prices as weights (i.e., are based upon one, or a series of comparisons in constant prices): in these respects their construction resembles that of our own output index. In contrast, the series published by the National Research Project was computed from gross output and used labor requirements as weights: in its methods of construction it therefore differs radically from the other indexes mentioned.

Unlike our own index, that computed by the Bureau of Agricultural Economics[1] takes no account of changes in livestock inventories. The differences on this account may be gauged from the comparison in Table C-2, where both indexes are broken down into their crop and livestock components. It will be seen that the series for crops agree much more closely than do the series for livestock products. The differences between the combined indexes (NBER and BAE) in Table C-1 are largely the result of this difference in the treatment of livestock. Thus, whenever we have allowed for a decrease in inventory, our livestock index falls below the corresponding BAE index—most strikingly

[1] *The Farm Income Situation* (U. S. Bureau of Agricultural Economics, Nov. 1941), p. 10.

TABLE C-1

INDEXES OF AGRICULTURAL OUTPUT, 1897–1939

1929:100

Year	*NBER*[a]	*BAE*[b]	*Strauss-Bean*[c]	*NRP*[d]	*Year*	*NBER*[a]	*BAE*[b]	*Strauss-Bean*[c]	*NRP*[d]
1897	66.0	..	69.4	..	1918	90.2	91.6	89.7	89
1898	69.5	..	73.2	..	1919	87.1	91.9	89.1	87
1899	69.5	..	72.3	..					
					1920	90.0	93.1	95.5	95
1900	70.1	..	73.0	..	1921	81.9	84.6	84.3	81
1901	68.8	..	70.7	..	1922	90.3	92.3	90.1	88
1902	71.8	..	74.1	..	1923	91.9	95.9	91.1	90
1903	72.5	..	73.6	..	1924	94.9	98.9	93.2	92
1904	75.7	..	77.5	..	1925	95.8	98.5	94.5	98
1905	75.3	..	77.5	..	1926	101.3	101.5	100.6	102
1906	81.7	..	82.3	..	1927	98.2	98.9	97.1	96
1907	76.3	..	76.2	..	1928	102.4	103.3	102.0	101
1908	78.1	..	79.6	..	1929	100.0	100.0	100.0	100
1909	77.4	79.9	78.1	78					
					1930	100.4	99.2	100.9	97
					1931	104.0	103.3	108.9	107
1910	79.4	80.2	79.9	82	1932	100.0	97.9	101.7	100
1911	81.5	83.8	81.7	85	1933	97.4	97.3	96.2	95
1912	85.6	86.2	85.5	90	1934	83.5	93.9	77.5	80
1913	82.8	82.5	83.4	84	1935	92.2	92.3	87.4	94
1914	89.6	87.5	91.2	92	1936	93.0	94.1	88.0	88
1915	89.9	87.7	90.4	89	1937	106.3	106.6	104.6	..
1916	82.3	84.1	82.3	85	1938	105.4	103.6	..	..
1917	85.9	86.6	84.9	89	1939	110.7	107.9	..	..

[a] Table 5; computed from data in Table A-1, Appendix A.

[b] Not available until 1909. For 1909–39 source is *The Farm Income Situation* (U. S. Bureau of Agricultural Economics, Nov. 1941), p. 10.

[c] Frederick Strauss and L. H. Bean, *Gross Farm Income and Indices of Farm Production and Prices in the United States, 1869–1937,* Technical Bulletin 703 (U. S. Department of Agriculture, 1940), Table 60, variant entitled "ideal index."

[d] Not available until 1909. For 1909 and following years source is R. G. Bressler, Jr., and J. A. Hopkins, *Trends in Size and Production of the Aggregate Farm Enterprise, 1909–36* (National Research Project, Philadelphia, 1938), Table 4.

during the period 1918–27—while it catches up with or exceeds the BAE index in years during which herds were being built up —e.g., 1913–18, 1928–33. In a number of years these discrepancies lead not merely to different rates of change, but to actual divergence in direction. This is not surprising. For the period 1909–16, for example, our livestock index shows an uninterrupted rise, while the BAE index records three years of decrease—1910, 1912 and 1914—decreases in the volume of slaughterings were more than compensated for by increases in number on hand. Thus, while slaughter of hogs fell by 7 percent between 1909 and 1910, there was an increase of 15 percent for hogs on farms during 1910, so that on balance net output of hogs increased 9 percent between 1909 and 1910. A similar situation exists between 1913 and 1914, except that in this instance decreases in slaughter and increases in herds occurred not only in hogs, but also in cattle. The quantitatively most important discrepancy develops for the period 1933–35. Inventory changes during those years were large, and their omission results in a rise in the BAE index from 1933 to 1934 and a sharp fall from 1934 to 1935, while our index records a contrary movement.

As is pointed out elsewhere [2] our index would show a smaller decline between 1933 and 1934, if we had included in our slaughter series the volume slaughtered for government account. Even then, however, there would still remain a drop instead of the increase shown by the BAE index. It is perhaps idle to argue over the "true" production index for this three-year stretch, 1933–35, since it presents very anomalous conditions which allow of a variety of interpretations. Once we have explained the difference between the two indexes in terms of their scope, the choice between them may be left to the reader.

We turn now to a comparison between our index and that advanced by Strauss and Bean.[3] The two indexes (Table C-1) resemble each other closely and observable differences of 2 or 3 points are difficult to trace; probably they result from

[2] P. 106, above.

[3] Frederick Strauss and Louis H. Bean, *Gross Farm Income and Indices of Production and Prices in the United States, 1869–1937,* Technical Bulletin 703 (U. S. Department of Agriculture, 1940), Table 60.

the combined effect of small differences in data and in weights.[4] Thus, the slightly faster rise shown by our index up to 1906 might be due to our higher estimates, for the later years, of corn and livestock production, and a smaller drop in non-citrus fruit. A somewhat larger difference occurs in 1920 when the Strauss-Bean index exceeds ours by more than 5 percentage points. This seems traceable to a discrepancy between the two livestock indexes, which in turn must be ascribed—as far as the authors can determine—to some errors, typographical or otherwise, in the Strauss-Bean bulletin.[5] But for these discrepancies, the Strauss-Bean index would not, for instance, exceed our index in 1920 and 1931 by around 5 percentage points.

Differences between our index and the National Research Project index [6] remain within 5 percentage points, but are hard to track down since they are due to differences not only in data but also in weights. Indeed, it must be considered astonishing that the use of an entirely different weighting system—manhours per unit instead of value per unit—results in an index which reports very similar movements for the period as a whole.

[4] The Strauss-Bean index takes account of changes in livestock inventories, as does our own. However, the former uses Fisher's "ideal" formula (Strauss and Bean, *op. cit.*, pp. 19-20) instead of the Edgeworth formula used here (pp. 326-27 above).

[5] From the data as given in Strauss and Bean, *op. cit.*, Tables 72 and 89, it is not possible to reconstruct the series for the "ideal" index, for 1910 and later years, given in Table 73.

[6] R. G. Bressler, Jr., and J. A. Hopkins, *Trends in Size and Production of the Aggregate Farm Enterprise, 1909–36* (National Research Project, Philadelphia, 1938), Table 4.

TABLE C-2

NET OUTPUT OF CROPS AND LIVESTOCK PRODUCTS, 1909-39[a]

1929:100

Year	Crops		Livestock Products	
	NBER	BAE	NBER	BAE
1909	84.7	82.5	71.5	78.4
1910	86.2	83.5	73.9	78.2
1911	89.2	86.6	75.3	81.9
1912	97.9	95.3	75.9	80.5
1913	88.4	85.4	78.0	80.7
1914	102.8	101.0	79.7	79.0
1915	100.0	96.4	82.1	82.2
1916	83.0	83.0	82.4	84.8
1917	90.2	89.6	82.5	84.7
1918	95.1	93.7	86.4	90.4
1919	93.2	93.1	82.1	91.2
1920	101.6	104.5	81.0	86.1
1921	79.5	81.7	83.1	86.4
1922	91.1	92.0	89.3	92.4
1923	91.7	92.5	91.9	98.0
1924	99.0	97.6	91.2	99.7
1925	102.1	101.0	90.7	96.9
1926	109.5	107.3	95.0	97.8
1927	98.4	98.2	97.8	99.2
1928	108.0	107.6	98.4	100.6
1929	100.0	100.0	100.0	100.0
1930	99.3	98.0	101.2	99.9
1931	106.9	106.5	102.8	101.3
1932	94.5	94.3	103.2	100.1
1933	87.0	86.3	104.4	104.1
1934	72.8	73.7	91.2	106.5
1935	90.6	90.6	93.3	93.3
1936	83.0	83.7	100.1	100.7
1937	121.3	119.7	97.4	98.3
1938	108.4	106.6	102.8	101.8
1939	111.1	109.0	109.4	107.0

[a] For the National Bureau of Economic Research indexes see Table A-3, above. For the Bureau of Agricultural Economics indexes see *The Farm Income Situation* (U. S. Bureau of Agricultural Economics, Nov. 1941), p. 10.

Appendix D

Charts: Sources and Notes

Appendix D

Charts: Sources and Notes

1 Table 1.
2 Table 1; for population estimates see Appendix B.
3 Table 6. For composition of the partial indexes shown in this chart, see p. 331.
4 Table 2.
5 Tables 4 and 5.
6 Table 5 and Appendix A.
7 *Agricultural Statistics, 1940,* Table 5.
8 Reproduced, with permission, from material furnished by the Corn Industries Research Foundation.
9 Table 5 and Appendix A.
10 U. S. Bureau of Agricultural Economics release, "Consumption of Agricultural Products" (1941). Calendar year data.
11 Table 5.
12 Frederick Strauss, *The Composition of Gross Farm Income since the Civil War,* Bulletin 78 (National Bureau of Economic Research, 1940), Table 7; *Agricultural Statistics, 1941,* Table 654. Data relate to year beginning July.
13 Strauss, *op. cit.,* Table 6; *Agricultural Statistics, 1941,* Table 223. Data relate to year beginning July.
14 Table 5 and Appendix A.
15 Strauss, *op. cit.,* Table 7; *Agricultural Statistics, 1941,* Table 654. Data relate to year beginning July.
16 Strauss, *op. cit.,* Table 6; *Agricultural Statistics, 1941,* Table 151. Data relate to year beginning August.
17 *Agricultural Statistics, 1941,* Table 153.
18 R. B. Evans and R. F. Monachino, *Trends in the Consumption of Fibers in the United States, 1892–1939,* U. S. Bureau of Agricultural Chemistry and Engineering (New Orleans, 1941), Tables 18 and 19. Data relate to fiscal years ending June, 1899–1917; calendar years 1918–39.

19 Evans and Monachino, *op. cit.,* Tables 16 and 17. Data relate to fiscal years ending June, 1892–1917; calendar years 1918–39.

20 Table 5.

21 Evans and Monachino, *op. cit.,* Tables 26 and 27; and material supplied by these authors. Data relate to fiscal years ending June, 1892–1917; calendar years 1919–39; no data available for 1918.

22 Evans and Monachino, *op. cit.,* Tables 18 and 19. Data relate to fiscal years ending June, 1892–1917; calendar years 1918–39.

23 Table 5 and Appendix A.

24 U. S. Agricultural Marketing Service, *Sugar Cane for Sugar and Sirup: Acreage, Production and Disposition, by States, 1909–39* (Washington, 1941).

25 Table 5 and Appendix A.

26 Cattle (other than milk cows) on farms, *Agricultural Statistics, 1941,* Table 458; *Crops and Markets,* February 1942. Population estimates, Appendix B. Data relate to January 1.

27 Cost to packers, *Agricultural Statistics, 1940,* Table 557; meat produced, *ibid.,* Table 554; beef cattle on farms, *ibid.,* Table 463.

28 Table 5 and Appendix A.

29 Table 5 and Appendix A.

30 Appendix A, Table A-4.

31 Table 5 and Appendix A.

32 *Agricultural Statistics, 1940,* Table 657. Data relate to year beginning July.

33 Table 5 and Appendix A.

34 U. S. Bureau of Agricultural Economics, *The Fruit Situation,* November 1941.

35 Table 5 and Appendix A.

36 Bureau of Agricultural Economics, *The Vegetable Situation* (December 1941), pp. 26-27. Data cover 17 vegetables for fresh market shipment (asparagus, snap beans, beets, cabbage, cantaloups, carrots, cauliflower, celery, cucumbers, eggplant, lettuce, onions, peas, peppers, spinach, tomatoes, watermelons) and 8 vegetables for manufacture (asparagus, snap beans,

cabbage for kraut, sweet corn, cucumbers for pickles, green peas, spinach, tomatoes).

37 Table 5 and Appendix A.

38 Table 21.

39 Table 23.

40 Table 24.

41 Table 24.

42 Table 24.

43 Table 24.

44 U. S. Bureau of Agricultural Economics release, "The National Food Situation" (December 1941), Figure 1.

45 Tables 31 and 35.

46 Table 38.

47 *Agricultural Statistics, 1941,* Tables 1, 49, 75, 151, 223, 335; *Crops and Markets* (December 1941), p. 273.

The average yields per acre for the period 1866–1941, shown in the chart, are as follows: wheat, 13.6 bushels; oats, 28.4 bushels; corn, 26.0 bushels; potatoes, 95.4 bushels; cotton, 181.7 pounds; tobacco, 783 pounds.

Index

RELATION OF THE DIRECTORS TO THE WORK AND PUBLICATIONS OF THE NATIONAL BUREAU

1. The object of the National Bureau of Economic Research is to ascertain and to present to the public important economic facts and their interpretation in a scientific and impartial manner. The Board of Directors is charged with the responsibility of ensuring that the work of the Bureau is carried on in strict conformity with this object.

2. To this end the Board of Directors shall appoint one or more Directors of Research.

3. The Director or Directors of Research shall submit to the members of the Board, or to its Executive Committee, for their formal adoption, all specific proposals concerning researches to be instituted.

4. No report shall be published until the Director or Directors of Research shall have submitted to the Board a summary drawing attention to the character of the data and their utilization in the report, the nature and treatment of the problems involved, the main conclusions and such other information as in their opinion would serve to determine the suitability of the report for publication in accordance with the principles of the Bureau.

5. A copy of any manuscript proposed for publication shall also be submitted to each member of the Board. For each manuscript to be so submitted a special committee shall be appointed by the President, or at his designation by the Executive Director, consisting of three Directors selected as nearly as may be one from each general division of the Board. The names of the special manuscript committee shall be stated to each Director when the summary and report described in paragraph (4) are sent to him. It shall be the duty of each member of the committee to read the manuscript. If each member of the special committee signifies his approval within thirty days, the manuscript may be published. If each member of the special committee has not signified his approval within thirty days of the transmittal of the report and manuscript, the Director of Research shall then notify each member of the Board, requesting approval or disapproval of publication, and thirty additional days shall be granted for this purpose. The manuscript shall then not be published unless at least a majority of the entire Board and a two-thirds majority of those members of the Board who shall have voted on the proposal within the time fixed for the receipt of votes on the publication proposed shall have approved.

6. No manuscript may be published, though approved by each member of the special committee, until forty-five days have elapsed from the transmittal of the summary and report. The interval is allowed for the receipt of any memorandum of dissent or reservation, together with a brief statement of his reasons, that any member may wish to express; and such memorandum of dissent or reservation shall be published with the manuscript if he so desires. Publication does not, however, imply that each member of the Board has read the manuscript, or that either members of the Board in general, or of the special committee, have passed upon its validity in every detail.

7. A copy of this resolution shall, unless otherwise determined by the Board, be printed in each copy of every National Bureau book.

(Resolution adopted October 25, 1926 and revised February 6, 1933 and February 24, 1941)

NATIONAL BUREAU OF ECONOMIC RESEARCH PUBLICATIONS IN REPRINT

An Arno Press Series

Barger, Harold. **The Transportation Industries, 1889-1946:** A Study of Output, Employment, and Productivity. 1951

Barger, Harold and Hans H. Landsberg. **American Agriculture, 1899-1939:** A Study of Output, Employment, and Productivity. 1942

Barger, Harold and Sam H. Schurr. **The Mining Industries, 1899-1939:** A Study of Output, Employment, and Productivity. 1944

Burns, Arthur F. **The Frontiers of Economic Knowledge.** 1954

Committee of the President's Conference on Unemployment. **Business Cycles and Unemployment.** 1923

Conference of the Universities-National Bureau Committee for Economic Research. **Aspects of Labor Economics.** 1962

Conference of the Universities-National Bureau Committee for Economic Research. **Business Concentration and Price Policy.** 1955

Conference of the Universities-National Bureau Committee for Economic Research. **Capital Formation and Economic Growth.** 1955

Conference of the Universities-National Bureau Committee for Economic Research. **Policies to Combat Depression.** 1956

Conference of the Universities-National Bureau Committee for Economic Research. **The State of Monetary Economics.** [1963]

Conference of the Universities-National Bureau Committee for Economic Research and the Committee on Economic Growth of the Social Science Research Council. **The Rate and Direction of Inventive Activity:** Economic and Social Factors. 1962

Conference on Research in Income and Wealth. **Input-Output Analysis:** An Appraisal. 1955

Conference on Research in Income and Wealth. **Problems of Capital Formation:** Concepts, Measurement, and Controlling Factors. 1957

Conference on Research in Income and Wealth. **Trends in the American Economy in the Nineteenth Century.** 1960

Conference on Research in National Income and Wealth. **Studies in Income and Wealth.** 1937

Copeland, Morris A. **Trends in Government Financing.** 1961

Fabricant, Solomon. **Employment in Manufacturing, 1899-1939:** An Analysis of Its Relation to the Volume of Production. 1942

Fabricant, Solomon. **The Output of Manufacturing Industries, 1899-1937.** 1940

Goldsmith, Raymond W. **Financial Intermediaries in the American Economy Since 1900.** 1958

Goldsmith, Raymond W. **The National Wealth of the United States in the Postwar Period.** 1962

Kendrick, John W. **Productivity Trends in the United States.** 1961

Kuznets, Simon. **Capital in the American Economy:** Its Formation and Financing. 1961

Kuznets, Simon. **Commodity Flow and Capital Formation.** Vol. One. 1938

Kuznets, Simon. **National Income:** A Summary of Findings. 1946

Kuznets, Simon. **National Income and Capital Formation, 1919-1935:** A Preliminary Report. 1937

Kuznets, Simon. **National Product in Wartime.** 1945

Kuznets, Simon. **National Product Since 1869.** 1946

Kuznets, Simon. **Seasonal Variations in Industry and Trade.** 1933

Long, Clarence D. **Wages and Earnings in the United States, 1860-1890.** 1960

Mendershausen, Horst. **Changes in Income Distribution During the Great Depression.** 1946

Mills, Frederick C. **Economic Tendencies in the United States:** Aspects of Pre-War and Post-War Changes. 1932

Mills, Frederick C. **Price-Quantity Interactions in Business Cycles.** 1946

Mills, Frederick C. **The Behavior of Prices.** 1927

Mitchell, Wesley C. **Business Cycles:** The Problem and Its Setting. [1927]

Mitchell, Wesley C., et al. **Income in the United States:** Its Amount and Distribution 1909-1919. Volume One, Summary. [1921]

Mitchell, Wesley C., editor. **Income in the United States:** Its Amount and Distribution 1909-1919. Volume Two, Detailed Report. 1922

National Accounts Review Committee of the National Bureau of Economic Research. **The National Economic Accounts of the United States.** 1958

Rees, Albert. **Real Wages in Manufacturing, 1890-1914.** 1961

Stigler, George J. **Capital and Rates of Return in Manufacturing Industries.** 1963

Wealth Inventory Planning Study, The George Washington University. **Measuring the Nation's Wealth.** 1964

Williams, Pierce. **The Purchase of Medical Care Through Fixed Periodic Payment.** 1932

Wolman, Leo. **The Growth of American Trade Unions, 1880-1923.** 1924

Woolley, Herbert B. **Measuring Transactions Between World Areas.** 1966